LOCAL BUDGETING

Introduction to the Public Sector Governance and Accountability Series

Anwar Shah, Series Editor

A well-functioning public sector that delivers quality public services consistent with citizen preferences and that fosters private market-led growth while managing fiscal resources prudently is considered critical to the World Bank's mission of poverty alleviation and the achievement of the Millennium Development Goals. This important new series aims to advance those objectives by disseminating conceptual guidance and lessons from practices and by facilitating learning from each others' experiences on ideas and practices that promote *responsive* (by matching public services with citizens' preferences), *responsible* (through efficiency and equity in service provision without undue fiscal and social risk), and *accountable* (to citizens for all actions) public governance in developing countries.

This series represents a response to several independent evaluations in recent years that have argued that development practitioners and policy makers dealing with public sector reforms in developing countries and, indeed, anyone with a concern for effective public governance could benefit from a synthesis of newer perspectives on public sector reforms. This series distills current wisdom and presents tools of analysis for improving the efficiency, equity, and efficacy of the public sector. Leading public policy experts and practitioners have contributed to this series.

The first 14 volumes in this series, listed below, are concerned with public sector accountability for prudent fiscal management; efficiency, equity, and integrity in public service provision; safeguards for the protection of the poor, women, minorities, and other disadvantaged groups; ways of strengthening institutional arrangements for voice, choice, and exit; means of ensuring public financial accountability for integrity and results; methods of evaluating public sector programs, fiscal federalism, and local finances; international practices in local governance; and a framework for responsive and accountable governance.

Fiscal Management

Public Services Delivery

Public Expenditure Analysis

Local Governance in Industrial Countries

Local Governance in Developing Countries

Intergovernmental Fiscal Transfers: Principles and Practice

Participatory Budgeting

Budgeting and Budgetary Institutions

Local Budgeting

Local Public Financial Management

Tools for Public Sector Evaluations

Performance Accountability and Combating Corruption

Macrofederalism and Local Finances

Citizen-Centered Governance

PUBLIC SECTOR
GOVERNANCE AND
ACCOUNTABILITY SERIES

LOCAL BUDGETING

Edited by ANWAR SHAH

THE WORLD BANK
Washington, D.C.

©2007 The International Bank for Reconstruction and Development / The World Bank
1818 H Street, NW
Washington, DC 20433
Telephone: 202-473-1000
Internet: www.worldbank.org
E-mail: feedback@worldbank.org

1 2 3 4 10 09 08 07

This volume is a product of the staff of the International Bank for Reconstruction and Development / The World Bank. The findings, interpretations, and conclusions expressed in this volume do not necessarily reflect the views of the Executive Directors of The World Bank or the governments they represent.

The World Bank does not guarantee the accuracy of the data included in this work. The boundaries, colors, denominations, and other information shown on any map in this work do not imply any judgement on the part of The World Bank concerning the legal status of any territory or the endorsement or acceptance of such boundaries.

ISBN-10: 0-8213-6945-8
ISBN-13: 978-0-8213-6945-6
eISBN-10: 0-8213-6946-6
eISBN-13: 978-0-8213-6946-3
DOI: 10.1596/978-0-8213-6945-6

Library of Congress Cataloging-in-Publication Data
Local budgeting / edited by Anwar Shah.
    p. cm.
ISBN-13: 978-0-8213-6945-6
ISBN-10: 0-8213-6945-8
ISBN-10: 0-8213-6946-6 (electronic)
    1. Local budgets. 2. Local finance. I. Shah, Anwar.

HJ9111.L63 2007
352.4'8214–dc22

                                                                    2006101261

Contents

Part I Fiscal Administration

CHAPTER

1

Part II Local Budgeting

8

Local Budget Process   213
Daniel R. Mullins

9

Local Budget Execution   269
Kurt Thurmaier

BOXES

FIGURES

TABLES

Foreword

In Western democracies, systems of checks and balances built into government structures have formed the core of good governance and have helped empower citizens for more than two hundred years. The incentives that motivate public servants and policy makers— the rewards and sanctions linked to results that help shape public sector performance—are rooted in a country's accountability frameworks. Sound public sector management and government spending help determine the course of economic development and social equity, especially for the poor and other disadvantaged groups, such as women and the elderly.

Many developing countries, however, continue to suffer from unsatisfactory and often dysfunctional governance systems that include rent seeking and malfeasance, inappropriate allocation of resources, inefficient revenue systems, and weak delivery of vital public services. Such poor governance leads to unwelcome outcomes for access to public services by the poor and other disadvantaged members of society, such as women, children, and minorities. In dealing with these concerns, the development assistance community in general and the World Bank in particular are continuously striving to learn lessons from practices around the world to achieve a better understanding of what works and what does not work in improving public sector governance, especially with respect to combating corruption and making services work for poor people.

The Public Sector Governance and Accountability Series advances our knowledge by providing tools and lessons from practices in improving efficiency and equity of public services provision and strengthening institutions of accountability in governance. The series highlights frameworks to create incentive environments and pressures for good governance from within and beyond governments. It outlines institutional mechanisms to empower citizens to demand accountability for results from their governments. It provides practical guidance on managing for results and prudent fiscal management. It outlines approaches to dealing with corruption and malfeasance. It provides conceptual and practical guidance on alternative service delivery frameworks for extending the reach and access of public services. The series also covers safeguards for the protection of the poor, women, minorities, and other disadvantaged groups; ways of strengthening institutional arrangements for voice and exit; methods of evaluating public sector programs; frameworks for responsive and accountable governance; and fiscal federalism and local governance.

This series will be of interest to public officials, development practitioners, students of development, and those interested in public governance in developing countries.

Frannie A. Léautier
Vice President
World Bank Institute

Preface

Budgetary institutions at the local level serve to allocate community resources consistent with community preferences. The role and budget documents of these institutions have changed significantly in the past two decades. Local budgets have evolved from instruments of planning and financial control to tools of performance measurement, results management, and fiscal discipline. Local budgets now also serve to enhance citizen empowerment and results-based external accountability in the public sector. Citizens want these documents to be complete and accurate accounts of government operations and to be presented in user-friendly formats. This book documents the choices available to local governments to meet these demands and to ensure prudent and transparent fiscal management at the local level.

Local Budgeting provides a comprehensive guide for local administrators who are involved in designing and implementing budgetary institutions and who wish to improve efficiency and equity in service delivery and to strengthen internal and external accountability. It details principles and practices to improve fiscal management. It reviews techniques available in developing countries for forecasting revenues and expenditures, and it examines institutional arrangements for ensuring transparency and fiscal discipline. In addition, it outlines some strategies to deal with corruption in local revenue administration.

With respect to budgeting, the volume discusses the decisions that need to be made in determining budget format and layout, including the scope of the budget, the degree of transparency of the legal requirements underlying the budget, and the extent to which the budget will emphasize inputs, outputs, and outcomes. *Local Budgeting* also discusses the role of the capital budget. It details how performance budgeting can serve as a tool for results-based accountability to citizens. It helps the nonspecialist reader learn how to interpret budget documents to discover what the government is doing and how well it is performing its tasks. It highlights approaches to stakeholder inputs in the budget process. Finally, it explores the role of budget execution in ensuring management flexibility while enhancing democratic accountability.

Local Budgeting represents a collaborative effort of the Swedish International Development Cooperation Agency and the World Bank Institute to improve public expenditure management and financial accountability in developing countries, especially in Africa. We hope that policy makers and practitioners will find this volume a useful guide to reforming budgeting institutions.

Roumeen Islam
Manager, Poverty Reduction and Economic Management
World Bank Institute

Acknowledgments

This book brings together learning modules about local fiscal administration and budgeting that were prepared for the World Bank Institute's learning programs and were directed by the editor over the past three years. The learning modules and their publication in this volume were financed primarily by the government of Sweden through its Public Expenditure and Financial Accountability (PEFA) partnership program with the World Bank Institute, a program that was also directed by the editor. The government of Japan provided additional financial support for editing this book.

The editor is grateful to Hallgerd Dryssen, Swedish International Development Agency, Stockholm, for providing overall guidance and support to the PEFA program. In addition, Bengt Anderson, Goran Anderson, Gunilla Bruun, Alan Gustafsson, and other members of the PEFA external advisory group contributed to the program design and development.

The book has benefited from contributions to World Bank Institute learning events by senior policy makers and scholars from Africa and elsewhere. In particular, the editor would like to thank Tania Ajam, director, Applied Fiscal Research Center, Cape Town, South Africa; Paul Boothe, former associate deputy minister, Ministry of Finance, Canada; Neil Cole, director, South Africa National Treasury; Anders Haglund, PricewaterhouseCoopers, Stockholm; Professor Roy Kelly, professor, Duke University; John Mikesell, professor, Indiana University; Ismail Momoniat, director general, South Africa National Treasury; and Christina Nomdo, Institute for Democracy in South Africa, Cape Town.

The editor is grateful to the leading scholars who contributed chapters and to the distinguished reviewers who provided comments.

Anupam Das, Alta Fölscher, Adrian Shall, and Chunli Shen helped during various stages of preparation of the book and provided comments and editorial revisions of individual chapters. Kaitlin Tierney provided excellent administrative support for this project.

Thanks are also due to Stephen McGroarty for ensuring a fast-track process for publication of the book and to Dina Towbin for excellent supervision of the editorial process. Denise Bergeron is to be thanked for the book's excellent print quality.

Contributors

AMARESH BAGCHI is professor emeritus at the National Institute of Public Finance and Policy, where he served as director for 10 years. He began his working life as a tax administrator in the government of India and has been associated with tax policy formulation and implementation at different levels of government in India. He has written extensively on taxation and has served as a member of official committees on taxation of central, state, and local governments.

ALTA FÖLSCHER is an independent researcher and consultant. She has worked in Africa, Asia, the Balkans and Eastern Europe, the Caribbean, and the Middle East on issues of public finance and public policy. Her areas of work include governance, public accountability and fiscal transparency, public expenditure and financial management, pro-poor expenditure analysis, forecasting and costing, and education financing. She has published several papers and edited three books on public finance management in Africa. She has coedited books on economic transformation in South Africa. She has a master's degree in public policy and management from the University of London.

CAROL W. LEWIS is a professor of political science at the University of Connecticut, Storrs. With research interests in public budgeting and ethics, she has published in numerous scholarly and professional journals, including *Public Administration Review, Municipal Finance Journal,* and *Public Integrity.* Her most recent book, coauthored with Stuart C. Gilman, is *The Ethics Challenge in Public Service: A Problem-Solving Guide* (2005). A former local elected official, Lewis has served as a research consultant or developed and delivered training programs for the Brookings Institution, the Council of State Governments, the National Academy of Public Administration, and the World Bank, among others. She has numerous university and professional associations.

JOHN L. MIKESELL is professor of public finance and policy analysis and is director of the Master of Public Affairs program at the Indiana University School of Public and Environmental Affairs. He serves as editor-in-chief of *Public Budgeting and Finance* and has written widely on property and sales taxation, tax administration, and budget processes. His textbook *Fiscal Administration, Analysis, and Applications for the Public Sector* is a standard textbook in graduate public administration and public policy programs. He holds a doctorate in economics from the University of Illinois, Urbana. He received the 2002 Wildavsky Award for Lifetime Scholarly Achievement in Public Budgeting and Finance from the Association for Budgeting and Financial Management.

DANIEL R. MULLINS is associate professor in the Department of Public Administration and Policy at The American University. His research focuses include intergovernmental fiscal systems, tax and expenditure limitations, budgeting practices/reform, fiscal implications of demographic change, economic development, and metropolitan economic and spatial structure. His research has appeared in a variety of academic and professional publications, including *Public Administration Review, Policy Sciences,* and *Urban Affairs Quarterly.* He is managing editor of *Public Budgeting and Finance* and is coeditor of *The Evolution of Public Finance and Budgeting: A Quarter Century of Developments* (2006). He has served in advisory capacities at all governmental levels in the United States and has worked internationally with many governments. His research often focuses on public sector budgeting, intergovernmental fiscal relations, and problems of finance and service delivery in transitional economies. He holds a doctorate from the Maxwell School of Citizenship and Public Affairs at Syracuse University.

IRENE RUBIN is professor emeritus at Northern Illinois University, DeKalb. She has taught public budgeting and finance for her entire career. Much of her writing is on the relationship between politics and budgeting, especially on getting into and out of fiscal stress. Her books include *The Politics of Public Budgeting: Getting and Spending; Borrowing and Balancing* (2005); and *Class, Tax, and Power: Municipal Budgeting in the United States* (1998). Recent book chapters include "Does Process Matter? U.S. Budget Process 1998–2004" in *Handbook of Public Policy* (2006) and (with Joanne Kelly) "Budgeting and

Accounting Reforms" in *The Oxford Handbook of Public Management* (2005). Her doctorate is from the University of Chicago.

LARRY SCHROEDER is professor of public administration at the Maxwell School of Citizenship and Public Affairs of Syracuse University. A public finance economist, he has conducted research on a variety of state and local government fiscal issues both in the United States and in developing and transition economies. His research focuses on fiscal decentralization, intergovernmental fiscal relations, and institutional arrangements' effects on the provision of public services. He is the coauthor of several books and numerous articles addressing those subjects. He has consulted with and led policy research projects in many countries, including many in South Asia and Southeast Asia and some in Africa and Eastern Europe.

ANWAR SHAH is lead economist and program/team leader for public sector governance at the World Bank Institute in Washington, DC. He is a member of the executive board of the International Institute of Public Finance in Munich, Germany, and a fellow of the Institute for Public Economics in Alberta, Canada. He has served the Canadian Ministry of Finance in Ottawa and the government of the province of Alberta, where he had responsibilities for federal-provincial and provincial-local fiscal relations. He has written extensively on public and environmental economics issues and published books and articles dealing with governance, global environment, fiscal federalism, and fiscal management issues. He has lectured at leading educational institutions around the globe.

CHUNLI SHEN is a World Bank consultant on budgeting, public financial management, and fiscal decentralization issues. She has a master's degree in public management and is pursuing a doctorate from the School of Public Policy at the University of Maryland at College Park. She has worked for the government of Montgomery County, Maryland, and at the Center for Public Policy and Private Enterprise and the National Association of Housing and Redevelopment Officials. With Anwar Shah, she has coedited several World Bank–published books on China in the Chinese language: *Fiscal Federalism and Fiscal Management* (2005), *Local Public Finance and Governance* (2005), and *Regional Disparities in China* (2006).

KURT THURMAIER is professor of public administration at Northern Illinois University, DeKalb. His research interests include state and local public budgeting and finance, intergovernmental relations, and e-government, about which he has done extensive research, writing, and teaching. He has worked at the Wisconsin State Budget Office as a budget and management analyst; been a Fulbright Scholar at Jagiellonian University in Krakow, Poland; served as a consultant to local governments in Poland through the International City/County Management Association; and served as a consultant on U.S. city-county consolidation efforts. His books include *Policy and Politics in State Budgeting* (2001) and *Case Studies of City-County Consolidations: Reshaping the Local Government Landscape* (2004).

A. JOHN VOGT is professor of public finance and government at the School of Government of the University of North Carolina at Chapel Hill. He offers training on capital planning and finance for local government officials in North Carolina and across the United States. He teaches in the Master of Public Administration program at the University of North Carolina. His most recent book is *Capital Budgeting and Finance: A Guide for Local Governments* (2004). Other books include *A Guide to Municipal Leasing* (1983) and *Capital Improvement Programming: A Handbook for Local Government Officials* (1976). He has served as an adviser to the Government Finance Officers Association's Economic Development and Capital Planning Committee, and he regularly consults with local government officials on capital planning, budget, and finance.

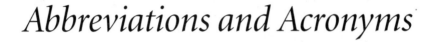

Abbreviations and Acronyms

ADB	Asian Development Bank
CDCs	community development committees
CEO	chief executive officer
CFO	chief financial officer
CIP	capital improvement program
COP	certificate of participation
ECA	Economic Commission for Africa
FIMS	financial information management systems
GAO	Government Accountability Office (United States)
GDP	gross domestic product
GFOA	Government Finance Officers Association (United States and Canada)
GO	general obligation
GPP	Government Performance Project
ICMA	International City/County Management Association
IDASA	Institute for Democracy in South Africa
IDP	Integrated Development Planning
LASDAP	Local Authority Service Delivery Action Plan (Nairobi, Kenya)
MDP	Municipal Development Partnership
MTEF	medium-term expenditure framework
MVT	motor vehicle tax
NASBO	National Association of Budget Officers
NGOs	nongovernmental organizations
NIE	new institutional economics
NPM	new public management (framework)
O&M	operation and maintenance

OECD	Organisation for Economic Co-operation and Development
OMB	Office of Management and Budget
POG	Priorities of Government
SNGs	subnational governments
ULBs	urban local bodies
VAT	value added tax

Overview

ANWAR SHAH

Local budgetary institutions serve as the medium for determining what local services will be provided and how they will be financed. Transparency of these institutions is critical to ensuring that local governments are responsive to citizen preferences; that they deliver local services efficiently, equitably, and with integrity; and that the electorate can hold them accountable for their service delivery performance. Open and transparent local budgeting is thus viewed as critical to the integrity of the local public sector and to citizens' trust in government.

Transparency of budgetary institutions is typically lacking in local governments in most developing countries, especially those in Africa. This volume attempts to provide practical guidance to local governments interested in establishing open and transparent budgetary institutions. This guidance is intended to provide assistance in establishing fiscal discipline, prudent allocation of public resources, and efficiency and equity in local public service provision. In this volume, leading international experts have contributed to all relevant aspects of local public budgeting: budget formats, including performance budgeting and processes; budget execution; capital budgeting; revenue and expenditure forecasting; fiscal administration; local fiscal discipline; and combating of corruption in revenue administration.

Chapter 1 by John L. Mikesell provides an overview of principles and practices in establishing sound fiscal administration at the local level. Reforms in fiscal administration should promote fiscal

1

discipline, sound allocation of public resources, and technical efficiency of service delivery. By enhancing transparency and accountability to citizenry, the reforms should enhance the responsiveness of local governments to citizen interests. Five core functions constitute local fiscal administration: budgeting, accounting, cash management, debt management, and revenue administration. Each is an important component of local fiscal responsiveness and control. In the context of developing countries, Mikesell notes that the system of fiscal administration must maintain a hard budget constraint, provide meaningful information for decisions, maintain public transparency, encompass all fiscal operations of the government, adequately regulate public borrowing, operate within a reasonable transfer system, and strengthen technical capacity for fiscal operations. With a strong system of fiscal administration in place, local governments can make an important contribution to citizen well-being by exploiting the advantages of having a government that is close to the public.

Chapter 2 by Larry Schroeder reviews the rationales for and techniques available to local government financial managers for forecasting revenues and expenditures in developing and transition economies. It illustrates how the techniques can be used and buttresses that discussion with illustrations of how they are actually used. Because few local governments in developing countries conduct systematic forecasting exercises, the examples are drawn from local governments in developed economies.

The annual budget requires that revenues for the next fiscal year be estimated so as to provide resource constraints for the formulation of spending plans. These revenue estimates should be as accurate as possible to avoid revenue shortfalls or excessively large revenue surpluses during the fiscal year.

Whereas all subnational governments engage in such forecasting efforts, fewer attempt to make systematic, longer-term (three- to five-year) estimates of revenues and expenditures. By projecting the likely flow of revenues over the medium term and comparing those revenues with the level of spending that would be necessary to maintain current levels of service, local officials can determine whether financing shortfalls are on the horizon and, if so, consider policies to overcome those potential deficits. Similarly, the revenue and expenditure impacts of investments in new capital infrastructure, including the operating and maintenance costs associated with that infrastructure, can be estimated and thereby inform policy makers of the fiscal effects of their plans for new capital investments.

Several techniques can be used to forecast both revenues and expenditures. They range from simple judgmental approaches that rely on the knowledge of experts to more sophisticated multivariate statistical techniques. For forecasts of revenues that are sensitive to economic conditions, statistical forecasting methods may be most appropriate. But statistical analyses require considerably more data and forecaster expertise than the alternatives: time trend analysis and deterministic approaches. In fact, the examples of actual local government forecasting efforts reviewed in the chapter reveal that the most commonly used approaches are deterministic approaches, in which forecasts of revenues or expenditures are based on simple links to variables assumed to directly influence revenues and expenditures. As fiscal decentralization policies give greater fiscal authority and responsibility to local governments in developing countries, the need for improved budgeting and financial planning will increase. The forecasting techniques discussed in the chapter should, therefore, become increasingly relevant.

Local governments in developing countries are facing increasing fiscal strain as cities and their infrastructure requirements expand and revenue growth lags behind. The avenues of response open to local governments are a function of the national environment within which they operate and of their local capacity and institutional arrangements. In chapter 3, Alta Fölscher explores how institutions at national and subnational levels affect local governments' capacity to operationalize fiscal discipline.

Fiscal discipline is a key value in public finance management at the national and the local levels. Given limited resources, expenditure claims would result in chronically high deficits and increasing debt and tax burdens if governments were not fiscally restrained. Fiscal discipline is inherently connected to notions of affordability: it has come to mean maintaining budgeted and actual spending, revenue, and borrowing at levels that are financially sustainable and compatible with short- and long-term economic objectives. However, the value of fiscal discipline lies as much in avoiding the negative external and internal impacts as in seeking the benefits of hard budget constraints for spending effectiveness and efficiency.

Fiscal decentralization—the transfer of expenditure responsibilities, together with some revenue-raising capability to lower levels of government— poses new challenges to the institutions through which governments manage macroeconomic stability and growth. The destabilization potential of local government fiscal operations is much higher when local governments have access to credit. When no borrowing is possible, local governments are forced to take difficult decisions sooner rather than later. However, options for financing their crucial development needs are fewer.

Many institutional tools are available to facilitate and enforce general government fiscal discipline in fiscally decentralized contexts. The design of any grant system is important. Intergovernmental fiscal relations should be based on stable, transparent, nonarbitrary, universal, and nonnegotiable rules, and the level of resources assigned to local governments should be sufficient to match expenditure responsibilities. When continuing expenditure responsibilities are assigned to local government, they should be matched by stable revenue sources. At the same time, local government budgets should have flexibility to meet local circumstances and needs.

The operational system that facilitates coordination and cooperation among levels of government is also important. Timely and comprehensive reporting of budget implementation should be based on a consistent system of national accounts and should include the transfer of resources from national government to subnational governments. Such reporting is necessary for earlier rather than later detection of fiscal stress and remedial action and for clear accountability among levels of government. In addition, the annual intergovernmental budget process should be cooperative.

Country systems that control subnational budgeting should pay attention to the ex ante incentives and ex post consequences that face both borrowers and lenders before the agreement to borrow. Relying on ex ante constraints without consequences after the fact gives irresponsible lenders and borrowers a big incentive to overcome initial obstacles. Relying solely on consequences may allow larger local governments to build up such large debts that the national government will not enforce the consequences. The history of subnational borrowing in newly decentralizing countries suggests that sole reliance on market discipline may not be sufficient to encourage local fiscal discipline. Many conditions must be satisfied if financial markets are to be an effective check on local discipline. These conditions include enforcement of contracts, level playing fields for local governments with other debtors, availability of adequate financial information on governments, no expectations of central government bailouts of lenders, and borrower capacity to respond to market signals. Very few countries meet these conditions. Therefore, fiscal discipline is best supported by rules or by greater central government oversight and control over subnational borrowing.

At the local level, own-revenue capacity and efficient local revenue administration are cornerstones of local fiscal discipline. Governments that deploy modern approaches to budgeting (including medium-term budgeting, modern classification systems, improved internal controls, and use of performance measures) are better placed to maintain fiscal discipline. A requisite for any of these constraints to be effective is local-level fiscal transparency. Merely the availability of accurate and timely information is insufficient, however. A strong civil society—independent media, responsive opposition groups, good research organizations, and respected commentators—complements such information. In summary, transparency of local government finances requires transparency in risk assessments and in medium-term fiscal assumptions, policies, and targets; comprehensive budget frameworks; comprehensive balance sheets; periodic, accurate information on budget execution; and robust auditing and oversight institutions.

The incidence of corruption in the assessment and collection of government revenues is known to be endemic, particularly in developing countries. Chapter 4 by Amaresh Bagchi examines the scope and prevalence of corruption in state and local revenue administration and strategies to combat the scourge. The chapter takes note of the principal revenue sources of state and local governments by examining practices in selected countries and the scope they offer for corrupt practices. In reviewing the recent literature on corruption to identify potential drivers of corruption in revenue administration, Bagchi concludes that the economic theory of crime (corruption thrives as long as the gains exceed the costs) provides a valuable clue to corruption's possible remedies. However, accountability and governance (the agency approach) also figure prominently among the factors underlying the widespread incidence of corruption in revenue administration. The prescriptions that follow from this insight are simultaneously to curb the gains from evasion of taxes by bringing tax rates down to acceptable and administrable levels and to raise the costs of evasion and bribery by adequately compensating tax officials. In this context, the chapter takes note of debate on the efficacy and ethics of providing incentives for tax inspectors in the form of a fraction of the additional revenue secured for government.

The message emanating from the agency approach is based on the celebrated Klitgaard formula: C (corruption) $= M$ (monopoly) $+ D$ (discretion) $- A$ (accountability). To explore the scope for containing corruption by curbing M and D, Bagchi examines corruption cases associated with a few major sources of revenue for state and local governments, such as the value added tax and the property tax. The chapter concludes that accountability depends critically on governance. In this context, it emphasizes the role of fair and free elections, civil society, and other institutions of accountability.

Chapter 5 by Irene Rubin examines the decisions that must be made in determining budget format and layout, including the scope of the budget, the degree of transparency of the legal requirements underlying the budget, and the extent to which the budget will emphasize inputs or outputs and outcomes. The chapter describes why these decisions are important, considers alternatives, and describes what each option is designed to achieve. It argues that decision makers should select options on the basis of the legal structure, the particular political and financial problems that they confront, and the political context in which they work. Ease or complexity of implementation is also a concern; decision makers should select formats matching the skills and experience of budgeting and financial management staff.

The budget layout can emphasize legal issues and fiscal controls to help prevent overspending, it can call attention to efficiency or effectiveness issues to improve management, and it can clarify where fiscal discretion lies and hence help hold administrators accountable not only for the funds they receive but also for a given level of performance with those resources. The budget document can be a major tool of accountability to the legislative body or to the press and the public. But typically, the budget cannot accomplish all these tasks equally well at the same time. Officials have to choose which goals are most important to them and orient the budget to achieve those goals; alternatively, they can develop hybrids that attempt to achieve multiple goals, rather than to maximize any one goal.

With enhanced emphasis on government accountability for perform-ance, a large body of literature has emerged on performance budgeting and related reforms at the national level. Although performance budgeting owes its origins to innovations in budgeting reforms at the local level, scant atten-tion has been paid to drawing lessons from these experiences for wider application. Chapter 6 by Anwar Shah and Chunli Shen provides an intro-ductory overview of performance budgeting at the local level and carries this work forward analytically by presenting a framework for the use of this tool for results-based accountability to citizens. Local-level citizen-centric performance budgeting, a framework introduced in this chapter, is intended as a tool for citizens to demand accountability from their local governments. This tool is pertinent to recent public management reform movements, which emphasize performance accountability and citizen participation. The chapter concludes that performance budgeting is an important tool for citizen empowerment at the local level. However, it must be an integral element of a broader reform package to create a performance culture. In the absence of incentives for both better performance and bottom-up accountability for results, the introduction of performance budgeting may not improve per-formance accountability.

A mirror of the rapid social and economic change in a development setting, budgeting in Sub-Saharan Africa is evolving to meet new challenges. Best budgetary practices are dynamic and, when transposed to the development context in Sub-Saharan Africa, require continuous adaptation for success, rather than simple importation or imitation. Although its core is political, budgeting demands some technical expertise. Drawing on budgets of various local authorities for illustrations, Carol W. Lewis in chapter 7 focuses on 10 features critical to understanding the budget document: reporting entity; fiscal year; operating budget and capital budget; legal status and budget cycle; balance or surplus/deficit; overall balance; funds; revenue reliance, central allocations, and local discretion; costs and budget share; and spotlighted concerns.

Chapter 7 notes that achieving results through budgeting requires effective and efficient financial and program management. The second part of the chapter is devoted to relating the budget to performance through a variety of internal and external assessment techniques and tools. The tools include financial measures and indicators of financial condition, and the techniques include citizen participation and engagement, performance measurement, and benchmarking.

Chapter 8 by Daniel R. Mullins is concerned with reform of the budget process. Much of the substance and significance of local government budgetary processes owe to the context of the intergovernmental structure within which the processes occur. Meaningful local processes require local discretion and authority to marshal and manage local resources in fulfillment of local needs and objectives. Simultaneously, effective modes of communication and coordination among levels of government are essential. Multitiered institutions and actors establish limiting elements of this process, resulting in complex and varied capacities for meaningful local budgetary choice. Excessively constrained local authority is widespread in Africa; however, the trend is shared authority and greater local discretion and capacity.

Cooperative intergovernmental systems are underdeveloped but evolving. A balance between hierarchal/coercive and cooperative/collaborative mechanisms (vertically and horizontally) has yet to be widely achieved. Nonetheless, the objectives and elements of effective budgetary processes at the local level are essentially the same as at other levels. The process should include mechanisms to establish needs, goals, and objectives to guide decision making and budget development; appropriate and effective programmatic and managerial responses; and spending plans consistent with available resources and managerial/programmatic means of goal achievement. The process should also incorporate a feedback mechanism to evaluate performance and ensure financial integrity. Effective systems are expected to promote fiscal discipline and expenditure control, strategic resource allocation, operational (managerial) efficiency, and responsiveness to local needs.

Process and environmental conditions are important elements of the local budget cycle. Critical factors are balanced institutional authority and proper representation of stakeholders. Fiscal discipline must be secured, but in a manner that ensures responsiveness to local populations. Effective budget formulation requires systematic incorporation of consultative local policy guidance, within the context of realistic appraisals of local resource availability. Likewise, administrative/managerial initiative and flexibility should be fostered in the development of programmatic options. Effective legislative review requires meaningful legislative authority and the availability of pertinent information on which to exercise policy choice and oversight, which in turn requires independent institutional capacity, submission of proposed expenditure plans sufficiently detailed to hold operating units accountable, and discretion in making final spending allocations. Mechanisms to ensure execution consistent with the approved budget are critical, as is balance between managerial flexibility and legislative control. Evaluation and reporting must be sufficiently robust to ensure accountability for programmatic performance and financial integrity, and reporting must be made public. Timetables and technical details are important, but proper institutional relationships, capacity, roles, and stakeholder participation are critical to effective outcomes.

Participatory processes provide significant potential for improved planning and budgeting. However, to be effective, participation must be broadly based. Too often, participatory processes provide access to only small subsets of local populations and can result in dominance of the local elite in a manner that channels resources away from populations in need. Mechanisms to promote open, communitarian participation are important to securing the benefits of participatory processes. Adequate social capital is a critical element. It both fosters and is fostered by meaningful local resource discretion and participation. Effective participation should be institutionalized in regular decision access for stakeholders as a component of the budget planning, development, and approval process. Governments may need to require procedures for ensuring adequate representation of groups that otherwise might be socially excluded.

Accountability among institutions, among levels of government, and between institutions of governance and the public is critical. Both rule-based and performance-based mechanisms are required. Significant steps in this direction are taken with participatory processes. However, accountability for results (ex ante) requires specific consideration. Accountability can be fostered through open reporting, meaningful sanctions, the appropriate organizational culture, program design and incentives, rule of law, and democratic institutions. Accountability requires measures to mitigate political capture and bureaucratic corruption. Mechanisms for independent evaluation and open information and voice are essential.

Mullins concludes that the establishment of proper process elements is one of the most important—and most complicated—aspects of effective local budgeting (and governance). It requires coordination across and between levels as well as among institutional actors, civil society, and the general local population. Establishment of proper process elements also requires the diligent performance of interdependent roles and functions by both those officially and those unofficially engaged in the process and across sometimes relatively independent institutions and individuals. It requires institutional and cultural development and sophistication. It could be the single most influential element in producing an effective and responsive local budgeting and governance system.

Citizens around the world have the same fundamental needs and rights to be able to know for what purposes they are paying taxes and fees and whether those taxes and fees are actually spent for the purposes determined by duly elected representatives. Local budgets speak to these needs and rights when the budget document is accessible and clearly communicates the sources of revenues and plans for spending them and when midyear and final reports on budget execution clearly present how the funds have been spent relative to the plan.

Chapter 9 by Kurt Thurmaier argues that budget execution should be understood and treated as a one of several instruments of administrative control to ensure democratic accountability and management flexibility. Producing the budget document and appropriate financial reports requires a managerial approach to local budgeting, whereby the chief executive and governing body develop and execute a budget that realistically strives to achieve the city's goals and mission. This approach recognizes political, legal, and management facets of budget execution. The politics of budgeting cannot be separated from budget execution any more than politics can be excluded from budget development. Budget execution is not simply an accounting function. It involves careful management of revenues and expenditures—and of the politics of budgeting.

Local budget execution requires discussion of national (and regional) budget execution. The relatively large dependence of many local governments on regional and central budget transfers for budget revenues means that local governments' capacity to effectively execute budget plans is dependent on central and regional governments' capacity to effectively execute budget plans.

Chapter 10 by A. John Vogt discusses the reasons that a local government would establish a special process for capital budgeting. The chapter defines what is meant by capital expenditure and considers which capital expenditures or projects belong in the capital budget. In addition, it advances a model or process for local capital budgeting that includes planning for needs, financing, decision making, and implementation.

Five conditions increase the likelihood that a local government will benefit from a separate and well-developed process for capital budgeting. First, the community is experiencing substantial growth, and local government must establish infrastructure and facilities to meet the growth, or the community is not growing, and local government is investing in infrastructure and facilities to spur growth. Second, local government faces large capital needs requiring the investment of substantial amounts of money. Third, meeting public capital project needs is likely to shape the most basic features of the community. Fourth, the community is using debt, capital leasing, and other methods of capital financing that involve long-term payment obligations. Fifth, the operating budget process is not well suited to planning and financing the local government's capital needs.

Under the conventional definition from accounting, a capital expenditure is spending of significant value that results in the acquisition of property that lasts more than one year—usually many years. Capital assets include land, buildings, infrastructure, and equipment. Not all capital expenditures need to be included in the capital budget. Spending for capital equipment that recurs annually or regularly and that is for ongoing infrastructure renovation programs can readily be planned and financed in the operating budget. The capital budget should be reserved for the more expensive capital projects or for acquisitions that have long useful lives and for expensive, irregularly recurring equipment and other capital acquisitions.

The chapter organizes the roles, policies, and procedures making up the process for local capital budgeting into five general stages, each with specific steps. Stage 1, organization, requires definition of the capital budget process and development of policies for capital budgeting. Stage 2, planning for capital needs, entails identification of needs; prioritization of capital requests; project evaluation, scoping, and costing; and preparation and approval of a capital improvement program. Stage 3, capital financing, requires assessment of a jurisdiction's financial condition and preparation of a multiyear financial forecast, identification of capital financing options, and development of a capital financing strategy and selection of financing for projects. Stage 4, project decision making, requires recommendation of capital projects and spending, authorization of capital projects and spending, and appropriation of money for them. Stage 5, implementation, involves obtaining and managing project financing, organizing and managing construction projects, and acquiring equipment and other capital assets.

In summary, this volume provides a comprehensive treatment of principles and practices in the reform of local budgetary institutions and fiscal administration and should serve as a useful guide to the policy makers, practitioners, and students of fiscal administration.

P A R T *One*

Fiscal Administration

1

Fiscal Administration in Local Government: An Overview

JOHN L. MIKESELL

Local governments can make an important contribution to public well-being through the execution of government policies and the delivery of public services that are important to the local citizenry. Their special fiscal advantage lies in the closeness of the citizenry to the decision makers and administrators of the programs that provide services. Local government has the potential to be the most transparent and accountable level of government in providing services to the citizenry. Full realization of that promise, however, requires strong fiscal administration so that citizen interests are reflected in local programs; so that policies are conducted in a fiscally sustainable way; and so that resources are not lost through inefficient, ineffective, wasteful, or corrupt operations. The potential of responsiveness to the citizenry means little if resources intended to provide services slip into the pockets of politicians and bureaucrats.

Local governments should seek to enhance the well-being of their citizens through the provision of public services consistent with the goals of the citizenry. If governments fail to provide these services, to pay for their provision in a responsible fashion, or to safeguard resources obtained to provide these services, the well-being of the citizenry, at present and in future, will be in jeopardy. The unique advantages of local government finance are that decisions can be made close to the citizenry and advantage taken of that closeness—to ensure that decisions respond to the preferences of the population—and that evaluation of the results of decisions involves the population. Citizen input can be included as a service program is being developed by administrative agencies, and it can be included through hearings conducted while legislation to enact those programs is deliberated. These inputs are much simpler for local governments to obtain than for regional or national governments, so local governments offer the best hope for direct citizen participation in the fiscal process. The participation of the citizenry in local fiscal decisions and their implementation is critical to improving the allocation of public resources and to increasing responsiveness to local citizens' concerns.

Special Fiscal Advantages of Local Government

The fiscal promise of local government reflects the several advantages of devolution of responsibility to governments closer to the population: improved delivery of services through greater citizen input, greater responsiveness in government action, and better accountability to the citizenry for public service outcomes. Local fiscal administration, implementing the policies and programs of local governments with devolved political powers, can provide a number of specific fiscal advantages. Some of these merit particular attention here.[1]

Choices and Responsiveness

Local governments permit fiscal diversity and choices about what government services will be provided to the citizenry. Indeed, their most fundamental strength is to permit people living in various localities within a country to receive somewhat different government services while continuing to be citizens of the larger nation. Localities that have a degree of fiscal autonomy can adjust both what levels and types of government services are provided and how they are financed, as they respond to the preferences of a heterogeneous population. Residents of different localities are unlikely to reach the same conclusions about what services government should provide, so a degree of fiscal autonomy means greater diversity both in what services are provided and in how they will be financed. That diversity provides something like the product and price selection afforded by a private market, in which many possible suppliers offer their products to the buying public. Local fiscal administration provides the structure through which these governments can respond to the service preferences of their residents in a fashion that is fiscally responsible, financially sustainable, and consistent with standards of transparency and democratic governance.

Local governments may make little difference when a country is small and has a homogeneous population and geography and an undifferentiated economy. But if there are major differences within the country—for instance, some rural areas and some urban areas—the variation in governmental services and means of financing them signifies that having independent local governments can be ideal for accommodating citizen preferences. The sorts of services that are most important to the population are not likely to be the same in all parts of the country. Local governments provide the institutional mechanism for responding to those differences. They become the governance mechanism that best serves the interests of the citizenry. And the system of local fiscal administration is the means for responding efficiently and effectively to those different interests. A system of decentralized branches of the national government cannot hope to provide the diversity that is possible with devolved local sovereignty. Indeed, the variation can extend to the localities themselves; for example, Swaziland uses one form of local government in urban areas and another form in rural areas.

Citizen Participation

Local governments provide the opportunity for political participation. Such governments enable citizens to participate in the political process in their own areas, thus giving greater vitality to democracy. Rather than government decisions being made in some distant capital, real sovereign choices are made closer to the people. The citizenry has a better chance of influencing the democratic process and the choices emerging from it when the decisions and the decision makers are closer and more accessible. Participation in the decision process (through local fiscal administration), not receipt of better information about government activities, is what empowers people in participatory governance. Even though communications technology has made available better, cheaper, and more accessible mechanisms for dealing with a central government, those mechanisms do not fully substitute for the regular, face-to-face contact that a physically accessible government provides.

Experimentation and Innovation

Local governments provide natural laboratories for governmental experimentation and opportunities for governmental innovation. Multiple sovereignty means that local governments may develop their own approaches to dealing with public issues. Some experiments will be successful; some will have problems. The innovations will not put the nation at risk—as would attempts at new practices at the national level—and those that are successful can become best practices for the rest of the country. Because multiple local governments are working for the best interests of their citizenry, there are strong competitive incentives for these governments to strive for efficiency and effectiveness: their citizens will see what other governments are doing and will demand similar or better responses from their leaders.

Accountability

When governmental decisions are made closer to the citizenry, rather than in the national capital, the public is likely to keep careful track of decisions about government services and taxes to finance them, to communicate their concerns and interests to government representatives and officials, and to be watchful as policies are put into practice by the government bureaucracy. That attention is an important contributor to accountability. Lawmakers can be part-time legislators and remain fully involved in the local community and economy, rather than professional legislators who live in a distant capital and connect with their districts only remotely. The citizenry, not an external audit agency, keeps watch on the implementation of government programs, so the feedback is immediate, not the product of some report eventually released by specialists. Direct accountability is to those people for whom the government services are intended and to whom the government will be accountable in the next election. Furthermore, the person passing a law lives in the community and must abide by that law and suffer its consequences.

Improved Revenue Mobilization

The citizenry is more inclined to accept increased tax payments when it sees a clear link between payment of the tax and improved government services. When taxes are levied and collected at the central government level, that link can be hard to see. Payments disappear into the national treasury, and the funds get used in ways that have little identifiable consequence or impact on the taxpayer.

The relationship can be radically different in the local fiscal structure. The governing body levies a tax for local roads, for example: the tax is collected locally, the money is spent on the local roads, and the citizenry can see the link between the tax and the service. The citizenry may be more willing to accept imposition of a tax if the link between it and a particular service is apparent. The effect is both on the politics of getting taxes adopted and on compliance. Any local taxpayer will be a greater relative contributor to the local budget than he or she is to a national budget, and any tax not paid will make a greater difference to that budget. The consequence of nonpayment seems more apparent, so compliance is more likely. The cheater on local taxes is stealing from neighbors, not some distant central bureaucrats. And noncompliance may be more visible to the general public, with some resulting prospect of social pressure to comply. Revenue mobilization involves politics and compliance incentives, not only technological capacity, and local governments can have the advantage in those other areas.[2]

Easier Monitoring of Results

The government services that normally become the responsibility of local governments are services that are close to the people: primary and secondary education, local transport, protective services, local cultural and recreational facilities, housing and utilities, water and sewerage, waste management, and the like. The citizenry are immediately influenced by the services provided, and there is little need for sophisticated measurement instruments to judge the success of the services. The citizens receive the services and can reach easy conclusions about their quality and reasonableness. They can police the results of the government agencies' actions without any survey or reporting lags.

Communication of evaluations is also easy. Local lawmakers and administrators are easier for citizens to contact than are comparable officials of regional or national governments. Except for the governments of the largest localities, there is no distant chain of command between the field and the administration. Problems and results can be communicated simply and quickly, making for high responsiveness. This is critical for establishing citizen-oriented public governance. Because citizen monitoring of results is relatively easy at the local level, it is reasonable for citizen participation to be a regular component of the local budget process. This is important for the formulation of budget programs as well as for the monitoring of program execution and for the evaluation of program results.

Subnational Minority Majorities

Ethnic, religious, linguistic, or social groups may be a majority of the population in certain regions, although distinct minorities in the nation as a whole.[3] Their special interests may well be submerged by the majority in national politics, and they may become alienated from the life of the nation. Local sovereignty gives these citizens the opportunity to govern and to provide local government services, often with a style and substance differing from those in other regions, without the need to break away and form their own country. Because of this ability to adjust government services to local tastes and preferences, local government with decentralized responsibility can be a great accommodator of regional differences and a moderator of regional tensions. The decentralized structure can give regional majorities a role in governance that they would almost certainly never enjoy at the national level. In rural Africa, providing a degree of self-governance has often "been a response to the need to provide an often ethnically diverse population with greater 'voice' and representation in the political process—without dismembering the state as a geographical unit" (Winter 2003: 10). Indeed, decentralization has been the stabilizing result of long civil wars in Mozambique and Uganda. Of course, decentralized governance offers no panacea, as the continuing dissatisfaction of the province of Quebec with its place in Canada demonstrates. But without the degree of sovereignty over many governmental services that provincial government provides, citizen dissatisfaction there would likely be even greater.

Some Disadvantages of More Responsible Local Government

Autonomy in local fiscal administration can improve the provision of government services to the citizenry. But the devolution of greater authority to local units of government is not without problems—and some have proven significant.

Duplication and Responsibility

Seldom are divisions of governmental responsibility among tiers of government so clean that duplication of effort (and the accompanying waste) is totally prevented. Agencies from more than one government may have authority in a particular field—criminal investigations, for instance—with the result that some responsibilities get taken care of twice, while other important functions may get neglected. A centralized government would likely have better control and reduce the duplication of effort.

Just as local governments can create duplication of governmental effort, they also can cause confusion about responsibility for public problems, with the result that inadequate attention is given to some services. The central government may believe that localities are satisfactorily handling an issue, and localities may believe that the issue is a central government responsibility.

More important, the citizenry may be confused about which government is responsible for providing particular services. In a nation with tiers of government, "the government" is never a single entity but multiple governments with differing roles and responsibilities. It is not surprising that an ordinary individual would be confused about which tier of government is responsible for certain duties and which level should be blamed for service failures. Hence, transparency of operations and a clear understanding of assigned responsibilities between governments are important for accountability.

External Impact of Local Decisions

When substandard local provision of services has an adverse impact on the growth prospects and economic productivity of the nation as a whole, local decisions have national importance. Many services that may be provided by local governments—education, environmental protection, public health, and the like—have impacts outside the political and geographic jurisdictions of localities. Local fiscal decision makers have every incentive to pay less attention to external beneficiaries than to the local citizenry, who have a direct impact on the fate of local politicians. In that democratic environment, it is natural that external effects will have limited impact in the fiscal decision-making process and on policy outcomes. At a minimum, such external effects create a strong reason for having special features in the intergovernmental fiscal system to induce localities to take account of these effects in their decisions—whether the features are mandates, controls, or transfer programs.

Another type of external impact from decentralized finances is the macroeconomic impact. When local governments have fiscal autonomy, it is possible that their actions may make national economic stabilization more difficult.[4] There is concern that uncoordinated decentralization creates a bias toward deficits, particularly in developing countries. The problem is particularly acute when the governments with new responsibilities lack the capacity and resources to deal with them. The ultimate danger is that local governments will be unable to practice fiscal discipline and will run uncontrolled deficits, and so may ultimately need to be bailed out by the central government. Unless there is a perceived hard budget constraint on local governments, the sustainability of the national system of government finance is then in jeopardy.[5]

Technical Capacity and Economies of Scale

A frequent objection to expanded local fiscal authority is that local governments lack the technical capacity to handle the tasks needed for responsive, honest, and efficient management of public resources. Personnel may lack the qualifications needed for the work, local governments may lack appropriate information technology, and local lawmakers may lack the experience needed for balanced fiscal decision making. As a result, the local citizenry will not be adequately served if government finances are placed under local responsibility. Rather than start the process of developing local capacity to handle these tasks and provide the citizenry the advantages of having public choices locally, national governments choose to retain fiscal choice at the central level. This occurs in the face of abundant evidence that local authorities are able to develop appropriate capacity. However, without a well-developed and transparent system of fiscal administration, inefficiency, corruption, and ineffective provision of services are distinct possibilities.

A related concern is that of lost economies of scale from having smaller governments provide local services. However, scale economies come from the size of the producer of a service, and smaller local governments might contract for services with larger governments or with private enterprises for production of services, while retaining local government control over the terms and conditions of provision of those services.[6] That arrangement, popular in many jurisdictions in the United States, permits local control over the service while earning the cost and technological advantages associated with large-scale production. It is limited only by the capacity to design a production contract that includes all relevant terms of supply expectations for the quality and quantity of the government service. If intangibles are associated with the service, it may be more difficult to develop an appropriate contract because those intangibles are not easy to capture in contract language—and the contractor will focus on performance of those expectations set out explicitly in the contract.

Horizontal Fiscal Balance

Horizontal fiscal balance—a problem in countries that have substantial regional economic differences—considers the extent to which the distribution of revenue resources (or local tax bases) across local governments can leave some units with great fiscal affluence while others have little capacity. Tax bases are not evenly dispersed because there is an unequal geographic distribution of natural resources (oil, water, and fertile soil); hubs of commerce; and people within countries. A pattern of fiscal imbalance will emerge with almost any local tax source, although this will happen to a greater extent for certain sources (natural resource taxes are one example) than for others and where the geographic scope of the localities is smaller.

Significant disparity in fiscal resources means that the residents of some localities will have better governmental options available to them than will others. Localities that have high fiscal endowments may offer more governmental services at a standard tax rate, standard governmental services at a lower tax rate, or various combinations between those limits. This puts their citizens at an advantage in comparison with citizens of less well-endowed jurisdictions. Such a result may be accepted as an element of the working of the market economy, except to the extent that localities are charged with the provision of services of national importance (primary and secondary education or basic public health, for instance). In these services, the limited endowment of localities can produce public service issues for the nation as a whole—because low-quality public service there can have effects on the rest of the nation—and some national intervention may be needed.[7]

Many higher-tier governments establish intergovernmental transfer schemes to mitigate horizontal imbalances, so that the public services provided by local governments do not vary as widely as their fiscal endowments. Of course, if local government finances are not supported by local resources—in other words, if they are financed exclusively by transfers from a higher tier of government—the horizontal imbalance problem will not arise, unless the higher-tier government is insensitive to imbalance in its transfer programs. However, local governments lose a considerable degree of fiscal autonomy when they lose the ability to adjust the size of their budgets and the distribution of program costs among the population.

Maintenance of National Standards

A national structure with local fiscal autonomy encourages the formation of local identity and local response to special issues confronting localities. However, this responsiveness to local situations may conflict with a spirit of national unity and the need to maintain certain government service standards throughout the nation. Local governments may have different service levels and standards as a result of local disparities in government affluence, competence of local government bureaucracies and officials, rules or their interpretation, and political choices made by the citizenry. Governmental policies and programs will likely differ according to the locality in which a business or individual is located. Therefore, public service responsibilities that are determined to be those of local governments must be those in which national variation will be acceptable.

Expectations from Local Fiscal Administration

Local fiscal administration encompasses the several tasks associated with the delivery of a program of government services to the citizenry, including planning the program, executing it, financing it, and evaluating its results. Proper implementation of local programs should contribute to the well-being of the citizenry and ensure the fiscal sustainability of the operations of the government and local economy. The administrative tasks may be done by the central government (possibly through its local offices), by the local government, or by some cooperative arrangement involving both levels. Examples of each combination appear across industrial, developing, and transition countries. Regardless of the arrangement, the tasks must get accomplished in order for the finances of the government to be managed. The tasks are interrelated components of a functioning program of fiscal administration. Because the size, assigned responsibilities, political constraints, and legislative structures of local governments vary dramatically, even within a single country, the articulation of fiscal administration will itself be subject to great variation. However, the tasks identified here are basic to all local fiscal administration.

The system of local fiscal administration is expected to provide fiscal discipline and responsibility, responsive resource allocation, and efficient and effective government operations (Campos and Pradhan 1996; Schick 1998). The system should function with transparency of policy decisions, program results, and finances, both within the government and to the community at large.

Fiscal Discipline

Local fiscal administration should provide a structure for restraining expenditures to the revenue available, should ensure that expenditure and revenue plans are executed as adopted, should preserve the legality of agency expenditures, should establish a clear trail of agency responsibility for resources intended for use in provision of public services, and should accommodate a system of governance in which government finances serve the interests of the citizenry. It should serve as the first line of defense against public corruption. By erecting a sound system of internal controls to check the execution of the budget, a strong system of internal audit to prevent misuse of resources, and a strong system of external audit to verify the proper use of resources and to implement corrective actions if misuse is discovered, the local government provides a system that serves as protection against theft, misappropriation of funds, and misuse of government resources. A structure for fiscal discipline is the most fundamental element of fiscal administration because it contributes long-term fiscal sustainability and is the first barrier against corruption.

Resource Allocation

Local fiscal administration should provide a structure for choosing policies and for identifying trade-offs in the use of government resources. Resources are limited, opportunities for provision of useful government services are broad, and the budget process should provide a structure for ensuring that resources are allocated to the uses of greatest importance for the citizenry. Because not all worthwhile services will be affordable with the resources available, the fiscal process needs to include a balanced system for making choices from among the several alternative uses of those resources. The choices will emerge largely from political deliberations, not scientific analysis, so the process must be structured to allow as much open identification of alternatives and trade-offs and flexibility for response as possible to improve the chances that broad citizen interests will have bearing on the final choices. Local budgeting provides the greatest opportunity for obtaining direct citizen input into the allocation of these resources, because the decision process is closest to the people and input can be obtained at relatively low cost. Citizens need not travel to a distant capital to be heard by lawmakers in budget deliberations or to hire professional representation to communicate their interests. The potential for citizen participation and for transparency of both decision-making and service results for the citizenry are greatest at the local level.

Technical Efficiency

Local fiscal administration should be a mechanism for providing efficient implementation of the local government's fiscal plans. Once agencies have received resources for the provision of government services, the fiscal process should not discourage the agencies from using them most efficiently. Although it is important that resources not be diverted away from public use, agencies should focus on providing services that have been approved by lawmakers and not on determining exactly how resources are used. Attention needs to be on the results of the use of resources, not on the resources themselves. The process should encourage agencies to be efficient in their provision of services, direct agency attention toward the services of greatest value to the citizenry, encourage use of the best available technological strategies for providing service, and foster quick response when demands for service or provision alternatives change. Control over resources is critical for fiscal discipline, but that control should not be so rigid that government agencies are unable to respond flexibly, quickly, and efficiently in the delivery of services to the citizenry.

Transparency

The process should be transparent to the citizenry if the advantages of public input are to accrue. Citizens should understand when in the process public input will be considered by administrative bodies, and lawmakers and public bodies need to be transparent in their operations. Transparency is a critical element of greater involvement. Otenyo and Lind (2004) helpfully identify five phases of transparency reforms in government: (a) transparency as representative government (government legitimacy); (b) transparency as a means of judging the distribution of policy benefits (service delivery); (c) transparency as a response to maladministration (eradicating corruption); (d) transparency to enhance accountability (information and decision-making disclosures); and (e) transparency as open government (technology, electronic democracy, and governance).[8] Each aspect links to the process of fiscal administration for local governments because that process provides the best opportunity for communicating fiscal results and intentions to the local citizenry and for receiving communications from the citizenry.

Even when lawmakers are effectively operating as the agents of those who have elected them, it is critical that the population understand the fiscal decisions made on their behalf, if for no other reason than to allow them to make informed choices in the next election. For transparency to be effective, fiscal decisions—on taxing, spending, and borrowing—need to be made in an open process, not in closed hearing rooms or so quickly that there is no opportunity for public scrutiny. And fiscal information needs to be publicly and freely available to the general public and, most important, to the media. At the local level, transparency provides the means of communication between government and citizenry regarding priorities, plans, decision making, and evaluation of results and, hence, can become an important foundation for responsive, responsible, and effective public services. Published budgets that include both plans and results in transparent language are important for encouraging local citizen input. A provision for local citizen input is one of the great advantages of making fiscal decisions at the local level, and transparency is the tool for achieving the advantage of citizen participation in the fiscal process. How much information is provided and how usable it is depends on local political will, the cost of providing information, and higher-tier legal requirements. The last is least effective because local transparency is seldom an important concern for higher-tier lawmakers.

Core Functions of Local Fiscal Administration

Local fiscal administration encompasses five distinct core functions. In some countries some may be undertaken by a national administration, while in others they are local responsibilities. It is not apparent that one division of responsibility for the functions is always superior to another. However, the returns from local fiscal autonomy in terms of close responsibility to the local population will be greater as more functions can be devolved to the locality.[9] The core functions include budgeting, accounting, cash management, debt administration, and revenue administration.[10] Each should contribute to the achievement of the overall expectations of fiscal discipline, responsive resource allocation, and efficient operations, as well as to some specific objectives for each function.

Although each function has its own processes and procedures, their roles and operations are closely interrelated as part of fiscal administration. For instance, the preparation, execution, and audit of budgets relies on the government accounting system; revenue administration links closely with cash management operations, as does execution of the adopted budget; and debt management must be connected to budget planning and execution. The operation of an independent local government hinges on the successful operation of the systems that are components of fiscal administration. Each is outlined here.[11]

Budgeting

Budgeting is the process of planning, adopting, executing, monitoring, and auditing the fiscal program for the government for one or more future years. The local budget process is the core of the system of fiscal administration, because that is where the broad financial policies and programs of the government are developed and the size of government is established, with the other functions contributory to its operation.[12] There are certain fundamental principles for the design of a modern local budget system:

- The budget process is comprehensive, including all fiscal entities associated with or connected to the government, and there are no extrabudgetary funds to interfere with fiscal discipline, transparency, accountability, and the struggle against corruption.

- The budget minimizes the use of earmarked funds that reduce the capacity to allocate resources to areas of highest priority.
- The budget is intended to be an operations guide and to be executed as it was enacted.
- The budget process is an annual one, to maintain control, but is adopted in a multiyear financial framework to facilitate planning.
- The budget is based on a realistic forecast of revenues and of the operating environment.
- The budget serves as a statement of local policy.
- Expenditures in the budget are classified according to the administrative unit that is legally responsible for the funds and according to the basic purpose (or program) of the spending.
- The budget is provided in an intelligible format as a communication device with the public, both while it is considered and after it has been adopted.
- The budget process is focused on performance results, not only on inputs purchased by the government.
- The budget process incorporates incentives for lawmakers to respond to citizen demands for services and for agencies to economize on use of resources.

The adopted budget is expected to provide hard constraints on agency resources while giving them flexibility in exactly how they use the resources for service delivery. It is particularly critical that planning efforts be linked to the budget to keep both efforts realistically on track, sometimes working through a formal medium-term budget framework to put everything together. The link makes planning more meaningful and the budget better informed.

The budget process itself is a recurring cycle in which (a) the chief executive of the government, with the operating agencies, develops a service plan to respond to the conditions anticipated in the upcoming year; (b) the appropriate legislative body reviews that plan and adopts a program response based on that plan; (c) the administration puts the adopted program into effect; and (d) an external review body audits and evaluates the executed program and reports its findings to the legislative body and the citizenry.[13] In contrast to the informality and uncertainty found in many developing countries, local governments in Uganda follow a standard budget process and face no need for approval from the central government (Obwona and others 2000)—a good beginning, because an established budget process is a fundamental requirement of local fiscal administration.

The process may provide different budgetary paths for capital (or developmental) expenditures and operating expenditures. Such dual budget systems have created problems in a number of developing countries because the recurring funds needed to operate developmental capital projects are ignored in the budget process,[14] because coordination between donor-financed (mostly developmental) and domestically financed (mostly operating) programs is not undertaken and priorities get distorted from local choices, and because development programs are often planned without regard to resource constraints (Alm and Boex 2002; Sarraf 2005). Indeed, failure to integrate the two budgets and to recognize their total cost of implementation has historically been a fiscal problem in several African countries.

The need to integrate the two types of expenditures in the budget of a government, whether done in a single or a dual budget, is unquestionable. The traditional logic of the capital budget (not development budgets, which also include expenditures for development of human capital) is that infrastructure projects get purchased once and then yield a flow of returns for many years without the need to pay for the project again. A major infrastructure project is likely to be sufficiently expensive to disrupt the finances of the locality if paid for in a single year and so permanent that extraordinary reviews should be undertaken before including it in a spending program. These features are distinct from spending that develops human capital (teacher and physician salaries, for instance) and give rise to the special budgetary treatment of capital spending in local fiscal systems in industrial countries. Fiscal logic accepts that capital budgets may be financed (that is, paid for by issuing debt), so that the facility is being paid for throughout all the years of its life, whereas operating expenditures need to be paid from revenues received during the current year. Whether dual budgets are maintained or not, there is no doubt about the need for local governments to integrate both types of spending in the overall budget process, to link budgets to planning, to maintain processes that reflect the interests of the citizenry, and to maintain budgets within available resources.

In local government budgeting, the citizenry can be involved in each stage of the process, as a means of making the government responsive to public interests and a means of monitoring the results of government programs. Citizen participation has traditionally been political—that is, involving campaigning, voting, lobbying, and sometimes testifying at hearings—but it has been thought of as aimed at influencing public representatives and officials. However, a new philosophy and system—participatory budgeting—incorporates citizen views as agencies develop their budget proposals, so citizen input is considered earlier in the process than has traditionally been the case. Citizens participate directly in deliberations and negotiations over the distribution of local resources, usually in neighborhood meetings, and also in the monitoring of public performance. Participatory budgeting has been successfully used by local governments in Brazil, Canada, China, the Dominican Republic, Ecuador, India, Indonesia, the Philippines, Serbia, South Africa, Sri Lanka, Tanzania, the United Kingdom, and Uruguay.[15]

As Andrews and Shah (2005) point out, budgets and budget processes in developing countries have typically not been citizen friendly. To make participation functional, several significant revisions are needed: (a) budget data must be classified in ways that are meaningful to the citizenry; (b) the budget needs to be prepared in a way that is accessible to the citizenry; (c) the budget must clearly communicate the core responsibilities of officials; and (d) the budget must clearly report crucial features of fiscal operations (outlays, revenues, deficits or surpluses, performance outcomes, and so on).[16] Most often, participatory budgeting has focused on investment spending, first on general priorities and then on specific projects. The budget process needs to ensure complete, timely, and easily accessible provision of information relevant to both intent and execution of service delivery.[17] The best presentations include information about outcomes or results of public programs, along with the traditional financial information about operations. These information flows can be more directly meaningful to local citizens than information about national patterns from the central government—a particular advantage of providing authority and responsibility to local governments.

A global trend in budgeting and public expenditure management is to move the locus of concern from a focus on control of budgetary inputs (emphasizing fiscal discipline) toward a focus on responsibility for service outcomes (the desirable results that emerge from governmental operations, emphasizing resource allocation) or results-oriented management and evaluation. While local governments may have fewer technical skills in statistical monitoring and sophisticated evaluation of results, they can make up for that by greater proximity to the citizenry being served: by paying attention to public response and integrating public input into the monitoring process, a results or outcome orientation emerges.[18] However, Schick (1998) forcefully points out that control of inputs is critical and must be assured before governments move to the more risky task of control of outcomes or results in the budget process. Local services are, however, somewhat more susceptible to the results focus than are central services.

Accounting

Accounting is the application of the system and procedures that record, classify, control, and report on the finances and operations of the government.

Trustworthy accounting systems that track financial transactions by agency, function, and object classification are needed to provide the government, the citizenry, and various third parties with reliable information about the finances of the government for three reasons: as a historical record, as a guide to current operations, and as an input to future financial plans. If the system is to play its appropriate role in local fiscal administration, the financial statements produced by the accounting system should be (a) relevant, in the sense that they include all information that would be helpful in making a decision and are available in time to influence the decision; (b) reliable, meaning that the information is verifiable by independent audit, free from bias, and provides a faithful representation of what has happened; (c) comparable across similar entities so that statements can be benchmarked; and (d) consistent across accounting periods.

Without a trustworthy accounting system and the fiscal reports that system generates, it is not possible to judge the fiscal health of a locality. This ability to judge is important for local lawmakers, for any central overseers of local government finances, for any entities interested in doing business with the locality, and for the citizenry in general. The financial record is needed as new budgets are prepared, so that the fiscal circumstances of the government are understood and so that historical information can guide the preparation of program proposals to be included in the budget. The accounting system also contains various internal controls and checks to protect public funds, to prevent allocation of those funds in ways inconsistent with the legally adopted budget, to provide information that helps prevent spending beyond the amounts available in the budget, and to prevent fiscal gimmicks from giving a misleading impression of the government's financial condition.

The accounting systems and standards should be prescribed by the central government, to ensure comparability and to improve transparency, or, if the profession is sufficiently developed, by a semipublic national accounting standards board.[19] Problems in developing and transition countries include incomplete coverage (funds outside the budget and omission of donor-funded projects); cash reporting only; information gaps (government guarantees and quasi-fiscal activities); data inconsistencies (failure to reconcile debt with financial flows and failure to reconcile budget and actual data); and lags in issuing reports (IMF 2006). Accounting systems that are not amenable to internal and external audit or that generate audited reports only years after the end of the accounting period, as has been the case in municipalities in some Indian states, do not serve the public interest. External audits verify that transactions have been made in compliance with relevant laws. The external audit body in developing and transition countries is usually a central government entity—for instance, the National Auditing Office in Croatia (Ott and Bajo 2001)—but in industrial countries, the body sometimes is a private audit firm working under contract.

Cash Management

Cash management includes operations within the budget year that handle cash flows into the government, payments made by the government, use of funds while they are held by the government, and accommodation strategies when revenues fail to cover approved expenditures. Payments in and out should be made through a single treasury account, not through individual agency accounts, to maintain control and accountability and to obtain the advantages of cash pooling. Revenues must be received and recorded to the appropriate accounts, and payments must be made on a timely basis to legitimate claimants. The timing of revenue flows into the treasury will seldom match payments from the treasury and, even in a government with a balanced annual budget, there will be periods in which accumulated revenue will be less than accumulated expenditures. One task of cash management is to develop short-term mechanisms to bridge those differences without payment arrears (forced loans from suppliers).[20] During other periods of the year, the treasury will have cash balances, and the second task of cash management is to make productive use of those funds in secure short-term investments.[21] Balancing the return from those assets with the need for cash to meet payment obligations is a fundamental resource management issue.

An alternative approach is used in parts of Francophone Africa. Disbursements and revenue remain centralized for local governments,[22] and the national treasury is responsible for managing all these cash flows. That method reduces the need for local capacity in this component of fiscal administration—because the capacity remains centralized. In general application, this approach will almost certainly lead to concerns about lack of financial control by localities and suspicions that funds are not being credited properly (Winter 2003). In this scheme, other elements of fiscal administration can be local while cash management remains centralized.

Debt Administration

Debt administration is the management of government borrowing and of servicing of the outstanding debt. In general, local governments may be permitted to borrow for legitimate infrastructure purposes if they have the capacity to service their debt without requiring assistance from higher governments.[23] The key to borrowing is to convince prospective lenders that they will be repaid on schedule. The fundamental objectives of debt management are effectiveness (the ability to meet the medium- and long-term needs for the finance of infrastructure development); efficiency (borrowing at lowest possible net cost); equity (distribution of infrastructure cost fairly across generations); and accountability (adequate disclosure of debt and debt service program to officials, citizenry, and relevant third parties). Debt management avoids imprudent debt structures and strategies that might threaten fiscal sustainability and future access to debt markets.

Although borrowing can be an excellent way to finance the development of long-life capital infrastructure, it does carry a long-term first claim on public revenues and can create continuing problems for fiscal sustainability if localities borrow to finance continuing operations. Furthermore, local government borrowing can conflict with a national macroeconomic stabilization policy that is designed to constrain inflationary pressures. Such borrowing is self-limiting, in the sense that doubts about the ability to service debt will ultimately exclude the government from debt markets.[24] No amount of manipulation of debt terms or special enhancements will succeed in maintaining access to debt markets if there is doubt about the reliability of debt service.

Proper debt and borrowing policy is crucial for local governments because high debt-service costs can crowd out local spending for continuing services, including those that are absolutely crucial for the citizenry (education, poverty reduction, public health, public safety, and the like). Misuse of borrowing can put the fiscal viability of a government in jeopardy—misuse meaning the use of borrowing to finance operating expenses of government (an operating deficit) and expansion of debt for capital infrastructure that exceeds the debt service capacity of the government. Nonetheless, debt issuance is an appropriate mechanism for financing long-life government capital assets.

Because the proper use of borrowing is the nonrecurring acquisition of long-life capital infrastructure, it is normal that there be a close link between development of the local capital (or development) budget and debt management. Debt management information can help guide the cycle of asset acquisition to avoid high debt burdens, bunching-up of debt issues, and other features that may cause necessary interest rates to increase. Because of the long-term consequences of local government debt and the attractiveness of borrowing to local politicians, local borrowing, debt policy, and debt management are subject to considerable central control and supervision in many countries.

A responsible local debt-management policy embodies principles of fiscal sustainability and discipline:

- Long-term debt should be used only to acquire capital infrastructure that has a useful life longer than the maturity of the debt.
- Debt should not be refinanced to extend its maturity (although it may be refinanced to take advantage of lower interest rates).
- Nonrecurring revenue should be used for capital spending or debt reduction rather than for operating expenditures.
- Short-lived capital assets should be financed with current revenue rather than by borrowing.
- Local governments should integrate capital asset planning and financial planning to ensure the affordability of long-term infrastructure programs.
- Debt should be issued on a competitive basis.
- Localities should practice complete, comprehensive, and clear debt reporting.

Within those principles, debt managers should manage borrowing and debt to minimize the interest, issuance, and servicing cost of debt. Even though borrowing can be subject to great political abuse and corruption, the use of debt is an element of sound local fiscal administration, and it is important to establish controls sufficient to allow governments to borrow in a responsible way.

Some countries have developed systems to facilitate local borrowing by pooling risk, to obtain lower interest costs and provide technical efficiencies in borrowing. In the United States, a number of states have created state bond banks that consolidate the infrastructure offerings of local governments, thus permitting a larger debt issue over which to spread administrative costs and allowing the greater expertise of specialized state staff to be used to manage the issue. The debt issues are consolidated without evaluating the projects, except to determine their legality. In South Africa, a private corporation—Infrastructure Finance Corporation Limited—provides a similar function. It raises funds from international financial institutions and shareholders and lends to municipalities, water boards, and other public institutions for infrastructure development. Similar infrastructure development funds operate in India; the Tamil Nadu Urban Development Fund is one of the best examples (Venkatachalam 2005). All these mechanisms assist with local debt management by providing expertise and economies of scale and allowing some reduction in borrowing cost through technical efficiencies. Of the many development funds around the world, however, few have become truly market-driven intermediaries capable of bringing private savings into the debt markets.

Revenue Administration

Revenue administration implements the system of taxes and charges enacted by the government to provide funds for the operation of government programs, seeking to do so at reasonable cost without biases toward certain taxpayers or types of economic activities. The functions of revenue administration include taxpayer registration and service, tax declaration or assessment, revenue and taxpayer accounting, delinquency control, audit, enforcement, and appeal or protest (Ebel and Taliercio 2005; Mikesell 2007a).[25] Local taxes have successfully been administered by local governments acting alone, local governments working cooperatively, higher-tier governments acting alone, and higher-tier governments working cooperatively with local governments.[26] User charges are, however, usually administered by the government that applies the charge. The extent to which revenue administration is decentralized depends on a mix of technical and political considerations. Although local administration contributes to local control of the revenue program, central administration can permit advantages of scale and specialized expertise; the exact balance between the two options depends on the nature of the particular tax and how it is structured. The guidance that Bahl and Linn (1992) offer for local government tax policy in developing countries applies equally to administration of that policy: keep it simple, and focus on revenue production to the exclusion of other social or economic objectives.

In many developing countries, including those in Africa, revenue sources that local governments are allowed to use typically have limited yield potential even if perfectly administered. Rather than allow the levy of one or two productive taxes, localities are allowed a multitude of unproductive taxes (as many as 60 in Tanzania). They are costly to collect relative to their yield, so local governments are discouraged from levying them or, if they do levy them, from rigorously administering them. The revenue simply does not justify much collection effort. Experience with autonomous local revenue programs, including responsibility for self-administration, under these circumstances should not be taken as evidence of what would be possible if the localities were allowed to use a productive revenue source (a broad tax on land or real property, for instance).[27] Reforms in Tanzania show the potential for improving real property tax revenue by making sure that all properties are on the tax rolls, assessing properties at realistic values, levying a meaningful rate on the tax base, and vigorously collecting the tax that is levied (Kelly and Musunu 2000). Similar prospects for improved revenues have been demonstrated for Kenya (Kelly 2000).

It has been said that "tax administration *is* tax policy" (Casanegra de Jantscher 1990: 179), and this is never more true than for property tax, which is usually identified as the best tax choice for collecting autonomous local government revenue. The property tax base is normally established by government agents (either government employees or private contractors working under government standards), not by taxpayers, so their determinations of value—the values that establish what tax policy is—emerge directly from administrative rulings. In this context, transparency, accountability, and openness of appeal are crucial for acceptable administration and for some assurance to taxpayers of equitable treatment. The inseparability of policy and administration is far more pronounced for revenue administration than for any of the other tasks of local fiscal administration.

The Legal and Institutional Context for Local Fiscal Administration

Local governments in most countries operate within two legal frameworks, one adopted by the national government (or regional governments, in federal systems) and one adopted by lawmakers at the local level. Those frameworks include the local fiscal law and the fiscal administration that implements the law. Fiscal administration must be consistent with any constitutional requirements, must meet regulatory and other oversight standards, and must operate within legal structures erected at national and local levels. The structures include (a) rules regarding budget processes, accounting standards, treasury management, debt management, and revenue mobilization; (b) the context for internal and external audit and enforcement systems; and (c) responsibilities for any special agencies that have oversight of the fiscal functions. Seldom will local governments have free reign in fiscal decisions and how they will be implemented.

Open Borders, Open Internal Markets

The boundaries between local governments within a country are generally open.[28] People and products can freely move from locality to locality. Such free movement is important for the development of national markets in goods, services, and employment and facilitates the flexible movement of capital investment to options that show the greatest potential return. Barriers to movement interfere with the allocation of resources and constrain the growth of the domestic economy. Although local governments may attempt a modern version of mercantilism to gain economic advantage, such practices hinder the overall growth and development of the nation. Hence, constraining practices in fiscal administration, whether they involve budget programs, revenue structures, or debt management, are contrary to the national interest, and central governments usually seek to prevent them. Similarly, local expenditure and taxation programs may be fashioned to distort the movement of resources from one region to another when local governments have substantial autonomy of fiscal choice. Full flexibility of choice may create interjurisdictional competition for mobile factors of production, which creates considerable economic inefficiency. However, this problem is less one of fiscal administration than one of fundamental fiscal policy.

Expenditure and Revenue Assignment

The sorts of services that citizens expect local governments to provide and the revenue resources those governments have available are systematically different from those of central governments. Local governments, either through formal legal assignment or through practice and tradition, are normally responsible for the services that relate closest to people and property, which may include social services (education, public health); infrastructure (roads, water, sewerage, waste management, housing, heating, telecommunications); the environment; social safety nets; and protective services—in varying shares, with private responsibility for some of them. Such services are where the potential advantage of local responsibility is the greatest. National and regional governments are responsible for services with broader impact (national security, interregional transportation, international affairs, monetary and fiscal policy, and the like). Those governments also assume responsibility for transfer expenditure programs, to deal with imbalance and spillover issues involving local governments.

Experience shows that governments in developing countries decentralize responsibility more eagerly than sources of revenue. There is general consensus that neither assigning all revenue mobilization to the central government nor allowing local governments complete freedom to exploit tax bases represents sound fiscal policy. A more reasonable program is one in which each tier of government has access to certain productive tax sources, supplemented by a transfer program to handle horizontal imbalances. Even when localities are allowed to tax a potentially productive base (such as real property), the problem is not fully resolved, because some localities are likely to lack fertile land, commerce, natural resources, or other activities that lead to tax potential. If local governments are expected to provide services to the citizenry, they will require transfers.

Some countries practice complete separation of resource bases by tier of government (for example, India). Others permit considerable tax overlapping (for example, Canada and the United States), although often with considerable cooperation between tiers in structuring and administering the overlapping taxes. Given that local governments usually lack the flexibility to deal with considerable swings in revenue collections from year to year, they are best assigned access to tax bases that are generally immobile (real property, for instance) and that have considerable revenue stability. Inefficient decisions and ineffective administration are likely to result if those general assignments are violated. As economic activity becomes less tied to physical locations and more easily located anywhere in the world, local governments face increased challenges in the independent administration of most tax bases. Productive local revenue structures typically begin with a property tax.

One important issue involves balance between revenue availability and expenditure assignment. As Sevilla (2005: 10) summarizes: "A certain balance between subnational competences and allocated financial resources is necessary to avoid additional problems and funding shortages in public service delivery that sooner or later would create budget deficits." Clarity of assignment and balance between expenditure and revenue are important conditions for orderly local fiscal administration.[29]

Controls and Mandates in Budgeting

The extent to which local governments have autonomy as they develop, adopt, and execute the service provision components of their budgets differs across countries. While some countries follow a practice of only limited guidance and control from the central government, others establish significant guidelines, constraints, and controls over local allocation decisions. Central guidance, controls, and standards seek to ensure that substandard local provision of critical governmental services does not create problems for the nation, but they also restrict the capacity of localities to respond to local conditions and citizen interests. A control framework includes restrictions that are constitutional (some broad principles on which local government will operate); statutory (definitions of the intergovernmental fiscal system, institutional details of government structure and procedures, accountability processes and structures, and remedies for violations); and regulatory (interpretations of the statutes).

Several sorts of intervention are used. First, the central government may impose uniform or minimum standards on the services provided by the local governments. These may be input quality standards, ratios between input classes, or financial requirements. Interventions in choices about education and public health are common, but they may involve other services as well. Unfortunately, national governments in transition countries frequently use input-based "norms" (Guess 2001: 423) that require local governments to spend according to certain physical input ratios (such as nurses to doctors in clinics), rather than focusing on performance-oriented standards that allow a degree of local creativity and responsiveness. That use of norms reduces the efficiency and effectiveness of the government service. Second, the central government may intervene in regard to service areas in which spillover benefits are received beyond the jurisdiction of the locality making the budgetary decisions. The intervention works to protect these services against reallocations toward services that give greater benefits exclusively to the local citizenry. Third, central governments may mandate spending in an area deemed to be of great national importance, often without making any financial provision to support that required expenditure. Some countries have passed laws that prohibit such unfunded mandates, but their effectiveness is usually limited.[30] Fourth, the central government may establish administrative policies in an effort to improve the efficiency of service provision. These programs may require cooperative arrangements between localities. Fifth, a central government entity may be charged with reviewing local budgets before they can become legally binding (as in Mali and Senegal). Unfortunately, these approvals are not always conducted on a timely basis, causing fiscal years to begin with no adopted budget in place. In Swaziland and Zambia, approval often comes several months into the fiscal year (Steffensen and Trollegaard 2000).[31]

The policy question is, how worthwhile are these interventions into the local budgeting process? Each intervention reduces the extent to which the gains from making fiscal choices closer to the people will be realized and increases the control that the central government has over the local decision-making process. The impact of control can be significant. For instance, if the central government establishes wage rates for local employees and drastically controls the ability of localities to dismiss staff, as has been the case in Lithuania, the local government loses a considerable degree of control over its spending—particularly in the provision of labor-intensive services. Although the controls increase the extent to which defined national interest will influence choices, they reduce the ability of the local government to respond to particular local concerns. Accordingly, modern concepts of democratic governance would support a minimalist approach to these controls. If systems to control corruption are in place, if the structures for public choice are robust, and if other elements of fiscal administration are serviceable, then a policy of limited intervention is advisable.

Special Concern with Borrowing and Local Debt

Governments at any level cannot casually borrow without a definite plan for debt service. Excessive debt can endanger fiscal sustainability because of the overburden of debt service on operating expenses; it can also hamper macroeconomic stabilization efforts as debt accumulates.[32] Even when debt is used only to finance, capital infrastructure, the burden of debt service can cripple local finances, and the consequences of mismanagement are high and long-term.[33] Default or repudiation of debt tarnishes the credit rating of a subnational government for decades. For instance, several American states defaulted on their debts in the 1840s—and those states continue to pay a premium on their debt more than 150 years later (English 1996). As a result, higher-tier governments typically control local government borrowing.

There are three patterns of borrowing constraint:[34]

1. *Capital market discipline.* This logic allows localities free access to capital markets. Borrowing is limited by lender willingness to loan. Credit ratings by such agencies as Standard and Poor, Fitch, and Moody's and their national affiliates provide market participants with guidance about default risk.[35]
2. *Higher-tier government review bodies.* Agencies in higher-tier governments, often the national ministry of finance, evaluate and approve local borrowing as to purpose and amount. For instance, in India the federal government must approve state borrowing if the state has debt outstanding to the federal government—and most do. Central controls on local borrowing are common in unitary states.
3. *Legal borrowing limits.* The simplest approach is to forbid local borrowing, but this policy rules out a potentially sensible tool of fiscal administration. A less stringent control is a rigid ceiling on outstanding local debt. For instance, Poland limits annual debt payments of a local government to no more than 15 percent of total forecast revenue. In the United States, almost all states constrain debt issued by their local governments, usually by limiting debt to a particular percentage of the local tax base. There is no debt service guarantee, although states do sometimes intervene in the finances of distressed localities. In Indonesia, borrowing limits for lower levels of government are established by the national government, which also implicitly guarantees the debt. Hungary similarly permits municipal borrowing within limits but explicitly provides no guarantee.

Higher-tier control is vital if there is an implicit (or explicit) guarantee that the higher tier will provide backup debt service. As Rodden (2002: 671) observes: "When the central government is heavily involved in financing subnational governments, it incurs moral, political, and practical obligations that make it difficult to commit to 'say no' to entities that overspend, generate unsustainable deficits, and demand bailouts." Hence, higher-tier governments have a degree of responsibility in ensuring that local governments maintain fiscal discipline: unless local governments see that they face a hard budget constraint, they have little reason to operate responsibly. The American experience is that local governments find ways around unrealistically strict controls, and localities in other countries are likely to be equally clever.

Market discipline may not adequately constrain local borrowing in developing or transition economies. Several conditions need to apply in order for that discipline to be effective (Lane 1993):

- Financial markets must be open. Financial intermediaries cannot be required to serve as purchasers of last resort through reserve or portfolio requirements, provisions of the tax system, or direct mandates.
- Lenders must have full information about the borrower's outstanding debt and capacity to service both old and new debt. Many local governments lack the capacity to forecast revenues and expenditures in the intermediate term, let alone over the life of a long-term bond issue.
- Financial markets must not expect that delinquent borrowers will be bailed out by the central government or by easy central-bank financing.
- Borrowers must be able to respond to indications that the borrowing limit is approaching. The response must become effective before the local government has been excluded from the market.

Loan sources can be difficult to monitor. In the developing capital market, sources for local governments may include other governments, foreign and domestic banks, international organizations, aid organizations, and so on. In that environment, financial control can be complicated; local officials may abscond with funds, leaving the next administration to handle the mess. Many countries apply more stringent controls on foreign borrowing than on domestic borrowing. Without these conditions, market discipline will be ineffective. Central governments need review bodies or legal limits to local borrowing if localities are to avoid fiscal problems associated with the misuse of debt. Clear limits on borrowing provide transparency and certainty and may prevent the political negotiation with central authorities that a review body could create (Ter-Minassian 1997). However, it is difficult to write a limit so binding that experts cannot evade that limit.

Transfer Programs

Local governments depend on transfers received from higher-tier governments to finance a portion of the cost of services they provide. That share will be considerable in instances in which there is a fiscal gap between the cost of delivering assigned service responsibilities and the revenue that can be generated from locally assigned sources. Such gaps can result from some combination of excessive off-loading of responsibilities to the local government or inadequate revenue capacity assigned by the central government.[36] These transfers use distribution standards enacted by the donor government and allocate fund amounts established by these governments, so localities lack direct control over these revenues. But there are sensible reasons for transfers beyond simply filling a gap. Some conditional transfer programs require certain actions by the recipient government (for instance, expenditure of required amounts of funds for a service category or achievement of certain performance measures in Mali and Uganda); with such programs, there is a degree of local control. These transfer programs are designed by central and regional governments to induce certain local actions that contribute to public services that have spillover effects beyond the boundaries of the local government. In that sense, they are intended to be optimizing for the broader nation, not just for the locality.

A second class of transfers mitigates some of the horizontal imbalance of fiscal resources among localities. When local governments finance a portion of their budgets from their indigenous resources, some will enjoy fiscal abundance from their local economies while others will suffer from limited resources. The second group will be hard pressed to provide minimal services to their citizens. This becomes a national problem when the consequences of these services have an impact outside the locality—as when students who were poorly educated in a low-affluence locality move to another locality and become a burden on the social infrastructure there. Therefore, central governments make transfers to provide a degree of fiscal equalization among local jurisdictions. These transfer programs require a standard for distribution (that is, criteria that determine the share received by a locality) and a mechanism for appropriating funds into the distribution formula.

Purely equalizing transfer programs provide local governments with funds that are not intended for any particular purpose but enter the general budget process, for allocation according to local citizen priorities. However, transfer programs intended to support only certain government services (the conditional programs previously described) may have equalizing components that provide greater support for programs in low-capacity localities.[37] Central government finances in many developing countries are themselves fragile, and these governments are likely to reduce the funds provided to transfer systems when they experience financial difficulty, which can be often.[38] That reduction creates extra insecurity for local government finances and threatens the execution of service delivery programs.

There are several desirable features for a transfer program. In general, the program should be (a) transparent and objective, so that localities will know and trust the program functions; (b) formula-driven, so that transfers can be removed from political bargaining between donor and local recipient; (c) stable, so that localities will be able to predict their budget constraint; (d) meaningful, so that the sums received do improve the fiscal condition of the localities; and (e) revenue stimulative, so that funds received do not dampen the incentive for localities to generate revenue from their indigenous resources.[39] In one reformed program, the South Africa central government distributes revenue transfers to local governments through a formula that is based on household per capita income, thus eliminating ad hoc fiscal transfers and providing transparency and a degree of predictability for the recipients.

Special Concerns for the Developing Country Context

Local fiscal administration has new importance for developing and transition countries as they tentatively move away from systems of centralized governance embedded in their colonial heritage or from command-and-control economic principles (Shah 2004). Local governments with greater fiscal responsibilities require improved administrative structures to allow the citizenry to enjoy the advantages of decentralized government while controlling to the greatest extent possible its disadvantages. However, local governments in many of these countries face a challenge that improved fiscal administration cannot correct. They operate in a situation in which all revenues are centrally controlled, except possibly for some low-yield nuisance taxes and charges. Major items of expenditure over which the local government nominally has authority are actually controlled by central mandates and regulations. As noted for municipalities in Lithuania, "local governments have no independent means to adjust to downturns in revenues or increases in costs. Faced with such events, their only option is to run up arrears or borrow from the [central] government or private lenders" (World Bank 2002: iii). In these circumstances, few of the advantages of local government can be realized, and little is to be gained from improved local fiscal administration.

When local governments have meaningful ability to respond to the demands of their citizenry for governmental services, they can make a contribution to public well-being. However, the system of local fiscal administration needs to be constructed to facilitate responsiveness and control over resource use. When the system is in place, local fiscal administration can contribute significantly to the well-being of the citizenry. Several lessons for structuring local fiscal administration run through the experience of many developing and transition countries:

- *Decisions within realistic hard budget constraints.* Many localities develop untenable expenditure plans on the basis of overly optimistic revenue forecasts. During budget execution, pre-expenditure controls on budget commitments are inadequate and arrears (effectively, forced loans) develop. Obligations get paid haphazardly, resulting in an executed budget that is inconsistent with the adopted plan. The problems of faulty budget development, late budget approval, inadequate monitoring of budget execution, and inappropriate execution controls are, unfortunately, common among developing and transition countries.
- *Meaningful information.* Budget classification, development, analysis, approval, and execution focuses on resource inputs, without attention to the services being provided to the citizenry. The information is not presented in a manner that is meaningful to the citizenry. The classic input orientation in the budget arises from a concern for fiscal discipline and control of government operations—from a concern that government and its corrupt employees should be constrained. That is, indeed, the first concern of a budget system, but it should not be the only concern. The attention on control should not crowd out the other foci of fiscal administration—namely, appropriate allocation of resources and encouragement of technical efficiency in operating agencies. Classifications that organize beyond inputs and legal compliance toward attention to the results or outcomes of government are an important reform for responsive local fiscal administration.
- *Transparency for participation.* Local governments provide inadequate dissemination of usable and relevant fiscal information to the public and inadequate direct citizen participation. Transparency of information is critical for accountability and democratic governance. It includes communication with the citizenry, local performance evaluations, and citizen participation in the tasks of fiscal administration. Providing accessibility—bringing citizens into the fiscal process—can be the unique contribution of local government to public service delivery. However, it

will not happen if the information for informed participation is inadequate and procedures for participation are not clear.

■ *Comprehensive coverage.* Local budgets suffer from incomplete coverage. Localities often create special funds from assigned revenues or autonomous agencies that are connected to the government but are seen as outside local fiscal controls. If operations do appear in local budgets, they may be included only on a net basis, thus concealing the true resource use by the agency. The intent is, presumably, to afford greater flexibility of operation, but such structures conflict with control and oversight by the government and with transparency of government operations. Sometimes the extrabudgetary funds emerge through donor-supported activities and a desire by the donors to control how the funds are used. Rather than create such funds, the appropriate response is to repair the regular fiscal system so that all resources are adequately protected. Local budgets need to be comprehensive if the objectives of fiscal administration are to be achieved.

■ *Borrowing.* Issuing debt for infrastructure development can be sound fiscal administration. Developing and transition countries need clear rules for regulating this borrowing, including at least ceilings and possibly review as to purpose.

■ *Transfers.* Local governments need intergovernmental transfers to correct fiscal imbalances and the external impacts of local decisions. Some localities have minimal indigenous resources. To assign them significant service responsibilities without providing resources through transfers would amount to a cruel hoax. Donor governments need transfer programs that are transparent, reliable, and stable if local governments are to have fiscal discipline and provide services efficiently. Transfers that are discretionary, negotiated, and variable do not provide a sound basis for responsible local government.

■ *Technical capacity.* A great concern in giving local governments more fiscal authority is that they will perform poorly because of low technical capacity. The decision to decentralize frequently involves the decentralization dilemma, described by Dillinger (1991: 29) as "a trade-off between indifference and incompetence." The central government is likely to focus less on local problems and preferences than would a local government, but the central government is likely to have greater technical capacity. Thus, central indifference is balanced against local incompetence. However, incompetence can be cured with training and experience, whereas indifference can be endemic.[40] Capacity can be learned through experience; this is probably the best approach to building capacity.

Notes

1. In these localities elected local councils have decision authority, responsibility over meaningful government services, limited mandates from higher authorities, some control over revenue, and a budget process for decision making, control, and monitoring. Not all localities have the same structure, of course.
2. Revenue mobilization prospects also depend on what alternatives the localities have. For instance, Livingstone and Charlton (2001) find that the local tax potential in Uganda falls considerably short of assigned expenditures, but other possible tax instruments show more promise.
3. Local governments may also provide stronger representation for the poor than is provided at the central level.
4. Empirical studies that provide evidence of the impact include DeMello (2000), Fornasari and Webb (2000), Hunther and Shah (1996), and Prud'homme (1995).
5. In the United States, however, state and local governments have a tradition of greater fiscal discipline than the federal government.
6. Some developing and transition countries have gone overboard in the creation of new local governments, establishing far more than are sensible. For example, Armenia, with more than 900 local governments; Croatia, with about 420; the Czech Republic, with 6,292 (Dabla-Norris 2006); and Georgia, with about 1,000, likely take it too far. Some thought about political rationalization should accompany discussions about improving local fiscal administration.
7. This unevenness of resources is a concern about decentralization of responsibility expressed in a recent review of results-oriented expenditure management in Burkina Faso, for instance (Mesple-Somps and others 2003).
8. Otenyo and Lind (2004) also offer specific examples of where transparency affects several tasks in local fiscal administration. For more attention to transparency as it applies to revenue policy and administration, see Mikesell (2007b, chapter 7).
9. The focus is primarily on devolved government finances—"the transfer of authority for decision making, finance, and management to quasi-autonomous units of local government with corporate status" (Litvack and Seddon 1999: 3). Other forms of decentralization involve significantly less scope for independent processes of local fiscal administration and practice under central fiscal systems.
10. Some might add physical asset management and procurement to the group of fiscal administration functions, although these important functions are not part of the normal group.
11. Each function is described in greater detail in Mikesell (2007b).
12. A comparison of national public expenditure management systems in Anglophone and Francophone Africa appears in Llienert (2004). Francophone countries have greater centralization of fiscal management than do Anglophone countries.
13. Legislatures maintain financial control through legal appropriations that are based on three principles: (a) funds appropriated for one purpose cannot be used for another, (b) funds appropriated are the maximum that can be spent, and (c) funds appropriated for one year will not be available for another unless specific provision has been made. Execution of those approved appropriations is in the hands of the administration. In some transition countries (for example, Albania), budgets approved at the local level must be reapproved at the central level.

14. Local governments in some countries—notably Mali, Senegal, and Uganda—frequently omit new operating and maintenance expenses that result when they develop infrastructure projects. This practice obviously threatens fiscal sustainability of the government (Winter 2003).

15. Ilala Municipal Council in Dar es Salaam, Tanzania, appears to have been a more successful experiment, as do Porto Alegre and Belo Horizonte, Brazil. More than 300 localities in 20 countries have used the system.

16. In a number of cities that use participatory budgeting, citizen involvement has concentrated on development expenditures rather than traditional operating programs. Because much of total spending is for salaries and traditional government overhead, there will be little room in such cities for programs deriving from citizen input unless there is willingness to redirect resources.

17. Low literacy rates in several Sub-Saharan African countries create a challenge to citizen participation in budgetary processes, in light of the normal means of communicating fiscal information.

18. Burkina Faso has some experience with bringing decentralized administration into a results-oriented expenditure management system. Its experience shows the need for involving local officials in developing their own performance information systems and budget structures in the implementation of such a management system (Mesple-Somps and others 2003). Guess (2001) cites Razgrad, Bulgaria, and Veles, Macedonia, as models, for linking financial data and physical results in their budgets.

19. The International Public Sector Accounting Standards Board develops high-quality standards for public sector financial reporting and works toward convergence between international and national standards, to improve financial reporting throughout the world. It is particularly concerned about the transition from cash-based accounting to accrual accounting, to improve the quality of reports of financial condition and to provide better tracking of government activities. The government does not set the accounting standards in countries that practice under the English common law system; these countries presume that allowing private bodies with better knowledge and resources to set the standards, rather than a government body, produces a more responsive outcome. The government may be involved in establishing the bodies, but the bodies are private.

20. The United States and Canada have well-developed short-term municipal debt markets, but most countries do not permit their municipalities to borrow for less than a year. That limitation poses extra challenges for cash managers.

21. Cash balances from a number of localities can be combined into a larger investment pool to be managed by a higher-tier government or by contracted professional managers.

22. Such centralized treasury management is far from rare in developing and transition countries. For example, a National Payments Office in the Ministry of Finance also performs treasury functions in both Macedonia and Serbia (Guess 2001).

23. Municipal bond markets are at different stages of development across the developing countries; they typically face a wide variety of institutional challenges before they can play a major role in infrastructure finance. Leigland (1997) reviews progress and barriers in Indonesia, the Philippines, Poland, and South Africa.

24. If it is believed that local borrowing will ultimately be covered by the central government, the moral hazard is obvious. Local governments will have no incentive for fiscal responsibility because their errors will be cleared up by the central government.

Easy access to loans from the central government can be as corrosive to fiscal discipline as central assumption of local debt, as seen in Lithuania (World Bank 2002).

25. For a summary of the process of property tax administration in developing countries, see Bahl and Linn (1992). Property tax administration is significant because this tax is particularly suitable for local government application, including administration, to provide fiscal autonomy.

26. A number of Sub-Saharan African countries (including Kenya, Malawi, Rwanda, South Africa, Tanzania, and Zambia), following the example of Indonesia in the early 1980s, have established national autonomous revenue agencies to improve tax collection performance by removing tax administration from political meddling, to provide greater flexibility in operations, to change the fiscal incentives under which the tax collectors operate, and, at least in part, to give a fresh start in dealings with taxpayers. There appear to be no comparable examples for local administration.

27. Even land or real property tax productivity is likely to be low in rural Africa because ownership is unclear and values are extremely low.

28. There are, of course, lingering exceptions, enforced to greater or lesser degrees in developing and transition economies. They include residency permit requirements in some transition countries, established ostensibly to ensure orderliness in labor markets and provision of local services, and local trade taxes (*octroi*) that apply to the movement of goods across municipal boundaries and that continue to exist in some countries of Asia and Africa. These exceptions inhibit the potential for economic development and improved living standards, although the trade taxes do have good revenue capacity.

29. A review of the decentralization process in Ghana, Senegal, Swaziland, Uganda, Zambia, and Zimbabwe showed imbalance between spending responsibilities and revenue resources to be a considerable problem (Steffensen and Trollegaard 2000). Lack of financial support for spending mandates is a problem for intergovernmental relationships throughout the world.

30. In Senegal, 80 to 90 percent of the aggregate budget is for compulsory spending (Alassane and others 1999). There is no space for meaningful local fiscal administration here.

31. Senegal uses a system of tacit approval to ensure timeliness: if the central government has not raised an objection by a certain deadline, approval is automatic (Steffensen and Trollegaard 2000).

32. Subnational government borrowing in Brazil was so excessive as to threaten national economic stability in the 1990s.

33. In contrast to national governments, localities lack the power of seigniorage. Financing through the creation of money is normally inappropriate—as countries of the former Soviet Union discovered in the early years of their independence—but it can be a tool of last resort, and that gives the national government an extra guarantee of debt service for local-currency debt. Its utility would deteriorate rapidly if it were used regularly.

34. Singh and Plekhanov (2005) examine the effectiveness of various borrowing constraints for controlling local fiscal deficits. They find no arrangement to be best under all circumstances; the best arrangement depends on a series of other institutional arrangements in the country.

35. The rating process and criteria used by one of the international rating agencies are explained in Fitch Ratings (2002). The report makes clear the great extent to which strong finances and strong fiscal administration contribute to the rating. Few

Sub-Saharan African countries have local government creditworthiness ratings from private entities (Zimbabwe is one exception).

36. The transfer program is important as a means of preventing local governments from dealing with the imbalance by borrowing to cover operating expenses and thus endangering long-term fiscal sustainability.

37. Some general transfer programs involve tax sharing, in which a defined portion of a national or regional tax is dedicated for distribution to local governments. The distribution may be made by formula (for example, based on population) or by place of collection (as in some countries of the former Soviet Union). The formula system is easier to administer and can contribute to a horizontal equalization program. The place system provides some explicit incentive for localities to encourage development of the national tax base.

38. For instance, Ghana had difficulty sustaining Common Fund payments to its districts in the recent past.

39. For instance, Alexeev and Kurlyandskaya (2003) found that the transfer system in the Russian Federation discourages lower-level government efforts to increase their tax bases. There is no logical sense to creating such disincentives.

40. There is evidence that greater accountability to constituents—greater responsibility for local governments—has induced improvements in staff competence and attention to quality of work (Campbell 1997; Tendler 1997).

References

Alassane, Papa, Jesper Steffensen, Svend Trollegaard, and Abdoul Wahab. 1999. "Senegal: Fiscal Decentralisation and Subnational Finance in Relation to Infrastructure and Service Provision." National Association of Local Authorities in Denmark, CABEX Sarl, and M. R. BEAL International, Senegal. http://www1.worldbank.org/wbiep/decentralization/africa/Senegal%20Report%20English.pdf.

Alexeev, Michael, and Galina Kurlyandskaya. 2003. "Fiscal Federalism and Incentives in a Russian Region." *Journal of Comparative Economics* 31: 20–33.

Alm, James, and Jameson Boex. 2002. "An Overview of Intergovernmental Fiscal Relations and Subnational Public Finance in Nigeria." International Studies Program Working Paper 02-1, Andrew Young School of Policy Studies, Georgia State University, Atlanta.

Andrews, Matthew, and Anwar Shah. 2005. "Toward Citizen-Centered Local-Level Budgets in Developing Countries." *In Public Expenditure Analysis*, ed. Anwar Shah, 183–216. Washington, DC: World Bank.

Bahl, Roy W., and Johannes F. Linn. 1992. *Urban Public Finance in Developing Countries.* Washington, DC: World Bank and Oxford University Press.

Campbell, Tim E. J. 1997. "Innovations and Risk Taking: The Engine of Reform in Local Government in Latin American and the Caribbean." Discussion Paper 357, World Bank, Washington, DC.

Campos, Ed, and Sanjay Pradhan. 1996. "Budgetary Institutions and Expenditure Outcomes." Policy Research Working Paper 1646, World Bank, Washington, DC.

Casanegra de Jantscher, Milka. 1990. "Administering the VAT." In *Value Added Taxation in Developing Countries*, ed. Malcolm Gillis, Carl S. Shoup, and Gerardo P. Sicat, 171–79. Washington, DC: World Bank.

Dabla-Norris, Era. 2006. "The Challenge of Fiscal Decentralization in Transition Countries." *Comparative Economic Studies* 48: 100–31.

DeMello, Luiz R. Jr. 2000. "Fiscal Decentralization and Intergovernmental Fiscal Relations: A Cross-Country Analysis." *World Development* 28 (2): 365–80.

Dillinger, William. 1991. *Urban Property Tax Reform.* Washington, DC: World Bank.

Ebel, Robert, and Robert Taliercio. 2005. "Subnational Tax Policy and Administration in Developing Economies." *Tax Notes International* 37 (March 7): 919–36.

English, William B. 1996. "Understanding the Costs of Sovereign Default: American State Debts in the 1840s." *American Economic Review* 86 (March): 259–75.

Fitch Ratings. 2002. *International Rating Methodology for Regional and Local Governments.* New York: Fitch Ratings.

Fornasari, Francesca, and Steven Webb. 2000. "The Macroeconomic Impact of Decentralized Spending and Deficits: International Evidence." *Annals of Economics and Finance* 1: 404–33.

Guess, George. 2001. "Decentralization and Municipal Budgeting in Four Balkan States." *Journal of Public Budgeting, Accounting, and Financial Management* 13 (Fall): 397–436.

Hunther, Jeff, and Anwar Shah. 1996. "A Simple Measure of Good Governance and Its Application to the Debate on the Appropriate Level of Fiscal Decentralization." World Bank, Washington, DC. http://www.worldbank.org/wbi/governance/pdf/wps1894.pdf.

IMF (International Monetary Fund). 2006. "Selected African Countries: IMF Technical Assistance Evaluation—Public Expenditure Management Reform." Country Report 06/67, IMF, Washington, DC.

Kelly, Roy. 2000. "Designing a Property Tax Reform Strategy for Sub-Saharan Africa: An Analytical Framework Applied to Kenya." *Public Budgeting and Finance* 20 (Winter): 36–51.

Kelly, Roy, and Zainab Musunu. 2000. "Implementing Property Tax Reform in Tanzania." Lincoln Institute of Land Policy Working Paper WP00RK1, Cambridge, MA. http://www.lincolninst.edu/pubs/dl/8_KellyMusunu00.pdf.

Lane, Timothy D. 1993. "Market Discipline." *IMF Staff Papers* 40 (March): 53–89.

Leigland, James. 1997. "Accelerating Municipal Bond Market Development in Emerging Economies: An Assessment of Strategies and Progress." *Public Budgeting and Finance* 17 (Summer): 57–79.

Litvack, Jennie, and Jessica Seddon, eds. 1999. *Decentralization Briefing Notes.* Washington, DC: World Bank Institute.

Livingstone, Ian, and Roger Charlton. 2001. "Financing Decentralized Development in a Low-Income Country: Raising Revenue for Local Government in Uganda." *Development and Change* 32 (1): 77–100.

Llienert, Ian. 2004. "A Comparison between Two Public Expenditure Management Systems in Africa." *OECD Journal on Budgeting* 3 (3): 35–66.

Mesple-Somps, Sandrine, Marie Eugenie Malgoubri, Jean Muguet, and Blaise Zongo. 2003. "Results-Oriented Expenditure Management: The Case of Burkina Faso." Working Paper 204, Overseas Development Institute, London.

Mikesell, John L. 2007a. "Developing Options for the Administration of Local Taxes: An International Review." *Public Budgeting & Finance* 27 (Spring 2002): 41–68.

———. 2007b. *Fiscal Administration, Analysis, and Applications for the Public Sector,* 7th ed. Belmont, CA: Thomson Wadsworth.

Obwona, Marios, Jesper Steffensen, Svend Trollegaard, Yeko Mwanga, Francis Luwangwa, Ben Twodo, Abdul Ojoo, and Fred Seguya. 2000. "Fiscal Decentralisation and Sub-National Government Finance in Relation to Infrastructure and Service Provision in Uganda." National Association of Local Authorities in Denmark and Economic Policy Research Centre, Uganda. http://www1.worldbank.org/wbiep/decentralization/africa/Uganda%20Annexes.pdf.

Otenyo, Eric E., and Nancy S. Lind. 2004. "Faces and Phases of Transparency Reform in Local Government." *International Journal of Public Administration* 27 (5): 287–307.

Ott, Katarina, and Anto Bajo. 2001. *Local Government Budgeting in Croatia.* Zagreb: Institute of Public Finance.

Prud'homme, Remy. 1995. "The Dangers of Decentralization." *World Bank Research Observer* 10 (3): 354–60.

Rodden, Jonathan. 2002. "The Dilemma of Fiscal Federalism: Grants and Fiscal Performance around the World." *American Journal of Political Science* 46 (July): 670–87.

Sarraf, Feridoun. 2005. "Implementation Note: Integration of Recurrent and Capital 'Development' Budgets: Issues, Problems, Country Experiences, and the Way Forward." World Bank Public Expenditure Working Group, Washington, DC. http//www1.worldbank.org/publicsector/pe/StrengthenedApproach/CapitalRecurrentIntegration.pdf.

Schick, Allen. 1998. *A Contemporary Approach to Public Expenditure Management.* Washington, DC: World Bank.

Sevilla, Joaquin. 2005. "Accountability and Control of Public Spending in a Decentralised and Delegated Environment." *OECD Journal on Budgeting* 5 (2): 8–21.

Shah, Anwar. 2004. "Fiscal Decentralization in Developing and Transition Economies: Progress, Problems, and the Promise." Policy Research Working Paper 3282, World Bank, Washington, DC.

Singh, Raju, and Alexander Plekhanov. 2006. "How Should Subnational Government Borrowing Be Regulated? Some Cross-Country Empirical Evidence." *IMF Staff Papers* 53 (December): 426–52. International Monetary Fund, Washington, DC.

Steffensen, Jesper, and Svend Trollegaard. 2000. "Fiscal Decentralisation and Sub-National Government Finance in Relation to Infrastructure and Service Provision: Synthesis Report on 6 Sub-Saharan African Country Studies." National Association of Local Authorities in Denmark. http://www.cddghana.org/documents/decentralization%20in%20subsahara%20africa_1999_PADCO.pdf.

Tendler, Judith. 1997. *Good Government in the Tropics.* Baltimore, MD: Johns Hopkins University Press.

Ter-Minassian, Teresa. 1997. "Decentralizing Government." *Finance and Development* 34 (September): 36–39.

Venkatachalam, Pritha. 2005. "Innovative Approaches to Municipal Infrastructure Financing: A Case Study on Tamil Nadu, India." Working Paper 05-68, Development Studies Institute, London.

Winter, Mike, ed. 2003. *Local Government Initiative: Pro-Poor Infrastructure and Service Delivery in Rural Sub-Saharan Africa, A Synthesis of Case Studies.* New York: United Nations Capital Development Fund.

World Bank. 2002. "Lithuania: Issues in Municipal Finance." Report 23716-LT, World Bank, Washington, DC.

2

Forecasting Local Revenues and Expenditures

LARRY SCHROEDER

Budgets are the heart of the financial management and fiscal planning process. Because budgets and plans are future oriented, forecasting upcoming expenditure requirements and resource availability is critical to the budgeting and planning process. This chapter focuses on advantages and shortcomings of methods that subnational governments can and do use to forecast revenues and expenditures.[1]

The chapter takes a normative (what ought to occur) and a positive (what actually happens) approach. The positive approach to subnational forecasting in developing and transition economies is stymied by the lack of empirical information on which to base analysis. It appears that local governments in developing and transition countries seldom attempt to forecast fiscal conditions in a systematic manner.[2] Even information on national level forecasting practices in low-income countries is quite limited. The literature on local government forecasting techniques and procedures focuses primarily on jurisdictions in the United States. Thus, many of the actual practices cited herein are drawn from U.S.-based experiences.

Fiscal forecasting is critical to good local financial management. At least in principle, local governments are required to ensure that expenditures do not exceed revenues. Therefore, realistic annual budgets require that revenues be forecasted as accurately as possible. If revenues are vastly overestimated, the locality will have to make unanticipated cutbacks in spending. Similarly, underestimates of revenues will lead to unexpected budget surpluses, which could tempt local decision makers to undertake pet projects that would have been rejected if scrutinized in the regular budget process. These undesirable outcomes imply that realistic and reasonably accurate revenue projections should be a primary objective of forecasts in the annual budget process.[3]

Ex post revenue forecasting accuracy is generally less of a concern for longer-term (three- to five-year) fiscal forecasts. Multiyear forecasting exercises are generally meant to assist in planning and policy making. Starting at a point of equality between revenues and expenditures (that is, a balanced budget), projections of revenues and expenditures several years into the future will most often lead to forecasts of a budget deficit. Such forecasts warn policy makers that they must enact fiscal policies to avoid revenue shortfalls. Such policies can include efforts to mobilize additional resources locally, garner additional intergovernmental transfers, and reduce spending. If the policies are undertaken and are successful, the forecast of a deficit will be in error in the sense that the deficit did not arise as was forecast. However, such an "error," which leads to prudent fiscal decisions, is preferable to emergency measures to avoid deficits.

The following section reviews the various techniques for forecasting revenues and expenditures. Subsequent sections discuss revenue forecasting and expenditure forecasts. Another section explores the challenges faced by forecasters in developing and transition countries.

General Forecasting Techniques

Some forecasting techniques may be more applicable to revenues or to expenditures.[4] Objective approaches are fairly easily explained and systematic; subjective approaches are based primarily on the forecaster's judgment. The choice of approach is likely to be based in part on the forecaster's judgment and various approaches' feasibility.

Judgmental Techniques

Judgmental forecasting essentially relies on the forecaster's special expertise—that is, knowledge of the local revenue system and the factors that tend to affect annual flows of revenue. Because this subjective approach is primarily dependent on the idiosyncrasies of the specific situation and forecaster, not much can be said about it other than that its implementation cost is likely to be low and that it can yield fairly accurate short-term forecasts. Stemaier and Reiss (1994) document evidence that a panel of local experts can generate annual budget forecasts as accurate as forecasts resulting from objective techniques.

Time-Series Techniques

Time-series techniques link expected future revenues or expenditures to past experience. These techniques can differ greatly in terms of complexity. This discussion is limited to the simpler approaches.

By far the simplest approach is to project the next year's flows purely on the basis of what happened in the very recent past—for example, the past two years for which data are available. The forecaster can predict that the change in the amount of a local revenue source will alter in the future year just as it has in the past. But the forecaster must decide whether to use the *absolute* change experienced or the *percentage* change in the data. That is, if a revenue source increased from 100 to 120 pesos between years t and $t + 1$, the forecaster can project that the series will increase in the future by 20 percent each year or by 20 pesos each year. (An absolute increase of 20 pesos from 120 pesos to 140 pesos implies only a 16.7 percent increase, because the base is now 120 pesos.)

If the forecaster can use data for many years in the past, he or she must select one of several techniques for analyzing revenue trends. One technique is to compute percentage year-to-year changes in the series and, if they are approximately equal for at least the previous four to five years, to use the average of those percentage changes. Alternatively, the forecaster could plot the series against time on a two-dimensional graph; if all points lie approximately on a straight line, the same linear trend might be used to project trends.[5] Computerized spreadsheet programs can project linear trends as well as linear growth on the basis of a statistical estimate of the past. Trend techniques are simple to use and to explain, but they rest on the assumption that the factors that have influenced a revenue or expenditure in the past will continue to exist.[6]

Deterministic Techniques

Forecasters may find variables other than the passage of time more realistic as determinants of future revenues or expenditures. For example, if a government transfer program is exclusively determined on the basis of the local population, forecasters can use a projection of population growth to drive the forecast. They can also use the technique to estimate future locally generated revenues. In Prince William County, Virginia (in the United States), forecasters assumed that the number of households in the county is directly related to retail sales tax collections and that the real (as opposed to nominal) per household sales taxes would be constant over the following five years. The forecasters then made assumptions about growth in the number of households and converted the projected real sales taxes into a nominal amount on the basis of expected future increases in prices (Prince William County, Virginia, 2002).

Forecasters use deterministic forecasts extensively in making projections of expenditures. Wages and salaries associated with a particular local government service equal the product of the average annual wages and salaries of those employed in producing the service multiplied by the number of employees. A forecaster can make assumptions about each of these variables, the product of which will constitute the expected level of spending on wages and salaries.

Deterministic techniques are often used at the national level in developing countries when revenue forecasts are made several years into the future. Typically, the government sets a target that national revenues will equal some proportion of gross domestic product (GDP). Forecasters multiply estimates of future levels of GDP by the targeted revenue proportion to forecast future tax and nontax revenues. Because local product data are relatively unlikely to be available, this technique may be less applicable for local government forecasting than for national government forecasting.

However, forecasters have a somewhat related deterministic approach for forecasting local revenues. A useful statistic in analyzing revenue data is the income elasticity of a revenue stream. The income elasticity coefficient measures the percentage change in past revenues relative to the percentage change in income (which might be approximated by the percentage change in a country's GDP). If revenue elasticity estimates are available, forecasters can combine projections of GDP to derive a deterministic forecast of a local revenue source.

Deterministic approaches to forecasting are quite simple (and hence forecasters can easily explain the underlying rationale to policy makers). Unlike time-trend techniques, they do not require that the forecaster assume that future revenues or expenditures will rise (or fall) inexorably as they have in the recent past. The technique does, however, require that the forecaster make explicit assumptions regarding the variable(s) thought to drive the revenue or expenditure being forecasted. Such assumptions may turn out to be erroneous.

Statistical Models

Statistical forecasting models, sometimes termed *econometric* models, constitute the most complex approach to forecasting and require the most extensive amount of data. They allow the forecaster to attempt to capture the effects of one or more variables that conceptually should affect a revenue or expenditure and to base the relationship between those variables and the one being forecasted on statistical estimation techniques. Because local economic conditions are likely to affect local government revenues, revenue forecasts from statistical modeling are more common than spending forecasts from such modeling.[7]

The most common statistical approach is linear regression analysis. First, the forecaster determines independent and causal variables to explain past and future changes in the revenue or expenditure to be projected. Second, he or she collects historical data on these variables and on the revenue and expenditure series to be forecast. Third, the forecaster uses linear regression analysis to estimate the statistical relationship between the revenue and expenditure series and the causal variables. Fourth, he or she makes projections of (or assumptions about) the future levels of the independent variables and inserts them into the estimated statistical relationship to forecast the revenue and expenditure series.[8]

The accuracy of forecasts from this technique relies on selection of reasonable independent variables, the correctness of the projected values of those variables, and the stability of the statistical relationship into the future. Unlike judgmental techniques, the method makes explicit the factors that the forecaster is using to generate forecasts and therefore permits ex-post analysis of erroneous forecasts so that future forecasts might be improved. Unlike projections from trend-based forecasts, projections from a statistical model will depend on the expected changes in one or more independent variables; hence, the revenue or expenditure series may show decreases as well as increases into the future. Unlike the deterministic approach, the statistical technique permits the analyst to learn whether the hypothesized relationships between the chosen independent variables and the revenue/expenditure series are statistically relevant (statistically significant).

To decide which technique is most reasonable in any locality, forecasters will have to rely on their own judgment as well as on some analysis of local budgets; the cost and feasibility of using a particular method will also enter into the decision. A single approach will not necessarily be the most appropriate for all local revenues or expenditures. Furthermore, the reasonableness of a technique may depend on whether the forecast is for a single budget year or multiple budget years.

Revenue Forecasting

In revenue forecasting for the annual budget, final estimates should include the effects on revenues of any policy changes, such as changes in tax rates and tariffs as well as changes in the definitions of local taxes and charges. Longer-term projections generally make no attempt to incorporate the revenue impacts of future policies; instead, the objective is to forecast revenues that would be realized by the local government if no changes in policies were made. Estimating the future flow of revenues in the absence of foreseeing future changes in policies is sufficiently difficult.

Although revenues can be forecasted in the aggregate, disaggregating them into their constituent parts is more reasonable. Only in this way can the forecaster analyze in some depth past forecast errors and use that information to improve future forecasts. Furthermore, different techniques may be more or less appropriate for different types of own-source and intergovernmental revenues.

Own-Source Revenues

Local governments use a variety of taxes. Because property-based taxes are particularly important local revenue sources in many developing countries, specific attention is given to forecasting such revenues.

The orientation of the discussion here is normative rather than positive. As Kyobe and Danninger (2005: 3) note, "little research has been carried out on the determinants of revenue forecasting practices" at the central or local levels in developing and transition countries. In a survey of forecasting practices in 34 countries (80 percent of which are developing countries and 20 percent of which are transition economies), Kyobe and Danninger found that revenue forecasts are the product of the consensus of technical experts in 64 percent of the countries. Kyobe and Danninger show that only 12.9 percent of the responding countries rely on statistical (econometric) methods to produce their revenue forecasts.

Researchers have conducted several surveys of state and local government revenue forecasting practices in the United States (see Jung 2002 McCollough 1990; Rubin, Mantell, and Pagano 1999). These surveys reveal that judgmental and trend techniques were, by far, the most commonly used approaches. Only 20 to 33 percent of the surveyed localities used statistical methods.

The task of forecasting own-source revenues generally focuses primarily on the major local tax and nontax revenues, because aggregate forecasting errors are little affected by minor revenues. With respect to major revenues, the types of factors that might influence changes in revenue flows from year to year are useful to consider. Some local revenues, such as an income-based tax or a tax on the revenues of local businesses, can be expected to change as economic conditions change; however, revenues from a vehicle parking concession may not be expected to fluctuate greatly from year to year (unless parking tariffs change).

Statistical modeling is a reasonable method for forecasting local taxes and some nontax revenues that are presumed to be sensitive to fluctuations in the state of the local economy. New York City uses this approach for forecasting important local tax revenues (see box 2.1).

B O X   2 . 1   New York City's Revenue Forecasting Effort

New York City, the largest city in the United States, annually produces a multi-year forecast of its tax revenues in accordance with the city's charter, which stipulates that revenue forecasts be generated for all taxes that constitute at least 5 percent of tax revenues. Furthermore, the Office of Management and Budget (OMB) must make the forecast available to the public.

The OMB relies heavily on statistical forecasting methods. The OMB's Economic Analysis Unit maintains a 77-equation econometric (statistical) model of the New York City economy. Among the economic variables forecasted from the model are employment in 14 major sectors of the local economy; wage rates for the finance, private nonfinance, and government sectors; consumer price index; personal income; gross city product; and some real estate market indicators, such as vacancy rates and rental rates for office space. Analysts use output from this model as input for the tax revenue forecasting equations.

The retail sales tax, levied on retail sales in the city, generates approximately 14 percent of New York City's tax revenues. In the statistical model used to project annual sales tax revenues, these revenues are a function of the wage rate and total employment in the city. Analysts use regression analysis to estimate that statistical relationship between those two variables and past sales tax revenues.

New York City is allowed to collect tax levied on the personal incomes of city residents (who also pay taxes on their incomes to the federal government and the state of New York). This tax constitutes approximately 17 percent of total tax collections for the city. The forecasting model for the personal income tax is more complex than the one used for sales tax. From projections of personal incomes, a micro simulation model maintained by the New York State Department of Taxation and Finance is used to estimate total tax liability. Most taxes

(Box continues on the following page.)

on wage and salary incomes are paid on the pay-as-you-earn or withholding basis. The model to estimate these taxes stipulates that the logarithm of withheld taxes is a function of the log of wage earnings plus dividend, interest, and rental incomes and the log of the maximum city personal income tax rate. Other income taxes are paid directly by the taxpayer during the fiscal year; to forecast these payments, analysts use three independent variables: dividend, interest, and rental income; net capital gains realization; and the maximum city income tax rate. Analysts estimate the second of these independent variables using a statistical model with five independent variables.

New York levies a tax on corporations doing business in the city. To forecast this tax revenue, which makes up more than 6 percent of total tax revenues, the OMB divides firms into two groups: financial firms and nonfinancial firms. For financial firm corporate tax revenues, analysts consider two variables: profits of New York Stock Exchange member firms and the GDP (for the country). For corporate taxes of nonfinancial firms, analysts use three explanatory variables: gross city product, before-tax corporate profits relative to GDP, and employment in professional services within the city.

The final tax forecasted by OMB is the property tax. This tax on the assessed value of real property generates more than 40 percent of the city's tax revenues. Because the tax is not closely linked to current economic conditions, analysts use a combination of judgmental and deterministic methods to forecast its revenues.

The complexity of the forecasting effort described above reflects New York City's large annual tax revenues (exceeding US$28 billion) and heavy reliance on own-source revenues necessary to provide public services.

Source: New York, New York 2005.

Statistical techniques require a level of technical sophistication not always available at the local level in developing countries. Potentially even more constraining are the data requirements necessary for such a technique to be useful. First, a time series of revenue data for the revenue stream being forecasted is necessary; generally, the series should be at least 15 years long. (This series of data will have to be "cleaned" for past policy changes that have significantly affected local revenues; see box 2.2.) Second, a set of variables that can reasonably be hypothesized to influence those revenues must be available for the same period of time. Finally, projections of those explanatory or independent variables must also be available.

At the local level in most developing countries, use of nationwide economic indicators—for example, GDP or national income or national price levels—may be the only feasible way to implement the statistical approach, because local-level data are unlikely to be available. Even then,

BOX 2.2 Preparing Time–Series Data for Forecasting

If a statistical (econometric) model or long time–series model is to be used for forecasting revenues, a substantial data preparation effort is necessary. First, the revenue data must be reported consistently over the entire time period. Major revenue sources are likely to have been reported consistently over a long period. But financial managers sometimes record minor revenues somewhat randomly from year to year.

Second, the data should be "cleaned" for past changes in the rate or definition of the base of the revenue source. Consider the following example: a tax rate is doubled in between fiscal years 2000 and 2001. Such a large rate increase should result in a substantial increase in revenues derived from that revenue source. If the analyst were to look at a plot of the flows of revenues from 1990 through 2005 and fit a trend line to those data, the slope of the trend would overestimate how much the revenues have been increasing from year to year. Similarly, if the definition of the base of the tax had changed at some point during the series—for example, certain types of fuels were made exempt from a fuel tax—the time series of actual collections would reflect that policy change.

To obtain a more realistic estimate of the trend in revenues from a tax for which rates or bases have changed, the analyst, who wishes to use the time series of data, should adjust the data to reflect revenues from a consistently defined set of tax rates and tax bases. Similarly, if a statistical model is to be used to forecast revenues, the analyst must clean the data of the effects of rate and base changes. The task is not too difficult if only one or two rate or base changes were made during the time series of data collected; however, it can be considerably more difficult if numerous changes were made. First, the analyst must review the history of changes in tax rates and base definitions—changes not always regularly recorded. Second, the analyst must make estimates of the revenue effects of those changes and adjust the time series accordingly. This task may not be particularly difficult for changes in tax rates; as suggested, if the tax rate had been doubled in 2001, the analyst can assume that in the years before 2001 revenues would have been twice as large as they were had the higher rate been in effect. (Such an adjustment is, however, based on the questionable assumption that the rate change would have had no effect on the behavior of taxpayers.) Adjusting for changes in the definition of a tax base requires estimating the revenue effects of the change in base definition not only for the year in which the change took effect but also for all years before that change. When such estimates are made during the year in which the policy change is implemented, the analyst can use the results to adjust the revenue data for the years before the change.

Analysts can use many methods to clean revenue data. Gamboa (2002) summarizes the alternatives. For additional information, see Bahl (1972), Harris (1966), or Prest (1962).

Source: Author.

analysts must recognize that forecasts made from such equations can be in error. Given the difficulties associated with using statistical models for forecasting own-source revenues, many revenue forecasts rely on deterministic or trend-based approaches.

Although statistical or econometric forecasts of local revenues may not be feasible in most developing or transition countries, systematic forecasts using deterministic techniques can provide a reasonable alternative that links local revenue forecasts to projections of the national economy. Stated in the form of a simple equation,[9]

$$Rev_{t+1} = Rev_t \times [(1 + GDPGro) \times J1],$$

where Rev_{t+1} is the forecasted amount of revenue expected to be collected in year $t + 1$, Rev_t is the amount of revenue collected in year t, $GDPGro$ is the projected rate of growth in the nation's GDP during year $t + 1$, and $J1$ is an adjustment factor.

$J1$ can be set on the basis of the forecaster's best judgment. If $J1$ is set equal to 1.00, the assumption is that local revenue will grow exactly as fast as growth in GDP for the nation. The $J1$ factor is equivalent to the income (GDP) elasticity of the local tax yield; thus, if $J1 = 1$, the forecaster is assuming a unitary income elasticity for that local revenue source. Any other estimates of the income elasticity of a local tax can be substituted in the equation for the $J1$ adjustment factor.[10]

Some local revenues may be immune to fluctuations in the national economy. Parking fee revenues, for example, are probably invariant to changes in GDP. Analysts can use local variables such as projected population or number of registered vehicles to forecast these particular revenues.

Accurately forecasting property tax revenues can be challenging, particularly if the base of the tax is defined as the value (capital or annual) of the property. Analysts might expect property values to be highly correlated with local, and perhaps national, economic conditions. But local property taxes are seldom closely linked to short-term fluctuations in the national economy, because the base of the tax is the assessed value of the property; in most cases assessed values do not coincide with market values of the property.[11]

Good projections of property tax revenues will depend on the forecaster's knowledge of how the tax is administered locally.[12] Property tax revenues (like revenues from other taxes) are the product of the tax base times the tax rate times the collection ratio.[13] Changes in any of these factors will determine the degree to which actual revenues are likely to grow; thus, the forecaster needs to know how each factor is likely to change. If assessed values of property keep pace with inflation (not common in most developing countries), expected inflation can be used to project the tax base. However, if reassessment intervals are long, the base will grow only to the extent that new taxable properties are added to the tax roll. In this case, projections of revenues can rely on forecasts of new construction and additions of new properties to the tax roll. Likewise, changes in efforts to collect current property tax liabilities (as well as delinquent taxes) can significantly affect actual collections. Only forecasters familiar with local assessment practices and tax collection efforts are likely to make reasonably accurate projections.

Intergovernmental Transfers

Intergovernmental transfers dominate local government revenues in many developing countries. Even in supposedly highly fiscally decentralized countries, intergovernmental transfers may constitute two-thirds to three-quarters of the revenues available to subnational governments. To forecast accurately the revenues to be received both in the next fiscal (budget) year and over the longer term, a local government forecaster must estimate the revenue flow under the control of a nonlocal level of government. To do this, he or she must have knowledge of the two factors that determine the flow of transfers to a particular local government: the size of the total pool of money to be transferred to all localities under a particular intergovernmental transfer program and the mechanism used to allocate that money to all eligible subnational governments.

One type of transfer closely related to own-source revenue is a shared tax distributed to local governments on the basis of where the tax is collected.[14] Forecasters can project shared tax revenues using the methods discussed above, particularly when the shared tax is likely to be highly correlated with the national economy. But they could in some cases rely on the central government's forecasting efforts. If the central government is projecting a 5 percent increase in a tax shared with subnational governments, forecasters could reasonably assume that a comparable percentage growth rate holds at the local level. When the local government derives the entire proceeds from the "shared" revenue source, the techniques discussed above are probably reasonable for forecasting future revenues.

Some countries rely on transfer programs under which the total transfer pool is set at some percentage of national tax collections and allocated among local governments according to a well-defined formula with transparent variables. In the Philippines, 40 percent of tax collections by the Internal Revenue Bureau are distributed across provinces, municipalities, cities, and barangays (geographic subdivisions of cities and municipalities) according to well-defined formulas that include only two variables: population and area of the jurisdiction (plus an equal amount to all jurisdictions). According to the Internal Revenue Allotment, the transfer pool for a particular fiscal year depends on internal revenue collections in the fiscal year completed three years before the budget year in question. That is, the transfer pool for fiscal year 2007 is based on actual collections in 2004. Thus, projecting IRA revenues for 2008–11 requires an estimate of tax collections for 2005, 2006, and 2007; if such a forecast is made in 2007, information on tax collections for 2005 and 2006 will already be available.

Where the size of the transfer pool is determined annually as part of the state budget process, projecting the size of the pool is considerably more difficult. If the government conducts multiyear planning and budgeting exercises by constructing a medium-term expenditure framework (MTEF), this planning document might provide a reasonable approximation of the size of the pool.[15] Because intergovernmental transfers from the central government are simultaneously revenues to local governments and "expenditures," projections of the transfer pool may be directly available from the MTEF. In that case, the local forecaster must forecast the share of that pool that the local government will obtain. Alternatively, the local forecaster may use past trends or expert opinions regarding the amounts to be transferred or, using a conservative scenario, assume that the transfer pool will remain constant in nominal terms, or, less conservatively, will remain constant in real terms—that is, will grow only to keep pace with inflation.

Another type of intergovernmental transfer program is specific-purpose transfers—that is, grants that must be spent for particular purposes. Again, forecasting is likely to be judgmental or trend based. In many countries, local governments receive pass-through transfers to be spent for specific purposes mandated by the central government. In these instances, the revenues will have no net effect on the budget, because they are offset by an equal amount of spending. The forecaster must retain that balance on both the revenue and the expenditure sides of the budget.

Another type of transfer program with direct links to expenditures is a cost-sharing transfer whereby the local government matches some proportion of the transfer with its own expenditures. If revenue forecasts include such a transfer, analysts must adjust expenditure forecasts in a corresponding manner to reflect the local share. Cost-sharing transfers are most commonly used to help finance capital investments. These investments are likely to have long-term effects on recurrent expenditures—effects for which analysts must account in multiyear forecasting efforts.

Expenditure Forecasts

The term *forecasting* is less appropriate for the process that yields estimates of expenditures as shown in the annual budget than for the process that yields estimates of revenues. Generally, writers of the operating budget for the next fiscal year rely on forecasts of revenues and, in an environment with a hard budget constraint, derive budgeted amounts equaling those revenue forecasts. Expenditure forecasting, in the sense of developing estimates of spending that might occur, is most closely tied to long-term forecasts of spending.

As noted, multiyear spending forecasts are not really predictions of the amounts that will actually be spent but rather predictions of the cost of providing a certain level of public services. Most state and local governments in the United States forecast what it will cost in the future to provide the level of services provided today. They then compare their estimates with long-term projections of revenues to determine whether, in the absence of policy changes on the revenue side, budgetary deficits will result. Alternatively, these governments use a deterministic model to generate alternative expenditure policy scenarios.

An accounting identity approach to expenditure forecasting disaggregates spending by department, agency, or program and by object of expenditure (for example, labor or materials). This approach recognizes that expenditures will be the product of the quantity of each input times its price or cost. The forecast of these detailed expenditures can be as disaggregated as the accounting or financial management system permits.

Personnel Expenditures

The deterministic approach to forecasting expenditures on labor can be built from the accounting identity that labor expenditures in year t (LE_t) equal the product of wages or salaries (W_t) times the amount of labor used (N_t). That is,

$$LE_t = W_t \times N_t.$$

This calculation can be performed for each functional area. If sufficient data are available, the wage and employment information within a functional area can be disaggregated into various categories of employees. For completeness, wage and salary data should include the costs of any fringe benefits associated with employees—for example, contributions toward retirement programs.

For the purpose of forecasting, the analyst must make assumptions about the future values of W and N. Regarding future levels of wages and salaries, one assumption is that these levels will just keep pace with the expected level of inflation—that is, real wages will remain constant over the forecast period. If the analyst uses assumptions about future increases in prices to generate revenue forecasts, he or she should reflect those assumptions in expenditure forecasts.

Projections of the amount of labor to be employed should be linked to the underlying assumption about service levels. As noted above, the assumption of a constant service-level budget is commonplace. Determining exactly what that assumption means for projections of public employment levels is hard to specify for some services. In the case of public education, it might mean that employment must increase at the same rate that student-age population is expected to increase. For other services, population may be considered a reasonable determinant of future employment requirements (under the assumption of constant services). That is, if the local population is increasing annually by 1 percent, the forecaster could assume that local public employment needs to increase by 1 percent.

Mandated or local policies that have been adopted but not implemented should also be built into expenditure forecasts. Thus, for example, if the local government has passed legislation that commits it to provide two additional health centers, the forecaster must include the additional employees necessary to operate those centers in the forecast. Similarly, if policies decrease needs for public employees, the forecaster must reflect a reduced number of employees in the forecast.

As noted, analysts can use a deterministic model to project expenditures under policy scenarios other than those based on the assumption of constant services. This task is particularly easy if the entire model is computerized. The accounting identity approach makes computerization on commercial spreadsheet programs feasible.

Nonpersonnel Current Expenditures

The costs of materials and supplies associated with the production of local services can be forecast in a manner comparable to personnel expenditures. The following accounting identity can be used for the forecast:

$$O_t = P_t \times Q_t,$$

where O_t is other current expenditure in year t, P_t is the price of those nonpersonnel expenditures, and Q_t is the quantity of nonpersonnel inputs.

The degree to which these expenditures are disaggregated by functional area depends on the forecaster's ability to assign materials to relatively homogeneous groups of goods, the availability of price indexes for the different types of supplies, and the level of detail needed to make the forecast realistic. The lack of disaggregated price indexes is generally the primary obstacle to a full disaggregation of current expenditures. For many categories of goods used in governmental production, no good price indexes exist; thus, analysts make assumptions about future increases in general price levels or simply use their judgment to project these prices. However, if certain inputs such as electricity tariffs are recognized to increase more rapidly than general price levels, that assumption can be built into the forecasts.

Direct Payments to Special-Needs Households

Local governments in some countries are required to make either direct or in-kind payments to individuals and households, such as the low-income elderly, with particular special needs. When such payments are financed through intergovernmental transfers from the central government, forecasts of expenditure requirements will be offset by equal increases in transfer revenues with no net effect on local government budget deficits or surpluses. When special-needs payments are not financed through intergovernmental transfers from the central government, the forecaster must project both the numbers of individuals or households eligible for such payments and the levels of those payments.

The number of individuals or households entitled to special-needs payments depends on the basis of eligibility. If eligibility is based primarily on age, analysts can use forecasts of the eligible population to carry out the forecast. Other programs may depend on the state of the economy, in which case the number of individuals or households eligible for the program will likely depend on macroeconomic forecasts. That is, if major economic growth is projected, the number of eligible recipients for the program may be expected to decrease. The analyst must link the expenditure requirements to the macroeconomic forecasts that underlie the revenue forecasts.

Capital Expenditures and Debt Service

Projections of capital expenditures are linked directly to formation of a capital budget (see chapter 5). Consequently, no special methods are necessary for generating a forecast. Instead, the forecaster may simply assume that the capital expenditures will occur as stated in the capital budget. However, analysts should consider certain details in making the forecasts.

The presumption in the present discussion is that revenue and expenditure forecasts will focus on the general fund budget (the primary budget of a local government). Capital expenditures are *lumpy* in that they constitute large, one-time-only outlays. Such outlays may be financed directly from general fund revenues; in general, neither annual own-source revenues of a local government nor ordinary transfers can meet the expense of large outlays. Such funds must come from accumulated surpluses (balances) in the general fund, capital expenditure transfers from the central government, or debt.

If all or the bulk of capital expenditures are funded directly from transfers, the forecaster can include the total capital expenditure in the general fund forecast, because the revenue side of the forecast will include a comparable revenue flow. If capital expenditures are financed from accumulated surpluses, the forecasting model should include carryover balances on the revenue side of the ledger.

If the capital expenditure is to be financed from local government debt, the revenue estimates should include only the flow of revenues into the general fund and not include funds obtained through credit from a lending agency. To include the entire capital expenditure in the fiscal forecast would indicate a large negative difference between revenues and expenditures. Therefore, the preferable approach is to exclude the capital outlay from the expenditure forecast and to exclude funds from the lending agency from the revenue side of the forecast. In addition, "spending" on the capital project should be included in the multiyear expenditure forecast under the heading of debt service. That is, in the years following the receipt of credit, the local government will be required to pay the principal and interest associated with the debt. Such debt service will, therefore, be an additional entry on the expenditure side of the fiscal forecast.

If local governments are allowed to borrow, forecasting of debt-financed capital expenditures will focus exclusively on expenditures on debt service. For previously incurred debt, the expenditure forecast will include the principal and interest payments associated with that debt. The forecaster will have to make assumptions regarding the terms associated with the new anticipated debt during the forecast period. That is, the new debt will require both principal and interest expenditures that the forecaster will need to include in forecasts for subsequent years.

Potentially as important as the additional interest and principal payments associated with debt are any additional recurrent expenses associated with the additional capital as debt is most commonly used for capital investments. Indeed, one of the acknowledged benefits of longer-term fiscal forecasting is that it requires policy makers to recognize additional spending for the operation and maintenance (O&M) of new capital infrastructure. When the additional recurrent spending for O&M and the costs of servicing the additional debt are included in the out-year estimates of spending requirements, a local government might recognize that it cannot afford the investment at the present time or that it has the financial capability to carry the debt load.

The need for reasonably accurate estimates of O&M costs suggests that the chief financial officer (CFO) is not the only individual who must be involved in producing forecasts. Seldom will the CFO have the requisite knowledge to derive reasonable estimates of each department's operating costs. This task can be delegated to the departments directly overseeing operation of the infrastructure.

In summary, most forecasting of expenditures is of primary interest in multiyear projections, because the annual budget is generally determined from anticipated availability of revenues and specific policy initiatives. Multiyear projections of spending are generally built from accounting identity models under specific assumptions regarding levels of service. Analysts can compare results from these projections with multiyear forecasts of available revenues produced under similar assumptions. If projected expenditures exceed forecasted revenues, the results can serve as a warning to the local government that it should reduce its planned spending, undertake policies that will enhance revenues, or both.

Bexar County, Texas (2002:1) summarizes the objective of multiyear forecasts:

> *Forecasts are not predictions!* Forecasts are projected end results that may occur based upon stipulated assumptions.... [C]hange the assumptions and the end results will change. The value of forecasts is that they allow policy makers to anticipate potential issues and take a proactive stance, enabling greater success when mitigating problems and maximizing opportunities.

Oklahoma City, Oklahoma, and Champaign, Illinois, are two U.S. cities that use multiyear forecasts to inform the policy-making process (see boxes 2.3 and 2.4).

Challenges Facing Local Government Forecasters in Developing Countries

In developing countries, the task of forecasting revenues and expenditures at the local level is particularly challenging. Already emphasized in the discussion of revenue forecasting is the issue of data availability. Without adequate data,

BOX 2.3   Oklahoma City's Revenue and Expenditure Forecasting

Oklahoma City, a city of approximately 500,000 residents, is the capital of Oklahoma. For many years, the city has forecast general fund revenues and expenditures to show policy makers the sorts of challenges they are likely to face in maintaining a balanced general fund budget while meeting public service needs.

Rather than use a formal forecasting model, the city relies primarily on judgment and examination of past trends. First, it considers the economic outlook for the nation, the state of Oklahoma, and the city, as well as the county in which Oklahoma City is located. It examines population (including the age composition of that population), inflation (as measured by the consumer price index), personal income, occupancy rates for local hotels and motels, unemployment rates, and anticipated future job growth.

Oklahoma City, unlike most U.S. cities, does not rely on property taxation for general fund revenues. Instead, the retail sales tax is the primary source of own-source revenues. In fiscal year (FY) 2005, the city derived 54 percent of its revenues from the retail sales tax.

The city links revenue forecasts for sales taxes to population growth of approximately 1 percent per year and inflation of about 2.5 percent per year. These assumptions led the city's forecasters to project sales tax revenue growth of 2.3 percent in 2006 and an average of 3.5 percent per year for FY 2007–10. Similarly, they forecast other tax revenues on the basis of judgment, past performance, and anticipated policy changes.

Expenditure projections rely heavily on spending for employees, because personal services constitute nearly three-fourths of all general fund spending. After decreasing employment by more than 6 percent, Oklahoma City realized that further cuts in the number of employees could reduce the quantity and quality of public services. Furthermore, with the assumed increase in population, a constant city labor force might have to increase productivity to maintain constant services.

To project spending on personnel, the city's forecasters assumed that direct wages and salaries would increase at the assumed rate of inflation (no real increases or decreases in salaries); however, they recognized that insurance costs (primarily health insurance costs) in the United States have been increasing more rapidly than inflation in general. Thus, the forecasters predicted that insurance costs would increase by approximately 9 percent per year. Forecasters also used their judgment to project other services costs (including service contracts, utilities, and professional services not provided by city employees), supplies and capital expenditures, and transfers.

The most interesting aspect of the Oklahoma City forecasting effort concerns the projected gap between revenues and expenditures. Revenues

(Box continues on the following page.)

were projected to increase by about 3.3 percent per year, whereas spending was projected to increase by about 5.2 percent per year. Although the current surplus of revenues over expenditures meant that forecasters were not projecting deficits to occur immediately, they expected that spending would exceed revenues by about US$38 million by 2010. To address this possible deficit, the city's forecasting document describes ways in which the city could hold down increases in spending and find alternative revenue sources.

Source: Oklahoma City, Oklahoma 2005.

BOX 2.4 **Champaign's Revenue and Expenditure Forecasting**

Like large cities, some relatively small cities in the United States carry out multiyear fiscal forecasting. Champaign, Illinois, makes five-year financial forecasts to allow the City Council to make decisions about the annual budget, growth issues, and goals in the context of the city's anticipated ability to fund programs.

The forecasting process begins with an assessment of the state of the national and local economy. From their assessment of the future course of the economy, the city's forecasters derive a set of assumptions for both the revenue and the expenditure forecasts. Variables in their assumptions include inflation, cost of construction, interest rates, per capita income growth, and population growth. They also base expenditure forecasts on assumptions regarding increases in salaries, pensions, and health insurance.

The city's forecasters use past trends and judgment to project local revenues. For example, on the basis of assumptions about trends in per capita incomes, inflation, and population, they assumed that local sales tax revenues would grow by about 4 percent per year. For the property tax, the forecasters relied on information from the city's Planning Department concerning expected new construction and combined that information with estimates of increased property values.

One unique feature of the Champaign forecast document is its sensitivity analysis. As noted by the forecasters, the retail sales tax is a particularly important local revenue source, because it represents slightly more than one-half of the city's revenues. The forecasters illustrate how the difference between revenues and expenditures can become a large deficit under slow-growth assumptions regarding sales tax revenues. In addition, they examine scenarios for alternative rates of growth in the local property tax, which represents the second most important source of local revenues.

Source: Champaign, Illinois 2005.

forecasters are likely to be limited to purely judgmental projections or simple trend techniques. Long-term trend analyses require historical data consistently defined. Statistical forecasting requires not only that data, but also data on the variables used to explain past fluctuations in revenues.

Another challenge in many developing countries is local governments' heavy reliance on intergovernmental transfers. As suggested above, the many types of transfer programs, all with their own rules concerning allocation mechanisms and amounts to be transferred, complicate forecasting of transfers. If a subnational government's revenues are to be forecasted reasonably accurately, determinants of transfers must be analyzed.

Lack of control over revenue and expenditure policies is a challenge for local policy makers using fiscal forecasts. In many developing and transition countries, the central government regulates local governments' fiscal decision making. Local taxation and spending decisions are often particularly constrained. For example, statutes may specify that property taxes be set according to a specific schedule or that specific amounts not provided by the government be spent for particular purposes. In such circumstances, the payoffs from multiyear forecasting efforts may be diminished, except when local governments use their forecasts to lobby the central government for help in overcoming anticipated deficits. Such help might come in the form of fewer or relaxed constraints on local tax rates or redefinitions of the tax base, relaxed mandates regarding allocations of expenditures, and increased amounts transferred to local government.

Political and other nontechnical factors can influence expenditure and revenue forecasts. Forecasted revenues and expenditures can be intentionally under- or overstated. Much of the work on the subject of forecast bias at the subnational level has been conducted in the United States. Many analysts of subnational fiscal forecasts in the United States have argued that forecasters generally underestimate revenues (Bretschneider and Gorr 1987, 1992; Rodgers and Joyce 1996). Their argument is based on the presumption that locally elected decision makers prefer to avoid budgetary shortfalls, because a potential deficit could require those decision makers to rescind their budget decisions and could reflect negatively on their leadership. Furthermore, potential deficits can lead to lower credit ratings, which have a negative effect on taxpayers because they increase the interest on any new debt issued by the city. Finally, locally elected political leaders may prefer to have unexpected budget surpluses (because revenues were underestimated) that can be allocated through supplemental budgets in ways that give incumbents an advantage when they seek reelection to office.

Mocan and Azad (1995) do not support the hypothesis that fiscal forecasters will underestimate subnational governments' future revenues.

Cassidy, Kamlet, and Nagin (1989) find that forecast outcomes at the subnational level reflect both over- and underestimation biases, eliminating any real net effect.

Forecasters may be overly optimistic about future revenues at the national level in developing countries. National leaders in developing countries may be less risk averse than state and local leaders in the United States, or perhaps national leaders face fewer sanctions if the national budget is unbalanced. Central governments generally have greater freedom than subnational governments to incur short-term debt.

Danninger (2005) asserts another reason that national governments in developing and transition countries will overestimate revenues. He notes that revenue forecasts serve both as estimates for making budgets and as revenue targets. Using a case study of Azerbaijan, Danniger argues that because the government cannot directly monitor the collection efforts of tax administrators (a principal-agent problem), it overestimates revenues to pressure administrators to perform their task effectively.

Budgeted own-source revenues of local governments in developing countries could be similarly biased to provide an incentive for local tax collectors to put forth greater effort. But because own-source revenues are commonly much less important than intergovernmental transfers in the revenue structure of such governments, local forecasters are more likely to underestimate revenues. One reason for such bias could be aversion to the risk of deficits. In addition, forecasters and local politicians might believe that the central government will respond with increased transfers when deficit budgets are anticipated. If the central government does increase transfers, it encourages further underestimation of revenues.

Conclusion

Annual budgets require that revenues for the upcoming fiscal year be estimated to illuminate resource constraints as spending plans are formulated. These revenue estimates should be as accurate as possible to avoid revenue shortfalls or excessively large revenue surpluses. Either of these outcomes will require that local authorities revisit the allocation of funds, potentially disrupting provision of local services.

Although all local governments engage in some type of annual revenue forecasting, not all attempt to make systematic longer-term (three- to five-year) projections of revenues and expenditures. By projecting revenues over the longer-term and comparing them with the expenditures necessary to maintain current levels of service, local officials can determine whether financing shortfalls loom and consider policies to overcome them. Similarly, forecasters can assist local officials in their planning efforts by estimating the revenue and expenditure impacts of investments in new capital infrastructure, including O&M costs associated with that infrastructure.

Different techniques can be used to forecast both revenues and expenditures. They range from simple judgmental approaches that rely on the knowledge of experts to sophisticated multivariate statistical techniques. For forecasts of revenues that are sensitive to economic conditions, statistical forecasting methods may be most appropriate. But statistical analyses require considerably more data and forecaster expertise than the alternatives: time trend analysis and deterministic approaches.

Deterministic approaches are probably the most feasible alternative to statistical analyses of revenues when forecasts are based on simple links to variables assumed to directly influence revenues. The approach permits the forecaster to link future values of revenues to anticipated changes in the national economy and to other economic or demographic variables. The deterministic approach to multiyear expenditure forecasts has major advantages over alternative techniques and, once specified and computerized, allows the forecaster to consider the likely fiscal effects of alternative policy scenarios. Unlike simple time trend approaches, which rely solely on time to drive the forecast, the deterministic approach relies on variables that logically or conceptually ought to be linked to the revenue or expenditure being projected. And, unlike judgmental approaches, a deterministic model relies on explicit assumptions that permit analysts to examine forecast errors and alter the model to improve forecast accuracy.

The two most common revenue sources for subnational governments in developing and transition countries are intergovernmental transfers and property-based taxes. Neither is particularly easy to predict. Therefore, the forecaster should have in-depth knowledge of local administration of the property tax and of intergovernmental transfer programs that provide revenues to the local government.

As local governments in developing countries attain greater fiscal authority and responsibility, the need for improved budgeting and financial planning will increase. The forecasting techniques discussed here will become increasingly relevant.

Notes

1. This chapter uses the terms *subnational government, local government,* and *municipal government* interchangeably to denote noncentral government entities. Much of the discussion applies equally to single-purpose public authorities, such as water districts.

2. This conclusion is based on communications with colleagues who have worked or are working with local governments in developing and transition countries. None reported systematic efforts by these governments to forecast revenues and expenditures.

3. This chapter uses the terms *forecasts, projections,* and *estimates* interchangeably.

4. For good overviews of forecasting in general, see Makridakis, Wheelwright, and Hyndman (1998); Armstrong (2001); and http://www.marketing.wharton.upenn.edu/forecast.

5. When plotted against time, data lying on a straight line do not mean that the series is changing at a constant *rate;* instead, the rate of growth is decreasing. A series that is growing at a constant rate when plotted against time will be nonlinear and concave from above.

6. Even more complex time-series forecasting techniques are available but are seldom used at the state or local level in the United States. For an illustration of how such techniques could be used at the local level, see Cirincione, Gurrieri, and van de Sande (1999).

7. One exception to that generalization is forecasting of some social welfare expenditures, which tend to increase (decrease) during periods of economic decline (expansion).

8. Schroeder (2004) details the linear regression (statistical) approach to forecasting local government revenues and expenditures. For an example of a statistical model used for forecasting, see Wong (1995).

9. Research Triangle Institute (2002) suggests a more complex forecasting model that includes a real GDP component, an inflation component, and another subjective adjustment component.

10. So-called GDP buoyancy coefficients, which are commonly estimated as the percentage change in a revenue source divided by the percentage change in GDP, are not an appropriate substitute for an elasticity coefficient. To be a reasonably pure estimate of how changes in GDP affect revenues, the latter should be estimated from revenue data that have been cleaned of all rate and base definition changes.

11. Where the property tax depends on the floor area of a building or surface area of land, the property tax base is even less likely to be correlated with national economic conditions.

12. For a thorough discussion of local property tax administration and forecasting of property tax revenues in New York City, see New York, New York (2005).

13. Forecasts of property tax revenues must include the collection ratio. In some countries—for example, Romania—the budget law requires the budget to show aggregate tax levies (total property taxes to be paid) rather than a more realistic amount that reflects the fact that not all taxpayers will comply with the tax as levied (see ARD 2005).

14. Shared taxes are those imposed by a higher-than-local level of government (generally the central government) but shared with local governments on the basis of where they are collected. These revenues should be considered a form of transfer when the central government determines the base and rate of the tax as well as the percentage of the collections that local governments will retain. Although local governments consider these revenues their own, the central government retains full control of them. Therefore, the revenues should be considered a form of intergovernmental transfer.

15. For a review of experience with implementation of MTEFs, see Holmes (2003).

References

Armstrong, Jon Scott, ed. 2001. *Principles of Forecasting: A Handbook for Researchers and Practitioners.* Boston, MA: Kluwer Academic Publishers.

ARD (Associates in Rural Development). 2005. "Assessing the Borrowing Capacity of the Municipality of Iasi, Romania." Local Government Bridge Project, USAID Romania, Burlington, VT.

Bahl, Roy. 1972. *Alternative Methods for Tax Revenue Forecasting in Developing Countries.* Washington, DC: International Monetary Fund.

Bexar County, Texas. 2002. "Long-Range Financial Forecast and Strategies, FY 2002/03 through 2006/07." Planning and Resource Management Department, San Antonio.

Bretschneider, Stuart I., and Wilpen Gorr. 1987. "State and Local Government Revenue Forecasting." In *The Handbook of Forecasting*, ed. Spyros Makridakis and Steven C. Wheelwright, 118–34. New York: John Wiley and Sons.

———. 1992. "Economic, Organizational, and Political Influences on Biases in Forecasting States Sales Tax Receipts." *International Journal of Forecasting* 7 (4): 457–66.

Cassidy, Glenn, Mark S. Kamlet, and Daniel S. Nagin. 1989. "An Empirical Examination of Bias in Revenue Forecasting by State Governments." *International Journal of Forecasting* 5 (3): 321–31.

Champaign, Illinois. 2005. "Five-Year Financial Forecast." City of Champaign, Champaign, IL. http://archive.ci.champaign.il.us/archive/dsweb/Get/Document-3543/Five-year%20Forecast%20Att.pdf.

Cirincione, Carmen, Gastavo A. Gurrieri, and Bart van de Sande. 1999. "Municipal Government Revenue Forecasting: Issues of Method and Data." *Public Budgeting and Finance* 19 (1): 26–46.

Danninger, Stephan. 2005. "Revenue Forecasts as Performance Targets." Working Paper 05/14, Fiscal Affairs Department, International Monetary Fund, Washington, DC.

Gamboa, Ana Ma. 2002. "Development of Tax Forecasting Models: Corporate and Individual Income Taxes." Discussion Paper 2002–06, Philippines Institute for Development Studies, Manila.

Harris, Robert. 1966. *Income and Sales Taxes: The 1970 Outlook for States and Localities.* Washington, DC: Council of State Governments.

Holmes, Malcolm (with Alison Evans). 2003. "A Review of Experience in Implementing Medium-Term Expenditure Frameworks in a PRSP Context: A Synthesis of Eight Country Studies." Centre for Aid and Public Expenditure, Overseas Development Institute, London. http://www.odi.org.uk/PPPG/cape/publications/MTEF%20Synthesis%20Final%20Nov%2003.pdf.

Jung, Changhoon. 2002. "Revenue Estimation Practices and Budget Process in Municipal Governments." Paper presented at the 14th annual meeting of the Association for Budget and Financial Management, Kansas City, MO, October 11.

Kyobe, Annette, and Stephan Danninger. 2005. "Revenue Forecasting—How Is It Done? Results from a Survey of Low-Income Countries." Working Paper 05/24, Fiscal Affairs Department, International Monetary Fund, Washington, DC.

Makridakis, Spyros G., Steven C. Wheelwright, and Rob J. Hyndman. 1998. *Forecasting: Methods and Applications.* 3rd ed. New York: John Wiley and Sons.

McCollough, Jane. 1990. "Municipal Revenue and Expenditure Forecasting: Current Status and Future Prospects." *Government Finance Review* (October): 38–40.

Mocan, H. Nael, and Sam Azad. 1995. "Accuracy and Rationality of State General Fund Revenue Forecasts: Evidence from Panel Data." *International Journal of Forecasting* 11 (September): 417–27.

New York, New York. 2005. "Tax Revenue Forecasting Documentation: Financial Plan Fiscal Years 2005–2009." Tax Policy, Revenue Forecasting, and Economic Analysis Task Force, Office of Management and Budget, New York. http://www.ci.nyc. ny.us/html/omb/pdf/trfd5_05.pdf.

Oklahoma City, Oklahoma. 2005. "Five-Year Forecast, 2006–2010." Finance Department, Oklahoma City. http://www.okc.gov/finance_tab/five_yr_forecast/five_year_200610.pdf.

Prest, A. R. 1962. "The Sensitivity of the Yield of Personal Income Tax in the United Kingdom." *Economic Journal* 72 (September): 576–96.

Prince William County, Virginia. 2002. "Fiscal Year 2003–2007 Projections of General County Revenue." Prepared by the Department of Finance for the Board of County Supervisors, Prince William County. http://www.co.prince-william.va.us/ docLibrary/PDF/000930.pdf.

Research Triangle Institute. 2002. "Manual for the Municipal Financial Analysis and Planning Model Developed for Municipality of Nessebar, Bulgaria." Local Government Initiative Project, Municipal Finance Task Force, U.S. Agency for International Development, Research Triangle Park, NC. http://www.mftf.org/index.cfm.

Rodgers, Robert, and Phillip Joyce. 1996. "The Effect of Underforecasting on the Accuracy of Revenue Forecasts by State Governments." *Public Administration Review* 56 (January–February): 48–56.

Rubin, Marilyn, Nancy Mantell, and Michael Pagano. 1999. "Approaches to Revenue Forecasting by State and Local Governments." In *Proceedings of the Ninety-Second Annual Conference of the National Tax Association*, ed. Daphne A. Kenyon, 205–21. Washington, DC: National Tax Association.

Schroeder, Larry. 2004. "Forecasting Local Revenues and Expenditures." In *Management Policies in Local Government Finance*, ed. J. Richard Aronson and Eli Schwartz, 104–32. Washington, DC: International City/County Management Association.

Stemaier, James J. L., and Martha J. Reiss. 1994. "The Revenue Forum: An Effective Low-Cost, Low-Tech Approach to Revenue Forecasting." *Government Finance Review* (April): 13–16.

Wong, John D. 1995. "Local Government Revenue Forecasting Using Regression and Econometric Forecasting in a Medium-Sized City." *Public Budgeting and Financial Management* 7 (Fall): 315–35.

3

Local Fiscal Discipline: Fiscal Prudence, Transparency, and Accountability

Developing countries' local government budgets are coming under increasing strain. Rapidly growing urban populations are demanding more services, while tax bases are expanding slowly and central governments are decentralizing functions without additional intergovernmental transfers. Many cities not only face demand for higher levels of service provision, but also must come to terms with significant infrastructure backlogs and the need to allocate additional resources to maintenance and replacement of deteriorating or obsolete infrastructure.

Different local governments respond to fiscal stress in different ways. Avenues of response are a function of the national environment within which they operate and of local capacity and institutional arrangements. This chapter addresses four key questions. What is local fiscal discipline? What is the value of local government fiscal discipline? What are the consequences of poor local fiscal discipline? What institutions at the intergovernmental and local levels are important for local fiscal discipline?

Fiscal Discipline as a Value in Public Financial Management

In most contemporary text on public finance management, reference is made to fiscal discipline, allocative effectiveness, and operational efficiency as core desired outcomes of systems to plan for and allocate public resources.

When Are Governments Fiscally Disciplined?

Fiscal discipline is a key value in public finance management at national and local levels. Given limited resources, expenditure claims would result in chronically high deficits and increasing debt and tax burdens if governments were not fiscally restrained. Fiscal discipline pertains to all key measures of fiscal performance: the total revenue, the financial balance, and the public debt. Typically, fiscal discipline is achieved when constraints on one total (for example, revenue) are accompanied by constraints on other budget aggregates. If, for example, revenue alone is constrained, local governments may find it easier to meet deficit targets by increasing borrowing rather than by reducing expenditure.

But at what level would fiscal aggregates be considered fiscally disciplined? Under certain circumstances, governments may find it wise to borrow—for example, when the economic cost of raising additional tax revenue is likely to be more than the economic cost of borrowing or when borrowing allows two or more generations to share the cost of providing social and economic infrastructure.

Fiscal discipline is inherently connected to notions of affordability. When the budget aggregates are unaffordable, either ex ante or ex post, a government may be deemed to lack fiscal discipline. Affordability relates to how the level and distribution of public revenue, spending, and borrowing are likely to affect the macroeconomic environment and governments' own financial health in the short and long term.

In this context, notions of what counts as affordable spending have shifted (see Schick 1999). Before World War II, the balanced budget rule was an operating norm. This rule stipulates that spending during a fiscal year, including current and investment spending and revenue, should not exceed that year's revenue. A more relaxed form of the rule is that current spending should not exceed current revenue and that borrowing should be undertaken only to bridge short-term cash flow shortfalls or to finance investment expenditure that will increase revenues. Because the rule neither distinguishes between periods of economic growth and stagnation nor takes account of the short-term rigidity of public spending, governments infrequently adhered to it. However, it remained the ideal that shaped governments' fiscal policy efforts.

After World War II, governments shifted to a flexible rule that allowed budget totals to accommodate cyclical changes in economic conditions and changes in government policy. A typical version of this rule was that government should maintain fiscal balance over the economic cycle. Over time, the new approach came to mean that government should act through fiscal policy to reduce the gap between actual and potential output.

As ratios of debt and tax to gross domestic product (GDP) continued to rise and economic performance declined and as high deficits and high debt burdens came to be viewed as structural problems that persist through economic upswings, governments concluded that they required increased discipline of budget aggregates. The result was a strategy that permits controlled deficits expressly set by governments in light of fiscal sustainability and of macroeconomic stabilization and growth objectives. The use of modeling techniques to integrate the macroeconomic and public finance impact of target aggregates and to assess sensitivity to internal and external risks is common. Another feature of modern fiscal policy practices is the linkage of target setting with the formulation and implementation of budgets to ensure that actual levels of revenue, expenditure, and borrowing equal targeted levels (Schick 1999: 50–53).

At the national level, fiscal discipline has come to mean maintaining budgeted and actual spending, revenue, and borrowing at levels that are financially sustainable and compatible with short- and long-term macroeconomic objectives, given likely risks. Setting these targets optimally and achieving them is a function of the institutions of the budget process. Publicly available modeling assumptions, up-to-date and accurate macroeconomic and fiscal outturn data, and independent engagement with fiscal policy targets provide important checks on the robustness of governments' fiscal policy and the honesty of supporting projections.

Fiscal decentralization promises improved public services but also creates new challenges for the institutions through which governments manage macroeconomic stability and growth. Prud'Homme (1995), Tanzi (1995), and others warn that decentralization creates new risks. Lack of fiscal discipline at the local level and perverse fiscal behavior by local governments could lead to macroeconomic risk, for example.

The three major functions for public finance management in the public sector are macroeconomic stabilization, income distribution, and resource allocation. According to orthodox fiscal federalism theory, the stabilization function belongs to the national government. A key part of this function is controlling the fiscal aggregates to achieve an optimal balance between spending and taxes and to allow prudent use of borrowing. Local governments have few or no incentives to undertake economic stabilization polices, the impact of which would be limited. Furthermore, they often lack the necessary macroeconomic instruments to carry out such policies (Fjeldstad 2001; Pisauro 2001).

Whether local governments should be interested in managing local economies through their fiscal policies or whether they should have policy instruments to this purpose remains a much-debated issue in decentralization research, policy, and design. Many commentators appear to argue that local governments should manage local economies through their fiscal policies because of the need for regional stabilization (Shah 2004; Spahn 1997, 2005). Multiple layers of government have challenged the central government's capability to exercise national macroeconomic control.

Decentralizing expenditure responsibilities and revenue-raising ability means giving subnational governments the legal, political, and administrative authority to plan projects, make decisions, and manage public functions (Baltaci and Yilmaz 2006: 3). It also means transferring the risk of fiscal distress and imprudence to subnational governments. Fiscal decentralization programs implemented in many developing countries have given local governments additional service responsibilities, as well as access to greater public funding in the form of intergovernmental transfers or authority to raise taxes from a widened variety of local sources.

When local government conducts affairs such that expenditure responsibilities and costs systematically outstrip revenue, it comes under huge fiscal stress. Fiscal strategies to cope with this stress are important not only for local financial health and service delivery, but also for national economic and financial health.

Why Should Governments Pursue Fiscal Discipline?

The value of fiscal discipline lies as much in avoiding the negative external and internal impacts of high deficits and increased tax burdens that result from weak constraints as in seeking the benefits of hard budget constraints for spending effectiveness and efficiency. The fiscal history of developing countries is rich with examples of how governments in the short term fail to pursue prudent fiscal adjustment strategies in times of looming fiscal stress and thereby compromise their long-term development objectives. Unsustainable fiscal policies can jeopardize the country's international creditworthiness (increasing the cost of future borrowing) and macroeconomic stability.

The destabilization potential of local government fiscal operations is much higher when local governments have access to credit. Such access softens the budget constraint on them and allows postponement of painful expenditure or revenue adjustments in the face of fiscal imbalance, with potentially high medium- and long-term costs internally and externally. Without the possibility of borrowing, local governments are forced to take difficult decisions sooner, making adjustments less painful. However, they have fewer options for financing their crucial development needs.

Governments' borrowing can affect macroeconomic stability when the central bank's independence and monetary policy is compromised through a bailout of state or nonstate banks or local governments directly. A bailout can undermine the bank's role in ensuring price stability. Because fiscal decentralization requires clarity about roles and responsibilities, it can help the central bank pursue monetary and exchange rate policies that protect price stability (Shah 2005: 4). However, when subnational governments build up unsustainable indebtedness to local—and sometimes self-owned—banks, bailouts by the central bank can trigger monetary instability. In Brazil, for example, lending by banks to their own subnational governments without proper assessments of risk caused the 1995 state debt crises. A breakdown of arms-length relationships between governments and the financial system, whether at the national or local level, can threaten monetary policy and the financial system.

At the national level, high deficits and excessive government borrowing from domestic capital markets crowd out and drive up the cost of capital for private sector investment. In principle, excessive local government borrowing can have similar effects. When governments manage fiscal stress by borrowing internationally from banks or international capital markets, they face exchange rate and external instability risks. Only in a few developing countries are domestic capital markets sufficiently mature to allow local government use of capital market debt instruments; few local governments in developing countries have accessed international capital markets. In addition, local governments' failure to service international debt can negatively affect the national government's reputation, undermining the efficiency of the public sector's borrowing operations.

Rather than access credit directly, local governments in developing countries, particularly those in Africa, tend to receive development funds through onlending of international development finance by their national government. In countries that access concessional multilateral and bilateral development financing, prudent management of the total debt stock and of fiscal policy is key to ensuring budget and macroeconomic stability. In recent years, several countries, including Kenya, Malawi, and Zambia, have faced severe short-term instability and expenditure cuts because of the suspension of concessional finance and other aid flows from development partners after failure to meet fiscal or other policy targets. Although not strictly subnational borrowing, onlending is a source of potential instability, particularly when coordination mechanisms are inadequate to ensure the sustainability of projects or when local governments have to take on the operational cost of inefficient projects, because the national government failed to establish functional aid, investment, and debt management institutions.

Local governments that borrow excessively may find themselves in a debt trap, wherein outflows to redeem past debt are more than the inflows of new debt and debt service cost takes up an increasing proportion of spending, crowding out spending on infrastructure and services. When debt service cost exceeds current income, local governments' ability to deliver services is impaired. However, when local governments pursue fiscally sound policies and reduce their stock of debt (or replace inefficient debt instruments with more efficient ones), they can release revenue for investment without the need to access additional debt.

Fiscal crises exact a significant cost in terms of local government effectiveness. Failure to maintain fiscal discipline during implementation of local government budgets could lead to imposition of in-year expenditure cuts and disruption of local government services. Similarly, avoidance of difficult recurrent expenditure adjustments could lead to postponement or termination of discretionary types of expenditure, perhaps decreasing the quality and quantity of services.

Insufficient expenditure to build social and economic infrastructure has particularly negative consequences for service delivery and fiscal management. In the short term, it decreases the level and quality of service delivery. In the long term, lack of spending on local infrastructure will undermine local governments' economic competitiveness, affecting future revenues. Insufficient expenditure to maintain infrastructure reduces the lifespan of infrastructure, increases future maintenance costs, and can trigger crisis-spending outlays when critical infrastructure fails. Box 3.1 describes one alternative for funding some infrastructure investments.

Fiscal discipline not only helps governments avoid the negative consequences of extreme fiscal stress, but also makes a positive contribution to fiscal outcomes. At the macroeconomic level, fiscal discipline supports the fiscal stabilization function, as discussed. At the microeconomic level, fiscal discipline supports effective distribution and use of resources. In the absence of limits on spending, budget managers may lack incentive to suspend

BOX 3.1 Financing Critical Infrastructure

Petersen and Freire (2004) argue that subnational borrowing can be an alternative for funding some infrastructure investments, especially when the useful life of the investments (such as schools, roads, or public utilities) is long, and they highlight the need for developing efficient access to credit for local authorities. Some countries have begun developing credit markets by establishing municipal finance corporations operated on commercial principles. Municipal rating agencies could assist such corporations in helping local governments borrow for infrastructure investments.

Effective capital markets are dependent on subnational fiscal discipline. But they also contribute to such discipline by demanding transparency in subnational finances. Other necessary conditions for capital markets to develop include effective supervisory authorities, judicially enforceable contracts, tax decentralization, civic norms that promote fiscal prudence, and skilled staff, as well as adequate accounting, disclosure, and reporting standards (Petersen and Freire 2004: 4).

lower-priority activities or seek more efficient ways of achieving objectives so that they can fund new spending priorities. Failure to make difficult decisions about spending trade-offs results in incremental budget growth, which further threatens fiscal discipline.

Intergovernmental Context of Local Fiscal Discipline

Local governments' ability to control their fiscal balances is solely dependent on internal decision-making processes. Increasingly, the degree of spending decentralization tends to exceed the degree of devolution of revenue-raising responsibilities, putting strain on local budgets unless the fiscal imbalance is addressed through intergovernmental transfers. Some institutional arrangements are more likely than others to ensure that fiscal decentralization is consistent with fiscal discipline.

Pisauro (2001), Tanzi (2001), and Wildasin (1997) identify two potential sources of risk for local fiscal discipline that arise because of local governments' position as subparts of a larger state. The first risk is that local governments may behave in fiscally imprudent ways if they have the central government's implicit assurance that they will be bailed out if unable to meet their financial obligations (see box 3.2). The second risk is that local governments perceive the opportunity cost of nationally assigned and collected public revenues to be lower than the revenues' true social cost (the common pool problem). The larger the gap between local governments' expenditure responsibilities and assigned revenue bases, the worse the common pool

BOX 3.2 Hard Budget Constraints, Soft Budget Constraints, and Bailouts

When are budget constraints on subnational governments hard, and when are they soft? Wildasin (1997) argues that fiscal transfers altering the budget constraints of subnational levels of government are insufficient reason to assume that the constraints have become soft. As long as the transfer recipients perceive budget constraints to be binding, the constraints should be characterized as hard. A constraint becomes soft when "altered in some contingent fashion allowing an outcome to occur which would not have been attainable under the 'normal,' 'initial,' or 'announced' constraint" (Wildasin 1997, 6).

When the central government formally assumes the liabilities of the subnational government, the bailout is explicit. An implicit bailout can take many forms, including an increase in transfers, guarantees for debt rescheduling agreements, or a takeover of the local government's fiscal affairs (as when central government establishes independent bodies with exceptional authority to cut spending, reschedule debt, and boost revenues). Bailouts can occur through the fiscal system or the banking system. When the central bank steps in to bail out local banks—government owned or not—an implicit bailout has occurred. Bailouts may come with or without conditions, including political conditions such as the removal of key policy makers, and with or without a repayment requirement.

Central governments are more likely to step in to prevent debt crises if lower-level governments are too big to fail and provide public services that benefit the rest of society. A central government may also step in when it can reap a political advantage from doing so or will bear a high political cost from not doing so. The political cost of not providing a bailout may be greater for the higher-level government if the reason for the crisis can be traced, at least in part, to that government's actions. It may have been politically costly for Mexico's central government not to bail out the troubled states after devaluation of the peso in 1994. The higher the local governments' tax autonomy, the easier the central government will find it to deny bailouts.

Local fiscal crises' effects on reputation can be a factor in the central government's bailout decision. If the debt crisis of a large local government threatens the access of other local governments or the country to efficient sources of credit, a central government may decide that it cannot deny a bailout. Effects on reputation can also work for fiscal discipline. In South Africa, the central government's refusal to assume responsibility for a provincial government's bank overdraft soon after the 1994 political transition provided an effective signal to the market that circumstances had changed and was a key contributor to provinces' subsequent fiscal discipline.

Some experts argue for more central government control over lower-level governments to manage the potential negative impact on national

(Box continues on the following page.)

fiscal balances of poor local fiscal discipline. Other experts argue that the key problem may be insufficient subnational autonomy: smaller governments with higher local tax autonomy increase local political accountability and reduce incentives for bailouts, in turn strengthening fiscal discipline.

Source: Author.

problem. If local sources of revenue were sufficiently large to enable subnational governments to finance their expenditure tasks without having to depend on central government support, the gap between the local and the national opportunity cost of public funds would narrow. However, the moral hazard problem presented by the mere existence of a central government would persist: even if local governments can raise sufficient revenues, they may attempt to externalize the cost of their spending on the common national pool by failing to raise the revenues that will meet their financial obligations and leaving it to central government to bail them out.

Web (2004) identifies a similar free-rider problem that in theory affects local governments' deficit and borrowing decisions. In a national sphere, the central (or federal) government and subnational governments may share the same currency, central bank, and domestic and international credit markets. Thus, they have a common interest in maintaining sustainable country aggregate fiscal balances, price stability, a healthy financial system, and good access to international credit. But a single local government's interest may diverge from that of the rest of the country and prompt the government to behave in fiscally risky ways. If so, the government would receive all the benefits from its behavior but bear only a part of the cost—as long as the other governments continued their good fiscal behavior (Web 2004: 3).

Revenue and Expenditure Assignment and Intergovernmental Transfers

Whether local governments are likely to be fiscally solvent is as much a function of matching their expenditure obligations with sufficient revenue sources as of ensuring that the type of revenue sources matches those obligations. Different developing countries have different expenditure assignments. In many African countries, for example, the central government is responsible for education and health services, and local government is responsible for power, water, and waste management. The type of expenditure responsibilities that rest with local governments should determine in part the revenue sources assigned to those governments.

Spahn (1997) delineates two approaches to achieve stabilization under decentralized government. In the first approach, predictable revenue sources and cyclically stable expenditure responsibilities are assigned to local government. These assignments facilitate local budget planning and leave pro-cyclical budgetary policies to central government. The theory is that the steady behavior of local governments will become an embedded, cyclically neutral, and stabilizing force. In the second approach, expenditure responsibilities that are sensitive to the economic cycle, together with volatile taxes, are assigned to local government. In this case, budget flexibility, including the right to borrow, is needed at the local level. Shah (1998) notes that cyclically sensitive expenditure layouts and revenue bases are usually not assigned to local governments so as to insulate them from economic cycles and give national governments prominence in the stabilization function. Spahn (1997: 2) argues that local governments should carry out the allocation function and should provide cyclically constant public goods and services such as health and education. Stable local revenue sources, such as property tax or local fees for services, together with intergovernmental transfers that are not cyclically sensitive, should finance local governments.

Local governments need less budget flexibility when stable expenditure functions are financed through stable revenue sources, but too little flexibility can trigger fiscal distress. Consider the case of Colombia, where two nationally imposed restrictions on subnational budgets can cause fiscal strain. Colombian subnational governments have little autonomy in managing their expenditures. The revenue-sharing system stipulates how resources transferred by the central government are to be spent. Municipalities are required to spend 30 percent of transfers on basic education, 25 percent on health care, 20 percent on water supply, and 5 percent on physical education. The remaining 20 percent can be used for housing, welfare, debt service, and other uses. In addition, the central government earmarks revenues and makes strict expenditure mandates. Local governments have little control over key cost drivers. For example, subnational governments are responsible for paying teachers' salaries, but the central government determines the size of the salaries. The difficulty that subnational governments have experienced in managing the resulting budgetary inflexibility is reflected in rising levels of debt (Zabala 2004: 283).

The vague assignment of expenditure responsibilities without clearly assigned revenue sources can have equally deleterious effects. In Hungary, the 1990 law on local self-government devolved many expenditure responsibilities to local government but defined the tasks—and therefore the accountability for outcomes—vaguely within a framework of shared responsibilities.

Unconditional grants were to finance the expenditures. Between 1990 and 1998, when general government expenditure decreased, transfers to local governments decreased even faster as the central government struggled to fulfill its obligations. As tight fiscal conditions coincided with expanding fiscal responsibilities and growing investment needs for local infrastructure, local governments responded by becoming more efficient but also by reducing capital investments below replacement levels (Sood 2004).

Four considerations should enter into the design of any grant system:

■ Intergovernmental fiscal relations should be based on stable, transparent, nonarbitrary, universal, and nonnegotiable rules (Spahn 1997; 4). Transfers should be based on transparent, standard criteria for fiscal capacity or on expenditure needs that cannot be influenced through the strategic behavior of the central government or recipient governments.

■ Local governments should have sufficient access to resources to cover their expenditure mandates. Tanzi (2001) argues that decentralized countries, with the exception of Australia, Canada, and few others, have for the most part provided revenue sources insufficient for subnational governments to undertake their expenditure responsibilities. Consequently, these governments fail to deliver on their mandates or run into fiscal difficulties. The financial resources assigned in various forms (own revenues, shared revenues, and grants) should be sufficient to match expenditure assignments.

■ Local government budgets should be flexible to meet local circumstances and needs. The size of own revenues should be sufficiently significant to ensure flexibility and local-level accountability.

■ Expenditure mandates should not be too detailed. Local governments should have discretion in determining the mix of outputs or the means to deliver them. Central government's control over key cost drivers such as wages should come with a commensurate commitment to compensate local governments for cost-increasing decisions, particularly if taken in the absence of local government input.

A clear, workable, and substantive framework and rules are critical for a functional intergovernmental system but are insufficient to ensure optimal outcomes. An operational system that facilitates coordination and cooperation among the levels of government is needed. Pisauro (2001: 11) argues that a key objective of the intergovernmental system should be to shift the focus of fiscal policy to general government by building a framework for coordination of budget plans.

A prerequisite for an institutional framework that facilitates cooperation among levels of government is a system of public accounts that includes all levels of government and that makes expenditure and revenue classifications consistent. This system should provide frequent information on planned and actual revenue, expenditure, and borrowing of general government. Timely and comprehensive reporting of budget implementation, including the transfer of resources from the national government to lower tiers of government, is necessary for central government to monitor performance and to detect fiscal stress early on so that remedial action can be taken (box 3.3).

A system of public accounts clarifies accountability for poor fiscal and budgetary performance. In many developing countries with high revenue uncertainty, central governments pass on cash shortfalls to lower levels of government by postponing or suspending transfers, with disastrous consequences for service delivery. Regular publication of up-to-date and accurate information on intergovernmental transfers can act as a disincentive for such practices. Transparency in transfers also acts as a disincentive to aberrant local level behavior. Local authorities cannot plead resource shortfalls if local populations know the timing and level of transfers. In Uganda, transfers for health and education institutions are displayed in the institutions and published in a national newspaper.

Information alone is not enough to ensure cooperation among governments in coordinating fiscal policy. The annual budget process should be sequenced so that local governments can plan their budgets with reasonable certainty about the amount and timing of resource transfers from central

---

BOX 3.3 Impact of High-Quality Budget Institutions

A fiscal gap is not necessarily associated with lack of fiscal restraint. De Mello (quoted in Pisauro 2001; 15) estimates the effect of some decentralization indicators on the central government's budget balance in 30 countries, 17 of which are in the Organisation for Economic Co-operation and Development (OECD). In the OECD countries, fewer subnational taxing powers (and a higher fiscal gap) tend to improve fiscal outcomes. In the non-OECD countries, tax autonomy does not affect the government deficit, whereas dependency on transfers worsens it. De Mello considers these results evidence that common pool problems are more serious in non-OECD countries than in OECD countries, but Pisauro points out that what really makes the difference may be the quality of budget institutions, which, on average, is higher in OECD countries.

government and that information from local-level fiscal plans can inform the national budget process. Like rules for the payment of grants and sharing of revenues, rules that govern the budget process should be transparent.

In South Africa—where gaps between expenditure responsibilities and transfers from the central government are large for provincial governments but much smaller for local governments—a clear legal framework, cooperative budget structures, and good transparency arrangements help shift the fiscal policy focus from the central government to the general government level. The vertical and horizontal distributions of revenue strike a good balance between predictability in resource allocation and flexibility to respond to changes in the macroeconomic environment. For example, although the distribution of transfers between provincial and local governments is formula driven (minimizing opportunities for any one subnational government to maximize its share), the size of the pool to be distributed is dependent on fiscal policy and a negotiated assessment of expenditure needs at each level. Use of a medium-term framework and the ex ante and ex post publication of the criteria driving the vertical division of resources between governments facilitates transparency, predictability, and policy coordination. Intergovernmental forums that combine political and administrative leadership—for example, the Budget Council—are active throughout the budget process. Final decision making rests with a session of the extended national cabinet—a session that provides for subnational political representation. The Finance and Fiscal Commission, an independent constitutional body, plays an important advisory role: it annually advises the national parliament on the vertical and horizontal divisions of revenue. Given that parliament is still a relatively weak voice in public finance decisions, the real check and balance is that the commission's research and recommendations are made public and that the national ministry of finance responds to them formally in budget documentation, facilitating further transparency and buy-in by subnational governments. The system, which was initially developed for coordination between national government and provincial governments, now includes local governments, which play an important role in pro-poor service delivery.

In summary, fragmented budget processes, in which decisions about intergovernmental fiscal affairs are murky, contribute to poor local fiscal discipline. Budget institutions and procedures that are aimed at coordination and cooperation can support and may be necessary for fiscal discipline in a decentralized environment. Good information on actual transfers and expenditure, revenue, and borrowing outturns throughout the fiscal year is equally important.

Subnational Borrowing

The discussion above touched on the implications for subnational borrowing of revenue and expenditure assignment and the system of intergovernmental transfers. The operations of local government can have significant macroeconomic effects even under balanced budget conditions (Ter-Minassian 1997). A balanced budget expenditure increase by subnational governments can boost aggregate demand counter to stabilization efforts by the national government if, for example, the multiplier effects of the expenditures of subnational governments outweigh those of their revenues. However, the destabilizing potential of subnational governments is much greater if they do not operate under a hard budget constraint and can access additional financing in times of fiscal stress.

How do intergovernmental institutional arrangements for regulating subnational borrowing affect local fiscal discipline? Web (2004) identifies several channels for strengthening such discipline. He makes two important distinctions in sketching a framework for analyzing country conditions governing subnational borrowing. First, controls on subnational borrowing can operate before or after the fact. Ex ante controls usually are rules, regulations, and procedures determined by the central government, whereas ex post controls are sanctions that come into play when local governments behave imprudently. Second, controls can be directed at borrowers or lenders. Web argues that lending should be subject to ex ante and ex post constraints on both borrowers and lenders. Reliance on ex ante constraints without consequences after the fact gives irresponsible lenders and borrowers a big incentive to overcome initial obstacles. Reliance on consequences alone may allow large local governments to build up debts so large that the national government will not enforce the consequences.

In economies in which governments own banks and financial institutions and financial markets are not fully liberalized, ex ante controls are critical, because market constraints do not operate effectively. Under such conditions, credit allocation decisions are not strongly driven by considerations of protecting lenders' interests. Sole reliance on constraints on borrowers could lead lenders to push loans and local governments to borrow despite the rules. Constraints on borrowers may include higher ex ante capital requirements for risky lending to local governments or commensurate capital write-offs for loans not repaid. Fiscal responsibility laws or other rules, regulations, and procedures encourage fiscal restraint by borrowers. Restraints can be formulated using balance sheet items—for example, debt stock or money flow indicators such as debt service. Table 3.1 lists control options.

The ease with which a country can achieve fiscal coordination is not solely a function of its fiscal institutions. Political factors affect the urgency of the need for fiscal control institutions and the likelihood that the institutions will succeed. One obvious factor is the constitutional autonomy of subnational governments (see table 3.2). Other important political factors are whether a majority party is in control or whether government is a coalition or is divided between legislative and executive branches; the strength of party identities and unity; and the strength of the legislature over the executive. Insofar as the constitution, party system, and the politics of the day lead to a centralization of power, the country will have less need for special institutions to coordinate fiscal discipline among levels of government.

T A B L E   3 . 1 Ex Ante and Ex Post Controls on Subnational Borrowing

Control	On borrowers	On lenders
Ex ante controls	Debt ceilings Deficit targets Restrictions on international borrowing Regulation of subnational borrowing on the basis of fiscal capacity criteria (regulations by the central government, the central bank, or another institution)	No direct central bank financing Restrictions on international borrowing Regulations by the central bank or another institution Financial supervision agency Credit rationing to states Increased capital requirements for lending to risky subnational governments
Ex post controls (monitoring and consequences to enforce ex ante rules)	Limits on central bank financing No bailouts (from central government or from international community) and no debt workout without adequate conditionality Central government refuses to accept subnational debt Debt service withheld from transfers to subnational governments Publication of detailed fiscal results	Strong supervision of banks Regulations require capital write-off for losses from subnational debt

Source: Web 2004: 5.

The effectiveness of controls on general government borrowing is dependent on the presence of modern, comprehensive, standardized, and transparent budgetary and accounting procedures and information systems. Establishment of cooperative approaches to fiscal management is also critical. When local governments, particularly large cities, are actively involved in the process of formulating macroeconomic and fiscal objectives and the key parameters for general government fiscal policy, they are made co-responsible for their achievement (Ter-Minassian 1997: 8).

A good example of the possible benefits of a cooperative approach is Australia's Loan Council. The council is a cooperative forum for analyzing financing requirements of the states and the federal government in the context of general government fiscal policy and for allocating planned public borrowing over the medium term. These activities allow for trade-offs between competing claims. In addition, the council monitors subsequent loan activity; when a government is unable to keep its borrowing within its allocation, it must provide a formal explanation to the council (Pisauro 2001).

A cooperative approach promotes dialogue among levels of government and makes subnational governments aware of the macroeconomic implications of their budget choices. It works best where fiscal discipline is already widely accepted as a driving value in public finance choices. In countries where capital markets are lacking—and where poor discipline's

TABLE 3.2 Different Demands in Different Political Systems

Federal systems	Unitary systems
Greater policy, expenditure, and tax autonomy to subnational governments	Greater powers to central government
High local discretion to set budget limits, determine output mixes, and make operational choices	Limited sources of own revenue
	Less discretion in budget planning
	More binding guidelines controlling budget preparation and implementation
Higher risk of unfunded mandates	Centralized monitoring
Centralized monitoring not guaranteed	Centralized accountability
Accountability decentralized, often shared	Direct central government control over subnational borrowing
Greater ease of bailout denial	Higher risk of bailouts
Greater opportunity for local-level accountability to constrain local-level fiscal decisions	Less opportunity for local-level accountability

Source: Author.

effects on reputation are therefore weaker—or the leadership of the central government is weak, incentives and opportunities for cooperation are lessened (Ter-Minassian 1997).

The history of subnational borrowing in Brazil illustrates these principles. The 1988 Brazilian Constitution gave subnational governments, including large cities such as São Paulo, a lot of authority and resources. Over the next decade, Brazil had three major subnational debt crises, driven mainly by the largest states' use of their own banks to finance their operational deficits. The crises triggered agreements, but with the negative effect of reinforcing subnational governments' expectations of bailouts from the federal government. The agreements rescheduled debt, allowing debt stock to grow while ensuring that most of the repayment burdens fell on subsequent state and city leaders rather than on those leaders who defaulted and rescheduled debt. The rescheduling placed limits on debt service, thereby reducing the expected future cost of current borrowing. In effect, the agreements meant that both subnational borrowers and lenders suffered few consequences.

In the late 1990s, Fernando Cardoso was elected president because of his achievements as an effective finance minister. Fiscal prudence suddenly had political currency. Cardoso formed an alliance with the four largest debtor states, including São Paulo, and the government instituted five measures affecting borrowers and their creditors. The senate tightened its constitutional control over the fiscal activities of subnational governments with a new framework placing limits on borrowing. It forbade certain types of borrowing altogether. The rescheduling agreement of 1997 established much tighter constraints on subnational governments in default, increasing the cost of fiscal imprudence. The agreement set targets for decreases in debt and deficit ratios, ceilings for personnel spending and investment, growth in own revenue, and the privatization of state enterprises. It also stipulated consequences: no federal guarantees for debt, interest rate penalties on existing debt held by the federal government, increases in the debt service ceilings agreed earlier, and deductions of subnational debt directly out of federal transfers.

At the same time, the National Monetary Council ordered the Central Bank to limit banks' total lending to the public sector and to prohibit lending to any state in default or in violation of the debt and deficit ceilings issued by the Senate. The privatizations required in the rescheduling agreements included the state-owned banks, eliminating them as a source of financing.

Finally, in 2000, Brazil passed fiscal responsibility legislation, setting minimum standards for state budgeting and personnel and debt management. The legislation required that

- the annual budget of each government be in line with the government's multiyear budget and the federal fiscal program;
- all moneys owing to the federal government and its agencies be deducted from fiscal transfers;
- subnational governments seeking loans prove their compliance with the law to the Ministry of Finance;
- all borrowing above the Senate ceilings be paid in full and without interest, penalizing both borrower and lender;
- subnational governments be ineligible for discretionary transfers or federal guarantees and undertake no new debt until they repay all excess borrowing; and
- governors and mayors contract no obligations during their last six months in office.

The law also made debt and labor contracts that violate its provisions invalid—a heavy penalty on lenders, who would effectively lose their money (Web 2004: 8). Another law specified criminal penalties for officials who violate the law. In combination, these measures reduced general government debt and adjustments in personnel spending and public pensions.

The history of subnational borrowing in newly decentralizing countries suggests that sole reliance on market discipline may not be sufficient to encourage local fiscal discipline. Colombia's 1991 constitution brought greater freedom for subnational borrowing, mostly in the form of cash advances by banks. In 1997, Colombia introduced the traffic light law, creating a rating system for subnational borrowing on the basis of debt to current revenues and indicators of interest for operational savings. Highly indebted local governments got a red light and were prohibited from further borrowing. Yellow-lighted governments had to get permission from the finance ministry. In practice, lenders continued to provide credit to red-lighted governments, and some local territories offered inaccurate financial information to avoid a yellow-or red-light rating. Because most of the lending originated from banks, bank regulations were another way of controlling subnational borrowing. Since 1999, banks have been required to provide fully for the debt of any red-lighted subnational government, increasing the cost of lending. Legislation in 2000 imposed restrictions on the operations of subnational governments in an attempt to constrain the drivers of cost increases. In addition, the legislation required subnational governments to obtain satisfactory credit ratings from international rating agencies before borrowing.

Petersen and Freire (2004), Ter-Minassian (1997: 9), and Ter-Minassian and Craig (1997) suggest that many conditions must be satisfied if financial markets are to be effective in disciplining local borrowing. These conditions include free and open markets and no regulations that make local governments privileged borrowers, adequate information on governments' current financial position and past history, no expectations of bailout by the central government, and borrowers' capacity to respond to market signals before reaching default. Few countries meet these conditions. Even in Canada, where market discipline is the only constraint on subnational credit operations, provincial debt rose in the 1990s, despite a sophisticated market and no history of bailouts, deteriorating ratings, or increases in the cost of bonds.

Petersen and Freire (2004: 4–5) highlight the need for arms' length relationships between governments and between markets and banks, as well as civic norms for fiscal discipline, legal enforcement of contracts, and central government oversight of subnational borrowing. Developing countries typically do not meet these conditions: regulations on financial intermediaries make placement of government securities relatively cheap, timely information on the financial operations and health of local governments is not regularly available and may be inaccurate and incomplete, the state has ownership interests in financial institutions, and a history of soft budget constraints on local governments sometimes may be established. In such cases, local fiscal discipline is best supported by rules or by greater central government oversight of or control over subnational borrowing.

Rules to strengthen market discipline take many forms. Some rules set limits on absolute level of debt or on debt service cost ratios. Others allow borrowing only for specific purposes—for example, investment in infrastructure or short-term borrowing to cover cash flow shortfalls. Yet others limit the types of credit that subnational governments can access, banning international borrowing or borrowing from state banks.

However, local governments can be adept at circumventing fiscal discipline rules and putting off painful expenditure-reducing or revenue-raising decisions, particularly when transparency requirements are inadequate. For example, some governments may reclassify expenditures from current to capital to escape current budget balance requirements. Some may use own enterprises to borrow or may create off-budget entities whose debts are not included in debt stock assessments for debt ceilings. Some may use debt and investment instruments that are not included in balance sheet assessments. Some may borrow from their own capital spending allocations during the fiscal year to finance recurrent spending overruns. Some may run up huge stocks of arrears to contractors; these arrears will not show up in cash-based accounting systems.

These practices highlight the need for comprehensive monitoring of local governments' financial operations. The effectiveness of any monitoring is in turn dependent not only on appropriate frameworks, capacity, and willingness at national level, but also on the quality of local-level budgeting and accountability institutions.

Local Fiscal Discipline Institutions

Local governments can respond in several ways to fiscal pressure without resorting to debt financing. First, they can seek to raise additional revenue by increasing their user fees and charges, creating additional local taxes, or selling off assets such as land. Second, they can seek to improve the efficiency of their financial operations by improving their planning, programming, and budgeting capacity and by deploying productivity programs or seeking out lowest-cost means to deliver services. Third, they can enhance private and nongovernmental participation in the provision of services. To undertake each of these strategies successfully, local governments must have the capacity to assess their revenue streams and expenditure demands accurately and to make the difficult choices and control expenditure in accordance with those choices. Whether local governments have sufficient incentive to build these capacities depends on many factors.

Importance of Flexible Own-Revenue Sources

The discussion above highlighted the need for higher own-revenue financing of expenditure responsibilities at the local level to counter the common pool problem. The discussion on deficit financing made a similar point: local governments require some budget flexibility and autonomous revenue sources to support their credit market credibility. A third function of allowing local governments sufficient own-revenue sources is local governments' accountability to local communities.

When communities bear the cost of local services through local tax and user charges, citizens will realize the true budget constraint and will discipline their demand. Moreover, citizens are likely to place high value on their local governments' fiscal prudence. Local autonomy accompanied by accountability to citizens for service delivery provides robust opportunities for oversight (Shah 2004: 30). In a study of public organizations in six developing countries, Grindle (as quoted in Shah 2004: 30) found that where local autonomy and oversight matched decentralization, governments were "good performers."

Own-revenue capacity is a cornerstone of local fiscal discipline, particularly in a decentralized environment. Without access to their own revenue, local governments have fewer options when faced with fiscal pressure (or even with year-to-year infrastructure development needs). Local governments can respond to fiscal pressure optimally when national legal frameworks give them the flexibility to set local tax rates, determine user fees and charges, and identify additional resources. Typical local government revenues are property taxes, services charges, fees and licenses, rent for the use of facilities, and interest on investments. Some local governments also receive income from business enterprises they own, but ownership of enterprises can also result in contingent liabilities that trigger fiscal crises when they fall due.

Efficient Tax Administration

Flexibility in determining tax and other revenue bases and rates is usually outside local governments' direct control. Efficiency of revenue administration, however, is under local governments' control. Effective collection of tax and user charges and fees involves regular updating of tax rolls and evaluations for property tax. Local governments can increase tax collection on existing tax bases by reducing or removing exemptions and can often gain a lot by tailoring revenue arrangements to their collection capacity. Box 3.4 provides three examples of improved revenue collection.

Improvement of Public Financial Management Systems

As noted, local requisites for fiscal discipline are authorities' capacity to assess accurately their likely revenue inflows and expenditure outlays over the medium term and to undertake disciplined budget implementation. Modern approaches to budgeting involve use of fiscal and budgeting frameworks with a medium-term horizon, development of resource-constrained spending plans, modernization of budget classification and accounting systems, improvement of internal controls, use of performance measures, and establishment of institutions to improve transparency and accountability. Such approaches are critical for maximizing local government effectiveness in the context of limited resources.

As explained, local fiscal discipline is a function of political, administrative, and market constraints on the fiscal operations of local authorities. A requisite for any of these constraints to be effective is local-level fiscal transparency. Systematic political accountability for the outcomes of local financial

---

B O X   3 . 4 Examples of Effective Local Tax Collection Reforms

Much can be gained from compromises on the design and implementation of local taxes. In each of the three cases below, tax bases may yield revenue less than that collectable through a perfectly implemented ideal system. However, in each case the revenue collected represents a significant improvement over previous performance.

Hyderabad, India, had great success by deploying a collection strategy for property taxes that was suited to its capacity. Property taxes are, in principle, a good local revenue source, because they are stable and local citizens can perceive direct links between costs and benefits. However, they require frequent updating of tax rolls and tax evaluations. For two decades, Hyderabad did not undertake these two tasks, leaving the city with outdated tax rolls and little success in enforcing payment. The city then introduced a system requiring property owners and occupiers to file returns, assessing themselves on the basis of strict criteria and with assistance from local residence association committees, which exerted moral suasion to draw all liable owners and occupiers into the net. Tax revenues increased by 50 percent within a few months.

Vitória da Conquista, Brazil, had a culture of debt and fiscal deficits and a culture of nonpayment for services and of tax. To address the endemic tax evasion, the municipality began charging the service tax before businesses filed returns. The municipality made preassessments of the likely liability of 100 types of businesses and sent out accounts. Businesses had the right to object but had to provide receipts to prove that they had been overcharged.

In Kenya, a major source of local revenue is business licenses. Over time, the system became encumbered with many different licenses and provided opportunities for rent seeking by officials. Businesses could obtain licenses only after fulfilling conditions such as obtaining health certificates. The solution was to simplify the process by separating out the regulatory functions and creating a single unconditional business permit that all businesses had to obtain but could do so easily. Each municipality had to establish a standard set of tariffs but could choose one on the basis of its circumstances and revenue needs. The new system has significantly increased revenues.

Source: Mase and Devas 2004.

---

management is unlikely to be present unless citizens are constantly made aware of how well localities are being managed. Transparency can prevent problems from developing into crises. The benefits of local fiscal transparency are enhanced when the availability of accurate and timely information is complemented by the presence of a strong civil society—independent media, responsive opposition groups, good research organizations, and respected commentators.

To make local government finances transparent, the following are needed:

- *Transparency on medium-term fiscal policy and targets.* Several benefits accrue when local governments publicize medium-term revenue targets and expectations, expenditure projections, and financing needs. Transparency encourages investment by making tax burdens predictable, enhances fiscal credibility by lowering borrowing costs, creates an integrated framework for planning of local spending, and enhances the opportunity for local engagement with fiscal projections and targets.

- *Transparency on risks associated with the fiscal aggregates.* Discussion of medium-term targets for the budget aggregates should include discussion of risks, including price risks (for example, risks associated with the on-selling of utilities) and interest rate and exchange rate risks.

- *Transparency on the assumptions and models used to project revenues and expenditures.* Assumptions and models used to project revenues and expenditures should be open to scrutiny by higher levels of government and local stakeholders.

- *Budget comprehensiveness.* Budget and balance sheet frameworks should include all sources of revenue, all expenditure outlays, and all liabilities, including revenues and expenditures of arm's length agencies and other off-budget instruments.

- *Transparency on assets and liabilities.* Care should be taken to make transparent all current debts and all current liabilities, including arrears and contingent liabilities. Local budget statements should include a comprehensive statement of flows and a comprehensive balance sheet statement. Publicizing all planned fiscal operations and the impact of all past fiscal operations makes local governments hesitant to circumvent constraints on main budget operations by creating off-budget operations.

- *Information on budget execution.* The credibility of budget execution is important for local fiscal discipline. Frequent information on local governments' progress in meeting macro fiscal targets should be provided during the spending year.

- *Institutions to guarantee the credibility of financial information.* To deliver on transparency requirements, local governments need sound forecasting, budgeting, and debt and asset management, as well as internal control, accounting, and reporting systems. In addition, external audit practices must be robust to ensure the integrity of revenue and expenditure information.

Conclusion

Across the world, local governments are bearing increasing responsibility for the provision of public goods and services and the management of public moneys. To meet this responsibility effectively, they must have fiscal discipline—that is, the ability to spend only as much as is affordable in terms of their own future financial health and as in accordance with national or local macroeconomic objectives.

Local governments must contend with many exogenous factors that affect their fiscal health. As a subpart of a larger fiscal and monetary entity, local governments are highly vulnerable to national shocks, they are often heavily dependent on sometimes unpredictable fiscal transfers from other levels of government, and they may labor under highly rigid expenditure mandates. However, local governments' perverse fiscal behavior can adversely affect national fiscal and monetary conditions.

No matter the country or fiscal management system, all institutions that govern decisions affecting local fiscal balances—at all levels of government and across all sectors of the economy—must be incentive compatible if local governments are to maintain fiscal discipline and have the fiscal capacity to develop their localities. Whether incentives are effective is often dependent on whether the financial affairs of local governments are subject to scrutiny and whether those who undertake the risks are made to pay the price.

References

Baltaci, M., and S. Yilmaz. 2006. "Keeping an Eye on Subnational Governments: Internal Control and Audit at Local Levels." Stock 37257, World Bank Institute, Washington, DC.

Fjeldstad, O. 2001. "Intergovernmental Fiscal Relations in Developing Countries: A Review of Issues." Working Paper 11/2001, Christian Michelsen Institute, Bergen, Norway.

Mase, K., and N. Devas. March 2004. "Building Municipal Capacity in Finance." *IDD Research News,* March, International Development Department, University of Birmingham, Birmingham, U.K.

Petersen, J., and M. Freire. 2004. "Fiscal Devolution." In *Subnational Capital Markets in Developing Countries,* ed. M. Freire and J. Petersen, 11–28. Washington, DC: World Bank and Oxford University Press.

Pisauro, G. 2001. "Intergovernmental Relations and Fiscal Discipline: Between Commons and Soft Budget Constraints." Working Paper 01/65, International Monetary Fund, Washington, DC.

Prud'Homme, R. 1995. "The Dangers of Decentralization." *World Bank Research Observer* 10 (2): 201–20.

Schick, Allen. 1999. *A Contemporary Approach to Public Expenditure Management.* Washington, DC: World Bank Institute.

Shah, Anwar. 1998. "Fiscal Federalism and Macroeconomic Governance." Policy Research Working Paper 2005, World Bank, Washington, DC.

———. 2004. "Fiscal Decentralization in Developing and Transition Economies: Progress, Problems, and Promise." Policy Research Working Paper 3282, World Bank, Washington, DC.

———. 2005. "Fiscal Decentralization and Fiscal Performance." Policy Research Working Paper 3786, World Bank, Washington, DC.

Sood, P. 2004. "Hungary Case Study." In *Subnational Capital Markets in Developing Countries,* ed. M. Freire and J. Petersen, 525–44. Washington, DC: World Bank and Oxford University Press.

Spahn, P. B. 1997. "Decentralized Government and Macroeconomic Control." Infrastructure Notes, Urban No. FM-12, World Bank, Washington, DC. http://www.worldbank.org/html/fpd/urban/publicat/rd-fm12.htm

Tanzi, V. 1995. "Fiscal Federalism and Decentralization: A Review of Some Efficiency and Macroeconomic Aspects." In *Proceedings of the 1995 World Bank Annual Conference on Development Economics,* Washington, DC: World Bank.

———. 2001. "Pitfalls on the Road to Fiscal Decentralization." Carnegie Paper 19, Carnegie Endowment for International Peace, Washington, DC.

Ter-Minassian, Teresa. 1997. "Decentralisation and Macroeconomic Management." Working Paper 97/155, International Monetary Fund, Washington, DC.

Ter-Minassian, Teresa, and Jon Craig. 1997. "Control of Subnational Government Borrowing." In *Fiscal Federalism in Theory and Practice,* ed. Teresa Ter-Minassian, 156–72. Washington, DC: International Monetary Fund.

Web, S. 2004. "Fiscal Responsibility for Subnational Discipline: The Latin American Experience." Policy Research Working Paper 3309, World Bank, Washington, DC.

Wildasin, D. E. 1997. "Externalities and Bailouts: Hard and Soft Budget Constraints in Intergovernmental Fiscal Relations." Policy Research Working Paper 1843, World Bank, Washington, DC.

Zabala, R.T. 2004. "Colombia Case Study." In *Subnational Capital Markets in Developing Countries,* ed. M. Freire and J. Petersen, 279–98. Washington, DC: World Bank and Oxford University Press.

4

Combating Corruption in State and Local Revenue Administration

AMARESH BAGCHI

"One of the areas of government where the impacts of corruption loom largest is in the assessment and collection of taxes."
—Galtung (1995)

Corruption, or the abuse of public office for private gains, is a ubiquitous phenomenon. Public servants at all times and in all civilizations have been tempted to make personal gains at the cost of the public. Kautilya, the adviser to the Indian King Chandragupta Maurya, had discerned this tendency on the part of public officials some 2000 years ago: "Just as fish moving under water cannot possibly be found out either as drinking or not drinking water, so government servants employed in the government work cannot be found out [while] taking money [for themselves]" (Bardhan 1997: 1320–346).

Governments everywhere live with this reality. Although industrial countries have, by and large, succeeded in keeping corruption at bay, no nation in the world can claim to have achieved total success. In the United States, regarded as the country with the least corruption, over 10,000 government officials were convicted of that crime by federal prosecutors between 1990 and 2002 (Glaeser and Saks 2004). The scourge is most virulent in developing and transition countries—presumably the reason that the World Bank brought corruption activities into the mainstream of its aid program. Recognizing the urgency of the need to combat corruption, the Asian Development Bank (ADB) in 2001 pledged support for the Anticorruption Action Plan for the Asia and the Pacific region, which ADB members have since endorsed.

Opinions differ as to whether corruption is an unmitigated evil in all situations. According to some, corruption may not be all that bad for a country seeking private investment for growth as it serves to grease the wheels of administration. Examples of Suharto's Indonesia and China are cited to show that corruption may not be an obstacle to growth in all cases.[1] Arvind Panagariya (2006) has argued that empirical evidence in favor of making anticorruption policies the center of efforts to achieve rapid growth in developing countries is far from conclusive. He concludes that scope for corruption will decrease as liberalization reduces tariffs and calls for free play of the private sector (Panagariya 2006). The dominant view, however, is that corruption is inimical to growth and welfare in the long run.[2] Therefore, initiatives to curb corruption are to be welcomed.

Some observers view decentralization as a good way to reduce corruption, because it improves the performance of the public sector and enhances efficiency in public spending, delivery of public services, and welfare by bringing governments closer to the people, thereby making them accountable.[3] Although skeptics point to the negative effects of decentralization on growth and the high incidence of corruption in local governments,[4] many observers acknowledge the efficacy of decentralization in improving service delivery and plugging leaks from public spending programs by increasing public officials' accountability.

Whether decentralization reduces corruption in revenue collection at subnational levels of government has received little attention. Ample evidence shows that corruption in revenue administration is extensive and endemic.[5] The malaise appears to afflict all levels of government, particularly the government at the lowest level because of its relatively poor administrative resources.

This chapter explores corruption in revenue administration, particularly at the lower levels of government, and makes suggestions on combating the scourge. It first examines the principal revenue sources of state[6] and local governments across the world, their revenue significance, and the scope they offer for corruption. The chapter then reviews the literature on corruption. It concludes with a discussion of remedies.

Tax and Revenue Powers of Subcentral Governments and Scope for Corruption

State and local governments (SNGs) derive their revenue from a variety of sources, tax and nontax. In general, taxes raised at the local level are not significant in terms of revenue. Typically, substantial revenue is raised at the state level. Local governments depend heavily on transfers from above. Even so, considerable scope for corruption exists at the local level.

Revenue Sources of State and Local Governments and Their Relative Importance

Given considerations of economies of scale and efficiency, the national government usually levies major revenue-yielding taxes, such as customs duties and taxes on personal and corporate incomes, as well as social security levies and excise taxes on selected products. State governments typically have the power to tax consumption—sales tax and its modern variant: the value added tax (VAT). Local governments often levy land and property taxes. However, the pattern varies across countries.

In most countries, taxes on income and profits are levied at the national level. In some (for example, Switzerland and Nigeria), income tax is levied at the subnational level. VAT typically is levied at the national level. Where the powers are concurrent as in Brazil, Canada, and the United States, consumption taxes like the sales tax/VAT are levied at more than one level, and subnational governments derive revenue from income taxes (by piggybacking). In India, tax powers are vested in the union and state governments on the principle of exclusion—that is, concurrency is barred. Typically, only the central government can levy customs/excises and service taxes. States have the power to levy taxes on consumption (sales tax/VAT on goods) and on lands and buildings. The states also have the power to impose other taxes: vehicle taxes, excises on liquor, some types of stamp taxes, professions taxes, entertainment taxes, electricity duties, and so on. Taxes on land and buildings are levied at the local level, though at rates approved by state governments.

Local governments around the world also levy a variety of business taxes. The most common forms are corporate or enterprise income taxes, taxes on internal trade like octroi, gross receipts taxes, fixed or proportional taxes varying by type of business and location (for example, the *patente,* or fixed tax, levied in several Latin American countries), and taxes on nonresidential real property (Bird 2003). In China, the power to impose taxes belongs exclusively to the central government. Provincial governments can decide the rates but only within limits set by the central government. China's taxes include seven taxes on land and property, a business tax, an urban and township land use tax, a house property tax, an urban real estate tax, a farmland occupation tax, a land appreciation tax, and a deed tax. Revenue from all land and property taxes belong to subnational governments (Shanda and Duoshu 2004).

Nontax revenue sources are mainly interest on loans, fees, user charges for services provided by the local government, and fines and transfers from higher-level governments. Sale or transactions in publicly owned assets, particularly land, constitute a significant source of funds for governments at all levels but more so at lower levels of government, because local and state governments usually handle land matters. In China, lower-level governments run commercial enterprises, the profits of which contribute to the state and local exchequer. In several states in India, lotteries are a conspicuous nontax revenue source.

Table 4.1 presents some of the revenue sources of urban local bodies (ULBs). As the table shows, cities in the Philippines can levy as many as nine taxes; in Thailand, ULBs also have nine tax powers, five of which consist of levying a surcharge on taxes levied by the national government. In Korea, ULBs have many tax powers and also have several nontax heads on which to draw for revenue.

In developed countries, the revenue significance of taxes levied by SNGs varies. The share of state and local taxes taken together in the total tax revenue of general government (including social security contributions) ranges from 3 percent in the Netherlands and 4 percent in the United Kingdom, to 32 percent in Sweden and 38 percent in Switzerland (OECD 1999).

In developing countries, revenues raised at the subnational level as a proportion of total government revenue vary from 60 percent in China and around 35 percent in India, to 7 percent in Indonesia and 9 percent in Pakistan (Bird and Vaillancourt 1998: 19–20). The share of local government revenue in total government revenue is relatively small, averaging about 12 to 13 percent. Table 4.2 shows the importance of the revenue shares of three levels of government in selected countries.

Firm data on local government finances in developing countries are hard to find,[7] but it appears that taxes and revenues raised at the local level make up less than 1 percent of gross domestic product and less than 5 percent of total government revenues in most cases. But, as table 4.2 shows, in some countries (Mongolia), local governments raise over one-fifth of total revenue. However, the number of revenue heads available to local bodies (particularly in the case of ULBs) is not that small.

TABLE 4.1 Fiscal Domain of Cities

Philippines		Thailand			Rep. of Korea	
Taxes	Nontax revenues	Taxes	Surcharges	Nontax revenue	Taxes	Nontax revenues
Property	Fees for permits and licenses	House and building	Value added	Fees, fines, and licenses	Inhabitant	Rents, user charges, and fees
Business	Charges and rentals for recovery in public markets, slaughter houses, bus terminals, and so on	Land development	Liquor and beverages	Revenue from property	Property	Interest
Real property transfer		Signboards	Entertainment	Social or utilities service revenue	Auto	Stamp duties
Business of printing and publication		Animal slaughter	Gambling	Miscellaneous income	Farmland	Collection grants from higher-level government
Extraction of quarry resources			Excise		Butchery	Operating income from public enterprises (e.g., water and sewerage, hospitals, and subways)
Amusement					Tobacco consumption	
Professional					Workshop	
Delivery vans and trucks						
Community						

Source: Mathur and von Ein Siedel 1996.

TABLE 4.2   Share of Revenues Raised by Three Levels of
Government, Selected Countries, 1993–96

		Own revenues as percentage of total government revenues		
Location	Year	Central government	State government	Local government
Bolivia	1996	79.36	5.82	14.82
Botswana	1994	99.42	n.a.	0.58
Brazil	1993	72.42	23.27	4.31
Guatemala	1993	96.29	n.a.	3.71
India	1997	63.80	33.40	2.84[a]
Israel	1994	90.48	n.a.	9.52
Kenya	1994	94.03	n.a.	5.97
Malaysia	1996	86.97	9.74	3.29
Mongolia	1996	77.29	n.a.	22.71
Paraguay	1993	92.73	n.a.	2.27
Peru	1996	94.67	0.89	4.44
South Africa	1995	86.04	3.40	10.55
Thailand	1996	93.74	n.a.	6.26
United States	1995	58.68	25.45	15.87
Africa and Asia		84.53	1.64	13.83

Source: Ebel and Vaillancourt 2001.
Note: n.a. = not available.
[a] Includes revenue from municipalities only; revenue raised at the village level is not significant.

The relative share of individual taxes raised at lower levels of government also varies across countries. For instance, in some member countries of the Organisation for Economic Co-operation and Development (OECD), a large proportion of taxes raised at the subcentral level is derived from taxes on income and profits (100 percent in Poland and Sweden; 95 percent in Denmark), but SNGs often are empowered to set the rates only (OECD 1999). Next in importance are taxes on wealth and property, followed by taxes on consumption.

The dominant tax source of states where multilevel governance prevails is the sales tax or its modern variant, VAT. In India, nearly 60 percent of tax revenue raised by state governments comes from sales tax (now VAT). In Brazil, too, a substantial proportion of revenue collected at the state level comes from VAT.

The main source of revenue of local governments in developing countries is the property tax, although in some countries (Brazil, for example), other taxes are more important (Nickson 1995). According to a survey in the late

1980s, the median share of property tax in local taxes of municipalities is above 40 percent, irrespective of region or location (Bahl and Linn 1992). Many cities levy taxes on motor vehicles and on entertainment, the revenue contribution of which is insignificant except in a few cities (Bangkok and Jakarta, for example). In several countries, property transfer taxes constitute a local revenue source, and in several cities (including Seoul), revenue from this tax financed about 20 percent of total local government expenditure. Moreover, local governments levy nuisance taxes that are difficult and expensive to collect but that account for a significant share of local taxes (Bahl and Linn 1992).

A more recent study (Bird and Slack 2004) confirms that property tax continues to be the most important tax for local governments in developing countries. Institutional arrangements for implementation of the property tax vary. In some Latin American countries (such as Argentina), property tax is a provincial tax, and in others (such as El Salvador) it is a central government tax. In South Africa, local governments raise more property tax revenue than provinces (Bagchi and Chakraborty 2006).

In India, the proportion of tax revenue raised by local governments in aggregate tax revenue of state and local government was 4 percent as of 2002/03 (Oomen 2006), illustrating that few revenue-productive tax powers have been devolved to local Indian governments. The only significant tax that these governments (especially the ULBs) have at their disposal is the property tax, although octroi, or the tax on entry of goods into a local area, can fetch a significant amount of revenue for the local government in some cities (Mumbai, for example). In the case of rural local bodies, tax powers vary but are mostly restricted to powers of property tax and a few land-based taxes.

Room for Corruption

Where the SNGs piggyback on the tax (or the base) assessed by the national government, as in many OECD countries, tax administration poses no problem. So far as developed countries are concerned, even where SNGs levy the tax on their own, the incidence of corruption is low. Only VAT, which is levied in almost all advanced countries (but not the United States) and which accounts for about 25 percent of tax revenue, presents opportunities for fraud and evasion. However, in general, corruption in tax administration does not appear to be a major policy issue for advanced countries.

The picture is somewhat different in developing countries. In India, sales tax, the most important tax source for states, is rife with corruption, which is believed to be one of the main factors responsible for the failure of many state governments to realize the full revenue potential of the tax. A recent study of the tax system of one of the leading states of India (Government of Karnataka para 3.38.) notes widespread evasion, abetted by corruption, as a major factor underlying the stagnancy of revenues from sales tax for the state. Tempted by the gains from evasion, many traders do not mind paying a bribe to tax inspectors to avoid detection. Without bribe takers, evasion could not be practiced on such a large scale.

VAT is supposed to be less prone to evasion and corruption, because it has an internal mechanism to induce voluntary compliance. Nonetheless, the scope for fraud and evasion is not totally eliminated. In fact, VAT opens up new opportunities for evasion through exaggerated refund claims and input tax credit against false invoices. A recent International Monetary Fund survey revealed how VAT can generate false claims for refunds, especially in the case of exporters, through zero rating of exports. The survey authors called the refund process the "Achilles' heel" of VAT (Harrison and Krelove 2005).

At the local level, the property tax, the most important own-revenue source of local governments, provides ample opportunities for evasion and corruption. In India, corruption has been held to be partially responsible for the poor yield of the tax in most states. Assessment of the base of the tax involves valuation in which the scope for discretion and, hence, corruption is large.

Corruption is believed to be one of the main factors responsible for the property tax's poor revenue efficiency in Latin America. In a study of local government in Latin America, Nickson (1995) cites collusion between taxpayers and tax officials in assessment of property values and outright fraud by tax officials as largely responsible for the low effectiveness of property tax. Many other factors, such as haphazard revision of the tax base and delayed revision of rules by central government decree, have also been cited. But corruption figures prominently in the list.

Other taxes levied in many Latin American countries also have the potential to generate corruption. Such is the case of local business taxes unless levied on the basis of some objectively measurable indicators (such as size of shop or number of employees). Like urban property tax, land tax also involves valuation and so provides opportunity for corruption.

Stamp taxes and duties levied on transfer of properties (often at the state level but passed on to local governments) offer the same opportunity, because they, too, require valuation. But a big scam involving billions of rupees in stamp duty collection in India arose not so much from undervaluation, though that is believed to have been widespread, as from faking of the stamp papers on which the law requires property transfers to be recorded. Fraudulent production and use of stamp papers caught newspaper headlines across the country. The cost of the fraud is estimated to be as high as Rs. 780,000 million over a period of 10 years (Alm, Annez, and Modi 2004).

In South Asian countries, octroi has been a potent source of corruption. This tax is enforced with the help of check posts. These posts are known to be highly prone to corruption.

Local governments, like governments at other levels, usually raise revenue through user charges and fees. User charges are realized for providing services such as water supply and electricity. With the connivance of local officials, these services may be obtained at a charge lower than normal. Fees are levied for administrative transactions (such as granting a license for a shop) and are charged for operating market stalls (like rent), for operating kiosks in public places, and for hawking items in the streets. Allotment of stalls and kiosks provides room for corruption.

The scope for corruption in administration of fees and charges would appear to be limited. However, the cost to the local governments may not always be small, especially in the case of water supply and electricity. In India, nearly 40 percent of electricity generated is lost through theft, causing losses to electricity generators, which are usually owned by state governments (state electricity boards); these losses are believed to be the most important single factor in the huge deficits in India's state budgets (Rao and Chakraborty 2006). Theft is not confined to water and power. In the case of transport and some other utilities run by local (and also state) governments, valuable assets are pilfered, and the booty is shared with the utility employees.

Corruption can be rife in the sale or leasing of land and enterprises belonging to the government at throwaway prices or prices well below market rates. In India, land scams are reportedly widespread. Sale of public sector enterprises in Russia was widely reported to have resulted in siphoning off of large sums to politicians or mafia leaders.

Corruption in Revenue Administration: Driving Factors and Suggested Remedies

The objective of corrupt officials engaged in revenue administration is to profit by allowing taxpayers or users of public services to cheat the government through nonpayment of taxes or charges due under the law. In the case of taxes, the modus operandi is straightforward: the tax inspector turns a blind eye even when he or she finds a potential taxpayer not registering with the tax authorities as required by law, not filing a return of income or sales, not reporting true income or turnover, or not furnishing the particulars required for correct assessment of tax liabilities. In the case of nontax revenue, corruption thrives through the connivance of officials in a citizen's use of a priced public service without full payment for it. Much of the strategy for combating corruption in tax administration applies to combating corruption in nontax administration.

Drivers of Corruption

Drivers of corruption in government have come under rigorous economic analysis in recent years. Several explanations of corruption generators have been offered. One leading explanation comes from the theory of economic crime based on cost-benefit logic; another explanation is derived from the principal-agent framework.

Theory of economic crime

All corruption is essentially "a crime of economic calculation" (Klitgaard, Madean-Abaroa, and Parris 2000: 31). Gary Becker (1968) has noted that economic crime thrives when the gain exceeds perceived costs. Allingham and Sandmo (1972) expanded Becker's theory to explain income tax evasion. They note that a tax inspector is likely to allow a taxpayer to cheat on taxes if the offered bribe is higher than the cost of the inspector's loss of office with all its attendant benefits and the penalties or punishment prescribed for corrupt behavior. A taxpayer will find it economically beneficial to pay a bribe and default in complying with tax laws as long as the evaded tax is greater than the cost of the prescribed penalties. Viewed thus, the remedy for corruption in tax administration, at any level of government, would appear to involve three tactics: reduce the gain for the briber by lowering the level of the tax, raise the cost of noncompliance by raising the scale of penalties, or enhance the probability of detection and punishment by improving the efficiency of the tax enforcement machinery and by speeding up the judicial process.

Following cost-benefit logic, the benefit from evading a tax should be reduced to the minimum. Thus, the rates of taxes and charges should be set at a reasonable level. Excessively high rates and charges tend to promote evasion and corruption.

The appropriate or reasonable rate of tax depends on acceptability, which, in turn, depends to a considerable extent on the quantity and quality of services rendered by the government. Acceptability also depends on the capacity of the administration to enforce tax laws and on community members' ethical standards, which play a part in individuals' decision making. In countries where administration is weak, community values are permissive, or both, corruption tends to be endemic. In such countries, tax rates should be kept at an acceptable level and ways to reduce corruption must be found; otherwise, evasion will occur even in the presence of a low rate of tax.

To increase the perceived costs of evasion, the government should proceed simultaneously on three fronts. First, it should fix penalties and punishments on a scale that can deter potential evaders who are not risk averse. Second, it should enhance the probability of detection through better administration, which, in turn, requires attention to all the processes involved in implementing tax laws. Third, it should accelerate prosecution and adjudication of tax disputes.

Enhancing the scale of penalties may be self-defeating beyond a point. With disproportionate punishment, law dispensers tend to hesitate to deliver the verdict of guilty and to take even minor weaknesses in evidence as grounds for acquitting the accused. In India, penalties for evasion of income tax have been stringent—at one time, the penalty was to treble the amount of the tax evaded. Tax offenders are liable to be prosecuted and jailed if convicted by a court. Instances of evaders being made to pay the maximum penalty or of people being sent to jail for tax evasion are rare, although evasion has been known to be widespread (Acharya and Associates 1985). Compliance appears to have improved only after tax rates were reduced in the 1990s.

Tax evasion in developed countries like the United States is known to be low largely because of the high probability of detection and punishment. To deter evasion, the tax administration must have a good information system and an efficient audit system with scientific methods for selecting cases for scrutiny. It also must have capable officers to conduct the audit.

Even with efficient detection machinery, evaders may escape punishment because of onerous and time-consuming judicial procedures. The onus is usually on the prosecution to prove that the accused is guilty.[8] The judicial process can be streamlined if the parties to a tax dispute are required to submit their arguments in writing and hearings are kept to the minimum. Delays in proceedings may occur because of the small number of judges relative to the number of cases filed. Even so, modern technology, including e-libraries providing access to legal references and citations, should speed up the disposal of court cases. India's apex court has shown how computerization and strict rules for judges in matters of attendance and case disposal can reduce the number of pending cases and accelerate judicial decisions. Total pending cases in India's Supreme Court fell from 104,936 in January 1992 to 26,673 in September 1996 (Verma 2001).

The principal-agent framework

Another analytical approach to corruption is based on the principal-agent approach, an alternative that in some ways complements the strategy based on cost-benefit logic (Gurgur and Shah 2005). The essence of this approach, wherein citizens are the principal and officials are the agent, is largely captured in the celebrated formula enunciated by Klitgaard (1988): $C = M + D - A$, where C stands for corruption, M for monopoly, D for discretion, and A for accountability. The reasoning underlying the formula is simple: corruption is the combined result of the monopoly powers of the state, the discretion available to the government agent administering the law, and accountability. Corruption decreases when monopoly powers and discretion are reduced and accountability is enhanced.

Reducing monopoly powers in taxation may not be possible beyond a point, because the power to tax is the prerogative of the sovereign, although privatizing some of the functions pertinent to the levy of a tax or revenue raising should help to curtail monopoly. Government can circumscribe discretion by simplifying laws and introducing easily verifiable measures of the tax base. Accountability is enhanced when government supervises tax inspectors and promptly punishes corrupt officers. Klitgaard's formula suggests that corruption can be controlled if governance is rules based, leaving as little discretion to officials as possible, and if internal and external mechanisms enhance accountability.

In essence, the principal-agent approach explains corruption as an information problem. If the approach is valid, decentralization should provide an effective remedy for this problem. After surveying the literature on whether decentralization makes any difference to the incidence of corruption by alleviating the agency problem, Shah (2006: 485) concludes that "no definitive conclusion can be drawn regarding corruption and the centralization-decentralization nexus from agency-type conceptual models. These models simply reaffirm that the incidence of corruption is context dependent and therefore cannot be uncovered by generalized models."

Other Approaches
Decentralization, new public management, and new institutional economics

Other approaches to curbing corruption are provided by the new public management (NPM) framework and the new institutional economics (NIE). The NPM literature identifies a discordance among the public sector mandate, its authorizing environment, and operational culture and capacity. This literature avers that government officials will find it possible to indulge in rent seeking with little risk of citizen action to restrain them. The remedy is to appoint public officials on contract and make their continuance dependent on fulfillment of contracted obligations. Critics of the NPM framework argue that rent seeking may increase with separation of providers from service purchasers.

The NIE approach is more persuasive. Its proponents contend that officials find it possible to indulge in opportunistic behavior when citizens are not empowered or find it difficult to bring errant officials to book because of high transaction costs attributable to incomplete access to information. Citizen empowerment through devolution, citizens' charters, elections, and other forms of civic engagement can make public officials accountable to the people.

Good governance

Drawing on empirical literature, Shah (2006) concludes that the level of corruption is closely associated with the quality of governance. A high incidence of corruption is associated with poor governance, whereas a low incidence is associated with good governance. Hence, an anticorruption strategy should be based on reforms reflecting the broad institutional environment in each country (Shah 2006). Rule of law and citizen empowerment should take priority in reform efforts. Localization and decentralization would be of no avail in the absence of rule of law.

Ultimately, good governance is central to any anticorruption strategy, whether based on a crime and punishment, principal-agent, NIE, or NPM model. How to enlist the wholehearted cooperation of public officials in corruption control has been the subject of intense debate (see Mookherjee 2004).

Incentives for tax bureaucracies

One way to motivate public officials engaged in revenue raising to perform their duties honestly is to pay them adequate or reasonable salaries or to provide rewards for meritorious work. Mookherjee (2004) argues that government officials are self-interested individuals who cannot be expected to forgo moneymaking opportunities wherever they arise, unless incentives to act otherwise are strong. He notes that in societies where tax evasion is endemic, tax administration provides many opportunities for private gain at public expense.

One way to deter such corruption would be to relate the tax collector's pay to the revenue collected—for example, by offering the collector a bonus of, say, 20 percent of the collected revenue and fines. In the absence of any incentive, the bonus rate is zero; given privatization, the rate is 100 percent.

But a bonus scheme may merely increase the level of the bribe.[9] Corruption will survive as long as joint surplus (the combined gain of the tax evader and the corrupt official) remains positive.

The other alternative for government is to use the stick—that is, disciplinary action (such as dismissal), in which case salary constitutes the policy parameter. However, if the chances that corruption will be detected are small—one in a million—the salary, or what Besley and McLaren (1993) call the "efficiency wage," must be high. When the odds of detection are high, the efficiency wage can be smaller. Thus, Mookherjee (2004: 62) concludes that "whether it is desirable for the government to introduce an incentive policy that eliminates corruption depends on the 'institutional capacity' of the tax administration and wider society to police and penalize acts of corruption." The experience of Brazil, Ghana, Mexico, and Peru with incentives for tax collectors suggests that associated institutional reforms are essential for the incentives' success (Chand and Moene 1999; Chand, Moene, and Mookherjee 2003). Where institutional capacity is weak, such reforms may be too difficult and prohibitively expensive to implement.

Incentives to tax bureaucracies may be provided in the form of rewards linked to additional revenue collected. But performance measurement is not always simple. Short-term collection figures may be manipulated. Collectors might argue that measures other than increases in revenues collection ought to be rewarded as well. Moreover, rewards may have to be given to groups, rather than individuals, to avoid jealousies.

Fjelstad and Tungodden (2003a) argue that incentive schemes to enhance revenue collection are short sighted. Rewards or above-market wages for specific public sectors may induce seeking and payment of rents to secure attractive jobs. The apprehension is that the sale price of a post builds on the capital value of the salary, as is reported to be the case in some countries (Azerbaijan, for example).

Three points relevant in the present context emerge from the debate. First, poor levels of remuneration for tax officials (or any government official exercising some regulatory or law enforcement power) cannot but tempt officials to take bribes. They must be paid a greater-than-subsistence wage. Second, rewarding tax collectors by giving them a fraction of the additional revenue they collect may raise the cost of evasion for taxpayers by raising the bribe level and thereby the revenue level. Therefore, policy makers must weigh the likely revenue gain against the rise in bribe levels, though the number of corrupt tax officials may decrease as a result of incentive schemes. The impact on revenue of bonus payments is difficult to predict. Third, incentive schemes can be of no help unless accompanied by institutional and organizational reforms in tax administration. Institutional reforms are required to strengthen accountability.

Accountability

Accountability requires units and agencies to undertake investigations into allegations of corruption. Many countries have set up vigilance agencies or institutions of horizontal accountability for this purpose (Schacter 2005). But these institutions' success in bringing the corrupt to account is often limited by lack of political support and independence to conduct investigations (Pope and Vogl 2000). Another factor that undermines the efficacy of vigilance agencies is dilatoriness in following up cases identified for investigation.

Supplementary measures

Corruption in revenue administration is different in a crucial respect from corruption in other government activities. Diverting funds meant for public use or a poor relief program or exacting a bribe for granting a permit does not involve collusion between the official and the citizen, but corruption in revenue administration does. Corruption in which the official and the citizen are in conflict suggests remedies—such as transparency in governance and a voice for citizens in the running of public institutions—that may be inadequate for corruption characterized by collusion. When citizens engage in collective collusion,[10] intervention from a high-level authority may be required.

Overlap of local, state, and federal jurisdictions is another way of countering corruption at the local level (Rose-Ackerman 1994). This strategy has reduced police corruption in controlling illegal drugs in the United States (Bardhan 1997). To control corruption in tax administration in Singapore, customs officials work together in teams.

Recommendations to Combat Corruption at Subnational Levels

As noted, the taxes most associated with corruption are the sales tax/VAT, the property tax, local business taxes, excises on liquor, and transfer taxes. A strategy to combat corruption in state and local tax administration ought to focus on these types of taxes and on strengthening governance.

General Principles

Das-Gupta and Mookherjee (1998) describe the process of tax administration as identification of potential taxpayers; correct assessment of their tax liabilities; and follow-up through penalties, prosecution, and collection. These activities are facilitated by

■ an efficient system for collecting and storing information about the tax base, all potential taxpayers and their returns-filing status, pending assessments, and paid or pending taxes;
■ a monitoring mechanism for following up on the status of assessments, appeals, prosecutions, penalties, and final results in terms of taxes realized or due; and
■ definition of the tax base in a manner that allows for objective and unambiguous quantification of tax liabilities.

The last item calls for simplicity in tax laws and avoidance of exemptions or exclusions based on fine distinctions that allow for tax officials' discretion. The first two items are needed to establish accountability, which also requires clearly specified functions for officers at different levels, clearly delineated lines of control in the administration's hierarchy, and efficient channels of coordination among and within departments. Accountability also calls for a mechanism to respond to taxpayer grievances and a system to train tax officials.

Privatization and mechanization

Monopoly of the government can be reduced through privatization. But because revenue collection is a prerogative of the sovereign, it cannot be entirely privatized. However, some of the functions of tax enforcement or revenue realization can be outsourced, especially at the local level.

Giving areas of local revenue administration to private hands will not eliminate corruption. When regular employees of the Bombay Municipal Corporation went on strike and the corporation appointed temporary workers unfamiliar with corrupt practices to operate the check posts for enforcing octroi payment, collections quadrupled (Palkhivala 1994: 127). This experience suggests that local governments should avoid levies that call for physical inspection and instead rely on private agencies and on mechanized systems (for example, pilfer-proof meters for water and electric utilities) that reduce or eliminate human interference.

Hiring of a foreign agency for customs administration is sometimes advocated as a means to curb rampant corruption among customs officials. But after an unhappy experience with this remedy, Indonesia abandoned it. Sarkar (1989) notes that privatization of customs collection helped provoke the French Revolution. Sarkar (2006), citing an article in the London paper *The Guardian*, describes a huge scam that occurred when Pakistan contracted out preshipment inspection.

Clearly, privatized revenue collection activities offer opportunity for corruption. But corruption of such activities may be limited at the local level. Hence, wherever possible, tax authorities should explore the scope for privatization.

Transparency

The remedy for corruption, whether at the national or the local level, is transparency in the operations that beget the booty. Land and property deals and contracts for construction of public assets can potentially put large sums into the hands of senior government officials. If the government is to get its due, such transactions must be processed openly through tenders and advertisements in the media. The tenders must be opened to the public, and the public should have access to any information required to judge whether the transaction has been conducted in a fair manner. The Right to Information Act passed by the Indian Parliament is a milestone in the road to transparency and should help curb corruption at all levels.

Specific Anticorruption Measures

Some specific remedies may be needed for individual taxes levied at the state and local levels.

Curbing of corruption in VAT

In federal countries and economic unions like the European Union, VAT is levied at the state or member country level. This tax is found in more than 130 countries. It fetches, on average, 35 percent of government revenue in the western hemisphere—45 percent in Chile and Peru.

Although productive from the revenue angle, VAT offers scope for evasion and thereby corruption. The sharp decline in the revenue yield of VAT as a proportion of gross domestic product in Ukraine is attributed largely to corruption and the prevalence of a large underground economy (Bird and Gendron 2006). Although the European Union maintains high standards of tax administration, some observers fear that its operation of VAT has generated evasion of the tax by firms and households (Nam, Gebauer, and Parsche 2003).

Apart from the usual methods of evasion of traditional sales tax and direct taxes—nonregistration of businesses, nonfiling of returns, underreporting of gross receipts, abuse of multiple rates, and failure to remit the tax realized from customs to the Treasury—VAT offers scope for evasion through fraudulent claims for tax credit (using fake invoices), for refunds (showing intrastate sales as interstate sales), and for ineligible purchases.[11] In the

European Union, large-scale evasion of VAT has occurred through the carousel method—fictitious sales and purchases of goods through shell companies (Lienemeyer 1997). To check VAT evasion, subnational governments need an efficient system to track the sale and purchase of goods and an effective audit program. Modern technology should aid both these endeavors.

Electronic documentation of interstate transactions vastly reduces the scope for harassment and bribery and facilitates matching of sales and purchases. In the European Union, the VAT Information Exchange System supports the zero rating of intracommunity sales. Developing countries with a federal structure that have no such system should consider having an interstate sales tax on which purchasers can get a rebate. They should also consider a prepaid VAT on interstate sales.[12] Korea has attempted 100 percent matching of sales and purchases, but its system does not appear to be workable. República Bolivariana de Venezuela, where VAT evasion is estimated at 50 to 60 percent of the tax due, has introduced a system of tax withholding whereby the buyer must remit a portion of the tax charged to the Treasury (Evans 2003).

Tax laws usually prescribe one month or one quarter for depositing VAT collected on supplies. Ideally, the VAT audit would include short-interval checks during the year and some more comprehensive multiperiod multitax audits. The coverage rate for the VAT audit should be much higher than the coverage rate regarded as acceptable for income tax audits.

To facilitate compliance and minimize the scope for evasion in a state-level VAT system, the VAT base and procedures should be uniform across all states. The rates also should be uniform: only one rate for each state.

Property tax

Property taxation represents fertile ground for corruption in local revenue administration. Because the base of the tax is commonly derived from the rental or capital value of the property at current market rates, valuation invariably involves a large element of subjectivity and thus discretion. Many studies (including Bird and Slack 2004 and Municipal Corporation of Delhi 2003) have documented how this discretion has led to corruption, harassment, stagnation in property tax revenue, and inequity (because of disparity in the valuation of similar properties and so on).

The remedy is a unit area–based system. Under this system, a charge is fixed per unit area of land (such as square meter) and of building or some combination of the two. The per-unit assessment relates the tax liability directly to the size of the land and buildings. The rate per unit area can be adjusted to reflect location, the quality of the building, or other factors. The adjustment factor can reflect the market value as well. These factors are derived from average values of groups of properties within a given zone and may not reflect the characteristics of individual properties. Central and Eastern Europe, where the absence of property markets makes market values difficult to determine, generally use a unit area–based system, as does Chile, China, Germany, Kenya, and Tunisia (Bird and Slack 2004).

A unit-value assessment is used in the assessment of agricultural land. The land revenue system prevalent in South Asian countries such as Bangladesh, India, and Pakistan has long been based on the productivity of the land and the average value of the crops grown. Like the unit area–based system, this method of taxation is believed to curb corruption. With a unit area–based system, property holders can self-assess and pay the tax.

Value standardized though the unit-area system should be helpful in administering other taxes. A central valuation authority may help to establish standard values in a transparent manner and periodically undertake revisions. Anyone declaring the value of a property in a transaction below the standardized value may be subjected to scrutiny. It may help to curb evasion and corruption in taxes levied by the central government, like the income tax, in that it will provide a benchmark for judging the correctness of values declared in the sale and acquisition of properties.

A unit area–based system has its limitations. First, the benefits from services are usually more closely reflected in property values than in the size of the property. Moreover, market value has the advantage of reflecting the benefit of neighborhood amenities, which are usually created by government expenditure and local governments. Second, attempts to introduce adjustment factors in the unit area–based system create complications. In the Netherlands, the system became so complicated through adjustment that it was ultimately abandoned. Third, even this system offers opportunities for corruption. In Latin America, valuations of the size and characteristics of properties were often grossly underreported because of collusion between taxpayers and tax officials on self-assessment (Nickson 1995: 47). Like all tax systems, the unit area–based system calls for sample audits, supervision of lower-level officials by higher-level officials, and a system of quick punishment for false declarations.

Other taxes

The motor vehicle tax (MVT) is an important source of revenue for state and local governments. Based on ownership, use, or both, the MVT provides little scope for corruption. Nevertheless, it calls for audits, supervision of lower-level officials by higher-level officials, and disciplinary action for delinquent personnel.

Nontax revenues

Globalization is limiting taxation of capital, income, and commodities going into international trade. Hence, governments must turn to nontax revenue, the scope for which is large; Singapore derives a third of its revenue from nontax sources (Chia 1998). Interest, dividends, and profits of state-owned enterprises typically constitute the most important sources of nontax revenue. Other important sources are user charges for utilities and for minerals and forest products.

All these nontax revenues offer opportunities for corruption. As noted, the remedies are privatization and mechanization. But a system of supervision and inspection are needed to ensure that authority is not misused. Institutional reforms are also critical to minimize corruption in the administration of nontax revenues (Das-Gupta 2004).

Concluding Observations

The strategy for combating corruption in revenue administration must be multipronged. One prong is good governance. Another is creation of institutions of vertical and horizontal accountability (Schacter 2005). Yet other prongs are systems for collecting information about corruption and speedy legal proceedings to act on the information. Cooperation among levels of government is crucial in this regard. Simultaneously, governments must reduce the reward for corruption by setting moderate tax rates and creating simple tax laws on the one hand and must raise the cost of corruption by providing a decent salary to tax enforcers on the other hand. Finally, mechanization of information gathering and storage and of collection of tolls and fees and privatization of some of the activities involved in tax administration can be of considerable help.

Some researchers point to other remedies not discussed here. Henderson and Kuncoro (2006) report that Islamic values helped curb corruption in Indonesia's local governments in the post-Suharto era. Glaeser and Saks (2004) report that education largely explains the low incidence of corruption in the United States. Swamy and others (2001) suggest that greater involvement of women in elected bodies can reduce corruption.

Notes

1. Some empirical studies suggest that corruption is likely to be much more damaging to investment and growth in small as opposed to large developing countries; corruption increased growth in the newly industrializing East Asian countries. A recent study appeared to endorse these findings, although in a more ambiguous and nuanced manner (Rock and Bonnett 2004).

2. For a succinct exposition of how corruption impedes growth, see Mauro (1995). For a review of the issues pertaining to corruption and growth, see Bardhan (1997).

3. For arguments in support of this proposition, see Shah (2006).

4. In Japan, provincial governments have 3 times more officials than the national government but 15 times the number of corruption cases and 4 times the number of arrested officials. "Municipalities are often accused not only of mismanagement but of pouring public funds into private pockets" (Klitgaard, Madean-Abaroa, and Parris 2000). However, evidence across countries suggests a strong negative relationship between fiscal decentralization in government expenditure and corruption (Fishman and Gatti 2002).

5. According to studies of several developing countries, one-half or more of taxes due to government cannot be traced because of corruption and tax evasion. See Fjelstad and Tungodden (2003a).

6. *State* refers to all second-tier subnational governments, such as provinces, landers, and regional governments.

7. "[A]s a general rule, information on local taxes is often surprisingly difficult to secure and seldom easily comparable even within unitary countries" (Bird and Slack 2004: 4).

8. In income tax, the onus of proving the source of any receipt is on the individual. However, for prosecution purposes, the onus is on the department.

9. Mookherjee (2004) gives the following example: if the amount of the tax to be evaded is 1,000, and the penalty payable on detection of the fraud is 2,000, the joint surplus to be divided between the collector and the taxpayer is 3,000. In this example, a 20 percent bonus would reduce the joint surplus of the taxpayer and the tax inspector to 2,400, and the bribe would have to increase by 300 to 1,800.

10. Brosio, Cassone, and Ricciute (2002) suggest that tax evasion in Italy may have a regional dimension. People in poorer regions may rationally choose to evade taxes that, because they are levied uniformly across the country, impose a welfare burden on those regions.

11. For an exhaustive discussion of methods for evading VAT, see Mukhopadhyay (2005).

12. One alternative for tracking interstate sales and maintaining the VAT chain is the compensating VAT or the C-VAT (McLure 2000). No country has adopted the C-VAT.

References

Acharya, Shankar N., and associates. 1985. *The Black Economy in India*. Delhi: National Institute for Public Finance and Policy.

Allingham, M., and A. Sandmo. 1972. "Income Tax Evasion: A Theoretical Analysis." *Journal of Public Economics* 1: 323–38.

Alm, James, Patricia Annez, and Arbind Modi. 2004. "Stamp Duties in Indian States." Policy Research Working Paper 3413, World Bank, Washington, DC.

Bagchi, Amaresh, and Lekha Chakraborty. 2006. "Fiscal Decentralization and Gender-Responsive Budgeting in South Africa: Some Observations." National Institute of Public Finance and Policy, New Dehli.

Bahl, Roy, and Johannes Linn. 1992. *Urban Public Finance in Developing Countries.* New York: Oxford University Press.

Bardhan, Pranab. 1997. "Corruption and Development: A Review of Issues." *Journal of Economic Literature* 35: 1320–46.

Becker, Gary S. 1968. "Crime and Punishment: An Economic Approach." *Journal of Political Economy* 76 (2): 169–217.

Besley, Timothy, and John McLaren. 1993. "Taxes and Bribery—The Role of Wage Incentives." *Economic Journal* 103: 119–41.

Bird, Richard. 2003. "A New Look at Local Business Taxes." *Tax Notes International,* May 19.

Bird, Richard, and Pierre-Pascal Gendron. 2006. "Is VAT the Best Way to Impose a General Consumption Tax in Developing Countries?" *IBFD Bulletin* (July): 287–96.

Bird, Richard, and Enid Slack. 2004. *International Handbook of Land and Property Taxation.* London: Edward Elgar.

Bird, Richard, and Francois Vaillancourt, eds. 1998. *Fiscal Decentralization in Developing Countries.* Cambridge, U.K.: Cambridge University Press.

Brosio, Giorgio, Alberto Cassone, and Roberto Ricciute. 2002. "Tax Evasion across Italy: Rational Noncompliance or Inadequate Civic Concern?" *Public Choice* 42: 259–73.

Chand, S., and K. O. Moene. 1999. "Controlling Fiscal Corruption." *World Development* 27 (7): 1129–40.

Chand, S., K. O. Moene, and D. Mookherjee. 2003. "Fiscal Corruption: A Virtue or a Vice?—Reply." *World Development* 31 (8): 1469–72.

Chia, Ngee-Choon. 1998. "The Significance of Motor Vehicle Taxes in the Revenue System." *Asia Pacific Tax Bulletin* (July): 275–89.

Das-Gupta, Arindam. 2004. "Non-Tax, Non-Debt Government Revenue: Constituents and Principles." Report, Goa Institute of Management, Goa.

Das-Gupta, Arindam, and Dilip Mookherjee. 1998. *Incentives and Institutional Reform in Tax Enforcement.* New Delhi: Oxford University Press.

Ebel, Robert D., and François Vaillancourt. 2001. "Fiscal Decentralization and Financing Urban Governments: Framing the Problem." In *The Challenge of Urban Government: Policies and Practices,* ed. Mila Freire and Richard Stren, 155–70. Washington, DC: World Bank.

Evans, Ronald. 2003. "Focus on Venezuela's VAT Withholding Regime." *VAT Monitor* (March/April), 110–14.

Fishman, Raymond, and Roberta Gatti. 2002. "Decentralization and Corruption: Evidence across Countries." *Journal of Public Economies* 83: 325–45.

Fjeldstad, O-H, and B. Tungodden. 2003a. "Fiscal Corruption: A Vice or a Virtue?" *World Development* 31 (8): 1459–67.

———. 2003b. "Fiscal Corruption: A Vice or a Virtue? Reply." *World Development* 31 (8): 1473–75.

Galtung, F. 1995. "Current Strategies for Combating Corruption: A Study of Corruption in Tax Administration." Occasional Working Paper 8:95, Transparency International, Berlin.

Glaeser, Edward L., and Raven E. Saks. 2004. "Corruption in America." Working Paper 10821, National Bureau of Economic Research, Cambridge, MA.

Government of Karnataka, Bangalore. 2001. "1st Report of the Tax Reforms Commission 2001." para 3.38.

Gurgur, Tugrul, and Anwar Shah. 2005. "Localization and Corruption: Panacea or Pandora's Box?" Policy Research Working Paper 3486, World Bank, Washington, DC.

Harrison, Graham, and Rusell Krelove. 2005. "VAT Refunds: A Review of Country Experience." Working Paper WP/05/218, International Monetary Fund, Washington, DC.

Henderson, J. V., and Ari Kuncoro. 2006. "Sick of Local Government Corruption? Vote Islamic." Working Paper 12110, National Bureau of Economic Research, Cambridge, MA.

Klitgaard, Robert.1988. *Controlling Corruption*. Berkeley: University of California Press.

Klitgaard, R., R. Madean-Abaroa, and H. L. Parris. 2000. *Corrupt Cities*. Washington, DC: World Bank Institute.

Lienemeyer, Max. 1997. "The New VAT System and Fraud." *VAT Monitor* 8 (6): 270–75.

Mathur, O. P., and Nathaniel von Ein Siedel, eds. 1996. *Increasing the Income of Cities*. New Delhi: Centax Publications.

Mauro, Paolo. 1995. "Corruption and Growth." *Quarterly Journal of Economics* 10 (3): 618–713.

McLure, Charles Jr. 2000. "Implementing Subnational VATs on Internal Trade: The Compensating VAT (CVAT)." *International Tax and Public Finance* 7 (6): 723–40.

Mookherjee, Dilip. 2004. *The Crisis in Government Accountability: Essays on Governance, Reform, and India's Economic Performance*. New Delhi: Oxford University Press.

Mukhopadhyay, Sukumar. 2005. *Economics of Value Added Tax: Theory and Practice*. New Delhi: Centax Publications.

Municipal Corporation of Delhi. 2003. "Property Tax Reform." Report of the Expert Committee, Government of National Capital Territory, Delhi.

Nam, Chang Woon, Andrea Gebauer, and Rudiger Parsche. 2003. "Is the Completion of the EU Single Market Hindered by VAT Evasion?" Working Paper 974, Centre for Economic Studies and Information, Munich.

Nickson, R. A. 1995. *Local Government in Latin America*. London: Boulder.

OECD (Organisation for Economic Co-operation and Development). 1999. "Taxing Powers of State and Local Governments." Tax Policy Studies 1, OECD, Paris.

Oomen, M. A. 2006. "Fiscal Decentralization to the Sub-State Local Governments." *Economic and Political Weekly* 41(10): 897–903.

Palkhivala, Nani A. 1994. *We the Nation: The Lost Decades*. Delhi: UBS Publishers' Distributors Ltd.

Panagariya, Arvind. 2006. "Graft or Not to Graft Growth." *Economic Times*, New Delhi, 20 April.

Pope, Jeremy, and Frank Vogl. 2000. "Making Anticorruption Agencies More Effective." *Finance and Development* (June).

Rao, M. G., and Pinaki Chakraborty. 2006. "Multilateral Adjustment Lending to States in India: Hastening Fiscal Correction or Softening of the Budget Constraint?" Paper presented at World Institute for Development Economics Research Conference, Helsinki, June, 16–17.

Rock, Michael, and Heidi Bonnett. 2004. "The Comparative Politics of Corruption: Accounting for the East Asian Paradox in Empirical Studies of Corruption, Growth, and Investment." *World Development* 32 (6): 999–1017.

Rose-Ackerman, Susan. 1978. *Corruption: A Study in Political Economy.* New York: Academic Press.

_____. "Reducing Bribery in the Public Sector." In *Corruption and Democracy,* ed. Duc V. Trang, 21–28. Budapest: Budapest Institute for Constitutional and Legislative Policy.

Sarkar, S. B. 1989. "French Customs Administration under the French Revolution." *Excise Law Times* 40: A27–A39.

_____. 2006. *Words and Phrases in Customs, Excise and Service Tax Laws.* New Delhi: Centax Publications.

Schacter, Mark. 2005. "A Framework for Evaluating Institutions of Accountability." In *Fiscal Management,* ed. Anwar Shah, 229–45. Washington, DC: World Bank.

Shah, Anwar. 2006. "Corruption and Decentralized Public Governance." In *Handbook of Fiscal Federalism,* ed. E. Ahmad and G. Brosio. New York: Edward Elgar.

Shanda, Xu, and Wang Duoshu. 2004. "Land and Property Tax in China." In *International Handbook of Land and Property Taxation,* ed. Richard Bird and Enid Slack, 165–74. London: Edward Elgar.

Swamy, Anand, Stephen Knack, Young Lu, and Omar Azfar. 2001. "Gender and Corruption." *Journal of Deveopment Economics* 64: 25–55.

Verma, J. S. 2001. "The Judiciary and Judicial Reforms." In *Political Reform: Asserting Civic Soveregnty,* ed. V. A. Pai Panandikar and Subhash Kashyap, 144–80. Delhi: Konark Publishers.

Local Budgeting

5

Budget Formats: Choices and Implications

IRENE RUBIN

This chapter describes different local budget formats, their underlying assumptions, and likely consequences. It begins with decisions about budget scope (including time frame and items to be included in or excluded from the budget), moves on to the degree to which laws and regulations should be transparent in the budget, and concludes with the respective merits of organizing spending by departmental totals broken into line items or by lump sum allocations to programs. This discussion is intended to help budgeters select a format that speaks to their particular policy problems, legal environment, and implementation challenges. Even when the major formatting decisions are made at the national level, local officials can often supplement the official budget with annexes that address local issues and layouts that are comprehensible to local press and residents.

Budget format emphasizes some information and obscures other information and thus influences what people take away from reading the budget. It determines what kind of analysis is easy to do and, hence, what questions are easily answered. Some formats are user friendly, inviting not only elected officials but also reporters and citizens to take a look, and others are boring or intimidating. A budget document may match legal requirements but communicate well with neither elected officials nor the public, or it may communicate well with one group but not another.

The format of the budget does not necessarily affect the total amount of money spent, but it does frame decision making, influencing what comparisons will be made and directing elected officials either to the important policy considerations or to minor details without obvious policy content. In addition, some budget formats help teach stakeholders about fiscal constraints, laws, taxes, and intergovernmental relations. The format can help give citizens a sense of ownership and control or alienate them. It can illustrate open, transparent, and accountable government, or it can suggest the opposite.

The budget layout can emphasize legal issues and fiscal controls to help prevent overspending; it can call attention to efficiency or effectiveness issues to improve management; and it can make clear where fiscal discretion lies and hence help hold administrators accountable, not only for the funds they receive, but also for a given level of performance. The budget document can be a major tool of accountability to the legislative body or to the press and the public. But typically, the budget cannot accomplish all these goals at the same time. Officials have to choose which goal is most important and orient the budget to meet it or develop a hybrid format that goes some way in achieving multiple goals.

The choice of format depends not only on what policy problems are most important at the time, but also on the difficulty of implementation. Once established, some formats are more costly than others to maintain in terms of producing numbers and testing them for accuracy. Some are more susceptible to distortion or falsification than others. Maintaining a single format with which decision makers can become quickly familiar and on which they can rely for year-to-year comparisons may be more beneficial than sophisticated formats that are onerous to implement. Moreover, a budget office may not control some of the decisions that underlie some budget formats, such as whether programs cross the boundaries of administrative units or how flexible the accounting system is.

Scope

Decisions about scope have two major components. The first is the resources and expenditure programs to be included or excluded from the budget. The second has to do with the time frame covered and the number of years of data to be reflected in the budget numbers.

With respect to the decision concerning revenues and expenditures, should the budget encompass both capital projects and operating expenses, even though they may cover different time frames? Should it include borrowing and debt repayment, even though the time frame for loans may be longer than that for the operating budget or capital projects? Should the budget include grant income from other levels of government, even if such grants are earmarked for specific purposes and are out of the local government's discretionary control? How about funds for services run more or less like a business, like sewer and water, or for public hospitals charging fees for services, even if their revenues are unavailable for other types of spending? What about one-time revenues, such as those from the sale of property or equipment or from the prior year's fund balances? How should in-kind contributions be described? Should the budget include details on personnel, such as number, position, and cost? Should it include major contracts for services?

The minimum budget time frame is one year—the upcoming year or the so-called budget year. Should the budget include projections to show the impact of the budget year's spending on future budgets—for example, to show how a new capital project will increase or decrease operating expenses or how borrowing in the present fiscal year will affect borrowing in future years? Sometimes budget or finance offices make 10-year projections of revenues and expenditures to compare trends in each and thereby forecast expenditures as rising too rapidly or revenues as rising too slowly. Such an analysis should be included in the budget document if long-term budget balance is an issue.

Budgets normally include estimates of the present year's revenues and expenditures to allow decision makers to compare the present budget with the proposed one. Because the present year's figures are only estimates, budgeters may want to include last year's actual numbers as well. Inclusion of several years of historical data would help budgeters identify any items that are increasing out of control, any overall rise in expenditures, or any failure to keep salaries in line with price increases.

Generally speaking, more inclusive budgets are better than less inclusive ones, whether of scope or time frame. Budgets that include enterprise funds, grant revenues, loans and debt repayment, and contracts make apparent activities that, if left out of the budget, might disappear from public view, be poorly managed, and evade scrutiny. In addition, inclusive budgets clarify all sources of revenue and their use. Inclusive budgets can increase accountability and transparency and help maintain good financial management, especially if they include some estimate of budget decisions' impact on future revenue and expenditure trends.

Inclusive budgets also have disadvantages. Some details should perhaps be left out of the municipal budget, depending on the law and local circumstances. Comprehensive budgets may become too difficult to prepare or interpret, may mix data of varying degrees of quality, imply a level of municipal control that is not real or legal, or actually hide data in plain view because they offer so much detail.

Consider the comprehensive budget's challenge with regard to various kinds of resources, some of which are more constrained than others, and some of which have schedules that differ from the budget's time frame (see box 5.1). Some resources may be difficult to denominate in dollar terms. For example, how much are volunteer labor or in-kind contributions worth? In public-private partnerships, how should the private contribution be valued if given, say, in expertise or experience? On the expenditure side, a tax break or tax incentive may be a different kind of outlay than a dollar spent on garbage pickup or road repair. Putting incommensurate items in one budget and adding them up may be technically difficult or actually misleading, suggesting, for example, that the items are the same, that they may be in some sense interchangeable, that trades may be made between them, or that the city has the same degree of control over each of them.

Another disadvantage of a comprehensive budget is that including programs or projects for which the city has no legal responsibility may make the public think that the city can control the associated expenditures. Aside from raising false expectations, this practice may create some legal and financial

---

BOX 5.1 Handling Mixed Expenditures

Suppose that an association bought a piece of office furniture and paid for it over several years. Each year the budget listed the item, along with that year's payment, without indicating that the payment was partial or that another payment was due the following year. As a result, in any given year, it appeared as if the association had paid less than the real cost of the item. Anyone who examined several years' budgets would wonder whether one or several pieces of furniture had been purchased or if payment had been delayed (listed in a previous year but not paid until the current year).

The problem described in this example arises from mixing annual operating expenditures that fit neatly within a budget year with capital items whose cost is spread across years. The solution in this case might be to separate out capital and operating items. The capital items might be listed with totals and the amount to be spent each year, including the budget year.

Source: Author.

obligations for the city in the event that the programs or projects are badly managed or fail outright.

Finally, some information is difficult to obtain. When cities contract with the private sector, they often know little more than the amount they pay for the contract. Arm's length off-budget enterprises are semi-independent entities and may keep the details of their finances to themselves.

One way to minimize the disadvantages of a comprehensive budget is to make a distinction between inclusiveness and consolidation. That is, a budget may include many kinds of revenue and many kinds of programs and activities of different durations and with different time frames for decision making but without merging them, treating them as the same, or treating them as if trade-offs could be made among them. Capital items are routinely segregated because of their different time span and because they can sometimes be funded by borrowing. Similarly, special-purpose grants and enterprise funds can be included if they are segregated in the budget, because their revenue is not available to fund other governmental purposes. Supportive analyses and supplementary details, such as debt repayment schedules, can be included in appendixes to emphasize the relative independence and adequacy of revenue sources, while increasing the transparency of any cash flows into or out of each mini budget. Including these analyses in the budget can reveal not only the scope of government services, but also the services' fiscal condition.

Debt repayment schedules can be particularly useful, because they can be used in evaluating the fiscal health of a community and its debt burden, and hence its ability to fund future needs by borrowing. If excessive borrowing is or could be a problem, inclusion of debt repayment schedules in the budget is probably a good idea. For the many cities that do not borrow for capital projects, it would be unnecessary.

Human capital is a radically different resource than money. Personnel expenditures could be integrated into the budget or included in an appendix. If integrated into the budget, this information can be broken down into budget lines for each department or program, wherein the number and cost of temporary and permanent personnel and the costs of regular and overtime hours and benefits are listed. Sometimes this information is aggregated across the budget and included in an appendix so that only the dollar costs of personnel appear in the main budget document. Including a detailed listing of personnel might help control patronage by showing where positions are too many or too highly paid, but at the same time, it may detract attention from policy issues that require deliberation. To avoid wrangling over each position, incumbent, and salary, a personnel summary might be a better option.

In short, a budget can be inclusive and solve the problem of incommensurate or incomparable items by segregating some components. What should be included should depend somewhat on local problems, such as overstaffing or too much borrowing. Expenditures for which the city has no substantial responsibility or financial discretion should not be included.

Take the case of water service. A city can provide water directly, using a city department for labor, in which case the service should be included in the budget, or it can provide water through a publicly owned enterprise paid for by fees rather than taxes, in which case inclusion depends on whether the city is responsible for water provision or major revenues flow into or out of the water utility (see box 5.2). If the city has no responsibility for water policy, financial management, or personnel, and no interdependencies or transfers obtain between the water enterprise and other city funds, the water enterprise should be excluded from the city budget. In that case, the budget may refer the reader to a Web site or other location for information on the enterprise.

Many local governments are funded substantially by grants from the central government. These grants may be spent for anything or may be limited to special purposes, such as economic development projects. To the extent that the city has discretion about how the money will be spent, as well as responsibility for accounting for its expenditure, grant funds should be included in the budget. If the grant comes from the national or provincial level and is spent at the local level, but without any input from the city, it probably should not be listed as city revenue in the budget.

BOX 5.2 Example: When to Include an Enterprise

Citizens of Johannesburg, South Africa, have access to a limited amount of water free of charge and pay a fee for water use above that amount. Johannesburg Water, a utility that has an arm's length relationship with the city council, provides the water. The utility has its own staff and management, but the city is the company's sole shareholder and client. The city sets requirements, monitors performance, and maintains customer relations. To cover the cost of the "free" water, the city transfers money to the utility from its general revenues in the form of a subsidy. Given the subsidy and the city's control over requirements and performance, water provision should be included in the city budget. In fact, the revenues and expenditures of Johannesburg Water are included in the budget, as is the size of the annual subsidy.

Source: http://www.joburg.org.za.

Like level of responsibility and discretion, spillovers or interdependencies are another criterion for deciding whether grant funds ought to be included in the budget. Sometimes national or provincial governments provide funds for particular projects that a city must undertake. If the grant money requires additional spending from the city's own-source revenue, the budget should probably include the grant and, by implication, its accompanying mandate. Otherwise, the budget priorities will not make much sense, and national choices may be mistakenly attributed to the local government. Moreover, by showing how much local funding was required by the grant, a city is helping document the costs of unfunded mandates and helping to make the case against them. If unfunded mandates are an important problem, grants should be placed in a separate section of the budget, with one column for the intergovernmental revenues, a second for the projects being funded, and a third for the local match or additional payment. Another way to show the same information is to create a separate fund for earmarked grants and to provide a place in the budget to describe that fund, including transfers into the fund from general revenue that were necessary to carry out the mandated programs. Any transfers out of this fund would also have to be noted to indicate how much of the grant money was being used for, say, general administration. Making such transfers transparent might help ensure that grant money is spent according to the purposes of the grant.

Inclusiveness in terms of years of data allows both decision makers and the public to understand the consequences of present-day decisions. Making such costs visible when decisions are being made can help prevent elected officials from shifting a disproportionate amount of present expenditures to future taxpayers. Presenting several years of data allows readers to see trends, especially those regarding budgetary balance. Temporal inclusiveness also helps prevent shifting of expenditures back and forth across fiscal years to make the budget look more balanced than it is. This inclusiveness speaks to fiscal control, as well as to transparency.

Despite these theoretical advantages, temporal inclusiveness has its minuses with regard to long-term projections. First, long-term projections, with the exception of debt repayment plans and long-term contracts, are notoriously inaccurate, and the longer they go out in time, the less accurate they are likely to be. Putting unreliable numbers in the budget and failing to differentiate them from reliable numbers confuses the reader and may reduce the budget's overall credibility. Second, if long-term analyses reveal impending problems that are then averted, the lack of an actual crisis reduces the credibility of future warnings. Third, additional years of data do not necessarily make for a more informative budget. Many years of data can be overwhelming, hiding present-day decisions rather than highlighting them. Finally, long-term projections are notoriously sensitive to underlying assumptions and so can indicate whatever administrators want them to indicate.

But as noted, projections of the impact of the proposed budget on future spending and balance can be useful in highlighting the tendency to spend now without regard for future impacts. Projections can thus be useful in curtailing the tendency to grant entitlements that will increase with time, regardless of revenue growth, or to borrow, where that is legal, without sufficient attention to where the money will come from to pay off the debt. But this form of fiscal control can be overdone. In emergencies, expenditures need to be made, even when the source of the money to pay for them is unclear. Looking ahead at accumulating debt or projected fiscal imbalances can be paralyzing, limiting not only unnecessary or unaffordable benefits, but also those that are critical investments for the future. One resolution of this bind is to focus on estimating future returns on investment as well as future costs to see how well they match up. Such an analysis may be somewhat subjective, and hence should not be integrated into the harder numbers of the budget, but it can be helpful not only in revealing the assumptions underlying the budget and subjecting them to scrutiny and debate, but also in forcing decision makers to think about public spending in terms of investments.

An ideally inclusive budget, with many years of data and good projections, might be difficult to achieve. It would require a reasonably predictable revenue stream and a sufficient number of years of accurate data to use as a basis for projections. In addition, it would require no radical changes to the budget for political purposes, no changes in priorities, and no emergencies.

Revenues, particularly from national governments, have been unpredictable in some Sub-Saharan African countries. Elected officials sometimes intervene in budgeting decisions on an ad hoc basis, often during implementation, and insufficient revenue may stymie adherence to the formally approved budget. In Kenya in fiscal year 2004, the national government's payments to local governments were very near expectations, but local revenues were overestimated substantially in the budget, and combined national and local sources were only 73 percent of budgeted revenues (Commonwealth Local Government Forum 2005).

To the extent that revenue is unpredictable in any given year, projections are likely to be so far off target as to be useless. For now, in some countries, feasibility issues suggest reporting only one or two prior years, the present year, the budget year, and possibly one or two years thereafter. The South

African budget requirements for local governments include the budget year and two additional years.

Including off-budget enterprises or entities in the budget and making their operations transparent may be desirable but at times may not be feasible. The information necessary for a realistic budget presentation may not be made available to municipal budgeters. When services such as water or electricity are provided by the private sector under contract, cities may get only the financial information about operations that is specified in the contract. The city puts in the budget only the annual cost of the contract. But if the city is responsible for provision of the contracted service, it may need to know as much about the contract operations as it knows about its own operating department. For that reason, a city might consider putting requirements for providing such information into contract language. A situation in which the information would be useful is not difficult to imagine. In the event of a cholera epidemic, for example, a city with a private sector contract for water supply would want to know how many residents were receiving the service, how much of what chemicals were being purchased and used for water purification, and how and where sewage was being treated and dumped. How much was spent for which capital improvement projects would also be relevant.

Legal Structure

Budgets are always constrained by rules and laws, usually including a requirement for balance, however defined. The rules might specify the number of prior years' data and the number of years of spending and revenue projections to be provided. They might also specify how expenditures are to be grouped and spell out reporting requirements. Laws may regulate transfers between programs or funds.

Officials must decide whether to include in the budget general information not required by the rules, such as an explanation of revenue sources and of the source and likely accuracy of revenue projections. That is, they must determine whether the budget is to be purely a legal document listing expenditures and revenues or also a tool for educating the legislative body, the press, and the public. Should they include an explanation of their decisions or their prioritization process or identify performance targets not mandated by law? Budgets can contain all the information required by law but do so in a format that does not emphasize those rules.

The national government might dictate the format of the budget for all local governments or give cities complete freedom to determine their format.

If the national government dictates the format, budgeters' foremost concern might be compliance with legal requirements. But if cities have some discretion regarding format, local officials can emphasize conformity with the law or put information in a fashion that highlights other functions of the budget. The officials would likely choose the latter strategy if they disagreed with the national government about which problems were most important. The national government may be most concerned about fiscal controls, budget balance, and anticorruption measures, whereas the local government may be more concerned with government legitimacy, effective service delivery, and more broadly conceived accountability issues.

For some countries, decentralization has been a relatively recent phenomenon. Local governments may still be negotiating and establishing their independence. Local budgets that merely reflect compliance with national or provincial guidelines or rules may inadvertently convey the message that decentralization is in some way a sham. Such an impression can be particularly damaging if the public is involved in priority setting at the municipal level but cannot see the impact of its input on the budget. If a city needs to show some independence in budgeting, it might add sections of its own design to the forms provided by the national government or create a separate budget document for local consumption.

Even when city officials have considerable autonomy, they may want to demonstrate compliance with national budgeting laws. For example, they may think it important to show how money targeted for poverty alleviation or AIDS controls is being spent. They also may think it important to show national or provincial mandates for spending in the budget, because these mandates preempt local priorities and thus might temper public demand for redirection of those priorities.

Some elements of the legal structure normally figure prominently in budgets, such as the requirement that budgets balance. Budgeters not only need to make it clear how total revenues and total expenditures compare, but also to show the legal requirements for balance. For example, if a budget can be balanced by using savings from prior years, those prior years' balances should show up in the budget as available resources; if those balances are not allowable, they should not be included. If a budget can be legally balanced using borrowed revenue—the cash model—such revenue should be included, but if the balance is not cash based, borrowed money should be excluded. If departments are prohibited, under penalty of law, from overspending their budgets, the budget should report allocated and actual amounts by department for the previous year. This aspect of legal compliance simultaneously emphasizes accountability and financial compliance.

Cities can indicate that they have spent grants in accordance with national or provincial dictates by listing programs supported by grants in the expenditure section of the budget. For example, if a city receives grant funds for economic development, it can list an economic development program and include the grant money and any other funds it has allocated to that program. As long as the amount spent is as large as or larger than the grant amount, the city will be in compliance.

The Ilala Municipal Council in Dar es Salaam, Tanzania, lists all revenues and groups them by own-source funds and central government transfers. Then it lists all expenses paid for by own-source revenues and by central government grants. Within the central government grants category, it lists AIDS control as an expenditure. The amount of the spending exactly matches the amount of the central government grant for this purpose, which is listed elsewhere in the budget (Lubuva 2005). The budget makes it clear that the city plans to spend all of the money the national government gave it for AIDS control on an AIDS control program.

The central government may establish a fund structure, more or less visible in the budget, whereby it sets aside some revenue for specific accounts, such as debt repayment or employee benefits or for enterprises that charge fees. This structure may prohibit or limit transfers of revenues or surpluses in or out of these accounts. If legal compliance is an important issue and needs to be demonstrated, budgeters can divide the budget into funds and present revenues and expenditures for each.

If demonstrating compliance is not urgent, budgeters can devise user-friendly budget categories. Normally, revenues are listed before expenditures. Each may have internal divisions, so that like is grouped with like. For example, budgeters can group revenue by type—for example, by source of revenue, such as own-source revenues, intergovernmental grants, and donor contributions. Alternatively, budgeters can group revenue by its characteristics, such as degree of earmarking. Thus, own-source revenues might be divided into property taxes and investment income, both of which can be spent on nearly any need, and fee income, which can be spent only for the services for which the fees were collected. Grant money can be divided into equalization grants or general fund support on the one hand, and earmarked grants for narrower purposes on the other hand.

Budgeters may organize spending by city departments or by program. They can group it by the degree of control the city exercises over each function, in which case city departments would be in one category and enterprises or businesses bringing in their own revenue would be in another category. Aligning spending with administrative units emphasizes the accountability of administrators for the money they are spending; aligning the budget with programs emphasizes what is to be accomplished and aids planning.

In Sub-Saharan African countries, the central government typically mandates integration of a city plan into the budget, often through citizen input to the budget. In these cases, local governments should organize budgets by program and show how the budget allocation to each program is designed to address one or another of the city plan goals. That is, the budget format should blend formal compliance with local priorities.

Showing compliance with the law is usually technically easy and straightforward. It may involve use of forms provided by the finance ministry or local government ministry or use of reporting forms in lieu of a budget. Showing compliance without appearing to be merely a tool of the national bureaucracy is especially difficult. It may require greater attention to those items for which the city has discretion. For example, if a city has an economic development grant that does not specify how funds are to be spent, the budget could describe candidate projects, the decision-making process (including stakeholder input), and the resulting ranking of projects. This level of detail is likely to call attention to the grant portion of the budget, even if it represents only a minor portion.

Where formats are mandated, local governments may be able to add less constrained and more easily interpretable budget tables, appendixes, or volumes. As noted, they might provide one document to the central government according to its format requirements and a second, user-friendly document to local officials, stakeholders, and the media. In that way, local governments can be legally compliant and serve the needs of their citizens.

Input Budgeting versus Output Budgeting

Budget documents can emphasize inputs—that is, revenues, personnel, and equipment—or outputs, such as the level of services to be delivered (or outcomes, such as poverty reduction). Budgets rarely, if ever, emphasize both equally well at the same time. The reason is that input controls focus on the quantity and ways money is spent rather than what money is spent on, whereas output controls focus on what is produced rather than how it is produced. Input controls often put caps on each category of expenditure, or even each item of expenditure. Output controls, by contrast, attempt to use the inputs in a flexible fashion. These controls might make equipment and personnel interchangeable or substitute capital for operating costs, or vice versa, depending on objectives and costs. Input controls are easy to implement and easy to understand; output controls are more difficult to implement, and they require careful reporting and sensitive analysis.

A budgetary focus on inputs is oriented to fiscal control, ensuring that budgets are justified in terms of how much labor, equipment, fuel or electricity, insurance, and so on will be needed to accomplish a task. A budgetary focus on outputs is oriented to management: given total resources, what quality of services for what number of people can managers produce? Output orientation is not only focused on programs, but also on evaluation of the extent to which the targets in the budget were achieved.

The input model assumes that managers will waste resources if they are given more flexibility—they will hire too many staff or buy too many office supplies. The output model assumes that managers will use the resources they have in the best way possible to meet targets. The reason is that they will be held accountable, not for staying within the budgets for line items but for producing the quantity and quality promised within the resource packages they were allocated in the budget.

Each model uses a different planning concept. In the input model, managers calculate how much of each type of resource they will need to accomplish their tasks for the budget year; in the output model, managers ask how they can accomplish objectives such as improve public health. The input model often deteriorates; managers begin adding small amounts to each line item each year rather than recreating a plan or changing the targets or goals. This model tends to be more static. It requires less work, and any waste tends to stay in the budget from year to year. The output model, with its more flexible patterns of resource use to achieve what may be changing goals, requires more thought from year to year and provides greater opportunities for mistakes. Changing the amount of labor or the trade-off between capital and labor from year to year may be difficult, if not impossible, because of obligations to employees and an environment where a job is a precious resource. Thus, flexibility to operate an output model may not exist.

The assumption underlying the input model is that resources are scarce and that controlling the level of inputs and their distribution will enhance efficiency. Input controls are managed through line items. In a line item budget, the allocation to each department or program is broken down into the cost for each major purchase. In the lump sum budget, by contrast, the program or department manager is given a fixed sum that may be used in any of a variety ways to accomplish the task. With the line item budget, managers have little discretion once the budget year has begun; with the lump sum budget, managers have some ability to adapt to unforeseen circumstances.

Line item details allow readers to assess the reasonableness of the cost estimates and whether resources appear to be wasted. If, for example, budget lines show US$300 for paper supplies, US$200 for pencils, US$1,800 for three computers, and US$600 for two cameras, readers might wonder why a department needs US$200 worth of pencils or if the department is over-paying for that item. They might also wonder why the department needs two cameras. The drawback of a budget that provides this level of detail is that it can overwhelm readers and fail to sustain their interest.

Line item budgets have three other shortcomings. First, they tend to be bulky and, hence, costly to produce and distribute. Second, they focus decision making on small items—whether the number of pencils is appropriate and whether the number has gone up or down since the past year—rather than on whether the program is efficient and effective. Third, and most important, they are normally inflexible. If a manager has overestimated the number of pencils needed, and underestimated the costs of phone calls or postage, he or she will find it difficult to transfer funds for one item to another item without giving the impression of mismanagement or overspending. Even savings from careful use are hard to transfer into other budget lines, because all the estimates were (presumably) based on a plan for accomplishing a certain amount of work and with a certain amount of each resource.

Output budgeting focuses less on cost controls and more on whether programs are cost-effective. That is, it asks not how much a program costs but what citizens are getting for their money. Is the program a good deal? If money is scarce, a program's cost is important but so is getting the biggest possible bang for the buck.

Output budgeting affects format in three ways. First, it deemphasizes line items, reducing them to a handful or even eliminating them in favor of lump sums. Second, it emphasizes programs rather than administrative units such as departments. Instead of describing a public works depart-ment, the budget report details programs such as water purification and distribution, road construction and repair, or waste management. By dividing the budget in this fashion, the budget clarifies the cost of each function—for example, the cost of providing clean water on a per cubic meter basis.

The output budget emphasizes evaluation. It facilitates analysis of the cost of given quantities of given qualities. One implication of such analy-sis is that figures might be comparable among cities, enabling decision makers to identify cities that provide a better quality of services for a given amount of money or the same quality for less money and to copy what they have done.

Program budgeting is the basis of output budgeting. Performance measures help integrate multiyear, broad-scope planning into the annual budget. Suppose, for example, that a city planned to provide clean running water to all residents by 2016. For budgeting purposes, the city would have to determine how many homes would be added to the city water system each year and the cost. The city plan would include capital needs, in case additional wells were needed or greater purification capacity was required, as well as the number of water pipes necessary to reach underserved areas. The budget would reflect how much the city must spend to make a specific amount of progress on the plan each year—that is, the amount of money needed to provide clean water to a given number of households in the budget year. At the end of the year, the city would prepare a performance report that stated whether and why the number of newly served households met, exceeded, or failed to meet the target number. Planners could use the explanation to help determine the following year's budget allocation. If, for example, the cost of capital purchases was higher than predicted, the city might increase the following year's allocation or reduce the target number of households to which service is to be extended. If no explanation is adequate, the excess costs might indicate inefficiencies that a lower allocation might help wring out of the budget in the succeeding budget year.

Program budgeting is difficult to establish and maintain when performance measures are included. Because these measures highlight accountability, administrators may select measures on which they can succeed, rather than those that relate to accomplishment of the city plan. They may even attempt to falsify or distort their reporting to suggest that they are achieving their targets. When money in the budget is insufficient to do all that is needed, administrators may neglect basic but unmeasured tasks. They might trade quality, which is harder to measure, for quantity, which is easier to measure. Measures that have little meaning for quality of service provision are often discouraging to the administrators who have to live by them and to the budgeters who must use them to figure out whether programs need more or less funding.

Nonetheless, a program budget with performance measures unrelated to the city plan can be beneficial. For example, in the absence of a long-term citywide plan with which to integrate performance measures, each program not covered by the plan can establish its own measures, which may include efficiency gains or service quality improvements. Such measures need not be tightly integrated into the budget to be useful: a program can set a goal of responding to all citizen complaints within 24 hours without knowing the cost and can link that goal to the budget in the following year.

In addition, lack of performance measures for some programs need not affect the measures' usefulness to planners. Departments for which performance measurement is relatively easy can adopt and report performance measures, and the budget will still make sense, even if good performance is rewarded with budgetary incentives. Such incentives may make it desirable for other departments and programs to adopt some form of performance measurement.

[Performance measurement can be a powerful tool not only for public accountability and transparency, but also for governmental legitimacy] If citizens are involved in the creation of a plan for the city, and the performance measures help shape budget allocations in ways consistent with the plan, administrators can use these measures to demonstrate that they have taken the plan seriously. The result is likely to be a sense of ownership and control on the part of the citizens]

In summary, [input controls are much easier to implement than output controls] Although they aim to prevent overspending, their inflexibility can stymie good management and actually waste resources available in one budget line but needed in another line. They do not focus on the relationship between inputs and outputs and, hence, say nothing about how efficiently resources are used. To function as a cost-control device, line items need to be detailed, with the result that the budget document can be overwhelming to elected officials and the public alike.

[Output controls allow for more flexible use of resources and focus on the relationship between inputs and outputs, or efficiency, and sometimes also on effectiveness] But they are much harder to set up, integrate with an overall plan, and maintain, and are more susceptible to manipulation and mistakes. Fortunately, performance measurement can be integrated into the budget in piecemeal and experimental fashion, without harming the underlying budget structure or making it difficult to compare the present year with the budget year.

A typical input control budget would emphasize line items and would probably present past years' data to hold budget growth to prior years' levels. Any radical change would show up quickly. The formatting of expenditures would look something like that in table 5.1.

A typical output control budget might look more like table 5.2. In this table, items such as personnel, insurance, transportation, and communication are built into each of the program costs. These items can be broken out separately for each program, but doing so reduces the budget's flexibility.

The outcome-oriented budget normally includes the targets for each program's accomplishments. Sometimes it also reports last year's targets and the degree to which they were achieved. Under the fraud program, for

TABLE 5.1   Typical Line-Item Budget

Police department	Last year actual (US$)	Present year estimate (US$)	Budget year (US$)
Personnel	100,000	110,000	121,000
Communications	20,000	21,000	10,000
Vehicle purchase	40,000	44,000	40,000
Vehicle maintenance	5,000	5,000	5,000
Petrol	500	570	600
Uniforms	450	450	450
Insurance	1,000	1,300	1,400
Totals	166,950	182,320	178,450

Source: Author.

TABLE 5.2   Program and Performance Budget

Programs	Previous year actual (US$)	Present year (US$)	Budget year (US$)
Administration	16,950	17,000	18,500
Theft recovery	40,000	44,000	42,000
Crime prevention	40,000	42,000	40,000
Gang control	10,000	11,000	11,000
Arson investigation	10,000	11,000	10,000
Violent crime and drug control	25,000	32,000	33,000
Fraud control	25,000	25,220	23,950
Totals	166,950	182,220	178,450

Source: Author.

example, the budget might present the number of cases reported, the number investigated, and the number of cases disposed. Targets might include increasing the number of fraud cases reported by 10 percent, increasing the number investigated by 10 percent, and improving the clearance rate by 10 percent in the upcoming year. The budget might also provide explanations of failures to achieve targets.

Choosing a Format

In determining the format of the budget document, decision makers should keep three questions firmly in mind. First, what are their legal requirements and how much discretion do they have? Second, what are they trying to accomplish by using one or another format? Third, do they have or can they get the personnel, computational power, historical data, or accounting reports necessary to format the budget in the preferred manner? A format may be legal and desirable, but if the government lacks the capacity to implement it, or if a major portion of income is unreliable, it may not be practical. A format may be desirable, but if it contravenes regulations of the local or national government, it should not be selected.

In countries where corruption is a problem or where decentralization efforts have been recent and the level of incompetence or corruption at the local level is untested but anxiety provoking, accounting for every dollar may be of utmost concern. In these countries, input controls and line item budgeting may be useful to demonstrate that every dollar went where it was supposed to go. Clearly showing legal compliance with grant programs may be useful, but using only spreadsheet type forms may suggest that decentralization has not actually occurred. A tailor-made budget showing grant revenue in detail and by purpose, with line items for each program, may best serve the public's needs. The relative simplicity of input budgeting and its ease of comprehension by decision makers may be an advantage even if the budget is boring and attracts little public attention.

Where corruption may be a severe risk, the budget should include as many programs and resources as possible. Programs and resources left out of the budget are often nearly or completely invisible. They create tempting opportunities for cronyism, patronage hiring, overpayments, and unaccounted for fees.

National governments that are engaged in decentralizing efforts may not fully trust their local governments. To compensate, they may impose extra reporting requirements to ensure that local governments are complying with rules and not running deficits or raising taxes beyond citizens' ability to pay. In this case, a format that highlights the legal framework underlying the budget may be desirable even if the impression at the local level is that the national government is still calling the shots. As noted, one compromise would be production of one budget document for the national government and another tailored for local consumption.

If government legitimacy is a crucial issue, and citizen participation in and ownership of government is paramount, a format that links the budget to a long-term city plan through performance measures may be most desirable. Such a format lessens fiscal control and increases the risk of corruption (because it gives administrators discretion). But it increases transparency by identifying progress on public problems such as homelessness, lack of access to clean water, and AIDS.

If fiscal health is considered the most urgent problem, a format combining transparency and legal compliance with requirements for balance is desirable. In this case, the temporal scope of the budget is important not only to help identify and compare revenue trends and expenditure trends, but also to ensure that local government does not achieve a balanced budget by borrowing from the future and omitting that borrowing from the budget. A format that presents figures for the budget year and two following years can help ensure that expenditures are not shifted into the next year and that revenues from next year are not shifted into the budget year to achieve balance in the short run. Showing borrowing in the budget and the payback schedule is critical. Long-term contracts should be included, even if not in detail. If possible, the budget should highlight cost estimates for rapidly growing programs.

References

Lubuva, John M. 2005. "Subnational Experiences of Civic Participation in the Policy Making and Budgetary Process: A Case Study of Ilala Municipal Council in Dar es Salaam, Tanzania." Case Study, Africa Social Accountability Action Forum, Municipal Development Partnership for Eastern and Southern Africa, Harare, Zimbabwe. http://www.asaaf.org.zw/casestud1.htm.

Commonwealth Local Government Forum (United Kingdom). 2005. "Local Government System in Kenya." Commonwealth Local Government Forum. http://www.clgf.org.uk/userfiles/clgf/file/countries/Kenya.pdf.

6

Citizen-Centric Performance Budgeting at the Local Level

ANWAR SHAH AND CHUNLI SHEN

Interest in government accountability for performance has spawned a large body of literature on performance budgeting and related reforms at the national level (see Shah and Shen forthcoming). Performance budgeting, however, owes its origins to innovations in budgeting reforms at the local level. The literature has paid scant attention to these innovations or to the lessons that can be drawn from them.

This chapter provides an introductory overview of performance budgeting at the local level and carries this work forward analytically by introducing a framework for results-based accountability to citizens. Citizen-centric performance budgeting at the local level is intended as a tool to empower citizens to demand accountability from their local governments. This tool is pertinent to recent public management reform movements, which emphasize performance accountability and citizen participation.

This chapter presents motivations for the reform of local budgeting, introduces performance budgeting and contrasts it with line item and program budgeting, and identifies considerations that should guide adoption of performance budgeting. The chapter also presents a view of the practice of performance budgeting and draws lessons from this practice. Finally, it argues for institutionalization of performance budgeting as a tool for citizen empowerment through citizen-centric performance budgeting.

The chapter concludes that performance budgeting is an important tool for citizen empowerment at the local level. However, this tool must be an integral element of a broader reform package to bring about performance culture. In the absence of incentives for better performance and bottom-up accountability for results, the introduction of performance budgeting may not improve performance accountability.

Motivations for the Reform of Local Budgeting

Local public budgeting systems are intended to serve several important functions. These functions include setting of budget priorities consistent with any mandate of the government, planning of expenditures to pursue a long-term vision for development, exercise of financial control over inputs to ensure fiscal discipline, and management of operations to ensure efficiency of government operations. Another function is to enhance accountability of government performance to citizens.

Typically, a budgeting system cannot achieve all these functions equally well at the same time. The relative strength of each function depends on the budgeting tool and technique, but most critically on the issues in which the government takes the keenest interest. Budgeters can attempt to orient the budget to address those issues or to develop a hybrid budget that achieves multiple goals.

The traditional line item budget presents expenditures by inputs/resources purchased. It classifies disaggregated objects of expenditure and operating and capital expenditures. Operating expenses include cost objects for day-to-day operations, such as salaries, retirement, health insurance, office supplies, printing, and utilities. The capital outlays include purchase of long-lived assets, such as buildings, machinery, office equipment, furniture, and vehicles. A prominent feature of a line item budget system is to specify the line item ceiling in the budget allocation process and to ensure that agencies do not spend in excess of their caps. Hence, the budget facilitates a tight fiscal grip over government operations. The strengths of such a system are its relative simplicity and potential control of public spending through detailed specification of inputs.

The line item approach embodies several impediments to efficient and effective public planning and management, as well as to results-oriented accountability in public sector institutions. The line item budget emphasizes inputs and provides information on how much is spent and how it is spent rather than for what it is spent. The line item budget can say nothing about the efficiency of resource use, because it does not link inputs with outputs. The line item budget tends to focus decision making on inputs rather than on program efficiency and effectiveness. Line item control leads to micromanagement of agency operations by central budget offices and finance ministries and strengthens hierarchical controls within the agency. Public managers have very limited managerial discretion, and they cannot be held accountable for performance of government activities.

In summary, the line item budget is useful for setting priorities, facilitating planning, and maintaining financial control over inputs. That budget is less useful for managing operations and holding government accountable for its performance. Because decision making at the local level is closer to the people, the latter limitation makes a line item budget unacceptable to informed electorate at the local level. Hence, local governments in industrial countries—especially Denmark, Sweden, Switzerland, and the United States—have, over the past two decades, transformed local budgets as tools for popular support of their programs. Their innovations have yielded budget documents that detail not only spending but also information on the efficiency and efficacy of local spending (see table 6.1).

TABLE 6.1 Features of Alternative Budget Formats

Feature	Line item	Program	Performance
Contents	Expenditures by objects (inputs/ resources)	Expenditures for a cluster of activities supporting a common objective	Results-based chain to achieve a specific objective
Format	Operating and capital inputs purchased	Expenditures by program	Data on inputs, outputs, impacts, and reach by each objective
Orientation	Input controls	Input controls	Focus on results
Associated management paradigm	Hierarchical controls with little managerial discretion	Hierarchical controls, managerial flexibility over allocation to activities within the program	Managerial flexibility over inputs and program design but accountability for service delivery and output performance

Source: Authors.

Performance Budgeting: Basic Concepts

Performance budgeting is a system of budgeting that presents the purpose and objectives for which funds are required, the costs of proposed programs and associated activities for achieving those objectives, and outputs to be produced or services to be rendered under each program. A comprehensive performance budgeting system quantifies the entire results-based chain as inputs/intermediate inputs (resources to produce outputs), outputs (quantity and quality of goods and services produced), outcomes (progress in achieving program objectives), impacts (program goals), and reach (people who benefit from or are hurt by a program) (see figure 6.1).

As a byproduct of the information provided by the results-based chain, performance budgeting can yield useful indicators of the efficiency and quality of government operations. These indicators include quality (a measure of service such as timeliness, accessibility, courtesy, and accuracy), client satisfaction (rating of services by users), productivity (output by work hour), and efficiency (cost per unit of output).

In comparison to traditional line item budgeting, performance budgeting allows for more flexible use of fiscal resources and enhanced accountability for results. The performance budget shifts the focus of discussion from detailed line items to achievement of specific service delivery objectives and, therefore, facilitates informed budgetary decision making. Performance budgeting increases managerial flexibility by giving the program or department manager a fixed lump sum allocation that may be used for various needs to achieve the agreed-on results in service delivery. Public managers enjoy increased managerial discretion but are held accountable for what they

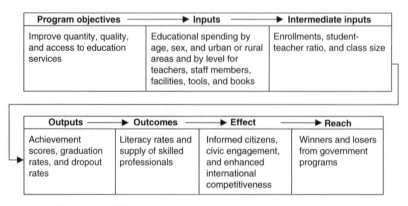

Source: Shah 2005: 217.

FIGURE 6.1 Performance Budgeting Results Chain

achieve in service delivery performance. Tables 6.2–6.3 and box 6.1 show, respectively, a line item budget, a program budget, and a performance budget of a police department.

Local governments are typically responsible for providing core public services such as solid waste collection and disposal, fire protection, and water supply and sanitation. These services tend to be highly visible, and their delivery is relatively easy to measure, making implementation of performance budgeting feasible. Performance budgeting not only serves the internal need for better government management, but also serves as a device to inform citizens about what the government is doing and how well it is performing and, therefore, such budgeting elicits citizen input.

In contrast to line item budgeting, performance budgeting applies lump sum allocations for programs instead of detailed line item classification. It emphasizes program objectives, which help citizens understand program costs and benefits. It relies on measurement, evaluation, and performance

TABLE 6.2 Line-Item Budget
(thousands of U.S. dollars)

Line item	2004 Amended budget	12/31/2004 Estimates	2005 Budget
Salaries and wages	741	741	1,002
Personnel	222	197	300
Uniforms	7	7	12
Office and operating supplies	3	4	5
Operating fuel	14	14	22
Small tools and minor equipment	2	2	2
Professional services	4	5	5
Communication and postage	19	13	25
Insurance	11	10	11
Utilities	—	1	20
Janitorial, HVAC, and facility maintenance	25	5	5
Miscellaneous	1	0	1
Government service dispatch	38	38	53
Equipment and furniture	9	9	12
Computer hardware and software	—	1	24
Drug awareness and resistance education	2	1	2
Travel	1	1	1
Training	8	8	9
Total police operations	1,107	1,057	1,511

Source: Adapted from Duvall, Washington 2005.
Note: HVAC = heating,ventilation, and air conditioning; — = not available.

TABLE 6.3 Program Budget
(thousands of U.S. dollars)

Program	FY2004/05 Actual	FY2005/06 Adopted	FY2005/06 Revised	FY2006/06 Projected	FY2006/07 Adopted
Custody management	104,770	128,156	139,790	133,769	144,025
Centralized operations	12,799	15,561	16,367	14,352	17,566
Enforcement	53,446	57,694	61,506	63,841	70,664
Building operations and maintenance	1,761	—	760	—	2,040
Administrative services	17,557	19,750	20,175	18,521	13,902
General government	—	—	—	—	8,619
Total programs	190,333	221,161	238,598	230,483	256,816

Source: Adapted from Maricopa County, Arizona 2006.
Note: — = not available.

BOX 6.1 Performance Budget

Mission Statement: Provide critical police services to ensure a safe community environment that protects the lives, property, and rights of all people who live in, work in, or are visiting Sunnyvale.
Program: Police Field Services
Program Outcome Statement: Provide police services that directly respond to emergencies and the general needs of the people and businesses within Sunnyvale.

Performance Objectives:

- Emergency events: response within 4 minutes and 30 seconds for 90 percent of events
- Urgent events: response within 11 minutes for 90 percent of events
- Fire emergency events: response within 6 minutes and 30 seconds for 90 percent of events
- EMS emergency events: response within 7 minutes for 90 percent of events
- Police-based traffic events: self-initiated or observed response 10 percent of the time
- All police events: 10 percent of responses will be self-initiated or observed

Activity	2004/05 Current (US$)	2005/06 Proposed (US$)
Activity 481100, 481101: Patrol response to public events		
Product: A number of incidents		
Costs	7,757,170	8,571,575
Products	45,000	45,000

Activity	2004/05 Current (US$)	2005/06 Proposed (US$)
Work hours	80,475	80,475
Product cost	172	190
Activity 481110: Patrol response to fire events		
Product: A number of incidents		
Costs	913,834	1,010,397
Products	650	650
Work hours	9,544	9,544
Product cost	1,406	1,554
Activity 481120: Patrol response to EMS events		
Product: A number of incidents		
Costs	913,834	1,010,397
Products	750	750
Work hours	9,544	9,544
Product cost	1,218	1,347
Activity 481130, 481131, 481132: Patrol response to traffic events		
Product: A number of incidents		
Costs	1,664,129	1,839,791
Products	7,500	7,500
Work hours	17,378	17,378
Product cost	222	245
Activity 481150: Ancillary activities		
Product: A work hour		
Cost	371,842	411,167
Products	3,733	3,733
Work hours	3,733	3,733
Product cost	100	110
Activity 481160: Nondirected patrol		
Product: A capacity hour		
Costs	3,014,636	3,332,610
Products	31,542	31,542
Work hours	31,542	31,542
Product cost	96	106
Totals for Service Delivery Plan 4810: Police field services		
Costs	14,635,445	16,175,937
Work hours	152,216	152,216

Source: Adapted from City of Sunnyvale, California (2005).

reporting, which help citizens assess government performance, influence budgetary decision making, and hold government accountable.

Simply changing the presentation of the budget from line items to a results-oriented structure will not change budget outcomes, the budget process, or the behavior of managers. An effective system of performance budgeting relies on performance measurement, strategic planning, and performance management. Strategic planning defines the performance to be measured; performance measurement and management are the prerequisites for a performance budgeting system, and they require reliable performance information and performance monitoring.

Budget Process under Performance Budgeting

Performance measurement plays an important role in the budgeting cycle. In budget preparation, budgeters can include performance indicators in budget instructions to demonstrate desirable performance levels; individual service agencies can use these indicators to demonstrate their past achievements and assist with their budget estimates and requests. In budget legislation, performance information facilitates informed budgetary decision making. Agencies can use performance information to justify their budget request, and legislators can use performance information to specify the expected service quantity and quality. Furthermore, performance information can facilitate communication between residents and governments and involve residents in budgetary decision making. At the stage of budget execution, managers can use performance indicators to clarify management goals, monitor achievement of these goals, and detect operational problems. When uniform performance information is available, it provides a standard for public managers to compare performance over time or across jurisdictions. In budget evaluation and auditing, performance indicators, along with information on budgeted funding, help policy makers gauge the efficiency and effectiveness of public programs.

Citizen Participation in Performance Budgeting at the Local Level

In the absence of citizen participation, performance budgeting runs the risk of becoming an internal bureaucratic exercise. Citizen participation has the potential of strengthening government accountability to citizens and making the government responsive to citizens' preferences.

Support from the electorate is necessary to sustain performance budgeting reform. Citizens' involvement also ensures credibility and improves

the reliability of the data that are collected, assessed, and reported. Participation in designing performance indicators, setting performance objectives,
and evaluating budgets gives citizens a sense of ownership. Furthermore,
citizen engagement provides an environment for sustainable performance
budgeting reforms, which tend to be costly to maintain. In the absence of
public support and assistance, managers and staff are unlikely to understand
the potential value of a results-oriented approach or to provide for its effective
implementation and use (Perrin 2002: 11).

Considerations in Performance Budgeting Reforms

Implementation of performance budgeting reforms entails many considerations.

Performance Measurement and Reporting

An effective performance budgeting system depends highly on reliable performance measurement and reporting. Because performance measurement
and reporting do not directly affect budgetary allocations, they do not
immediately incur financial risks for public managers and, therefore, serve
as an appropriate entry point for reforms. Construction of a performance
measurement and reporting system gives public officials an opportunity to
reach agreement on program goals and performance measures. In a survey
of local officials in municipalities in three counties in the state of Florida in
the United States, 93 percent of respondents stated that performance
reporting and management were more important than performance budgeting in their cities (Wang 1999: 543).

A performance budgeting system requires measures for gauging public
programs from a variety of lens, such as inputs, outputs (quantity and
quality of goods and services produced), efficiency (unit cost to produce
outputs), service quality (such as timeliness, accessibility, courtesy, accuracy,
and satisfaction), and outcomes (progress in achieving program objectives)
(McGill 2001; Wang 1999). Different measures assess different aspects of
budgeting practice. The use of multiple measures rests on the blurred
relationship among inputs, process, and results, an inherent feature of public
programs. In other words, the outcomes or service quality associated with a
government program cannot be inferred solely from outputs. Therefore,
managers must monitor the entire results-based chain to effectively manage
government programs.

Output-Focused Performance Management Paradigm

Performance management is a prerequisite for the success of performance budgeting. Governments that do not manage for results do not budget for results. Performance budgeting cannot thrive unless it is built into an overall managerial strategy for performance.

Donald Kettl (2000) distinguishes two sets of performance management strategies, one relying on market-like arrangements and the other relying on managerial norms and competence. The former strategy, "making managers manage," specifies contracts with budgetary allocations and competitive pressures and is practiced in New Zealand. The latter approach, "letting managers manage," is practiced in Australia and Sweden. Both strategies give public managers the flexibility they need to improve performance, but the former relies on incentives and competition, whereas the latter relies on good will and trust. In addition, the two approaches take different views on rewarding public servants. The market approach uses performance-based contracts to reward the chief executive financially if the organization achieves its performance targets. The empowerment approach holds that public servants are motivated more by the intrinsic rewards of public service than by material benefits.

To introduce a cultural change from input controls to output accountability in the public sector, New Zealand has transformed its public sector by taking a private sector management and measurement approach to core government functions. The country revamped a tenured civil service and made all public positions contractually based on an agreed set of results. Even the central bank governor was required to enter into a contract with the parliament. Under the terms of this contract, the governor's tenure was linked to limiting inflation to no more than 3 percent per year. The country decentralized program management at delivery points and gave managers flexibility and autonomy in budgetary allocations and program implementation within the policy framework and defined budget. In addition, the country introduced capital charging and accrual accounting to provide a complete picture of the resource cost of each public sector activity. It commercialized or privatized nonpublic functions. New Zealand's introduction of the contractualism version of outputs accountability in the public sector transformed the country's highly protected and regulated economy into an open and deregulated economy with a lean and efficient public sector (Walker 1996). More remarkable results were observed at the local level. For example, the new contractualism precipitated an astonishing turnaround in the fortunes of the town of Papakura by eliminating debt and reducing taxes while improving the quality and quantity of public service provision (Shah 2005).

Managerial accountability must be based on outputs rather than on outcomes, which are beyond mangers' direct control, difficult to define and quantify, and impossible to use as a costing basis. Linking outcomes directly with managerial actions and decisions is difficult or implausible, because outcomes are remote in time and space from a program's activities. Outcomes are difficult to identify and quantify, because the timescale for measuring them normally spans some time after the program's interventions and is generally not in sync with the program's budgeting cycle. Calculating the cost of the effort to achieve outcomes can be more difficult than costing outputs (Kristensen, Groszyk, and Bühler 2002: 16). Outcomes typically are not the result of a single intervention by one program in isolation but rather the result of the interaction of many planned and unplanned interventions and other factors. Hence, holding public managers accountable for outcomes is inappropriate and unrealistic. The focus on outputs as practiced in Malaysia and New Zealand offers greater potential for accountability. However, outcomes should be monitored; an exclusive emphasis on quantitative output measures can distort agencies' understanding of their programs' impact on society.

To foster outputs-based accountability, governments must relax central input controls to increase managerial flexibility. They can accomplish this task by consolidating various budget lines into a single appropriation for all operating costs (of which personnel cost is the largest component) and by easing a variety of central management rules. If such rules prohibit flexibility, consolidating budget lines makes little sense. Sweden's experience in dismantling central control over human resource management offers some interesting insights.

Performance Budgeting as a Tool for Informed Decision Making

Pursuing a direct link between performance and resource allocation is undesirable, because performance information does not constitute a sufficient basis on which to make budgetary decisions. At best, performance data serve as one factor to guide future directions. In addition, budgetary decisions involve value judgments. As past performance information provides some basis for considering what future priorities should be, policy makers must take into account divergent views about what future actions are most appropriate (Perrin 2002: 41). Furthermore, they must consider other factors—for instance, the legal or political imperatives that created certain government programs prevent abandonment of the programs for poor performance. No one would seriously suggest shutting down an ineffi-cient health care system unless better alternatives are available. Local governments in North America that are adopting performance budgeting create no direct link between performance and future budgetary allocations.

Performance Budgeting in Practice

The experience of U.S. local governments with performance budgeting sug-gests that such budgeting is relatively easy to implement at the local level and has high payoffs in terms of citizen support. Governments can implement it on a piecemeal basis for selected departments or agencies or for the local government as a whole. Alternatively, they can take a more gradual approach by instituting a performance management and reporting system and even-tually graduating to performance budgeting.

Many local governments in Canada, Denmark, Sweden, and the United States have adopted performance budgeting. These governments' budgets provide useful information on government performance (see annexes 6A and 6B for overviews of performance budgeting at the state, the city, and the country levels, respectively, in the United States). For example, the perform-ance budget of Fairfax County, Virginia, provides information on program objectives, budgetary allocations, outputs, service quality, and outcomes (see box 6.2 for an example of the county's police protection budget and annex 6C for additional examples of performance budgets).

Critical Conditions for Successful Implementation of Performance Budgeting

Several basic conditions are necessary to sustain the momentum of per-formance budgeting reform.

Motivation to Make a Change

Consensus among participants on the need for reform is critical to success-ful implementation. Public officials need to identify their motives for using performance measurement and performance budgeting. These motives may be external demands for service quality and accountability, as well as internal demands for efficiency and effectiveness (Wang 1999: 539). Public officials must also define the producers and consumers of performance-based

BOX 6.2 Example of a Performance Budget: Police Patrol
Services in Fairfax County, Virginia

As shown below, Fairfax County summarizes its funding for police patrol services
and articulates the overall goal and objectives of the services. In addition, it
identifies actual and estimated numbers for three types of performance-based
indicators: outputs, service quality, and outcomes.

Funding summary					
Category	FY2004 actual	FY2005 adopted budget plan	FY2005 revised budget plan	FY2006 advertised budget plan	FY2006 adopted budget plan
Total expenditure (US$)	93,518,475	84,535,731	86,954,912	94,807,577	94,827,577

Goal
The goal is to protect persons and property by providing essential law enforcement and public safety services, while promoting involvement, stability, and
order through service assistance and visibility.

The objectives include the following:
■ Maintain the rate of aggravated assault cases per 10,000 population at
4.0 or less.
■ Maintain the rate of burglary cases per 10,000 population at 17.8 or less.
■ Ensure that the rate of alcohol-related traffic crashes per one million vehicle
miles of travel is no greater than 32.9.

	Prior year			Current estimate FY2005	Future estimate FY2006
Indicator	FY2002 actual	FY2003 actual	FY2004 estimate/ actual		
Output					
Aggravated assault cases investigated	357	399	378/392	386	386
Burglary cases investigated	1,813	1,713	1,675/1,609	1,682	1,682
Alcohol-related driving arrests	2,536	2,815	2,665/2,899	2,698	2,69
Alcohol-related crashes	1,079	1,028	1,016/855	999	999

(Box continues on the following page.)

Indicator	Prior year			Current estimate FY2005	Future estimate FY2006
	FY2002 actual	FY2003 actual	FY2004 estimate/ actual		
Service quality					
Aggravated assault case clearance rate (%)	72.0	63.2	65.1/81.0	65.1	65.1
Average response time from dispatch to scene (minutes)	5.9	6.1	6.3/6.9	5.0	5.0
Burglary case clearance rate (%)	34.6	32.6	33.0/37.0	37.0	37.0
Outcome					
Aggravated assault cases (per 10,000 population)	3.7	4.1	4.0/4.0	4.0	4.0
Burglary cases (per 10,000 population)	18.9	17.5	17.8/17.6	17.8	17.8
Alcohol-related crashes (per million vehicle miles of travel)	37.4	34.9	33.7/27.7	32.9	32.9

Source: Adapted from Fairfax County, Virginia (2005).

information and provide an appropriate incentive strategy for that information's use. Finally, they must understand that performance-based information may be more helpful in improving management than in handling budgetary matters.

Legislative Support

⌈Strong and consistent political support from the legislature is critical for performance budgeting initiatives⌋Pursuit of internal rationality and efficiency criteria without regard to the political environment would jeopardize such initiatives. Legislators should be involved in establishing performance goals, developing performance indicators, monitoring the performance process, and evaluating performance results. Performance budgeting is unlikely to succeed if the executive and legislative branches have different ideas about the need for and objectives of the reform.

The legal stimulus to implement performance budgeting adds weight to the reform's expected outcomes. In a survey of state governments in the United States, Willoughby and Melkers (2000) found that of 15 U.S. states in which executive or legislative branch budgeters indicate that performance budgeting has been "effective" or "very effective," only 3 (Kansas, North Dakota, and Utah) have administrative requirements for performance budgeting. The other 12 states established performance budgeting by law. Budgeters from these states regard the effectiveness of performance budgeting more positively than budgeters from the other three states (Willoughby and Melkers 2000: 113–15).

Support and Engagement from Citizens

Aside from legislative participation on a limited scale, support from outside the administration is also necessary. Performance reforms should provide direct benefits to government stakeholders in exchange for their support (Wang 2000). Without at least some degree of public involvement, performance budgeting risks becoming an internal bureaucratic exercise detached from what the citizenry views as important. Moreover, in the absence of citizen support and assistance, managers and staff are unlikely to understand the potential value of a results-oriented approach or to effectively implement and use it (Perrin 2002: 11).

Administrative Capacity

The history of managerial and budgeting reforms indicates that the fate of a new initiative often does not depend on logical concepts, good intentions, and sound values but rather on operational issues: how well people solve practical problems and whether they can maintain support to sustain a reform's momentum. Mandating implementation of performance measurement and budgeting across the board, although politically popular, may not be administratively feasible. Political leaders and policy entrepreneurs who advocate implementation of performance budgeting must give agencies time to acquire the requisite capacities.

Rather than imposing a system for all programs to follow, the reform should respect agencies' institutional differences and help them, as Perrin (2002) notes, to develop an approach suitable for the agencies' situation and context. Such an approach can give agencies useful information for reviewing the impact of what they are doing and identifying how this information can aid them in their planning and budgeting. Building of administrative capacity—personnel, information systems, accounting standards, and most important, funding potential—is highly associated with the use of performance measurement in budgeting (Wang 2000).

One aspect of capacity building is development of a valid, reliable, and uniform financial and performance reporting system. Such a system provides a database for performance budgeting. It helps public managers understand how inputs are converted into outputs and outcomes.

Culture of Managing for Results

Performance budgeting must be an integral element of a broader reform package. Schick (2003) observes that every sustained implementation of performance budgeting has been accompanied and reinforced by transformations in public management. Governments that do not manage for results do not budget for results. Performance budgeting cannot thrive in the absence of incentives for improved performance and enhanced accountability for results. The "managing for results" reform that swept across industrial countries and some developing countries in the 1990s has shifted attention from bureaucratic processes and input controls to accountability for results (Shah 2005).

Citizen-Centric Performance Budgeting at the Local Level

Performance budgeting can prove costly and ineffective if the culture of governance is oriented toward command and control rather than accountability to citizens. Citizen-centric performance budgeting can be a starting point for citizen-centered governance. Citizen-centric performance budgeting at the local level is concerned with creation of an institutional environment in which citizens can hold government accountable for its performance (Andrews and Shah 2005; Shah 2005). Efficient and effective public spending in a manner responsive to civic demands is pertinent to recent public management reform movements, which emphasize performance accountability and citizen participation.

TABLE 6.4   Institutionalizing Citizen-Oriented Budgeting Process

Stage	Budget targets formulated	Budget bids and drafts formulated, reconciled, and finalized into budget proposal	Political representatives debate, amend, and approve budget	Budget is executed, in-year changes are made, and execution is monitored	Expost evaluation and control
Specific institutional requirements	**Revelation institution:** citizen input regarding resource availability	**Revelation institutions:** citizen input on service demand	**Reflection and revelation institutions:** citizen access to debate, as well as institutionalized transparency of debate process and outcomes and citizen-based approval process	**Reporting institutions:** citizen participation in and monitoring of projects, as well as response mechanisms	**Response and redress institutions:** citizen evaluation and response mechanisms
General institutional requirements	**Representative institutions** Rights-to-information institutions				

Source: Andrews and Shah 2005.

Budget and financial management processes at the local level in developing countries are typically managed in a closed-door fashion. Citizens are left to assess government performance on the basis of published budgets and financial statements that follow the line item format (Andrews and Shah 2005). Performance budgeting produces user-friendly budget documents and enhances government transparency through performance measurement and reporting, which facilitates citizen participation in budgetary decision making. Citizen-centric budgeting requires institutional arrangements that elicit citizens' input in budget approval and implementation and that provide avenues for citizens to evaluate performance and have grievances redressed (see table 6.4).

Citizen-centric budgeting requires some form of institutionalized citizen representation in the local government. Sometimes local governments are run by officials appointed by higher-level governments and are accountable to these governments rather than to local citizens. A government that does not represent local citizens in political matters is hardly likely to have a local citizen orientation when it addresses fiscal matters.

Governments attempting to orient their budgeting processes to meeting citizen needs must provide formal channels for citizen input. These channels largely come in two varieties: formal, institutionalized forms of representation or parallel, participatory mechanisms. The latter approach is reflected in a burgeoning literature documenting actual examples from around the world.

Some experts argue that the most appropriate basis on which to realize citizen-centric local budgeting is not parallel participatory structures but rather the formal representative local government. The first-best option for developing a citizen orientation in the budget involves citizens working within the political and administrative structures of representative local governments (Andrews and Shah 2005). To empower citizens, especially disgruntled citizens, local governments must be mandated to hold public hearings on budget proposals that are open to all. At these hearings, they must present a report on past performance. The budgetary proposals and performance reports must be made public well in advance of the hearings and must be made available in all local libraries and all local government offices as well as posted on the Internet. The local council should be required to include an annex to the budget that details its response to citizen input. Such a process can be a starting point for citizens' activism to reform their governments.

Conclusion

For local governments in industrial countries, performance budgeting is an important tool for connecting with electorates and building trust in governance. These governments have demonstrated the usefulness of this tool for communication as well as for management and external accountability. The benefits of this tool have been largely realized because of democratic accountability and administrative autonomy at the local level. In the absence of a strong institutional environment for bottom-up accountability and managerial flexibility, as is the case in many developing countries, performance budgeting will prove largely ineffective. In developing countries, citizen-centric performance budgeting that embodies institutional provisions for citizen input can help initiate a cultural shift from command-and-control governance to responsive, responsible, and accountable governance.

Annex 6A: Review of Performance Budgeting in the United States at the State Level

In the 1990s, many state governments embraced performance budgeting reforms (Flowers, Kundin, and Brower 1999: 618). All but three states (Arkansas, Massachusetts, and New York) have performance-based budgeting requirements. Of the remaining 47 states, 31 have legislated performance budgeting, and 16 have initiated it through budget guidelines or instructions (Willoughby and Melkers 2000: 106).

Many state (as well as local) governments have reported performance measures in their budget documents (Broom 1995; Melkers and Willoughby 1998; Tigue and Strachota 1994; Wang 1999). For many states, the motivation for developing such measures was not expressly to change appropriations. Maine's 2002–03 budget identified the purpose of its performance measures as "ensuring accountability, improving service delivery, communicating the agency efforts for the funds invested, and informing citizens about how their tax dollars are being spent" (Willoughby 2004: 24). Wisconsin considers performance information to be data that "should stimulate decision makers to ask questions about how well a program is working and to focus more on results" (Willoughby 2004: 24).

Generally speaking, performance information is not used for cost or program cutting or for changing spending levels, at least not immediately. Most of the research to date indicates that performance budgeting initiatives are more effective in managerial improvement than in budgetary decision making. Hager, Hobson, and Wilson (2001) found that only Texas and, to some extent, Michigan, use performance information in budgetary decision making. Texas is considered the leader among states in using strategic planning, performance budgeting, and performance monitoring to help policy makers understand how public funds can be used more efficiently and effectively. The state's executive branch budgeters claim that a decade after its implementation (in 1991), performance budgeting has changed appropriation levels (Willoughby and Melkers 2000).

The Government Performance Project (GPP), an academic-journalistic partnership that regularly assesses how states compare in the quality of their management, completed a new report card in 2005. The project gave five states—Louisiana, Missouri, Utah, Virginia, and Washington—an A in information, one of four examined areas (the others are money, infrastructure, and people). Seventeen states received a B, 26 received a C, and 2 received a D. Box 6A.1 describes the grading criteria for the information assessment category, which includes budgeting for performance. Budgeting practices in the five states scoring an A are summarized afterward.

BOX 6A.1 GPP's Grading Criteria for Information

The GPP describes its five grading criteria for information:
1. *Strategic Direction:* The state actively focuses on the strategic direction of its policy and on the collecting of information to support that policy direction.
2. *Budgeting for Performance:* State officials have appropriate data on the relationship between costs and performance, and they use these data when making resource allocation decisions.
3. *Managing for Performance:* Agency managers have the appropriate information required to make program management decisions.
4. *Program Evaluation:* The governor and agency managers have appropriate data that enables them to assess the actual performance of policies and programs.
5. *Electronic Government:* The public has appropriate access to information about the state, as well as the performance of state programs and state services, and is able to provide input to state policy makers.

Source: Government Performance Project 2005.

Louisiana

Lousiana established an electronic performance database, the Louisiana Performance Accountability System, to help state agencies file quarterly performance reports. The database is the depository of official performance information and the medium for public reporting of performance information. The legislative fiscal officer gives the Joint Legislative Committee on the Budget a summary of the data contained in each agency's performance progress report for the purpose of noting variances between actual performance levels and performance standards. The Executive Budget Office, the legislature, and a few executive agencies compare the cost of program results with the costs associated with specific activities. Officials in the state disagree about whether performance measures are routinely used in decision making.

Missouri

State agencies routinely produce performance information. They are required to report on actual versus projected performance for each budgeting unit when submitting their budget request document to the governor. The governor's budget contains output information across many policy areas, as well as outcome information from the Elementary and Secondary Education Department, the Department of Natural Resources, and the Department of Social Services. State agencies and the governor use performance information in the budgeting process to allocate resources.

Utah

Utah's agencies and budget process produce performance measures. These measures are available to the legislature and to the Governor's Office of Planning and Budget but are not published in the governor's executive budget. Utah's legislative fiscal analyst provides the appropriate performance measures to the appropriation subcommittees for use during budget deliberations. The subcommittees use the performance information to make precision cuts in funding rather than across-the-board cuts that could harm effective programs. The legislature is particularly interested in reviewing program measures and using them during budget deliberations.

Virginia

Elected officials, the state budget office, and agency personnel receive cost and performance data through a variety of means, including the Performance Management Index; reports of institutional effectiveness; and executive agreements among the governor, cabinet secretaries, and agency heads. Performance data also come from Virginia Results—agency and program-level performance measures, which are not always linked to budget requests. Agencies use performance and cost information when making resource allocation decisions, but the legislature rarely uses performance information to make such decisions. The budget office has made it a goal to more strongly link performance information with the budget process.

Washington

Washington has a long history of producing high-quality performance information. Its Priorities of Government (POG) system is regarded as one of the country's best examples of the use of performance information for budgeting on a governmentwide basis. Most agencies report on their performance quarterly; some of their performance indicators are directly related to the 11 POG results areas. Governor Gary Locke used the POG system in making budget adjustments to the 2003–05 biennial budget. The legislature was also engaged in the POG process.

Annex 6B: Review of Performance Budgeting in the United States at the City and County Levels

In the 1990s, many city and county governments implemented management and budgeting reforms (Cigler 1995). Among these governments, as among state governments, performance budgeting is more popular as an accountability and managerial tool in monitoring and evaluating service delivery than as means to improve budgetary decision making. Local governments use performance data to improve programs' efficiency and effectiveness, to enhance transparency of governance, to communicate with citizens, and (to a lesser extent) to inform budgetary decision making.

Integration of performance measurement into budgeting efforts is rare at local levels. Line item budgeting remains the dominant budget approach. On the basis of a national survey of governments of counties with a population over 50,000, Wang (2000) confirmed that some form of hybrid budget combining the traditional budget with some performance information is popular.

A survey of the finance directors of municipalities with a population of 25,000 to 75,000 in five contiguous southeastern states (Alabama, Georgia, North Carolina, South Carolina, and Tennessee) indicated that collection and reporting of performance measures for fiscal year 1996 was widespread but that city budgets did not incorporate performance data in any meaningful way (Rivenbark and Kelly 2000). Most cities (57.5 percent) used the line item budget; other cities used a hybrid budget, typically a line item budget with performance information attached. Seventy percent of respondents ranked prior-year expenditures as "very important" in driving preparation of the budget. In these cases, performance information, reported by department, was added at the presentation phase for explication and to conform to norms promulgated by professional budgeting organizations (Rivenbark and Kelly 2000: 74).

Wang (1999) surveyed local officials in municipalities with a population of 2,500 or greater in Dade, Broward, and Palm Beach counties, Florida, in 1996. All five cities used performance measures, but none used them in making resource allocation decisions. Some believed that budget decisions were political and that performance information was useful only if it fitted policy makers' political agendas. Some respondents expressed concern about the use of unreliable performance information resulting in an unfair distribution of budgetary resources (Wang 1999: 542).

Annex 6C: Examples of Performance Measurement and Budgeting

The following examples of performance measurement and budgeting are adapted from two U.S. county budgets.

Fire and Rescue Operations Division

			Funding summary		
Category	FY2004 actual	FY2005 adopted budget plan	FY2005 revised budget plan	FY2006 advertised budget plan	FY2006 adopted budget plan
Total expenditure (US$)	92.476,311	99,470,567	106,604,836	121,833,152	124,833,152

Goal

The goal is to provide emergency and nonemergency response to save the lives and protect the property of Fairfax County residents and visitors.

The objectives include the following

■ For emergency medical services (EMS), to provide on-scene advanced life support (ALS) capability within 9 minutes and a first responder with an automatic external defibrillator (AED) within 5 minutes (National Fire Protection Association response standards) to thereby achieve a cardiopulmonary resuscitation rate of at least 17 percent.

■ To maintain the emergency response rate of providing a hazardous materials (HazMat) team on scene within six minutes at 65 percent or better.

■ To deploy suppression resources so that an engine company arrives within 5 minutes of dispatch in at least 50 percent of cases and 14 personnel arrive within 9 minutes in 90 percent of cases (response and staffing standard of the National Fire Protection Association), holding citizen fire deaths to no more than 5, civilian fire injuries held to no more than 70, and fire loss to no more than $24 million.

		Prior year		Current	Future
Indicator	FY2002 actual	FY2003 actual	FY2004 estimate/ actual	estimate FY2005	estimate FY2006
Output					
Patients transported	39,211	39,078	39,652/40,949	41,768	42,603
Patients defibrillated	176	142	144/134	140	140
EMS incidents	60,685	60,306	61,192/62,420	62,115	63,358
Total incidents responded to	89,246	87,621	88,909/91,373	90,250	92,055
Suppression incidents	23,579	21,740	22,060/23,128	22,392	22,840

(*continued*)

(*continued*)

Indicator	Prior year			Current estimate FY2005	Future estimate FY2006
	FY2002 actual	FY2003 actual	FY2004 estimate/ actual		
HazMat incidents	613	136	150/126	130	130
Other responses by HazMat Response Team	3,460	4,577	4,600/4,714	4,800	4,900
Efficiency					
Average length of time of an ALS transport call (hours)	1:04:03	1:03:28	1:03/1:02:43	1:03	1:03
Cost per suppression and EMS incident (US$)	1,262	1,341	1,465/1,358	1,484	1,560
Average number of suppression and EMS calls per day	245	240	244/250	247	252
HazMat incidents per team	153	34	38/32	33	33
Other incident responses per HazMat Response Team	865	1,144	1,150/1,790	1,200	1,225
Service quality					
ALS transport units on scene within 9 minutes (percent)	87.08	85.49	85.00/85.27	85.00	85.00
AED response rate within 5 minutes (percent)	—	—	—/61.6	61.00	61.00
Fire suppression response rate for engine company within 5 minutes (percent)	53.93	53.64	53.00/51.38	50.00	50.00
Fire suppression response rate for 14 personnel within 9 minutes (percent)	—	92.75	90.00/94.83	90.00	90.00

(*continued*)

(continued)

Indicator	Prior year			Current estimate FY2005	Future estimate FY200
	FY2002 actual	FY2003 actual	FY2004 estimate/ actual		
Average time for emergency response to HazMat incidents (minutes)	5:30	5:11	5:11/5:29	6:00	6:00
Outcome					
Cardiac-arrest patients arriving at emergency room (percent)	16.5	19.6	17.0/20	17.0	17.0
Fire loss (US$ millions)	29.9	16.6	20.0/27.0	24.0	24.0
Fire loss as percentage of total property valuation	0.03	0.01	0.02/0.02	0.02	0.02
Total civilian fire deaths	7	5	5/7	5	5
Civilian fire deaths per 100,000 population	0.70	0.49	0.50/0.68	0.67	0.47
Total civilian fire injuries	84	51	75/64	70	70
Civilian fire injuries per 100,000 population	8.39	5.00	8.00/6.23	6.71	6.62
HazMat emergency responses within 6 minutes (percent)	66.2	65.4	65.0/65.8	65.0	65.0

Source: Adapted from Fairfax County, Virginia (2005).
Note: — = not available.

Montgomery County, Maryland, Solid Waste Services

Program
The Program involves residential refuse collection.
Mission
The Mission is to provide reliable, convenient curbside residential collection while achieving a high degree of customer satisfaction.

Community outcomes
The community outcomes that are supported include the following:
- Improved environment
- Enhanced quality of life
- Healthy children and adults

Program measures	FY2002 actual	FY2003 actual	FY2004 actual	FY05 budget	FY2005 actual	FY2006 approved
Service quality						
Number of missed collection complaints	1,686	3,245	2,614	3,135	1,741	3,000
Number of other customer complaints	507	652	485	650	422	600
Complaints per 1,000 households served	6.0	7.7	5.7	7.6	4.9	6.9
Efficiency						
Average cost per household served	60.03	63.02	63.08	62.79	57.73	63.05
Average cost per ton collected	68.74	67.75	64.51	73.75	61.87	63.07
Workload/outputs						
Households served	84,788	85,085	85,034	85,192	86,252	86,410
Refuse collected (tons)	74,044	79,153	83,152	72,531	80,472	86,382
Service requests	23,492	26,529	25,005	24,300	24,414	25,000
Calls for information	10,118	9,482	8,678	9,650	6,621	10,000
Inputs						
Expenditures (US$ thousands)	5,090	5,362	5,364	5,349	4,979	5,448
Work years	12.3	11.9	10.7	11.4	11.7	12.9

Source: Adapted from Montgomery County Office of Management and Budget, Maryland (2006).

References

Andrews, Matthew, and Anwar Shah. 2005. "Toward Citizen-Centered Local-Level Budgets in Developing Countries." In *Public Expenditure Analysis*, ed. Anwar Shah, 183–216. Washington, DC: World Bank.

Broom, Cheryle A. 1995. "Performance-Based Government Models: Building A Track Record." *Public Budgeting and Finance* 15 (4): 3–17.

Cigler, Beverly. 1995. "County Governance in the 1990s." *State and Local Government Review* 27: 55–70.

City of Duvall, Washington. 2005. "2005 Budget." http://www.cityofduvall.com/appsformspubs/2005_line_item_budget.pdf.

City of Sunnyvale, California. 2005. "Fiscal Year 2005–2006 Recommended Budget." http://www.sunnyvale.ca.gov/Departments/Finance/Budget/Recommended/ FY0506+Recommended/home.htm.

Fairfax County, Virginia. 2005. "FY 2006 Adopted Budget: Volume 1." Department of Management and Budget, Fairfax County, VA.

Flowers, Geraldo, Delia Kundin, and Ralph S. Brower. 1999. "How Agency Conditions Facilitate and Constrain Performance-Based Program Systems: A Qualitative Inquiry." *Journal of Public Budgeting, Accounting, and Financial Management* 11 (4): 618–48.

Government Performance Project. 2005. "Grading the States 2005." http://www. gpponline.org.

Hager, Greg, Alice Hobson, and Ginny Wilson. 2001. "Performance-Based Budgeting: Concepts and Examples." Research Report 302, Legislative Research Commission, Frankfort, KY.

Howard, Kenneth S. 1973. *Changing State Budgeting.* Lexington, KY: Council of State Governments.

Kettl, Donald. 2000. *The Global Public Management Revolution: A Report on the Transformation of Governance.* Washington, DC: Brookings Institution Press.

Kristensen, Jens Kromann, Walter S. Groszyk, and Bernd Bühler. 2002. "Outcome-Focused Management and Budgeting." *OECD Journal of Budgeting* 1 (4): 7–34.

Maricopa County, Arizona. 2006. "Fiscal Year 2006–07 Final Budget." Office of Management and Budget. http://www.maricopa.gov/Budget/BudgetDocument.aspx.

McGill, Ronald. 2001. "Performance Budgeting." *The International Journal of Public Sector Management* 14 (5): 376–90.

Melkers, Julia E., and Katherine G. Willoughby. 1998. "The State of the States: Performance-Based Budgeting Requirements in 47 of 50." *Public Administration Review* 58 (1): 66–73.

Montgomery County Office of Management and Budget, Maryland. 2006. "Montgomery Measures Up! For the Year 2007." Office of Management and Budget, Montgomery County, Maryland.

Perrin, Burt. 2002. "Implementing the Vision: Addressing Challenges to Results-Focused Management and Budgeting." Organisation for Economic Co-operation and Development conference on Implementation Challenges in Results-Focused Management and Budgeting, Paris, February 11–12.

Rivenbark, William C., and Janet M. Kelly. 2000. "Performance Measurement: A Local Government Response." *Journal of Public Budgeting, Accounting, and Financial Management* 12 (1): 74–86.

Schick, Allen. 2003. "The Performing State: Reflection on an Idea Whose Time Has Come but Whose Implementation Has Not." *OECD Journal on Budgeting* 3 (2): 71–104.

Shah, Anwar. 2005. "On Getting the Giant to Kneel: Approaches to a Change in the Bureaucratic Culture." In *Fiscal Management,* ed. Anwar Shah, 211–28. Washington, DC: World Bank.

Shah, Anwar, and Chunli Shen. Forthcoming. "A Primer on Performance Budgeting." In *Budgeting and Budgetary Institutions,* ed. Anwar Shah. Washington, DC: World Bank.

Tigue, Patricia, and Dennis Strachota. 1994. *The Use of Performance Measures in City and County Budgets.* Chicago, IL: Government Finance Officers Association.

Walker, Basil. 1996. "Reforming the Public Sector for Leaner Government and Improved Performance: The New Zealand Experience." *Public Administration and Development* 16: 353–76.

Wang, Xiao Hu. 1999. "Conditions to Implement Outcome-Oriented Performance Budgeting: Some Empirical Evidence." *Journal of Public Budgeting, Accounting, and Financial Management* 11 (4): 533–52.

——— .2000. "Performance Measurement in Budgeting: A Study of County Governments." *Public Budgeting and Finance* 20 (3): 102–18

Willoughby, Katherine, G. 2004. "Performance Measurement and Budget Balancing: State Government Perspective." *Public Budgeting and Finance* 24 (2): 21–39.

Willoughby, Katherine, G., and Julia E. Melkers. 2000. "Implementing PBB: Conflicting Views of Success." *Public Budgeting and Finance* 20 (1): 105–20.

7

How to Read a Local Budget and Assess Government Performance

CAROL W. LEWIS

Budgeting and budget documents in Sub-Saharan African countries reflect the diversity of local authorities in size and complexity and in functions and responsibilities, authority and autonomy, organizational and political structures and processes, legal and financial constraints and resources, intergovernmental relations and international arrangements, and social settings and other environmental conditions. Nonetheless, all budgets share core features. This chapter focuses on 10 such features: (1) reporting entity; (2) fiscal year; (3) operating budget and capital budget; (4) legal status and budget cycle; (5) balance, or surplus/deficit; (6) overall balance; (7) funds; (8) revenue reliance, central allocations, and local discretion; (9) costs and budget share; and (10) spotlighted concerns. Because budget formats vary, the budgets selected to illustrate these core features range from the complex and sophisticated budget of a large metropolitan center to the more basic documents of smaller municipalities.

The budget is a legally enforceable plan, expressed in currency, of operations for a fiscal period. In effect, a budget is a statement of public purposes and policies that are translated into the allocation of financial resources. Best practice recognizes the budget as a policy statement: "The budget is the government's key policy document.

It should be comprehensive, encompassing all government revenue and expenditure, so that the necessary trade-offs between different policy options can be assessed" (OECD 2001: 4). As an issues paper of the United Nations Economic Commission for Africa (UNECA) explains,

> the budget is the single most important policy document of governments, where complex development challenges are expressed in real budgetary terms. The national budget reflects the fundamental values underlying national policy. It outlines the government's views of the socio-economic state of a country. It is a declaration of the government's fiscal, financial and economic objectives and reflects its social and economic priorities. A national budget should be a translation of an inclusive policy making process into implementable and time bound projects (UNECA 2005: 2).

These observations apply to municipal budgets in South Africa: "The municipal budget is a policy document that encapsulates the activities and priorities of the municipality. . . . Moreover, the normative and ethical principles such as openness, transparency, and public accountability must be ensured in the preparation, execution, monitoring and control of the budget" (Kumar and Moodley 2003: 66).

Most local public programs and formal community services are funded largely or wholly through a budget. Spending public resources in ways and amounts other than set out in the budget is usually illegal. For many agencies, grants are legally binding contracts; contractors, donors, and oversight agencies scrutinize their practices and expect their money to go to programs as promised. As a result, most activities in the public sector live (and die) by this rule: if they are not in the budget, they are not going to be implemented. But this does *not* mean that if programs *are* in the budget that they will be implemented or will work. Effective and efficient financial and program management is needed to move from the budget to service delivery. The second part of this chapter is devoted to relating the budget to performance.

Questions Addressed by Budgets

A close reading of a budget provides answers to questions important to the local authority, its operations, and its relationship with its many stakeholders, including residents, taxpayers, community groups, and oversight agencies. The South African constitution mandates local government to encourage civic participation.

In Nairobi, the Local Authority Service Delivery Action Plan (LASDAP) is implemented through preparation and execution of the annual budget.

The plan has "several crucial components that would determine the outcome of the process," including preparing "the plan using a participatory process with local residents and stakeholder groups within the LA's [local authority's] area of jurisdiction" and "[b]eing realistic about the resources available" (Wamwangi 2004: 16–17).[1] The questions in table 7.1 help stimulate focused and realistic participation and help frame the tough choices for decision makers.

At a minimum, a sound budget document addresses the six sets of questions specified in table 7.1, which shows that the budget is linked to economic, social, and political factors.[2] The extent to which a budget responds to the questions in a comprehensive and comprehensible way is a measure of its excellence and usefulness. The Government Finance Officers Association (GFOA undated) applies a more elaborate set of standards than those reflected in the table.

TABLE 7.1 Budget Addressing Central Values and Questions

Value	Focus	Type	Concerns and Questions
Economy	Inputs and legal compliance	Economic or market	How much must we raise and spend?
Efficiency	Outputs and performance	Economic or market	What are we getting?
Effectiveness	Outcomes and problem solving	Social	What difference are we making? Are stakeholders satisfied?
Equity/fairness	Justice, due process, representation	Political	Is procedure followed? Is law? Are processes and outcomes fair?
Accountability	Disclosure, transparency	Political	Are records true, complete, open, and accessible? Are decisions traceable, declared, and understandable?
Responsiveness	Public participation, public opinion, and public demands	Political	Are decision makers paying attention? Is the decision-making process open and does it allow for direct and indirect public participation?

Source: Carol W. Lewis 2006. Reprinted by permission.

Values in the Budget

As a service plan, a record of political and financial compromises, and a declaration of public purposes and policies, a budget announces what—and who—is important to the local authority:

> In public discourse, the focus is often on operational issues such as poor revenue collection, unsustainable debt burdens, and lack of financial management capacity. In seeking to understand the financial challenges facing local governments, it is important to ask broader questions, namely: what is local government required to do? Where should the resources come from? (Appeah 2005:3).

The budget expresses where the local authority stands with respect to accountability, transparency, and scrutiny; equity, fairness, and responsiveness; public access and participation; and stewardship and managerial competence. When performance factors are added, the budget also addresses the other values shown in table 7.1: efficiency, effectiveness, and responsibility.

Typically, a budget does not proclaim all values with equal force. As a political document, the budget's emphasis tends to move in tandem with political agendas. In part because of the power and stakes involved, in part because of decentralization and democratization trends in Sub-Saharan Africa, and in part because of the influence of international and professional accounting and reporting standards,[3] the values of accountability and transparency are prominent on the development agenda. In its 2001 report on best practices, the Organisation for Economic Co-operation and Development (OECD) states,

> Transparency—openness about policy intentions, formulation and implementation—is a key element of good governance. The budget is the single most important policy document of governments, where policy objectives are reconciled and implemented in concrete terms. Budget transparency is defined as the full disclosure of all relevant fiscal information in a timely and systematic manner (OECD 2001; 3).

Therefore, financial reports should be publicly available at no charge.[4]

In his address to the founding Congress of the United Cities and Local Government of Africa (UCLGA) in May 2005, the Chairman of the African Union, President Olusegun Obasanjo, observed that

> local governments can only remain critical to sustainable development when they are efficient, well-led, effective, focused and dedicated to the values of transparency, accountability, inclusion, fair competition, equity, social justice and good governance. A corrupt and badly run local government is just as useless

to the people as a bad government at any level in society. A bad leader cannot run a good local government system. It is therefore critical that the mobilisation of the people, the strengthening of civil society, and the strengthening of oversight and democratic institution[s] are seen as central to the local government system (Obasanjo 2005:3).

The earlier-noted UNECA issues paper declares,

Transparency and openness to policy formulation and implementation is a key element of good governance. With this strong link between policy intentions and budget, the need to open the budget to public participation should be encouraged with the objective of ensuring greater accountability for the management of resources. Many countries are introducing changes to the traditional top-down budget process to bottom-up to make it more transparent and credible. What is also significant now is the linking of budgeting to a consultative process to get the input of the beneficiaries in the budget outcome (UNECA 2005:2).

A concern with accountability and transparency clearly is linked to a democratization agenda. For example, Obasanjo notes that the "core values of local self-governance permeate the practice of local government in Africa. These values include popular participation, human rights, service delivery, governmental responsiveness and accountability to citizens, and solidarity so important for the development of peaceful, sustainable, cohesive and inclusive societies" (Obasanjo 2005:2). Similarly, the Standards of Professional Conduct of the National Association of State Budget Officers in the United States instructs members to ensure that "government is conducted openly, efficiently, equitably, and honorably in a manner that permits the citizenry to make informed judgments and hold government officials accountable" (NASBO undated: 174).

Unfortunately, recent research on *central* government budgeting in 36 countries, including 9 Sub-Saharan nations (Botswana, Burkina Faso, Ghana, Kenya, Namibia, Nigeria, South Africa, Uganda, and Zambia) suggests that much work remains to be done in the area of budget accountability and transparency. The 2004 study identifies inadequate transparency in all four stages of the budget process: formulation, legislation, execution and monitoring, and auditing (Center for Budget Priorities 2004). Even so, the nine Sub-Saharan cases showed increasing civil society and legislative interest and demand for transparency, access and results (Claassens and Van Zyl 2005: 12).

Given that many central governments in Sub-Saharan Africa fall short of meeting best practices on budget transparency and accountability, it should come as no surprise that many local authorities also fall short. Many are small, resource-starved, and highly dependent on the central or provincial government or on donors or lenders for revenue. (See Kenya 2005, for example.) For many, this dependency translates into limited discretion over spending. With neither professional staff nor technical capacity to produce multiyear reports, analyses, and electronic budget documents, these local authorities tend not to meet the international standards on transparency and accountability (participation, documentation, execution, and verification). Their budgets may be nothing more than statements of planned aggregates for revenues and expenditures. Relatively few local authorities post even basic documents on the Internet, and the budget documents that exist may be difficult for those outside the executive branch to obtain.

Other local authorities—often large metropolitan centers with defined functional responsibilities in decentralized or decentralizing systems—enjoy relatively broad authority, coupled with some discretion over revenue sources and rates and over expenditures. Some of these authorities adhere to some best practices and pursue others. Their budget documents tend to be relatively accessible and are made comprehensible through the use of graphics and explanatory narrative; in some cases they include reports aimed at the popular audience.

It should be noted that best practices are moving targets: they develop in response to changes, which may be driven by increased technological capacity, economic and political developments (such as scandal, decentralization, and privatization), or fiscal pressure. As a result, best practices "are not meant to constitute a formal 'standard'" (OECD 2001: 3). They are more profitably viewed as a set of goals that promote quality and continuous improvement in budgeting.

How to Read a Budget

Because budgets are a statement of costs (allocations) and benefits (distributions), they record accommodations and agreements and wins and losses in a core decision-making process. The Institute for Democracy in South Africa (IDASA) defines budgets thus:

> No government in the world has infinite public resources at its disposal. At the same time, there is a boundless array of needs to be met through public expenditure. The budget thus always incorporates trade-offs between different spending priorities. It includes value judgements [sic] about which services, and whose interests, are most important. A government budget is therefore not

simply a technical document: it is also an important political instrument (IDASA 2004).

Budgets record the stakes and outcomes from this process. People cannot effectively participate in resource allocation and distribution if they cannot read and understand the budget.

Overview of Budget Documents

The budget is a series of documents. Of the more than one-dozen fiscal and budget reports that the OECD (2001) catalogues in its best practices, at least four relate to local authorities with limited functional responsibility and managerial capacity: (1) the overview of revenues and expenditures; (2) comprehensive, detailed estimates of revenues and expenditures; (3) a pre-budget report on budget policy and totals; and (4) a citizen's guide to or summary of the budget. Decision makers need the first three to make informed decisions. These documents are the focus of the following discussion.

Multiple documents, such as detailed estimates, usually are divided along organization lines, suiting legal and administrative purposes rather than programmatic purposes. (Chapter 5 discusses budget formats.) Although more than one-third of the 40 countries that responded to the 2003 OECD and World Bank survey on budget practices and procedures reported using a single document for the budget summary and its underlying details, more than one-half reported that the executive presents a general summary of revenues and expenditures to the legislature in one document and detailed estimates of expenditure in separate documents (OECD and World Bank 2003).

The citizen's summary is important for purposes of accountability and transparency. Such a summary is far less common among the countries in the OECD and World Bank survey and even more rarely required by law. With an emphasis on explaining rates and tariffs, Cape Town's citizen's guide is made available on the Internet. The GFOA (2001: 9–10) recommends a timely, concise, objective, and understandable report that encourages feedback from readers.

The budget generally consists of four main parts. The first is the budget message or prebudget report. Often in narrative form and in aggregate terms, this statement of priorities and key decisions usually emphasizes changes, especially in local taxes and rates (or charges and fees). According to the GFOA (undated: 2), "The message should describe significant changes in priorities from the current year and explain the factors that led to those changes". The second part of the budget is the budget summary that presents the overall fiscal plan for the local authority as a whole and usually for major spending categories (by object and function) and for major revenue sources such as local rates. The third part consists of detailed schedules, wherein expenditures are classified by organizational agency and revenues are reviewed in detail. The fourth and last part includes supplemental documentation and information, such as socioeconomic and legal information, that is material to understanding the budget plan, its adequacy, and its implications.

Major Technical Elements

In its "Budget Blinds or Budget Windows," IDASA's Africa Budget Project declares that the skill of "learning to speak the language of budgets" is "the spear and shield of a battle-ready budget advocate" (IDASA 2003a: 1–2).

Reporting Entity

What services or functions does the budget cover? To which legal reporting entity—the government or organization—does the budget apply? This information is important for comparing one local authority's budget to another local authority's budget, for comparing the current budget to previous budgets, and for understanding the exact use of the budget.

Reading a budget starts with two questions: "What is the local authority required to do? What is it expected to do?" The answers focus attention on legal compliance and stewardship, and they are not necessarily simple. According to Johannesburg's 2006 Integrated Development Plan, "Council-owned land is the responsibility of either the Johannesburg Property Company or City Parks, both wholly owned municipal entities of the City" (Johannesburg 2006: 25). Within one country, different local authorities may have different service responsibilities. In Kenya, for example, the Nairobi city government supplies water to residents, but the Mombassa city government does not (Habitat 1998: chapter 10).

The third question in reading a budget is "What else do we need to know?" This question is best broken into two parts. First, what information is missing that decision makers need to make sound decisions? Second, what is not on the budget that affects it? Consider the services delivered by parastatal or community organizations. Deficiencies in services that are not the local authority's responsibility affect the local authority's tax base and ultimately public confidence in public institutions.

Fiscal Year

Because legal authority to tax and spend often is limited to a specific period or fiscal year, using the budget for the correct fiscal year is critical. Local authorities may use a fiscal year different from that of the central government, community service providers, contracted partners, and donors. The convention is to designate the fiscal year as "FY" and to identify the year in which the fiscal period ends.

Operating Budget and Capital Budget

Many governments and other organizations use two broad types of budgets: the operating budget and the capital budget. The operating budget finances the goods and services consumed to provide services in the fiscal year, whereas the capital budget finances longer-lived and usually expensive projects with uneven ("lumpy") costs such as bridges and buildings. Paper for the printer belongs in the operating budget, along with employee salaries and wages, social contributions, and councilors' payments. The construction costs of a new facility may go in a capital budget.

Some localities have the authority to borrow for their capital expenditures. Under new legislation, Johannesburg brought the first municipal bond in South Africa to market in 2004 and is issuing its fourth in 2006. Figure 7.1 shows the operating and capital budgets for fiscal 2006. Although small relative to the operating budget, the capital budget affects the operating budget directly through debt service (the payment of principal and interest on the debt). Debt service appears as an operating expenditure in table 7.2.

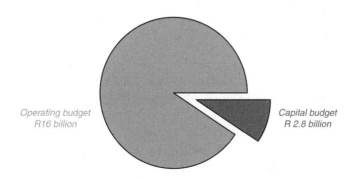

Operating budget
R16 billion

Capital budget
R 2.8 billion

Source: Johannesburg 2005: 138.

FIGURE 7.1   City of Johannesburg, South Africa, Integrated Development Plan, FY 2005–06 Budget

TABLE 7.2 Budgeted Interest Payments, Johannesburg, South Africa Integrated Development Plan, FY 2005–06

Details	Actual result, 2003/04 (R 000)	Budget, 2004/05 (R 000)	Adjusted budget, 2004/05 (R 000)	Budget, 2005/06 (R 000)	Percent	Budget, 2006/07 (R 000)	Budget, 2007/08 (R 000)
Interest on loans	546,360	586,165	586,165	611,327	4.3	630,384	635,390

Source: Excerpted from Johannesburg 2005: 141.

Legal Status and Budget Cycle

The formal budget process moves through a cycle: formulation and proposal, adoption, implementation, and audit. During formulation and proposal, the framework is constructed, but the budget is not yet official and binding. The adoption stage creates the legal authority to implement budget spending and revenue collections. Moving through the cycle from stage to stage, the budget's status changes along with the figures, and it is imperative to work with the correct figures in the correct document: requested; recommended; adopted; as amended, adjusted, revised, or estimated during implementation; and audited or actual.

A full budget process—from initial formulation to audit and issuance of the comprehensive financial statement—often takes nearly three calendar years to complete. Therefore, estimates and proposals are based at least in part on the most recent actual (from two fiscal years ago) and revised (from the prior fiscal year) figures. Budgetary decision making builds on previous years' data, and budget figures change throughout the cycle. Typically, each budget reaches through several years, and several budgets are in play—but at different stages—in a single fiscal year.

Balance (Surplus and Deficit)

Most local authorities are required to balance the budget—that is, an operating deficit is prohibited. A balanced budget is a core feature of professional budgeting standards. A budget is in formal balance when revenues equal expenditures for the fiscal year; surplus or deficit is the alternative. Most often, the proposed and adopted budgets are in balance, but only some local authorities and public agencies are required by law, regulation, or formal policy to end the fiscal year in balance. By definition, balance is relevant only to operating budgets. Most often, local authorities with borrowing authority are forbidden by law to issue debt of any kind to cover operating deficits.

Whether the budget is balanced is a critical piece of information, because budgetary balance is a popularly and professionally accepted gauge of financial responsibility and political leadership, as well as a basic goal and potent political issue. Deficits are all too common among local authorities:

> Most local governments themselves tend to fall victim to financial management crises often brought about by uncontrolled expenditure in the face of insecure revenue streams. Most of them consequently run deficit budgets because they are not prepared to take exceptional measures to collect tax arrears or deal with delinquent consumers of their services (Mabogunje 2005: 12).

Overall Balance

How do the effects of an operating deficit in a prior year affect future budgets? The answer is that the local authority must increase revenues by raising taxes or creating other revenue sources or must draw down the financial assets it has accumulated through transfers from reserves. The overall balance after transfers to or from reserves is available for use in future budgets—the financial bottom line—and may be drawn on to balance the budget in a future fiscal year.

Funds

Public budgeting and the political system it finances depend on proper stewardship of public resources. Controls to limit fraud, waste, and misman-agement include publication of the budget as a plan and publication of the financial report showing audited or actual results from implementing the budget. Another control involves dividing up public resources into funds. A fund is a self-balancing set of accounts established by law and dedicated to specific purposes. Local budgets typically segregate central government allocations or transfers by fund according to their intended and required use.

Expert players in the budget process know that money on the move warrants special attention. So, too, do transfers to and from different funds. One control is disclosure.

Revenue Reliance, Central Allocations, and Local Discretion

Central transfers and donor assistance are set aside or earmarked for specific uses (controlled through funds and program requirements), significantly reducing local officials' capacity to make budget choices and local stake-holders' influence over the budget. The local authority's capacity to make budget choices is referred to as *local discretion*. Reliance on own-source revenue—expressed as the percentage of total revenue raised under the local authority—serves as a rough proxy of local discretion: [own-source revenue/total revenue] = local discretion. The caveat here is that some local authorities (such as those in Swaziland) may require ministerial authorization for increases in rates and charges (Sabela 2003: 275).

Little reliance on own-source revenue and lack of discretion is more characteristic of Sub-Saharan localities than localities elsewhere, but the variation among Sub-Saharan localities is significant (Appeah 2005: 5; Habitat 1998; IDASA 2005; Mabogunje 2005). As Mabogunje (2005: 11) notes, "Intergovernmental transfers or subventions from higher levels of government have been important sources of revenue for local governments in most African countries, but their variability and unreliability from year to year put considerable strain and stress on capacity for performance in any one year." The impact of grants and donor assistance also must be considered. As Appeah (2005: 5) notes, "Grants also play an important part in the finance structure of local governments. Grants and donor support usually go to finance major infrastructural development and capacity-building efforts at the municipal level." The resulting lack of reliance on own-source revenue increases uncertainty (Habitat 1998), reduces accountability, and is associated by some observers with corruption.

Local revenue sources also present problems. For example, the property tax depends on expert and impartial administration, collection, and valuation (Bailey 2006: 1–2). Informal properties (those outside the property registration system and without planning permits) compound the problems. Therefore, uncollected and foregone revenues are important to consider. A savvy player in the budget process wants to know the collection rate calculated as the percentage of levied taxes that are actually collected.

Costs and Budget Share

Professional standards call for budgets to show *all* costs relating to the local authority's activities (provision of goods and services). But these costs need not be accounted for in the department or program to which they are related. For example, employees' pension or other benefits may be in a central account, with the result that a budget does not reflect a department or program's actual total costs. (Table 7.3 shows sample employee benefits, termed *social contributions*.) *Direct* costs are those that can be assigned specifically to a particular service or unit; examples include labor, equipment, and materials. *Indirect* costs cannot be assigned directly to one service or related directly to work performed. For full costing, indirect costs must be allocated or prorated.

TABLE 7.3 Excerpts from the Budget of Midvaal, South Africa

		Midvaal Local municipality consolidated estimate						
Vote number	Details	Actual audited 2004/05	Revised budget 2006/08	Full year forecast	Budget 2006/07	Budget 2007/08	Budget 2008/09

Expenditure (1)
Employee/councillors related costs

Employee salaries and allowances

Vote number	Details	Actual audited 2004/05	Revised budget 2006/08	Full year forecast	Budget 2006/07	Budget 2007/08	Budget 2008/09
6000 001 02 0001	Acting allowance	26,286	110,000	1,119	107,500	65,500	68,448
6000 001 02 0002	Basic salaries	34,487,271	40,806,854	35,669,296	43,568,363	45,631,876	47,685,310
6000 001 02 0004	Housing subsidy	834,910	881,328	725,296	865,728	906,707	947,509
6000 001 02 0005	Industrial council levy	13,986	15,420	13,670	15,450	16,177	16,905
6000 001 02 0006	Leave bonus	3,691,353	4,217,826	4,207,993	4,598,797	4,819,539	5,036,419
6000 001 02 0007	Overtime	3,004,964	3,948,650	3,806,368	3,235,000	3,390,280	3,542,843
6000 001 02 0009	Redemption of leave	1,114,452	1,120,561	1,045,179	1,075,615	1,127,245	1,177,971
6000 001 02 0010	Standby allowance	735,408	661,500	699,861	716,500	750,892	784,682
6000 001 02 0011	Telephone allowance	21,000	31,800	194,341	397,644	416,731	435,484
6000 001 02 0012	Traveling allowance	3,066,092	3,614,164	3,033,935	3,436,164	3,601,100	3,763,149
6000 001 02 0013	UIF	344,842	408,067	366,414	435,685	456,598	477,145
Total: Employee salaries and allowances		47,340,564	55,816,170	49,763,472	58,452,446	61,182,645	63,935,864

Employee social contributions

Vote number	Details	Actual audited 2004/05	Revised budget 2006/08	Full year forecast	Budget 2006/07	Budget 2007/08	Budget 2008/09
6000 001 03 0001	Group insurance	262,094	258,529	249,319	272,352	285,425	298,269
6000 001 03 0002	Medical fund	2,953,538	3,720,915	3,093,119	3,686,487	3,863,438	4,037,293

(continued)

TABLE 7.3 Excerpts from the Budget of Midvaal, South Africa (continued)

Vote number	Details	Midvaal Local municipality consolidated estimate					
		Actual audited 2004/05	Revised budget 2006/08	Full year forecast	Budget 2006/07	Budget 2007/08	Budget 2008/09
6000 001 03 0003	Pension fund	7,236,032	8,505,184	7,232,788	9,107,288	9,544,438	9,973,938
Total: employee social contributions		10,451,664	12,484,628	10,575,226	13,066,127	13,693,301	14,309,500
Remuneration of councillors							
6000 001 04 0001	Allowance: council members	1,685,907	2,224,445	1,737,509	2,950,293	3,091,907	3,231,043
6000 001 04 0002	Medical fund: councillors	69,597	172,800	55,539	1,319,440	1,382,773	1,444,998
6000 001 04 0004	Pension fund: councillors	148,121	172,800	131,598	0	0	0
6000 001 04 0005	Telephone allowance: councillors	179,056	155,000	0	169,536	177,674	185,669
Total: remuneration of councillors		2,082,681	2,725,045	1,924,646	4,439,269	4,652,354	4,861,710
Total: employee/councillors related costs		59,874,910	71,025,843	62,263,343	75,957,842	79,528,300	83,107,073

Source: Albert de Klerk, Chief Financial Officer, Midvaal Local Municipality, South Africa.

Different services and programs have different cost structures. The cost structure helps explain spending patterns. Many local authorities provide services that are labor intensive. As a result, personnel costs such as pay and retirement, health, and other benefits make up much of the authorities' operating costs.

Expressing spending categories—on a program or department or on personal services, for example—as a percentage of the total budget is standard practice in budget analysis. This so-called budget share is represented graphically as a piece of the total budget pie and is technique #1 in IDASA's toolkit for quantitative budget analysis (IDASA 2003b). The purpose is to see the local authority's budget priorities. Examining how these percentages change over several fiscal years reveals shifts in budget priorities. Changes in the costs of a particular program or demographic changes in the locality may drive budget change, which budget share highlights.

Budget share represents the local authority's priorities only where the local authority exercises decision-making discretion. If resources are earmarked by central government allocations or donors, or rates and charges are subject to central government approval, budget share is less useful as an indicator of the local authority's priorities.

Spotlighted Concerns

Budgets turn the spotlight on selected concerns. The format and array may be mandated by central law or regulation or developed by the local authority to highlight matters of local interest. The budget in table 7.3 shows a series of fiscal years and draws attention to percentage change over the previous year.[5] The analysis starts with the prior fiscal year as the point of departure for decision making. The National Association of State Budget Officers (NASBO) describes the base budget thus:

> The base budget is essentially the next fiscal year's cost of implementing this fiscal year's . . . decisions . . . The decisions typically reflect long practice and custom, and may at times seem "automatic." In fact, they are not. They are spending decisions. They represent an agreement on what kind of information is to be considered in subsequent decision making and how micro budgeting decisions are to be simplified (NASBO undated: 100).

Some budgets spotlight expenditures by financing source, which emphasizes the revenue structure and constraints as a core concern in decision making. As hints about both politically hot issues and decision-making perspectives, these spotlights are important to flag when reading the budget.

Analytic Constraints and Benefits

A budget's strong point is that it expresses political choices and priorities in currency, so comparisons can be made among different organizations, programs, and services and from one year to the next.[6] The budget's weakness is that it expresses only those factors and concerns that can be counted and expressed in monetary units. Because many important items are not readily translated into dollars, most budgets ignore them. Building budgets on the basis of prepared plans (such as Nairobi's LASDAP and Johannesburg's Integrated Development Plan) represents one part of the solution to this problem. Building budgets on the basis of plans promotes responsiveness to public needs as well as political demand and also speaks to the values of stewardship and accountability.

Some problems are specific to particular budget formats and others are specific to certain local authorities. Some budgets and related documents (such as cost estimates and comprehensive financial reports and audits) may frustrate full costing by failing to allocate indirect costs. Many budgets and financial reports simply ignore the buildup of outstanding legal financial responsibilities (accrued liabilities) such as pensions or other benefits and unpaid bills.[7] They also may disregard the deterioration of facilities for which the local authority is responsible. In summary, many budgets focus on inputs, some on outputs, and few on outcomes.

Although some budgets may spotlight legally binding obligations, other budgets may downplay them. Some emphasize the obligations flowing from central transfers and donor grants or other resources restricted to certain uses before the beginning of the budget cycle. Termed *uncontrollable*, these resources are restricted by law, regulation, or contract. They reduce the scope of current decision making and current discretion.

The broad adoption of professional budgeting and accounting best practices (see annex 7A) is one part of the solution to these problems. Another part of the solution is knowledge about the operation and the organization. For example, the budget may show a decrease in spending on a certain program, but this decrease does not necessarily translate into a program or service cut. Perhaps the decrease is attributable to the transfer of employees who were not contributing to the program but instead performing tasks more closely related to another program or administrative tasks better treated as indirect costs. According to NASBO, "Knowledge of agency history is commonly gained through review of available documents such as audit reports, program evaluation studies, and newspapers, and interviews with knowledgeable individuals" (NASBO undated: 68).

Numbers do not tell the whole budget story. To avoid false conclusions, sound budget analysis draws on both financial and program expertise:

> Each major decision point contains varying blends of technical, analytical, policy, communication, and political elements. Few decisions are solely technical. Most have larger implications than may be obvious (NASBO undated: 99).

Assessment Approaches, Tools, and Techniques

The point of reading a budget is to understand and influence the allocation and distribution of resources. But what do these resources accomplish when the budget is implemented? A budget is a statement of public purposes and policies. But are the policies put into action, and are the purposes met? Are resources wasted, or are operations efficient? What are the results—the benefits and weaknesses—of the programs financed by public resources? These questions of assessment turn the spotlight on accountability and results.

Best practices in budgeting include an assessment element. According to the GFOA (1998), "The budget process consists of activities that encompass the development, implementation, and evaluation of a plan for the provision of services and capital assets"; the fourth principle of its recommended budget practices is to "evaluate performance and make adjustments." This principle takes two steps to realize. First, performance is monitored, measured, and evaluated. Second, the learning is fed back into decision making and operations.

Although the idea of assessment may appear simple, a technically sound approach is difficult and some disagreement is likely. After all, assessment is political by its nature and purpose (as is budgeting) because, if successful, it alters services and resource allocations and distributions. According to the Johannesburg's Integrated Development Plan, "While the process of budgeting is inherently an exercise of political choice (allocating scarce resources among competing needs and priorities), performance information should be one of the decisive factors underlying decisions" (Johannesburg 2006: 55). As the GFOA (1993) notes, "Ultimate decisions on quality of service or 'outcome' measures need to be made by professionals with specialized expertise in the services under consideration, not by accountants."

Internal Assessment Approach

The conventional and now professionally outmoded approach to assessment looks primarily to the organization and its experts for evaluative data.

BOX 7.1 Obsolete Bureaucratic Assessment Technique

1. **Objective: gain in full-time positions over time**
   Establish number of authorized positions or funded permanent positions in current and for four prior years. (Use full-time equivalents.)
   Repeat procedure for selected comparable peer programs and agencies.
   Compute percentage change over five-year period for entire jurisdiction and for each selected agency or program.
   Compare agency or program to (1) overall change and (2) peer comparison units.
2. **Objective: gain in budget resources over time**
   Show agency or program budget total in current and for four prior fiscal years.
   Repeat procedure for selected comparable peer programs and agencies.
   Compute percentage and dollar changes over five-year period for entire jurisdiction and for each selected agency or program.
   Compare your agency or program to overall change and peer comparison units.

Source: Carol W. Lewis 2006. Reprinted by permission.

It may use the tools of cost accounting, financial analysis and reporting, and compliance auditing, among others. Box 7.1 shows one approach that emphasizes budget share and organizational or program growth. By drawing on available expertise and requiring relatively little time, this approach is efficient in a narrow, technical sense. By ignoring possible changes outside the organization and focusing exclusively on its own resources, the approach is both bureaucratic and inadequate to the complex task of modern management and to a dynamic budget process. When used alone, this internal, bureaucratic assessment technique simply is obsolete.

Financial Measures

A simple count of nominal currency has little meaning. Is the amount too little or too much? Is the growth (or decline) responsible or exorbitant? How do decision makers decide whether an amount of money is trivial or significant, affordable or extravagant?

Financial measures often are used to give meaning to budgetary and financial data. By standardizing budgetary data against another factor or sets of factors, analysts derive meaning, often stated as a ratio or percentage, from the relationship. Box 7.2 lists six types of conventional measures relevant to budgetary decision making and analysis. Different measures express different relationships. Because no single measure tells the whole story or answers all questions for policy makers, current best practice calls for use of varied budgetary and financial measures. Varied types and sources of information reduce the likelihood of error and distortion and increase confidence in the interpretation. Unfortunately, multiple sources of information are costly and trade simplicity for complexity.

BOX 7.2 Common Budget Measures

Budget Share
Measures function or category (activity, agency, and revenues or expenditures) as percentage of total revenues or expenditures
Shows relative priority within government (and excludes private sector activity); change in share shows shifting governmental priorities
Ignores amount, size of the budget, growth of budget, and size of economy

Share of Gross Domestic Product
Expresses function or category as a percentage of economic activity
Shows relative priority in society
Implies that the use is preferred to alternative uses in private and public sectors, but decision makers can allocate only the resources available to them; public budgeting concerns alternative uses among public resources

Per Capita
Measures function or category relative to residential population
Ignores impact on service demands of in-commuters, tourists, unofficial residents, and others

Constant Currency
Controls for price change; allows for inflation and deflation

Annual Arrays, Percent Change, and Rate of Growth
Uses history as the standard

Other Common Measures
Tax impact, usually on own-source revenue
Tax base, indicating ability to raise revenue
Wealth and income measures, indicating ability to pay
Political preferences, including legislative votes, citizen surveys, and demand indicators

Source: Adapted from Lewis (2003).

Financial Condition

When data are shown over time (preferably a minimum of five years), the trend indicates financial condition or fiscal sustainability. Financial condition "refers to a local governmental entity's ability to provide services at the level and quality that are required for the health, safety, and welfare of the community, and that its citizens desire" (Florida 2005: 1). The three aspects of financial condition are (1) financial solvency (a government's ability to generate enough cash to pay bills over 30 to 60 days), (2) budgetary solvency (a government's ability to generate adequate revenues over the budgetary period to meet expenditures and avoid deficits), and (3) long-run solvency (the long-run balance between revenues and costs, including incurred debt and accrued liabilities).[8] According to Groves and Valente (1994: 1–2), "financial condition refers to a government's ability to (1) maintain existing service levels; (2) withstand local and regional economic disruptions; and (3) meet the demands of natural growth, decline, and change."

The International City/County Management Association (ICMA) developed the financial indicators approach (Groves and Valente 1994; Nollenberger 2003); the GFOA similarly uses key financial indicators (Brown 1993, 1996). Although widely adapted for use by local public entities, the financial indicators approach has several shortcomings. First, it relies on ratios and five-year trends, meaning that comparisons are with the local authority's own history.[9] Second, it often uses per capita measures (see box 7.2 and table 7.4). Third, no single indicator drives the findings. The approach rests on the following principle: "No single financial indicator should be used to make conclusions regarding the entity's financial condition" (Florida 2005: 4; see also Hartford 2001). Table 7.4 details 13 financial indicators selected for analysis in Florida; the ICMA model employs 42 indicators of financial condition.

TABLE 7.4 Florida's Financial Indicators for Local Governments

Indicator	Warning trend
1. Unreserved fund balance + unrestricted net assets (constant $)	Declining results may indicate that the local government could have difficulty maintaining a stable tax and revenue structure or adequate level of services. Deficits may indicate a financial emergency.
2. Unreserved fund balance/ total expenditures	Percentages decreasing over time may indicate unstructured budgets that could lead to

(continued)

TABLE 7.4 Florida's Financial Indicators for Local Governments (*continued*)

Indicator	Warning trend
	future budgetary problems for the local government even if the current fund balance is positive.
3. Cash and investments/ current liabilities	Percentages decreasing over time may indicate that the local government has overextended itself in the long run or may be having difficulty raising the cash needed to meet its current needs.
4. Cash and investments/total expenditures or total operating expenses divided by current liabilities	
5. Current liabilities/total revenues or total operating revenues	Increasing results may indicate liquidity problems, deficit spending, or both.
6. Long-term debt (constant $)/population	Results increasing over time may indicate that the local government has a decreasing level of flexibility in how resources are allocated or decreasing ability to pay its long-term debt.
7. Excess of revenues over (under) expenditures/ total revenues	Decreasing surpluses or increasing deficits may indicate that current revenues are not supporting current expenditures.
8. Operating income (loss)/ total operating revenues	Decreasing income or increasing losses may indicate that current revenues are not supporting current expenses.
9. Intergovernmental revenues/ total revenues or total operating revenues	Percentages increasing over time indicate a greater risk assumed by the local government due to increased dependence on outside revenues.
10. Unreserved fund balances or unrestricted net assets/total revenues or total operating revenues	Decreasing results may indicate a reduction in the local government's ability to withstand financial emergencies or its ability to fund capital purchases without having to borrow.
11. Total revenues (constant $)/population	Decreasing results indicate that the local government may be unable to maintain existing service levels with current revenue sources.
12. Debt service/total expenditures	Percentages increasing over time may indicate declining flexibility the local government has to respond to economic changes.
13. Total expenditures (constant $)/population	Increasing results may indicate that the cost of providing services is outstripping the local government's ability to pay (i.e., the local government may be unable to maintain services at current levels).

Source: Excerpted from Florida 2005.

External Assessment Techniques and Tools

Current best practices call for varied and more useful assessment techniques, tools, and measures. "Non-financial performance data, including performance targets, should be presented for expenditure programs where practicable" (OECD 2001: 4). Exemplifying this approach, the Alaska Progress Report uses 49 measures classified as education, economy, environment, communities, and government. For education, the report argues,

> No single indicator adequately measures student performance. Dropout rates roughly indicate high school participation and completion. The best picture emerges from looking at a broad selection of factors such as attendance, test scores and the percentage of students who go on to college (Osterkamp 2006: 4).

External assessment turns attention to what is happening outside the organization. Although some of its elements date back many decades (for example, performance budgeting and management by objectives), the external assessment approach is especially important in the current development context, which is marked by donors, lenders, rapid social change, and infrastructure expansion, as well as by concerns with accountability, transparency, and civic engagement. A review of selected initiatives strengthens the link between assessment and development.[10]

Citizen Engagement

Techniques for involving citizens run from public meetings to participation in decision making through commissions, boards, and independent watchdog groups such as IDASA's Africa Budget Project. Johannesburg has developed an elaborate community consultation process as part of its performance management system (Johannesburg: 2006). The Internet has opened new opportunities. E-government provides a new tool for seeking citizen input, but a citizen-initiated tool for expression has emerged in Nairobi: http://bankelele.blogspot.com.

For local authorities in Kenya, "Monitoring and evaluation of the LAS-DAP process and the consequent implementation of the identified projects should be participatory, involving the local authority and the community" (Kenya 2005: 30). "The community . . . should be involved during the project's evaluation. This will also go a long way in improving accountability and transparency in the utilisation [sic] of public funds" (Kenya 2005: 32).

Citizen satisfaction with government performance often is solicited through public opinion polls, focus groups, and expert panels. These tools' usefulness depends on sound design, careful implementation, and meaningful assessment of public views (Charter Oak 2000, 2002). On a cautionary note, the OECD learned that

> Consultation, and even active participation in decision making does not mean that governments should surrender their responsibility for making final decisions. . . . And openness in itself does not necessarily improve governance, nor does it override all other public values. It should be balanced against other values of efficiency, equity, and responsibility (OECD 2005: 3).

Performance Measures

Evaluating service and financial performance and making adjustments are an accepted best practice (GFOA 2000; OECD 2001).[11] Performance measurement supplies quantifiable indicators of performance:

> Ideally, these indicators reflect the success or failure of an organization's progress toward its overall mission and align the incentives to enable sustainable success. Performance measures can also apply to tactical situations, providing government administrators with a "scorecard" of key performance metrics at an operational level (GFOA 2003).

In traditional use, performance measurement stressed the value of efficiency and addressed the question of what localities were getting for their resources. Today, performance measurement provides "*measures* or *indicators* of the volume, quality, efficiency and outcomes of public services," and its products "are yardsticks we can use to figure out if government is working well or poorly, or somewhere in between" (GASB undated). Performance measurement can incorporate seven types of measures: input and cost; activity/process; output; outcome; efficiency, quality and customer satisfaction; explanatory; and benchmarks. Input, output, and efficiency measures are the most common. Figure 7.2 features input, output, efficiency, and effectiveness measures.

Measures of volume, quality, efficiency, and effectiveness are among the basic building blocks of a performance management system. Based on subjective (for example, satisfaction levels) or objective data, measures should be quantifiable, valid, relatively inexpensive to operationalize, tailored specifically to the program and community, and replicable over time. Although many measures are output measures that center on what the agency or program is producing, outcome or effectiveness measures have been developed for a wide range of services and infrastructure projects (for example, Ammons

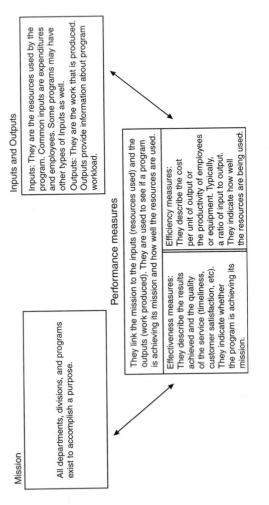

Mission

All departments, divisions, and programs exist to accomplish a purpose.

Inputs and Outputs

Inputs: They are the resources used by the program. Common inputs are expenditures and employees. Some programs may have other types of Inputs as well.
Outputs: They are the work that is produced. Outputs provide information about program workload.

Performance measures

They link the mission to the inputs (resources used) and the outputs (work produced). They are used to see if a program is achieving its mission and how well the resources are used.

Effectiveness measures: They describe the results achieved and the quality of the service (timeliness, customer satisfaction, etc). They indicate whether the program is achieving its mission.

Efficiency measures: They describe the cost per unit of output or the productivity of employees or equipment. Typically, a ratio of input to output. They indicate how well the resources are being used.

Source: Raleigh undated: 3.

FIGURE 7.2 Performance Measures

1995: 6–8). Measures should be both financial and nonfinancial. As the OECD (2001: 4) notes, "Non-financial performance data, including performance targets, should be presented for expenditure programmes where practicable."

Each jurisdiction is expected to develop its own measures for its own functions, missions, and strategies. Box 7.3 presents examples of performance measures.

BOX 7.3 Examples of Performance Measures

These examples of performance measures are from the Raleigh, North Carolina, police department.

Inputs
Sworn personnel per 1,000 population: Total number of sworn personnel divided by (total population divided by 1,000). Sworn personnel include all Park Police and sworn officers funded by city appropriations and federal and state grants.

Outputs
Community meetings and activities held: Total number of community events and meetings that officers attended.
Arrests made: Total number of physical arrests, citations to court, and summons to court issued.
Calls for service: Total number of calls for service logged to Raleigh officers by the Emergency Communications Center.
Accidents investigated: Total number of accident reports completed.
Special events handled: Total number of special events handled (parades, demonstrations, pickets, and sports events).
Reports filed by telephone response officers: Total number of case reports, not requiring an officer at the scene, that are completed by civilian telephone-response officers at the police desk.

Effectiveness
Average response time for emergency priority calls: The average time lapse for an officer to receive a call for service and arrive on the scene of a call.
Clearance rate for Part I offenses against persons: The percentage of homicides, rapes, robberies, and assaults that were cleared by arrest or exceptionally cleared.
Exceptionally cleared cases are cases in which there is sufficient evidence to prosecute an individual but the complainant or the court declined to prosecute.
Clearance rate for Part I offenses against property: The percentage of burglaries, auto thefts, and larcenies that were cleared by arrest or exceptionally cleared.

(Box continues on the following page.)

Exceptionally cleared cases are cases in which there is sufficient evidence to prosecute an individual but the complainant or the court declined to prosecute.

Recovery rate for stolen property: The percentage of stolen property that was recovered.

Compliance rate with accreditation standards: The percentage of applicable Commission on Accreditation for Law Enforcement Agencies' standards with which the department complies.

Efficiency

Training cost per police recruit: Cost for recruit training divided by the number of recruits trained. Costs include salaries and fringe benefits, personal equipment, supplies, and materials.

Calls for service per officer: Total number of calls logged to Raleigh officers by the Emergency Communications Center divided by the number of regular beat officers.

Source: Raleigh undated: 38.

According to GFOA (2000, 2001), best practice calls for performance measures to be used for budgetary decision making. According to GASB (undated), "Performance measures can be an important tool for understanding government performance, but without a process for using this information, it is only of limited value." An evaluation of OECD budget projects in Tanzania states that the ultimate objective is "to ensure that resources are used effectively and efficiently in the implementation of strategic priorities, and performance budgeting is relevant at this level" (Anderson and others 2000: 4).

To readily feed into decision making, performance measures should be developed within a performance management framework, as in Kenya (2005) and Johannesburg (2006). "A municipality's performance management system entails a framework that describes and represents how the municipality's cycle and processes of performance planning, monitoring, measurement, review, reporting and improvement will be conducted, organised and managed, including determining the roles of the different role players" (Ketel and van der Molen 2006). Figure 7.3 illustrates a generic framework of a type referred to as a balanced scorecard model.[12]

Responding to citizen input, shifting circumstances, and changing goals, performance measurement is necessarily dynamic—and difficult. Many organizations experienced with use of performance measures for

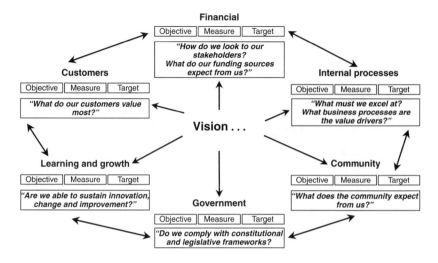

Source: Ketel and van der Molen 2006.

FIGURE 7.3 Balanced Scorecard Model

budgets admit that "[g]overnment performance is characteristically difficult to assess and, as a result, precise resource allocations are difficult to make" (GFOA 2003). As measures and systems evolve, flaws and even errors may emerge. One practitioner cautions, "Don't let the perfect stop you from the possible" (Pierce 2006: 39). The difficulties associated with performance measurement do not appear to have diminished its popularity; in May 2006 a search of the United Nations Online Network in Public Administration and Finance (http://www.unpan.org) for performance measures drew more than 7,500 results.

Benchmarks

Making comparisons with peer organizations or programs and using the results to improve performance is termed benchmarking (Ammons 1996). According to IPF Benchmarking in the United Kingdom,

> Benchmarking provides the evidence to answer the questions at the heart of Comprehensive Performance Assessment: How are we performing? Are we performing better year on year? How does our performance compare with our peer organisations? Can we learn anything from other organisations? (Institute of Public Finance 2007).

In its program for assessing the financial condition of local government, the state of Florida finds that

> Benchmarks provide a means of comparing financial indicator results for a local governmental entity to those produced for similar entities. Developing benchmarks involves determining benchmark groups (i.e., grouping similar local governmental entities together based on various financial and nonfinancial factors) and, for each benchmark group, calculating a benchmark for each financial indicator. Methodologies for calculating the benchmarks include using a fixed benchmark value by taking the average or median of the financial indicator calculations for the benchmark group or using a range of benchmark values selected from the benchmark group (Florida 2005: 3).

This tool obviously depends on collaboration among peer or related organizations. Potential users must view it as an opportunity for improvement rather than as a threat.

Conclusion

Budgeting is dynamic, and best practices are evolving to meet new challenges in changing societies (OECD 2005). Therefore, best practices transposed to the development context in Sub-Saharan Africa require continuous adaptation, not simple importation or imitation with a fixed and final destination in view. Although budgeting demands some technical expertise, its core is political. Politics is part of the institutional, legal, and social framework of budgeting. The successful transformation of budgeting in a development context demands the capacity to understand and work with political and administrative systems.

Local budgeting in Sub-Saharan Africa confronts complex pressures, the most formidable of which is resource scarcity. Therefore, realistic assessment approaches are critical. Given increasing decentralization and democratization and increasing demands for transparency and accountability in Sub-Saharan African countries, external approaches and especially citizen engagement techniques deserve attention. Best budget practices transposed to and developed in Sub-Saharan Africa are tailored adaptations of lessons learned and shared.

Annex 7A: Selected Internet Resources for Best Budget Practices and Innovations

United Cities and Local Governments of Africa on financial and other concerns: http://www.uclga.co.za.

Government Finance Officers Association on best practices in budgeting: http://www.gfoa. org/services/nacslb.

National Association of Budget Officers' training program on budgeting in the United States: http://www.nasbo.or/trainingProgra.php.

OECD's best practices for budget transparency: http://www.olis.oecd.org/olis/ 2000doc.nsf/ 87fae4004d4fa67ac125685d005300b3/c125692700623b74c1256a4d005c23be/ $FILE/JT00107731.PDF.

Database on budget practices from the OECD/World Bank survey: http://ocde.dyndns.org

OECD policy brief on governing for performance: http://www.oecd.org/dataoecd/ 52/44/33873341.pdf.

Africa Social Accountability Action Forum (ASAAF) on civic participation in subnational budgeting: http://www.asaaf.org.zw/casestud1.htm.

Institute for Democracy in South Africa (IDASA), its Africa Budget Project, and its online newsletter, *Africa Budget Watch*: http://www.idasa.org.za.

Professional association of municipal finance officers: http://www.imfo.co.za.

Overview of accountability from a lender/donor perspective: http://info.worldbank.org/ etools/docs/library/92650/assessing/pdf/pefa_pres.pdf.

Samples of city budgets: http://www.joburg.org.za/finance and http://www.capetown. gov.za/budget.

Clearinghouse for performance measurement (www.seagov.org) and systems of performance monitoring and reporting (http://www.seagov.org/sea_gasb_project).

Governmental Accounting Standards Board (1994) on financial and nonfinancial performance reporting ("Service Efforts and Accomplishments Reporting"): http://www. seagov.org/sea_gasb_project/con_stmt_two.shtml.

British performance assessment approach: http://www.audit-commission.gov.uk; http:// www.audit-commission.gov.uk/performance; and http://www.local-pi-library.gov. uk/ thelibrary.html.

Checklists for monitoring of local services (in Kenya): http://www.localgovernment.go.ke/ LASDAP%20Guidelines%20(MLG%20Manual%202).pdf.

Performance management (in Johannesburg): http://www.joburgarchive.co.za/2006/ pdfs/2006_idp_draft.pdf.

Integration of budget and performance in U.S. federal government: http://www.white-house.gov/omb/memoranda/m02-06_addendum.html, http://www.whitehouse. gov/results, and http://www.whitehouse.gov/results/agenda/ scorecard.html.

Assessment initiative by an independent public interest organization in the United States (at 2005–06 Alaska Progress Report): http://www.alaska2020.org/reports.htm.

International Monetary Fund principles of fiscal transparency: http://www.imf.org/ external/np/fad/trans/code.htm.

International Monetary Fund resources on international standards: http://www.imf.org/ external/np/fad/trans/site.htm.

Notes

1. See Kenya (2005: 40) for a sample public notice about calculating the resource envelope.
2. See NASBO (undated) module #4 on the impact of economic factors on budgeting.

3. See National Treasury of South Africa (2005) on implementation of the Municipal Finance Management Act No. 56 of 2003 and Generally Recognised Accounting Practice in South Africa. See OECD (2002) on models of public budgeting and accounting reform.
4. "All fiscal reports referred to in these Best Practices should be made publicly available. This includes the availability of all reports free of charge on the Internet" (OECD 2001: 9).
5. Cape Town's service element version at http://www.capetown.gov.za/budget is another example.
6. Accordingly, budgets must allow for changes over time in the value of money—inflation—and express current resources and costs in real terms. One resource on the methodology is the U.S. Bureau of Labor Statistics, especially the overview and frequently asked questions at http://www.bls.gov/cpi/home.htm.
7. Uncollected rates and charges also need attention. "The policy of full cost recovery for services in view of the declining purchasing power of people is reflected in the huge unsettled bills for utilities in African cities" (Appeah 2005: 7).
8. For a long-term fiscal plan emphasizing "fiscal sustainability," see http://www.toronto.ca/finance/long_term_fiscal_plan.htm. For long-term financial planning, see http://www.gfoa.org/rcc/services-fas.shtml.
9. Benchmarking deals with this problem and, for example, Florida (2005: 4) combines both.
10. Entire books have been written about assessing performance, including, for example, Ammons (1995, 1996) and Dilulio, Garvey, and Kettl (1993). Entire Web sites are devoted to the topic, including http://www.unpan.org/globalforums.asp, http://www.resultsaccountability.com, and http://www.seagov.org.
11. See also http://www.gfoa.org/services/rp/budget/budget-performance-management.pdf and GFOA (2000), principle IV and examples numbered 6.4.
12. A scorecard involves performance metrics at an operational level (GFOA 2003). For a how-to guide on the balanced scorecard, see Niven and Mann 2003.

References

Ammons, David N., ed. 1995. *Accounting for Performance: Measurement and Monitoring in Local Government.* Washington, DC: International City/County Management Association.
———. 1996. *Municipal Benchmarks: Assessing Local Performance and Establishing Community Standards.* Thousand Oaks, CA: Sage.
Anderson, Guy, Suzanne Flynn, Philip Harding, and Stewart Maugham. 2000. "Government Accounting and Interim Budget Development Projects in Tanzania." SIDA Evalution 00/14, OECD, Stockholm. http://www.oecd.org/dataoecd/49/29/35190386.pdf.
Appeah, Bernard J. 2005. "Local Government in Africa and the Challenge of Funding and Financing." Presented at the Founding Congress of the United Cities and Local Governments of Africa, Tshwane (Pretoria), South Africa, May 15–18. http://www.uclga.co.za/reports.html.

Bailey, Candice. 2006. "Blitz on R4.5bn Rates Debt." *Cape Argus*, April 5, 1–2.

Brown, Ken W. 1993. "The 10-Point Test of Financial Condition: Toward an Easy-to-Use Assessment Tool for Smaller Cities." *Government Finance Review* (December): 21–26.

———. 1996. "Trends in Key Ratios Using the GFOA Indicators Databases, 1989–1993." *Government Finance Review* (December): 30–34.

Center for Budget Priorities. 2004. "Opening Budgets to Public Understanding and Debate: Results from 36 Countries." International Budget Project, Center for Budget Priorities, Washington, DC. http://www.internationalbudget.org/openbudgets/ Summary.pdf.

Charter Oak Group. 2000. *Customer Satisfaction Handbook*. Glastonbury, CT: Charter Oak Group. http://www.charteroakgroup.com/pdf/csHandbook2.pdf.

———. 2002. "Quality Community Action Association System: Self-Assessment." Charter Oak Group, Glastonbury, CT. http://www.charteroakgroup.com/pdf/selfassessment_ Rev2.1.pdf.

Claassens, Marritt, and Albert van Zyl, eds. 2005. *Budget Transparency and Participation II, Nine African Case Studies*. Cape Town, South Africa: Albert Institute for Democracy in South Africa.

Dilulio, John, Jr., Gerald Garvey, and Donald F. Kettl. 1993. *Improving Government Performance: An Owner's Manual*. Washington, DC: Brookings Institution.

Florida, State of. 2005. "Local Governmental Entity Financial Condition Assessment Procedures." Auditor General. http://sun6.dms.state.fl.us/audgen/pages/pdf_files/ fca%20 procedures.pdf.

GASB (Governmental Accounting Standards Board). Undated. "Performance Management for Government." http://72.3.167.245/aboutpmg.

GFOA (Government Finance Officers Association). 1993. "Public Policy Statement on Service Efforts and Accomplishments Reporting." http://www.gfoa.org/services/- policy/ gfoapp1.shtml#plact6.

———. 1998, updated 2000. "Best Practices in Public Budgeting." CD–rom.

———. 2000. "Best Practices in Public Budgeting." http://www.gfoa.org/services/nacslb.

———. 2001. *Recommended Practices for State and Local Governments*. Chicago: GFOA.

———. 2003. "Performance Measurement." Management Consulting Services. http:// www.gfoa.org/rcc/services-fas.shtml.

———. Undated. "Awards Criteria. Distinguished Budget Presentation Awards Program." Government Finance Officers Association. http://www.gfoa.org/forms/documents/ BudgetCriteriaExplanations.pdf.

Groves, Sanford M., and Maureen G. Valente. 1994. *Evaluating Financial Condition*. Washington, DC: International City/County Management Association.

Habitat (United Nations Centre for Human Settlements). 1998. *Financing Cities for Sustainable Development*. Nairobi: Habitat.

Hartford, Connecticut. 2001. "Financial Trends." http://ci.hartford.ct.us/budget/ adopt- edfy2000-01/Trends/main-trends.htm.

IDASA (Institute for Democracy in South Africa). 2003a. "Budget Blinds or Budget Windows." Africa Budget Project. http://www.idasa.org.za/gbOutputFiles.asp? Write Content=Y&RID=555.

———. 2003b. "Quantitative Budget Analysis." PowerPoint presentation. http://www. idasa.org.za.

———. 2004. "What Is a Government Budget?" http://www.idasa.org.za/index.asp?
page=output_details.asp%3FRID%3D680%26oplang%3Den%26PID%3D18%26
OTID%3D37.
———. 2005. "Local Government in Budget 2005." Budget Brief 154, IDASA, Cape Town.
International Monetary Fund. 2001. Code of Good Practices on Fiscal Transparency.
http://www.imf.org/external/np/fad/trans/code.htm.
IPF (Institute of Public Finance). 2007. "CIPFA Benchmarking Clubs 2007, Corporate
Services." Brochure. http://www.ipfbenchmarking.net/pdf/Benchmarking%20
Brochure%20Nov%2006.pdf.
Johannesburg, South Africa. 2005. "Integrated Development Plan 2005/06." http://www.
joburg-archive.co.za/2005/pdfs/IDP-Chapter10.pdf.
———. 2006. "Integrated Development Plan 2006/11." http://www.joburg-archive.co.za/
2006/pdfs/2006_idp_draft.pdf.
Kenya, Republic of. 2005. "Guidelines for the Preparation, Implementation and Monitor-
ing of Local Authority Service Delivery Action Plan (LASDAP)." Ministry of Local
Government, Nairobi. http://www.localgovernment.go.ke/LASDAP%20Guidelines
%20(MLG%20Manual%202).pdf.
Ketel, Belinda, and Karel van der Molen. 2006. "Performance Management in Local
Government." Paper presented to the 10th International Winelands Conference,
Stellenbosch, South Africa, April 5–7.
Kumar, K., and S. Moodley. 2003. "The Theory and Practice of Local Government
Budgeting." In *Local Government Financing and Development in Southern Africa*, ed.
P. S. Reddy, D. Sing, and S. Moodley, 66–85. Cape Town, South Africa: Oxford
University Press Southern Africa.
Lewis, Carol W. 2003. "Updating State and Local Financial Indicators." *Municipal Finance
Journal* 24 (1): 17–35.
Mabogunje, Akin L. 2005. "The State of Local Government in Africa." Paper presented at
the UCLGA Founding Congress, Tshwane, South Africa, http://www.uclga.co.za/
reports.html.
NASBO (National Association of Budget Officers). Undated. "NASBO Training Curriculum."
http://www.nasbo.org.
National Treasury of South Africa. 2005. *Accounting Standards Implementation*. Municipal
Management Finance Act Circular 18, June 23. http://www.imfo.co.za/Documents/
AccountingStandardsCircular6July2005.pdf.
Niven, Paul R., and Steven V. Mann. 2003. *Balanced Scorecard Step-by-Step for Government
and Nonprofit Agencies*. Hoboken, NJ: Wiley.
Nollenberger, Karl. 2003. *Evaluating Financial Condition: A Handbook for Local Government*,
4th ed. Washington, DC: International City/County Management Association.
Obasanjo, Olusegun. 2005. "Keynote address by His Excellency, President Olusegun
Obasanjo GCFR, Chairman, African Union, at the Founding Congress of the United
Cities and Local Government of Africa (UCLGA)." Address to the founding Congress
of the United Cities and Local Government of Africa, Tshwane (Pretoria), South
Africa, May 15–18. http://www.uclgafrica.org/Documents/OfficialDocuments/
Keynote%20address%20by%20His%20Excellency%20Olusegun%20Obasanjo%2
0ENG.doc.
OECD (Organisation for Economic Co-operation and Development). 2001. "Best Practices
for Budget Transparency." Report JT00107731, OECD, Paris. http://www.olis.

oecd.org/olis/2000doc.nsf/87fae4004d4fa67ac125685d005300b3/c125692700623b7
4c1256a4d005c23be/$FILE/JT00107731.PDF.

———. 2002. "Models of Public Budgeting and Accounting Reform." *OECD Journal on Budgeting* 2 (Supplement 1), 3–354. http: // www.oecd.org/dataoecd/30/0/33684121.pdf.

———. 2005. "Public Sector Modernisation: The Way Forward." http://www.oecd.org/dataoecd/40/33/35654629.pdf.

OECD and World Bank. 2003. "Results of the Survey on Budget Practices and Procedures." http://ocde.dyndns.org.

Osterkamp, Ken. 2006. "Alaska Progress Report 2005–2006." Alaska 20/20, Anchorage. http://www.alaska2020.org/pdfs/2006/APR_2005-06.pdf.

Performance Measurement for Government. Undated. "Clearinghouse for performance measurement sponsored by the Governmental Accounting Standards Board." http://www.seagov.org.

Pierce, Karla. 2006. "Nine Habits of Effective Data-Driven Performance Management." *Government Finance Review* 22 (3): 36–40.

Raleigh, North Carolina. Undated. "Performance Indicators, Fiscal Year 2005–2006." http://www.raleighnc.gov/publications/Administrative_Services/Budget/2005-2006_Performance_Indicators.pdf.

Sabela, T. R. 2003. "Local Government Financing in Swaziland." In *Local Government Financing and Development in Southern Africa*, ed. P. S. Reddy, D. Sing, and S. Moodley, 273–83. Cape Town, South Africa: Oxford University Press Southern Africa.

UNECA (United Nations Economic Commission for Africa), Committee on Human Development and Civil Society. 2005. "Participation and Partnerships for Improving Development and Governance in Africa." Issues paper E/ECA/CHDCS.3/2, Addis Ababa, Ethiopia. http://www.uneca.org/chdcs/chdcs3/Issues_Paper.pdf.

Wamwangi, Kinuthia. 2004. "Sub-National Experience of Civic Participation in Policymaking and Budgetary Processes: The Nairobi Case Study." Africa Social Accountability Action Forum, Harare, Zimbabwe. http://www.asaaf.org.zw/casestud1.htm.

8

Local Budget Process

DANIEL R. MULLINS

L ocal budget systems, processes, and structures within and among nations reflect historical tradition and diversity in culture, capacity, national governance, and institutions. Thus, no single model of local government budgeting is best. That said, all effective subnational budget systems must contain certain elements that advance the three key objectives of public expenditure management: fiscal discipline/expenditure control, prioritized/strategic resource allocation, and operational (managerial) efficiency/effectiveness (Schiavo-Campo and Tommasi 1999: chapter 1).

Prescriptions for effectiveness include systems and processes that emphasize

- transparency in the definition of roles and responsibilities and decision making, the availability of information, openness of the budget process, and assurances of budgetary integrity
- comprehensiveness in the incorporation of all revenues and expenditures and full accounting of all budgetary transactions
- processes and methods to establish policy and priorities, including an outward-looking fiscal framework, focus on service outputs and outcomes, and a classification system that links expenditures to organizational units and purposes
- expenditure planning based on established priorities, relating spending to service levels and allowing flexibility in the use of resource inputs

- managerial efficiency supported by accountability for service levels and outputs and discretion in the relative use of inputs
- accountability and control reinforced by comprehensiveness; prioritization; and systematic budget and expenditure reviews, execution controls, and post-execution reporting and auditing (Mikesell and Mullins 2001: 564)

Each of these interrelated elements supports the accomplishment of the other elements.

The functions important at the subnational level in a developing context are the fundamental functions of all budgeting systems. According to Schick (2004: 84–85), these include

- establishing a fiscal framework that is sustainable over the medium term and beyond
- allocating resources to programs on the basis of governmental priorities and program effectiveness
- operating government and delivering public services efficiently
- ensuring that the budget reflects citizen preferences
- ensuring that spending units are accountable for their actions

In defining the essential elements of the local budget process, the National Advisory Council on State and Local Budgeting emphasizes decision making related to an assessment of needs and priorities, programmatic planning and management strategies directed at goal achievement, a process for constructing and adopting a consistent and realistic budget, and mechanisms to make adjustments and monitor and evaluate performance (see box 8.1) (NACSLB 1998). This implies the ability to make meaningful policy and managerial choices.

This chapter focuses on the broader context of the local budget process. The process is considered from the perspective of the most critical issues that shape it and its outcomes: the level and distribution of local authority, the importance of the local budget in a multitiered intergovernmental framework, coordination and cooperation mechanisms, planning and priority setting, participatory processes, and accountability and responsiveness.

Intergovernmental Framework

A nation's intergovernmental framework sets the stage for local autonomy and authority and, thus, defines the parameters within which local budgetary

---

BOX 8.1 Twelve Elements of the Budget Process

According to the National Advisory Council on State and Local Budgeting, the budget process "consists of activities that encompass the development, implementation, and evaluation of a plan for the provision of services and capital assets." The process includes a "long-term perspective" linked to "organizational goals," focuses on "results and outcomes," involves and communicates with stakeholders, and provides incentives to management and employees.

The twelve elements of the budget process fall into four categories.

The process should establish broad goals to guide government decision making as follows:

- Assess community needs, priorities, challenges, and opportunities.
- Identify opportunities and challenges for government services, capital assets, and management.
- Develop and disseminate broad goals.

The process should develop approaches to achieve goals as follows:

- Adopt financial policies.
- Develop programmatic, operating, and capital policies and plans.
- Develop programs and services that are consistent with policies and plans.
- Develop management strategies.

The process should develop a budget consistent with approaches to achieve goals as follows:

- Develop a process for preparing and adopting a budget.
- Develop and evaluate financial options.
- Make choices necessary to adopt a budget.

The process should evaluate performance and make adjustments as follows:

- Monitor, measure, and evaluate performance.
- Make adjustments as needed.

Source: NACSLB 1998: 3, 5.

---

processes function. This intergovernmental structure may be the single most influential element in defining the local budget process and its significance.

Scope of Autonomy

Local jurisdictions without expenditure and revenue authority and without discretion for use of funds are almost certainly hampered in their capacity to effectively budget. The scope of centralization and decentralization is, therefore, an important antecedent factor in local budget processes.

Decentralization implies meaningful choice and the ability to tailor local public sector policy and service delivery to the needs of local populations, as well as incentives for an effective, efficient, and locally accountable public sector. At the same time, mechanisms must be established to effectively link national and subnational planning and budgeting processes. This coordination becomes a defining element of subnational budgeting.

Decentralization's form is important. Most experts recognize three forms: political decentralization,[1] administrative decentralization, and fiscal decentralization (Gurger and Shah 2000; Rondinelli 1999; Tanzi 1995; von Braun and Grote 2000). Political decentralization "often requires constitutional or statutory reforms, development of pluralistic political parties, strengthening of legislatures, creation of local political units, and encouragement of effective public interest groups" (Rondinelli 1999: 2). It strengthens transparency, policy setting, expenditure planning, managerial efficiency, and accountability. Administrative decentralization redistributes authority and responsibility for public services among levels of government. *Deconcentration,* a weaker form of decentralization, shifts administrative responsibilities to subordinate units in regions, districts, field offices, or local administrations under supervision of the central government ministries. *Delegation* transfers functions and decision making to semiautonomous organizations accountable to, but not controlled by, the central government. *Devolution* transfers decision-making, finance, and management authority usually to local units with elected executives and legislative bodies with independent fiscal authority. It may have positive effects on local resource allocation, but lesser democratic processes will likely limit transparency and accountability.

Effective and meaningful political decentralization and administrative devolution require adequate revenue and expenditure authority. Without such authority, local decision making (including local budgeting) is meaningless. Fiscal decentralization requires discretionary access of subnational jurisdictions to significant revenue instruments (within a properly designed intergovernmental fiscal framework). This access—coupled with capacity to prioritize and make decisions regarding budgetary expenditures, use of factor inputs, and program operations—provides for meaningful local decision authority. Effective local budgeting is highly dependent on effective intergovernmental systems, and its prescripts are intertwined with prescripts of decentralization.

The beginning point for local budgeting varies substantially. In Africa, local choice (and, therefore, the significance of local budgeting and the local budgetary process) is greatest in South Africa and Uganda, followed by Kenya and Ghana. These nations couple significant political decentralization

TABLE 8.1 Profile of Decentralization in Africa

Country	Political decentralization	Administrative decentralization	Fiscal decentralization	Overall decentralization
South Africa	3.33	3.00	4.00	3.30
Uganda	3.33	3.00	3.50	3.15
Kenya	3.00	2.33	3.00	2.75
Ghana	3.00	2.33	2.50	2.60
Nigeria	2.67	2.67	4.00	2.60
Rwanda	2.67	2.67	2.50	2.60
Nambia	3.33	1.67	1.50	2.50
Senegal	3.00	1.33	2.50	2.50
Ethiopia	3.00	2.00	1.50	2.40
Tanzania	2.33	2.67	2.50	2.30
Zimbabwe	1.33	2.60	3.00	2.30
Côte d'Ivoire	3.00	1.33	3.50	2.20
Madagascar	2.67	2.00	1.50	2.20
Zambia	2.67	1.67	1.50	1.90
Mali	2.33	1.67	1.50	1.75
Guinea	1.67	1.67	2.00	1.75
Eritrea	0.33	2.00	1.50	1.67
Malawi	2.00	1.00	2.00	1.60
Burkina Faso	1.67	2.00	1.50	1.60
Mozambique	1.33	1.67	1.50	1.40
Rep. of Congo	0.33	1.33	2.50	1.40
Burundi	0.33	1.00	2.50	1.30
Angola	0.33	1.67	1.00	1.30
Cameroon	0.67	1.00	2.00	1.20
Dem. Rep. of Congo	0.33	1.33	2.50	1.20
Benin	0.33	1.67	1.00	1.20
Central Africa Republic	0.67	1.00	1.00	1.00
Niger	0.33	1.00	1.00	1.00
Sierra Leone	0.67	1.00	1.00	0.90
Chad	0.33	1.00	1.00	0.80

Source: Ndegwa 2002.
Note: All scores are on a 0–4 scale, with 0 representing the lowest level of decentralization and 4 the highest. Scores were estimated on the basis of a graphic presentation provided in Ndegwa (2002). Scores for overall decentralization are a composite based on an averaging of the variables used to create the scores for political, administrative, and fiscal decentralization, plus additional indicators for upward and downward accountability and the stability of the intergovernmental system.

with fiscal decentralization. Little local choice is provided in the Central African Republic, Chad, Niger, and Sierra Leone (table 8.1).

The gap between the devolved democratic authority in Uganda and South Africa and that of other African nations is considerable. The authority and autonomy of local jurisdictions also varies widely within nations. For example, in Swaziland, local authorities are largely centrally controlled, but city councils are relatively autonomous. City councils have discretion over management and operational systems and the authority to develop capacity, whereas town councils are much less autonomous. Central ministries completely control the operation of local town boards (Gamedze 2001).

Mozambique illustrates the evolution taking place in local governance more broadly across Africa. The country's central government nominates and appoints local district and borough leaders and administrators. In 1994, parliament provided a framework for establishing municipal districts with greater autonomy and began a local government reform program. In 1997, local authorities legislation was approved, and in 1998, the first municipal elections were held in 33 municipalities (Antonio 2001). Municipalities enjoy greater autonomy to raise revenue and conduct their fiscal affairs, are required to develop financial plans consistent with a municipal five-year plan, can levy taxes (collected by the central government), and can establish fees. Municipal governance structures include a municipal assembly (elected by the population from a party list), the elected municipal council president or mayor (the municipal executive), and the municipal council (an executive body headed by the mayor and composed of mayorally nominated town councilors, of which 50 percent must be from the elected municipal assembly). These are the requisites of meaningful local budgeting.

Mozambique has been following a "principle of gradualism," promoting local capacity building before giving a local jurisdiction the status of municipality. This approach has demonstrated that civic groups can be instrumental in promoting "management efficiency, accountability of public funds, [and] revenue generation" and that civic education is needed to sustain the contributions of stakeholders and civil society (Antonio 2001: 15). It has also demonstrated the need for clarification of the relative roles of institutions at various levels of government, the need for strengthened force of municipal legislation, the importance of improved technical qualifications and capacity building, the need for transparency in the use of public funds, and the importance of the municipal budget and funds for investment projects.

Implication of Constrained Authority in Africa

Reviews of local authorities across southern and eastern Africa by the Municipal Development Partnership (MDP) indicate that localities generally experience the same difficulties in coping with their responsibilities. Prominent among these difficulties are dependency on central government allocations because of inadequate local tax resources and authority, failures in administrative capacity, and lack of autonomy and thus inability to effectively budget and plan (Mosha and Mabaila 2003). The inadequacy of financing systems is common across lesser-developed nations and is a function of constrained resource bases and failures to provided appropriate levels of decentralized authority.

MDP finds that the primary difficulties for municipal governments in Botswana, for example, include inadequate levels of legislative and policy autonomy, insufficient own-source financial resources and poor financial administration, and capacity constraints regarding social service provision and infrastructure. In Gaborone, Botswana, the city council prepares annual budget estimates but cannot, according to MDP, implement proper budgeting and planning processes because of uncertainty about central government resource transfers and mandated expenditures. The absence of local legislative and administrative autonomy makes meaningful long-term planning and priority setting impossible. Personnel and capacity issues reinforce these problems. "Personnel for the council are employed by a central agency . . . and only limited powers have been decentralized to the Councils" (Mosha and Mabaila 2003: 2). MDP recommends that the city council be given greater autonomy in planning, budgeting, and funds administration. It also recommends that fiscal decentralization, reforms in personnel employment structure, and revisions to the statutory authority of local governments be accelerated.

Rural district councils in Zimbabwe face similar challenges. The country's five-year (1996–2001) Rural District Council Capacity Building Programme found that most problems typically experienced by the 57 rural districts involved deficiencies in both human and financial resources. The program's focus was improved planning, financial management, revenue generation, community participation, social and economic infrastructure, public transparency and accountability, and public-private partnerships.[2] An evaluation of the program found "outstanding progress . . . in the areas of strategic planning, monitoring and evaluations systems, staff restructuring and labour relations, [and] committee and budget restructuring" (Musekiwa 2002: 12–13). It concluded that capacity support can aid effective performance, that local authorities should be challenged to perform through provision of a legal mandate and resources to implement projects, that capacity building "by doing" "promotes local democratic governance" and "downward accountability," that empowering local institutions requires sophisticated guidance from the center, that capacity building can spur decentralization, and that coordination across programs and jurisdictions is critical (Musekiwa 2002: 12–13). The evaluation also underlined the importance of local autonomy.

These issues and recommendations mirror those found throughout lesser-developed and traditional settings and highlight the importance of the intergovernmental dimension for local governments. Reforms of the 1990s have established local jurisdictions with significant discretion to legislate, collect revenue, and budget. However, levels of actual local autonomy vary significantly. For example, in Namibia, municipalities are fiscally autonomous, town councils are partially autonomous, and villages are fully dependent on the central government. Local authorities in Botswana are budgetarily dependent on the central government for both recurrent and development spending and its allocation. Dependency is a major impediment, reinforcing vertical accountability at the expense of horizontal accountability to local citizens. Local capacity building for participatory budgeting is essential (Wamwangi and Kundishora 2003).

Complexity and Restructuring in Intergovernmental Management

Intergovernmental transition appears to be the norm in the developed and developing world. A decade ago the Organisation for Economic Co-operation and Development (OECD) noted that subnational jurisdictions are becoming more important partners and that the center is struggling "to retain some overall control of expenditures and revenues" (OECD 1997: 15). Experience in OECD countries highlights a variety of tensions in establishing an appropriate balance between increased local autonomy and direction from the central government, local service differentiation and flexibility and some degree of uniformity, and greater responsiveness to local desires and maintenance of economy and efficiency in service delivery. Similar tensions exist in developing countries. In OECD nations, the tensions required

■ adjusting financial and administrative *controls* away from detailed, top-down requirements and toward broadly agreed frameworks and ex post, results-oriented instruments
■ developing culturally and administratively appropriate *coordination and consultation* mechanisms for a comprehensive and coherent approach to target-based governance
■ promoting *accountability* procedures that combine managerial responsibility for financial results with political accountability to the public and that are in accordance with the shift toward citizen participation (OECD 1997: 70)

Unique economic, cultural, political, and capacity issues determine what is possible and desirable. Unfortunately, initiatives to increase local resource allocation roles have often not lived up to their promise, particularly in the developing world. The main factors hindering success are an inadequate institutional framework to oversee and facilitate decentralization, central government's conflicting political and bureaucratic incentives, limited local managerial and technical capacity, and inadequacies in local government accountability to local constituencies (Smoke 2000). These problems permeate local budgetary processes.

Coordination of Multitiered Institutions and Actors

Effective local budgeting requires central and regional governments to promote the development of local jurisdictions as effective governance institutions. Higher-level jurisdictions are critical in establishing procedures and standards for improved local operations and transparency and for promoting the accountability of local officials to local constituencies (Smoke 2000). "New skills are needed to manage multi-tiered systems with diverse, fragmented and interdependent components" (OECD 1997: 15). Central governments must conduct analytic studies to monitor and evaluate the decentralized system, determine tax effort, track subnational budgets, evaluate fiscal alternatives, establish and administer transfer systems, regulate local borrowing, establish fiscal information systems, and establish audit procedures. In addition, they must establish personnel and environmental regulations, qualifications for public employees, minimum service standards, mechanisms to resolve intergovernmental disputes, and sanctions (World Bank 2000). Reforms in Brazil, Cambodia, and Kenya have included central and provincial facilitation as a major element in local capacity building (Smoke 2000).

Because effective local budgeting necessarily involves the devolution of fiscal and sectoral responsibilities, a wide range of central government agencies and officials are implicitly involved (see annex 8A for a description of South Africa's sophisticated approach to intergovernmental relations). Therefore, important elements of local budgeting processes may require coordination by a local government planning or finance ministry and should generally include sectoral ministries to ensure harmonization of policies across levels of government. Nongovernmental organizations, civic groups, and private organizations should be effectively involved. Critical to coordination are clarity about the role of each level of government; measured subnational revenue and expenditure authority and proper fiscal structures; and administrative capacity, democratic and participatory institutions and societal norms, appropriate budget processes and procedures, and institutions to ensure cooperation among levels of government (Norris, Martinez-Vazquez, and Norregaard 2000; Shah 1998).

Local Budget Cycle

Any government budget process entails a cycle: preparation and formulation, approval, execution, and audit and evaluation (see figure 8.1 and see also annex 8B for a description of Estonia's local budget process). Preparation is often viewed as predominantly an executive role and includes the planning (sometimes referred to as pre-preparation) and the linkage of plans through a medium-term fiscal framework to a medium-term expenditure framework for the annual budget, establishment of priorities and resource and spending envelopes, instructions for agency budget submissions, and administrative review of the budget request. Approval is a legislatively driven stage and is highlighted by submission of the budget to the legislative body or council for consideration. The stage is defined by the scope of budget coverage and level of documentation of requests, by the scope of approval authority and legislative discretion in budget adjustment, and by the timetable for legislative action. The execution stage includes warrants issuance, mechanisms to ensure executive accountability to legislative policy, apportionment, administrative discretion and midyear adjustment procedures, treasury management, and financial controls. The audit and evaluation stage is a verification stage and includes execution reporting, independent verification of accounts, financial and performance reporting, and public disclosure. The essential elements are common across levels of government, but their implementation is far from uniform. As noted earlier, variations in intergovernmental, institutional, political, and civic contexts are significant, and these variations, rather than technical system variations, are among the most critical elements in the budget process in the developing country context.

The budget cycle must be supported by a budget calendar that specifies the staging of each element in the budget cycle (see annex 8B). The complete calendar reflects both legislatively and administratively established timetables for step completion. It identifies the roles and responsibilities of actors and institutions at each step as well as the information and procedural requirements for the completion of each step. Best practices recommend openness in budget processes as a vehicle for improved outcomes.

Process and Environment

Process issues permeate all elements of the budget cycle. However, the process is most identified with the rules and procedures and inputs and timetables of actor involvement in budget formulation and approval stages (see box 8.3).

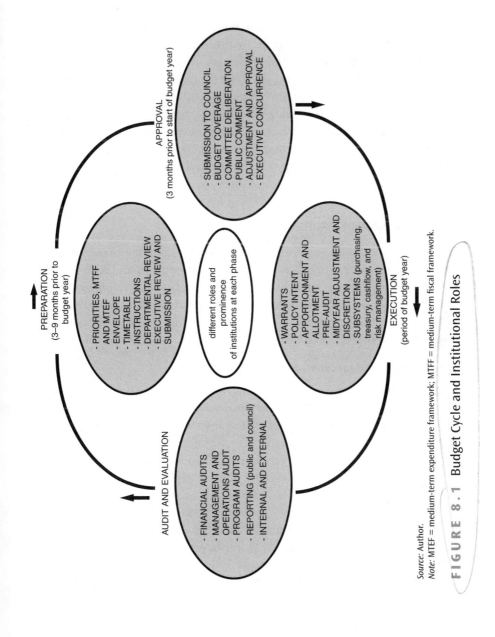

PREPARATION
(3–9 months prior to
budget year)

- PRIORITIES, MTFF
  AND MTEF
- ENVELOPE
- TIMETABLE
- INSTRUCTIONS
- DEPARTMENTAL REVIEW
- EXECUTIVE REVIEW AND
  SUBMISSION

APPROVAL
(3 months prior to start of budget year)

- SUBMISSION TO COUNCIL
- BUDGET COVERAGE
- COMMITTEE DELIBERATION
- PUBLIC COMMENT
- ADJUSTMENT AND APPROVAL
- EXECUTIVE CONCURRENCE

different roles and
prominence
of institutions at each phase

EXECUTION
(period of budget year)

- WARRANTS
- POLICY INTENT
- APPORTIONMENT AND
  ALLOTMENT
- PRE-AUDIT
- MIDYEAR ADJUSTMENT AND
  DISCRETION
- SUBSYSTEMS (purchasing,
  treasury, cashflow, and
  risk management)

AUDIT AND EVALUATION

- FINANCIAL AUDITS
- MANAGEMENT AND
  OPERATIONS AUDIT
- PROGRAM AUDITS
- REPORTING (public and council)
- INTERNAL AND EXTERNAL

Source: Author.

Note: MTEF = medium-term expenditure framework; MTFF = medium-term fiscal framework.

FIGURE 8.1 Budget Cycle and Institutional Roles

Within these two stages, budgetary choices take shape and are finalized in an official government budget.[3] Effective budgeting requires an initial identification of priorities and goals. Effective identification of goals and priorities requires appropriate input from the numerous stakeholders in local government—identification informed by a realistic assessment of community conditions, opportunities, and challenges. According to the National Advisory Council on State and Local Budgeting (NACSLB), a good budget process "incorporates a long-term perspective, establishes links to broad organizational goals, focuses budget decisions on results and outcomes, involves and promotes effective communication with stakeholders, and provides incentives to government management and employees" (NACSLB 1998). Processes and procedures for budget formulation and approval must reinforce these elements.

Balanced Institutional Authority

Budget processes can be classified according to the relative dominance of or balance among institutional actors in budget formulation and approval. Some processes exhibit extremes of executive and administrative dominance; others processes are legislatively dominated. Good arguments can be made for balanced levels of executive influence and legislative influence in budget development and adoption (see box 8.2).

Administrative and executive dominance

Administrative- and executive-dominated systems are typified by closed processes of executive budget development and review and by limited options for further council priority setting, review, or budget initiative. In such systems, the executive (mayor or chief administrator) is responsible for formulation outside legislative consultation. Completed budget proposals are forwarded to the legislative body (or council) for consideration. These proposals report gross aggregate revenue and spending totals, possibly classified by function. They neither detail spending plans nor present departmental or organizational units' mappings of resource flows. They include no analytical presentation. The legislative body has no capacity to perform its own review of the proposals and often is required to consider the budget as a whole, without pubic hearings, and its ability to amend the document is frequently severely limited. In some cases, the legislative body is given authority only to approve or reject the budget. In other cases, the body can only *advise* approval or rejection. Intergovernmental structures for

BOX 8.2 Fiscal Discipline: Budgetary Institutions
and Procedures

Hierarchical and centralized procedures heighten the authority of the
executive and fiscal institutions, promote fiscal discipline, and strengthen
the link between planning and execution. Legislative influence emphasizes
democratic control, checks and balances, and collegial relationships, but
decreases discipline. Open rules invite a more equitable distribution of
outcomes (and likely less capture) at the expense of possible delay and
expansion of spending. Closed rules limit spending prerogatives and, when
they provide ceilings for expenditures or floors for revenues or restrict
amendments, they favor executive authority.

Voting on aggregate revenue and expenditure totals before considering
specific spending proposals is thought to enhance discipline. Political actors,
however, often oppose transparency on budgetary matters to obscure difficult
decisions. They may promote fiscal illusion through use of optimistic revenue
and expenditure (cost) projections, off-budget accounts, and multiyear budgets
that postpone difficult choices.

Legal requirements for balance may speed responses to fiscal shocks
and promote fiscal discipline, although they may ultimately work against
transparency. Hierarchical procedures may enhance discipline, but reduce
democratic access. According to Dethier (2000a), hierarchical procedures are
often preferred when a government faces several years of fiscal austerity.

Multiyear plans can promote budget expansions legitimized simply by
the plan's existence. Budget discussions focused on current actions and
verified forecasts promote spending restraint.

Source: Author.

local budget review may further limit both local administrative and
legislative discretion.

Legislative dominance

In legislatively dominated systems, administrative agencies directly transmit
budget estimates to the council and its committees. If an executive budget
is prepared, a parallel legislative budget is also developed. The legislature
has the authority to develop the budget through input from the executive
or to supplant the executive budget with its own. The legislature plays a
heightened role in budget planning and formulation, and the legislative
chamber has staff assistance to aid in its direct budget development
responsibility. Legislatively dominated systems exist in environments in
which administrative authority and legislative authority are not clearly

separated. Community forums with legislative roles typify one system (town meeting). In legislatively dominated processes, the legislature has unlimited authority to establish spending requirements and has authority over both budgetary totals and the details of agency authorizations.

Balanced processes

Balanced processes avoid the excesses of both executive and legislative dominance. Under these processes, the legislature and the executive collaborate (sometimes in joint executive and legislative budget committees) in budget development, merging budget formulation with legislative approval. Sometimes one or the other has greater authority for particular tasks in the budget cycle, and each has independent investigation and review authority. When the executive formulates the budget, it provides detailed estimates and analytical support, allowing the legislative body to evaluate priorities and to map expenditures to programs and administrative units. This system allows the legislature to benefit from the informed position of the executive and to hold the executive accountable. In balanced systems, the council has amendatory power, often within limits established to promote fiscal responsibility. Some systems give councils the authority to reallocate spending across functions, programs, and activities, as long as the original aggregate budget ceiling is not exceeded. Other systems might require councils to offset aggregate spending increases and aggregate revenue reductions with corresponding revenue increases and spending reductions.

Conditions of local governance and comparative levels of authority

The comparative levels of legislative authority and administrative and executive authority are often a function of the economic environment and the level of discretion and autonomy enjoyed by local government. Administrative- and executive-dominated structures frequently exist where the central government maintains control over local government operations and management. These structures are routinely expected to produce relatively conservative local fiscal outcomes. However, central control can seriously limit innovation and the efficiency of local service delivery such that a fixed level of spending might provide for a level of local welfare lower than the level achieved through a lesser-controlled structure. Legislative authority is associated with increased local autonomy and is often perceived to be a risk to fiscal discipline. It is also associated with public participation and potentially improved targeting of scarce local resources to local needs. Balanced processes are preferred for their capacity to bring greater representation of needs, priorities, and operational modes into the budgeting arena. They allow legislative and executive actors to serve as a useful check on the otherwise unconstrained authority of the other. The relative authority of the executive and the legislature depends not only on the purview of local government, but also on local economic and social conditions, the capacity of actors and institutions, the budget's stage of development, the general environment of local governance, and general political conditions.

Budget Preparation and Formulation

Administrative structures are necessary to coordinate the preparation and approval of local government budgets. Elements range from the rather mundane need to identify, establish, and adhere to a timetable of steps, to inputs required for budget formulation, to varied processes of stakeholder and civil society participation.

Policy guidance and outlook

Effective budget development requires establishment of expenditure priorities. This process begins in a planning or preplanning stage and is often dominated by executive actors. Information flows are both top down and bottom up. In more ideal systems, policy guidance is given in a top-down process through establishment of expectations and parameters for budget development. These expectations and parameters take the form of directives to agencies and spending divisions from the executive administration. The directives regard the fiscal framework, resource and cost forecasts and assumptions, the budget envelope, and broad policy priorities.

How this framework is established varies from narrow participation in executive-driven systems to broader stakeholder and council involvement in participatory systems. Some frameworks use a committee composed of executive and council leadership. Relatively closed systems are thought to advance fiscal restraint. Relatively open systems are thought to identify and express community needs and interests. The range of interests and views reflected in the process determines the degree to which the process is representative.

This planning stage establishes the parameters for spending units' budget requests and influences the efficacy of the entire process in creating a reasonable, realistic, and responsive local policy agenda and executable budget plan. This stage is typically closed to the direct involvement of non-governmental actors. Wider participation is often achieved in goal-setting and community priority-setting processes, which, although providing input to budget development, are separate from the budget development process.

Essential bottom-up flows occur in this planning stage through the submission of broad departmental and spending unit policy and expenditure priorities and estimates of expected revenue outcomes. Administrative actors' views of policy initiatives and directions are captured through the submission of programmatic priorities. Bottom-up, top-down, and lateral (participatory) information flows are important to establishing an effective framework. Specific (top-down) budget instructions are established from this planning stage, and detailed department, agency, and spending unit (bottom-up) submissions follow.

Instructions and expenditure standards

From policy guidance comes instructions for spending units in developing spending requests. These instructions should not be so detailed as to limit the process's capacity to benefit from assessments of program and unit managers. These managers need flexibility in establishing spending plans to marshal scarce resources as effectively as possible in the pursuit of program objectives.

Budget instructions should identify programmatic priorities, the fiscal environment (restraint, retrenchment, expectations for budget reduction, threshold limitations on requests, and constraints), executive receptivity (or lack thereof) to spending initiatives, assumptions for cost increases (for critical inputs), expectations for personnel allocations, and information required for budget requests. In addition, instructions should specify the form that spending submissions should take, the type of justification required for continued and new spending initiatives, and the timetable for submission. The timetable should identify the dates when detailed submissions are to be made, submissions will be reviewed, and administrative hearings and appeals will occur. This timetable should also place the submission, review, revision, and appeal phase in the context of the timetable for the complete budget development cycle. In an ideal structure, preliminary expenditure envelopes will be established for department and agency submissions consistent with the aggregate budget envelope.

Review and compilation

Agency budget requests should be reviewed along programmatic, technical, and managerial dimensions. A review oriented toward the relative value of objectives should take precedence over a review of methods for achieving objectives. Technical review ensures that the figures and estimates of requirements are accurate and consistent with prior direction and assumptions regarding input costs, historic spending, and spending envelopes. Managerial review ensures that managers adhered to administrative mechanisms, systems, processes, procedures, and guidelines in the proposed method for conducting administrative and programmatic operations. Programmatic review ensures consistency of spending proposals with policy guidance and policy priorities.

All dimensions of this review are critical for effective budget development. Any errors must be corrected. Proposed resource inputs must be scrutinized. Acceptable managerial practices must be ensured. Programmatic activity must be scaled to fit within the established aggregate spending envelope within and across agencies.

Review should be multitiered. Development of budget requests should proceed from lower-level spending units and managers, and detailed internal review of requests should occur at each administrative level. This review should be directed at ensuring economy, efficiency, and effective resource deployment and an appropriate trade-off of resource requirements across competing claims on the public sector budget at each tier. Final review at the executive stage (in an executive budget development process) or at a committee stage (in a mixed executive-legislative process) should focus on broad trade-offs of spending priorities and managerial operations. The most common element of the review stage is sharp budget reductions at each successive level of requests. These reductions can only be made in an informed manner if spending requests are made in an appropriate programmatic context and with the necessary supporting information on costs and expected outcomes. Effective review trades off relative costs and outcomes across spending units and program objectives. Review should also be recursive, with opportunities to appeal or reconstitute requests (based on feedback from earlier review), at each stage of the process. Final review results in compilation of all spending requests in the working budget proposal.

Legislative Review and Approval

In representative systems, an elected legislative body (municipal council) is intended or expected to dominate the budget approval stage. For approval to be distinct from formulation, this body must have authority separate from that endowed to the executive. For approval to be meaningful, the council must have the authority to substantively alter the budget presented to it. This authority varies. As noted earlier, some councils have little to no amendatory powers and must vote on the submitted document as a whole. Others have authority to replace the submitted budget with one developed legislatively.

Even in instances of significant legal authority, practical authority is conditioned by the characteristic of the budget submitted for consideration and the procedures established for legislative consideration and amendment (such as open or closed amendment rules and length of time for legislative consideration). Budgets with limited information content provide little foundation for meaningful legislative policy consideration. Closed amendment rules tend to favor the budget as transmitted and as reported from specialized budget committees, whereas open rules are expected to favor participation and potentially lessened fiscal restraint.

More time for consideration means more time for amendment. Outcomes are also conditioned by the representational structures within the legislative body. At-large seats have different implications for fiscal restraint than ward-based seats. Ward representation provides greater potential diversity of represented views, but it may lead to greater pressure to move away from fiscal discipline.

Committee jurisdiction is also an important element in budget approval. Local councils have less ability to develop expertise, and modes of budget consideration vary from deliberations by a committee of the whole to parceling out of elements of the budget to distinct legislative committees. Legislative fiscal discipline may be enhanced by committee specialization.

Budget coverage

A critical element in the legislative review and approval stage is the quality of budgetary information. Informed review is information intensive. If budget deliberations are to meaningfully reflect the municipal government's priorities and policies, complete information must be provided. The budget must include all municipal revenues and expenditures; any special funds or extra budgetary accounts; all dedicated revenue and funds; all charge revenue; all operating expenditures; all capital expenditures; and all loans, grants and contingent liabilities. Classifications must allow resource commitments to be compared with realistic estimates of available resources and must allow mapping of resource commitments to accountable spending units and to priorities, objectives, and programmatic activities.

Review

The council must have authority to collect information and request testimony of administrative officials on the merits of all elements of the proposed budget. The council needs an independent means of information analysis. Appropriate personnel assistance to the legislative body in budget review is critical, as are timetables that allow sufficient time for consideration of policy and programmatic alternatives but that are not so lengthy as to render estimates obsolete. Review should be open and include input from civil society and the community at public hearings on the proposed budget.

Scope of approval

Legislative authority must be meaningful. Council deliberations should include consideration of aggregate revenues and expenditures, as well as spending at the programmatic and organizational unit levels. The legislature should have the authority to amend budgetary submissions. In the most open systems, this authority is boundless. However, economic circumstances and desires for balanced control frequently lead to restrictions on legislative authority. Authority is commonly limited by the aggregate revenue and expenditure envelope, as is appropriate when the council has participated in establishment of the envelope and as is often considered necessary for the purpose of fiscal discipline when it has not. In environments of greater legislative discretion, legislative establishment of a framework for aggregate revenues and spending is desirable before consideration of amendments to the submitted budget.

Legislative discretion, limited or not, over the spending mix is essential. Without such discretion, the executive cannot be held accountable to the council for expenditure policy or for the satisfaction of programmatic objectives. Mechanisms for meaningful legislative control over spending outcomes are needed if input from open processes of comment and representational systems are to be effectively transmitted to local policy.

Execution and Evaluation

Budget execution is often considered administrative and technical rather than policy determining. To the degree that the execution phase reflects implementation of aggregate plans and programs, this view may be accurate. However, effective implementation requires administrative discretion, and discretion allows policies to be altered through implementation. A balance is required in the relative authority of the executive body and the legislative body, and appropriate vehicles for and limits to administrative discretion in budget execution are also required (Forrester and Mullins 1992). This balance necessitates an understanding of the legal status of appropriations, the level of detail of legislative control entailed, and enforcement mechanisms. Structures range from legal controls over economic expenditure articles (ranging from personal services, to contractual services, to supplies) to lump sum appropriations for broader functions. Intermediate positions include legal authorization for program and spending units, with administrative discretion in the actual mix of inputs necessary to achieve approved objectives. Too-restrictive legislative control handcuffs management and creates inefficiencies in implementation. Too-lax legislative control jeopardizes consistency with legislatively established policy.

Rules are often developed to allow reprogramming of a portion of funds in execution so that effective managerial discretion can be achieved. Even for budgets presented in detail, the actual appropriations legislation is often broad enough to allow transfers among economic expenditure articles as needed. Shifting of resources among programs within functions may also be allowed, but transfers among functions are normally constrained. Mechanisms must exist to officially (legally and legislatively) amend the budget during implementation, and processes must ensure that resources cannot be expended until and unless necessary and only after appropriate amendments have been authorized. Process requirements must also be established. The process for midyear budget adjustments is appropriately closed.

Strong and comprehensive audit and evaluation requirements are necessary to ensure that the executed budget is consistent with legislated policy and to guard against malfeasance. Internal and external audits should support all other elements of the budget cycle by providing appropriate information for review of financial compliance and performance. Audit reports must be timely

---

BOX 8.3   Process Issues Permeate the Budget Cycle

In the United States, the National Advisory Council on State and Local Budgeting (NACSLB) focuses its recommendations regarding best practices on priority setting and on stakeholder and community involvement in budget development. These activities drive all subsequent budgetary activities, and they permeate the cycle of budget preparation, adoption, execution, and evaluation. For the NACSLB, budget development emphasizes process. Critical steps include

- developing a budget calendar
- developing budget guidelines and instructions
- developing mechanisms for coordinating budget preparation and review
- developing procedures to facilitate budget review, discussion, modification, and adoption
- identifying opportunities for stakeholder input

The emphasis of the NACSLB is on processes of stakeholder involvement and their incorporation into these critical steps.[a] The emphasis is on the expectation of improved budgetary outcomes with wider community participation. The challenge is to effectively channel that participation into budget development. This challenge exists across budget contexts and is a critical element in all budget processes.

a. For an example of incorporating stakeholder input consistent with NACSLB recommendations, see Calia, Guajardo, and Metzgar (2000).

Source: Author.

(initial reports should be completed within three months of the end of the fiscal year) and must be widely disclosed within the government and to the public. The legislative body must have independent ability to ensure the veracity of administrative implementation of the approved expenditure plan and the proper stewardship of resources. Without this verification of outcomes, legislative approval of plans has little practical meaning.

Integrating Priorities, Planning, and Budgeting across Levels

Subnational resource allocation requires coordination to ensure that local authority is not exercised in a manner incompatible with national objectives. Coordinating mechanisms include regulation, fiscal inducement, and hierarchical accountability structures. Regulatory models are varied. In some OECD countries, regulatory responsibilities are shared across levels of government. In others, authority is centralized. The trend is toward a middle position "as decentralized countries attempt to reduce duplication and regulatory costs by creating national standards, and centralised countries move towards power-sharing arrangements and a shift of responsibility away from the central government" (OECD 1997: 48).

Representation of National Interests

The basis of plan and priority coordination is information exchange and understanding of the purview and legitimate interests of different levels of government. The two bases for models demarcating intergovernmental authority are legal tradition and managerial culture (OECD 1997: 28). Each is dependent on representation of national policy and priorities at local levels to preserve national objectives in the execution of local authority.

At least one of the two main forms of demarcating intergovernmental authority—deconcentrated administrations and prefect systems—exists in virtually all nations. All OECD nations (unitary and federal) use deconcentrated administration, and most have a prefect system. The former represents central policies through a deconcentrated placement of central government agencies at the subnational level. These field offices' range of responsibility, local impact, and discretion varies considerably but is increasing. Unitary nations without central representatives at the local level (such as the United Kingdom and New Zealand) rely heavily on the legal status of central agencies.

In the prefect system, an official representative of the central government is charged with conveying that government's interests at the subnational level. This representative has two principle responsibilities: overseeing or administratively supervising subnational governments and acting as an intermediary between governmental levels. Typified by the Napoleonic model first employed by the unitary states of continental Europe, prefect systems have been retained even within moves for greater local decision autonomy. However, in many countries, the prefect system plays a role only in areas of shared responsibility and has lost its coercive powers. In any regard, the prefect acts as a communication conduit between levels of government.

Coordination, Consultation, and Collaboration

Coordination through consultation and collaboration has displaced direction in evolved governance structures. For administrative deconcentration and prefect systems, the intention is vertical coordination through consultation, which entails both vertical and horizontal collaboration. The more complicated the intergovernmental distribution of responsibilities, the more important and difficult coordination of tasks becomes. Traditional vertical mechanisms of direction are not sufficient. Responsiveness and relevance require a local perspective, but coordination remains necessary to clarify national policy goals, to establish agreement (if not consensus) regarding the contribution of individual programs and levels, and to communicate and learn from local experiences and progress toward objectives. Coordination and consultation considerably facilitate identification and elimination of overlaps, duplication, and competition among program activities.[4]

Consultation can, however, slow decision making and may provide relatively greater access for self-interested parties. Not all models are highly collaborative. Consultation ranges from the cooperative to the adversarial, is augmented through formal and informal mechanisms, and can be influenced by societal norms. Cooperative approaches seek consensus and collaboration; the adversarial approach favors decisive decision making involving legal procedures and is not as attuned to the growing complexity of intergovernmental arrangements.

Forms of coordination and consultation are varied and not mutually exclusive. Some are less formal, others use structural bodies or procedural means, some are mandatory, others are nonbinding, and some use consultation as the primary mode of policy making (OECD 1997). Consultation must have limits, particularly in areas relating to economic policy, citizen rights, internal and international trade, citizen mobility, and residency. "[T]he central government should reserve to itself the authority to undo local actions whenever they demonstrably injure clear national interests" (Goodpaster and Ray 2000: 2).

Coercion versus Cooperation in Planning and Budgeting

A planning framework is useful for classifying cooperative extremes relevant to local budgetary processes and autonomy. Intergovernmental coordination often "entails the imposition of procedural and/or substantive requirements by a higher-level government on subnational (state or local) governments, either as conditions for [fiscal] assistance or as [administrative] direct orders" (May 1998: 4). This coordination can take a coercive or cooperative form and conditions the relative role across tiers in policy development, implementation, and innovation (see table 8.2).

Coercive frameworks treat local jurisdictions as regulatory agents charged with following standards and procedures and enforcing prescriptions of higher-level governments. Monitoring of local compliance often focuses on prescribed actions, plans, and processes. Local compliance is enforced by the threat of sanctions for deviation from roles, procedures, prescriptions, or policy mandates.

Cooperative models attempt to stimulate local interest, support, and capacity to facilitate achievement of higher-level policy goals. Local-level goal commitment is assumed, and local jurisdictions function as regulatory trustees in pursuit of shared goals. Monitoring focuses on levels of substantive achievement and building of local capacity to play assigned roles. Local innovation is encouraged.

Constraints, Dilemmas, and Conditions of Efficacy

Each form of coordination suffers its own constraints and dilemmas. The coercive regime may discourage and sacrifice local innovations in pursuit of state-initiated innovations. Procedural compliance may be emphasized over substantive compliance, because straight-jacketed local jurisdictions are expected to employ cookie-cutter approaches. Coercive models require constant monitoring, and compliance may erode if monitoring or enforcement agencies become complacent, or if the local predisposition toward compliance changes.

The cooperative regime attempts to capitalize on local innovation. But attempting to foster local ownership of broad policy objectives could open procedural and policy compliance gaps if local government is reluctant to follow policy and process prescriptions and if parochial interests dominate the process. Absence of sanctions creates difficulties in motivating compliance. Higher-level governments must instead rely on incentives. Coercive models better secure procedural compliance, but cooperative models may produce

TABLE 8.2 Coercive and Cooperative Intergovernmental
Policy Designs

Features	Comparison of policy features	
	Coercive policy design	Cooperative policy design
Role of lower-level governments (state, regional, and local)	Regulatory agents: Enforce rules or regulations prescribed by higher-level governments	Regulatory trustees: Develop and apply rules that are consistent with higher-level goals
Emphasis of intergovernmental mandate	Prescribe regulatory actions and process; specify regulatory actions and conditions, along with required process or plans	Prescribe process and goals; specify planning components and considerations, along with performance goals
Control of lower-level governments	Monitoring for procedural compliance; enforcement and sanctions for failing to meet deadlines, for not adhering to prescribed process, or for not enforcing prescribed rules	Monitoring for substantive compliance with more limited monitoring for procedural compliance; monitoring systems for assessing outcomes and progress toward them
Assumptions about intergovernmental implementation	Compliance is a potential problem; need for uniformity in application of policies	Compliance is not a problem; need for local discretion in policy development
Source of policy innovation	Higher-level governments	Lower-level governments
Implementation emphasis	Induce adherence to policy prescriptions and regulatory standards; build calculated commitment as a primary means of inducing compliance	Build capacity of subordinates to reach policy goals; enhance normative commitment as a primary means of inducing compliance

Source: May 1998.

greater substantive compliance when local and higher policy interests and incentives are aligned. Cooperative systems may degrade if policy interests and priorities diverge across levels (May 1998).

The potential capture of the decision-making process by any one interest is greater when heterogeneous policy positions exist and when individual local stakeholders have inequitable input into decision-making. In both coercive and cooperative decision-making models, open, participatory processes are important. In cooperative models, participation results in policies comparatively more responsive to local needs. If participation is broad, it can work to limit capture but can also generate conflict. In coercive models, participation can mobilize community groups' support of policy objectives and increase the commitment of local officials to higher-level policy goals.

The overall efficacy of coercive versus cooperative decision-making models hinges on many factors. Cooperative approaches require shared policy objectives. "When there is fundamental disagreement over policy objectives or the allowable means for meeting them, the cooperative nature of the intergovernmental partnership will be doomed" (May 1998: 15). Cooperative approaches are more likely to be effective if precision can be avoided in defining policy or methods without risking realization of policy goals. If a cooperative model is to have meaning, real responsibility must be devolved to local jurisdictions. Devolution may impede the coercive model. Coercive approaches "require a higher-level authority to carry out monitoring of compliance by lower-level governments and the power of . . . enforcement" (May 1998: 15). Cooperative models require implementing agencies to be strongly committed to and capable of facilitating local performance. When local policy commitment exists, the results at least rival the results of coercive mechanisms, and over the long-term, such commitment may increase (May and Burby 1996).

Link between National and Subnational Budgets

Effective coordination among levels of government is critical. The link between national and subnational budgets is strongest in centralized systems in which subnational units function as administrative divisions of the central government. Central ministries establish priorities, and often subnational budgets are centrally approved. In decentralized systems, national and subnational budgets may not be formally coordinated (as in the United States) or these budgets may be integrated into one framework (as in Germany). In the United States, the national government uses fiscal incentives to entice states and localities to conform to national policy, and the national constitution and statutory legislation somewhat limits subnational units' budgetary purview. Mechanisms of direct budgetary coordination are absent.

Germany's 1969 Law on Budgetary Principles created a framework for coordinating budgetary processes and establishing uniform budgetary principles across levels of government. General provisions establish requirements for fiscal year, gross estimates, comprehensiveness, spending authorization, efficiency, and cost-effectiveness. Specific provisions establish budget preparation means, the accounting structure, budget classification, auditing, execution and reporting, and the role of special funds. The legislation requires multiyear financial planning and the exchange of budget information among levels of government (Spahn 2001).

The law's premise is that realization of national policy goals requires effective and standardized monitoring of central and subcentral governments' budgets, which, in turn, requires uniform budget classification in categories related to the national accounts. Revenues and expenditures are comprehensively accounted for in gross, full-cost (rather than net) terms and are subject to national consolidation. Special and off-budget funds are highly controlled. Annual budgets must be reflected in a medium-term financial plan established cooperatively by all three levels of government and a financial planning council. This financial plan is, however, only advisory in nature.

Participatory Planning and Budgeting: Issues, Modes, and Cautions

Greater levels of participation in planning and budgetary decision making are generally advocated. However, participation must be inclusive and properly structured (see annex 8C for a description of participatory budgeting in Uganda). Outcomes are dependent on the range of community views, the institutional framework for articulating these views, and the ability of the political actors and institutions to process inputs and deal with any conflict. A progressive political environment cannot alone ensure the superiority of participatory outcomes. Even an elaborate participatory mechanism can exclude large segments of socially and economically disadvantaged elements of society, as well as produce perverse effects in the form of increased conflict and stymied decision making (Campbell and Marshall 2000).

Campbell and Marshall (2000) note that public participation can be *self-interested* or *community focused.* They categorize self-interested participation as *instrumental participation,* which is predicated on a basic right of the individual to pursue his or her own self-interest; *consumer politics,* which emphasizes the rights of consumers to pursue freedom of choice and express preferences; and the *politics of presence,* which conveys the right of inclusion for groups excluded from the decision-making process. They note that community-focused participation takes two forms: *communitarian participation,* which stresses the obligation of individuals to contribute to collective well-being, and *deliberative democracy,* which stresses process and the development of institutions to promote open dialogue, shared solutions, and new forms of knowledge.

Local participatory processes may still exclude, producing little-altered outcomes while perversely limiting access, maintaining dominant motivations, and producing increased conflict and instability in decision making (Campbell and Marshall 2000). Rights-based motivations can undermine institutional structures intended to promote deliberation and can reduce local democratic processes to "confusion and noise." Improperly structured participation can leave existing power structures relatively unchallenged and can diminish the voice of the disadvantaged. Participation must be managed as an input to, not a substitute for, democratic decision making.

Participation is a function of both formal institutions and informal elements of social capital. Social capital is comprised of trust, norms, and networks "that foster mutually beneficial cooperation in society" (de Mello 2000). Social capital functions as a civil society coordinating mechanism promoting governance, performance, and accountability, and its development is expected to improve the outcomes of governance. Social capital is related to social status, educational attainment, religion, and income distribution. It is also related to the structure of governance. The characteristics of local decision making (relatively committed government, democratic institutional development, and trust in government and civil servants) are catalysts for increased social capital formation and reinforce (and are reinforced by) its positive effects. Local authority positively affects civic cooperation, civic association, and social capital formation. Participation not only influences but is influenced by local choice. Responsible, participatory local government is a vehicle for building civil society (Crook and Manor 2000). Civil society organizations improve the effectiveness of government, and properly structured participatory budgetary processes allow civil society to exercise influence in an orderly and focused manner.

Improperly structured local decision-making processes can, however, divert resources "from the poor, needy, and powerless to the rich, replete, and dominant" (Parker 2001: 1).

Institutionalizing of Access

For participative budgeting to be most effective, consultation is insufficient; "presence and representation" are needed to "institutionalize regular decision-making access for certain social groups" (ECA 2004: 11). This presence and representation may require quotas for "socially excluded groups or . . . structured access for a wide variety of neighborhood associations to municipal planning and budgeting debates" (ECA 2004: 11).

Forty countries, beginning with Australia, have adopted gender-responsive budgetary processes. According to the Economic Commission for Africa (ECA), these processes "are an innovative tool that empower civil society to hold public spending accountable to international and national commitments for promoting gender equality" (ECA 2004: 12). The commission notes that "the gender-budget initiative [in Porto Alegre, Brazil] is part of a broader process of municipal participatory budgeting involving [nongovernmental organizations], delegates, council members, community leaders and citizens" (ECA 2004: 12). This broader process includes an assembly to review the previous year's budget and elected representatives to identify spending priorities. Three months are spent in consultation with civil society, neighborhood organizations, and generally disempowered social groups (such as the poor) to construct an issue report covering transportation, health, education, and sanitation for consideration at a second assembly, in which priority sectors are identified and ranked. The result has been budget initiatives sensitive to the needs of a greater cross-section of the population and more responsive to local needs.

Bolivia has taken participation a step further. The 1994 Law of Popular Participation (renamed the Law of Organization in 1997) empowered community-based organizations to participate in community planning processes and in the establishment of municipal five-year plans. More radically, it required establishment of *vigilance committees* made up of community-based organization leaders to monitor municipal councils' allocation of resources. These committees review the use of central government transfers (including procurement plans), which are released only on the committees' approval. In instances of irregularities or fraud, the committees can petition the national government for a freezing of disbursements to the municipal government (ECA 2004: 35). According to ECA, Bolivia's participatory budgeting shows that

> citizens can actually exert influence in the decision-making process affecting the delivery of services to them. Such influence brings citizen engagement to the point where groups can translate access and presence into a tangible impact on policy-making and the organization of service delivery. This can happen when accountability mechanisms incorporate citizen concerns and preferences, by, for instance, engaging citizens in financial audits at local levels, or incorporating client satisfaction measures into new performance indicators for public servants, or even providing citizens with formal rights to litigate in the event of non-delivery of services (ECA 2004: 13).

Access in Environments of Limited Discretion and Emerging Participation

A case study of planning in Mbabane and Manzini, Swaziland, suggests the potential importance of access even in environments of limited discretion. Service delivery in the two municipalities was paralyzed by weak administration, antiquated equipment, and poor financial systems and procedures. In response, the two cities assembled a strategic planning team composed of staff from all levels and departments and headed by the office of the city manager. A workshop attended by representatives of stakeholders produced a strategy to address community problems (Gamedze 2001: 15).

In Rwanda, civic participation is rooted in a tradition of collective action connected with the harvest. District community development committees (CDCs) guide development and are the basis for decentralized local planning and budgeting, which feeds directly into a district-level medium-term expenditure framework. The objective is a process in which district-level plans (filtered through central-level sectoral ministries) are developed through "social mapping, seasonality, preference scoring and process techniques" (Kanyankole and Nzabakwiza 2005: 33). A central information center develops "information packages" to track problems identified by communities (Kanyankole and Nzabakwiza 2005: 33). Cell councils, sector councils, and CDCs provide for the expression of local views. The district is the administrative unit for local implementation and monitoring. Although national ministries establish national policy, the details of administration are a local responsibility. Empowering local populations has promoted popular and civic participation. The CDC and the district accountant are responsible for preparing the development budget and financing program for cells, sectors, and the district. The CDC is also charged with training and coordinating activities of stakeholders and is accountable to the executive committee, which is accountable to the district council. The executive committee also reports to the central government.

Accountability, Control, and Evaluation

Accountability in local governance occurs on at least two levels: accountability between institutions—for example, between agencies and executives and legislative bodies and between governmental levels—and accountability between the public (however defined) and institutions of governance. Effective local government is monitored for results by and is accountable to citizens, markets, and superior-level jurisdictions (Peterson 1997). Accountability requires established missions and goals and published measures of service quality.

Evaluation and accountability should be "embedded in the public sector organizational culture . . . by building institutional capacity for evaluation" (Shah 1998: 17). Evaluation capacity is critical to citizen participation and vertical oversight and requires an evaluative methodology and independent higher-level assessment.

Performance should be linked to budgeting. Accountable and responsive service delivery requires local innovation and adaptation. At the same time, control functions such as audit and inspection must be strengthened to ensure "freedom and responsibility within boundaries" (Peterson 1997: 19).

Balance in Local Discretion

Accountability is a function of design. Control over resources engenders and requires local officials to be accountable for outcomes. In local governance systems with inadequate resource authority, fiscal dependency promotes central control and regulation, limiting local autonomy and local accountability (Gooptu and others 2000).

Because many local services have implications beyond local boundaries, local officials must be accountable to central and regional institutions as well as to local institutions. Such accountability requires limitations on local discretion. Central regulation, minimum service standards, and conditional transfers limit local budgetary choice and are often used to promote broader national objectives. In structures transitioning to greater local control, ministries often resist the transfer of service delivery authority to local jurisdictions and attempt to retain de facto policy and delivery control through administrative regulation. Ministerial regulatory directive should not replace direct central responsibility.

Dividing authority over local services to locally and nonlocally elected or appointed officials interferes with local accountability. When nonlocal officials have responsibility for decisions affecting local service delivery, citizens may have difficulty holding these officials accountable (Edmiston 2000). True local accountability requires local capacity and discretion and political systems for holding local officials responsible for outcomes. As an accountability mechanism, election of local officials is superior to centralized, hierarchical administrative controls (see box 8.4).

Range and Basis of Central Control

Reporting and steering systems are needed to gauge fulfillment of public objectives and to maintain control over aggregate public sector expenditures. According to the OECD, the redesign of information and accountability systems is key to "contemporary inter-governmental management" (OECD 1997: 54). The two basic forms of control are performance-based control and more traditional administration- or rule-based control. The latter is based on institutional oversight mechanisms emphasizing the legality, regularity, and appropriateness of subnational actions.

BOX 8.4 Accountability in African Local Government

The Economic Commission for Africa (2004) finds that "Most African countries have tried to resolve the problem of accountability of local governments by asserting central government hierarchical control over local governments." Control mechanisms include "inspectorates, approval processes for local government decisions, deployment of central level personnel to local governments and, in extreme cases, use [of] powers of suspension and dissolution of local government councils." Internal accountability mechanisms include budgetary control and internal audit.

The commission notes that central governments often misuse their powers of control over local governments. It reports that legislative controls can be abused and "are not sufficient to ensure good governance when they are not subject to appropriate central or citizen accountability mechanisms." Experiments with more direct voice-accountability systems have had various degrees of success. According to the commission, "it appears that mechanisms involving elections, political parties, civil society and/or the media are more effective vehicles for accountability than, say, public hearings or opinion surveys."

Source: ECA 2004: 36–38. Reprinted with permission.

Modes of administrative control, or vertical monitoring, range from independent local audit commissions that establish financial integrity and value for money (United Kingdom) to prefect-style forms of guardianship (Belgium and Spain). Prefect-style monitoring is increasingly being replaced by a focus on results. In addition, blurring of tasks among levels in intergovernmental structures has resulted in less hierarchical forms of monitoring. Some of these forms are quite informal and use joint financing as a vehicle for vertical coordination (as in Canada, Denmark, Sweden, Switzerland, and the United States).

Performance-based controls are increasing in use, reflecting a movement away from financial control and detailed regulation. Their focus is on process and outputs and outcomes. General intergovernmental grants are displacing specific grants to allow more intergovernmental consultation on minimum standards and guidelines, but information and monitoring requirements are stringent.

Performance-based controls are often based on benchmarking and consultation, but require clear lines of accountability to be effective. Distinctions must be made between "the public accountability of elected officials and that of managers who are hierarchically accountable for results" (OECD 1997: 66). Accountability for managerial performance is salient to intergovernmental relationships.

Local budgetary authority has implications for monitoring resource use. In Australia and the United States, states establish their own audit requirements and have their own auditors. In France, regional chambers of accounts verify local finances and report to the national Court of Accounts.

Citizen Participation and Civil Society

Citizen participation and accountability are reinforcing (World Bank 2000). Catalysts are vehicles to register citizen complaints, to recall elected officials, and to provide for third-party critical thought and evaluation, judicial independence, and a free press. Citizen participation requires strong local institutions, a "class-less" society, political stability, and political freedom (Shah 1998: 21). A meaningful local budgeting process requires these conditions and can, itself, promote them (see box 8.5).

Public accountability is key. Kingsley (1996: 421–22) identifies (in addition to the free election of local leaders) the elements required to hold public

---

BOX 8.5 Role of Civil Society in Intergovernmental Budget Tracking: Uganda

The following is an excerpt from an unpublished case study by the World Bank in which the authors describe the role of Ugandan civil society in intergovernmental budget tracking.

In 1998, the Ugandan government established the Poverty Action Fund (PAF) as a mechanism to target, protect and monitor funds released by the HIPC initiative and donors for poverty programs including water, health, education, roads, and agriculture. The PAF is integrated into the budget and sent as fiscal transfers to local governments, hence the importance for local people to monitor its use. The government involves civil society organizations in monitoring the impact of PAF expenditures by allocating 5 percent of the fund to monitoring activities. Monitoring is coordinated by the Uganda Debt Network (UDN), and is undertaken through quarterly field surveys by a team of researchers and community members through Poverty Action Fund Monitoring Committees (PAFMCs) in 12 districts in Uganda.

PAFMCs are voluntary civil society groups participating in PAF monitoring, anti-corruption campaigns, and advocacy for accountability and transparency. The committees are diverse groups including women, youth, disabled people, religious leaders, and the elderly. In order to make monitoring more participatory, UDN introduced Community Based Monitoring and Evaluation System (CBMES) approach. Through CBMES the communities are engaged in continuous monitoring and evaluation of government programs.

During the inception of CBMES Pilot in Tororo District in November and December 2002 a meeting was organized by Budget Community Monitors to present their findings to local leaders and community members. Particular concern was raised about poor management, procurement, and control systems in the Mulanda Health System where 31 mattresses out of 40 had disappeared and 7 out of 8 bicycles purchased were also missing in less than a year. The monitors found that there was no evidence of purchase of health materials; they could not ascertain the cost of drugs and other utensils. The local officials . . . expressed a willingness to correct the situation. The Chief Administrative Officer interrogated the health center authorities and the stolen materials were recovered in less than a month.

UDN's model of PAF monitoring has proved to be successful as seen in the requests from around the country by various stakeholders, including the government. The initiative also tracks monthly expenditure releases from the central government to local governments and reconciles these with releases from the central bank. Quarterly progress reports are presented at multi-stakeholder meetings. In a relatively short period of time, this initiative has helped identify problems in funding to local government, increased funding to poverty relief programs, and shifted expenditures towards priority sectors.

Moreover, the Ministry of Finance, Planning, and Economic Development has opened its budget reference groups meeting to civil society consultations, which creates an entry point for civil society to join discussions previously reserved for policymakers and technocrats. This represents an additional opportunity to monitor government actions toward development obligations. In addition, by making information on the budget more accessible to civil society, UDN has strengthened the campaign for pro-poor budgets by promoting collaboration between civil society and government officials and by enabling groups to lobby more effectively for resources to be channelled to previously overlooked areas.

Source: Campos and Krafchik 2005: 8–9. Reprinted with permission.

officials accountable for performance: "performance measurement" of the output of all agencies, "independent and objective audits" of performance and financial management, "performance contracts," "decentralization of responsibilities within government" to give lower-level officials discretion in determining how to achieve targets, "customer orientation and access" through publication of operating plans and performance reports, and "a competitive mode of service provision" (contracting and use of nongovernmental organizations). He considers the most important element to be "a strong civil society" (Kingsley 1996: 421–22).

Accountability and Responsiveness

The appropriate balance of upward accountability (through regulation) and downward accountability (to constituents) is critical. Greater relative local (as opposed to central) accountability should not be taken as a given. Evidence suggests that democratic institutions, rule of law, and bureaucratic culture are more important to increased accountability and reduced corruption than the level of centralization and decentralization (Gurgur and Shah 2000).

Accountability failures exist because of political capture or bureaucratic corruption (Bardhan and Mookherjee 2000).[5] The assumption is that local governments are more prone to capture. Whether or not this is the case is dependent on the degree of voter awareness, the cohesion of special interests, the heterogeneity of districts, and the electoral system and its competitiveness (Bardhan and Mookherjee 2002). Local officials are expected to more accurately perceive the preferences of local populations than nonlocal officials (Azfar and others 2000). Acting on these perceptions may be a different matter when democratic accountability mechanisms are absent.

Local political accountability is undermined by poorly developed local democracy (see box 8.6). Alternative and supplementary means to promote accountability include participatory budgeting. "Yardstick competition," in which the performance of public officials in one jurisdiction is used as a standard for evaluating the performance of public officials in another jurisdiction, is another potential vehicle for holding local officials accountable for outcomes (Bardhan 2002: 12–13).

Supportive formal and informal institutions are necessary. Decision-making transparency is critical. "[I]nstitutions and mechanisms for citizen voice and exit, [and] norms and networks of civic engagement" (Shah 1998: 15) can overcome barriers to citizen participation and transparency in decision making. To achieve "direct citizen participation requires that citizens have clear information regarding the municipal budget and service costs and that they participate in actual budget choices" (Peterson 1997: 20). Formal structures identifying the role of community organizations and citizens are also important.

Service Efficiency and Effectiveness

World Development Report 1994: Infrastructure for Development identifies numerous examples of improvements in service delivery through expanded local discretion and authority. According to the report, a review of 42 developing countries found that "where road maintenance was decentralized, backlogs were lower and the conditions of roads were better" (World Bank 1994: 75). The report notes that "per capita water production costs are four times higher in centralized than fully decentralized systems and are lowest when decentralization is combined with central coordination" (World Bank 1994: 75).

BOX 8.6 The Budget Process and Accountability in Kenya

The following is excerpted from a report by the U.K. Department for International Development.

> The idealised model of representative democracy in local government suggests that, through regular, free and competitive elections, citizens make known their needs and priorities. The councillors they elect then formulate strategies, make key decisions and prioritise [sic] expenditure choices through formal policy and budgetary processes, with officials (who are politically neutral) advising them and implementing the decisions.
>
> The reality is generally rather different. Whilst local elections in Kenya are held regularly, and are generally free and fair, issues are highly aggregated, with candidates rarely presenting clear manifestos or choices. Together with the fact that elections are held only once in five years, this means that local needs, priorities and choices are not identified through the electoral process in sufficient detail for the purposes of planning and budgeting.
>
> Meanwhile, councillors are often poorly equipped to formulate strategies or make key choices, but instead tend to intervene on an ad hoc basis, often at the implementation stage. As a result, there is distrust between officials and councillors, with officials driving the agenda, and both sides accusing the other of vested interests and malpractice. In practice, much decision-making is informal, while formally approved budgets are often not adhered to because of the lack of financial resources.

Horizontal accountability—between officers and elected councillors

- there is a general lack of transparency over decisions and actual use of resources
- there is a profound distrust between officials and councillors in most [local authorities (LAs)], each accusing the other of malpractice
- councillors complain of not being provided with information, of council decisions not being implemented, and of officers not being accountable, e.g. for budget implementation
- councillors also accuse officers of secrecy, obstruction and corruption, and complain that corrupt officers are simply moved by the Ministry to different LAs
- officers often regard councillors as ill-educated and so unable to understand policy choices or read a budget (although officers rarely seem to make serious efforts to engage councillors in strategic decision-making)
- officers accuse councillors of being interested only in their direct benefits (allowances, corrupt awarding of tenders, appointment of staff), and of not following due procedures
- officers in some LAs see the [Local Authority Service Delivery Action Plan (LASDAP)] process as a way of holding councillors to account.

Vertical downward accountability—council's and elected councillor's accountability to citizenry

- there has been no tradition of reporting back to citizens on the work of the council

(Box continues on the following page.)

■ a lack of transparency and a tradition of secrecy, with budgets not being publicly available, and accounts not being produced, never mind audited (until now); "the council operates like a casino" was a comment of one citizen
■ although full council meetings are open to public, key decisions are usually made in closed meetings
■ almost all LAs have failed until recently to produce accounts, let alone have them audited
■ although some LAs put some information on their notice boards, this is often not in a form which can be readily understood, and few people are aware of it
■ the media can play an important role in building local accountability, although much media reporting in Kenya lacks proper investigation; local radio potentially offers opportunities for local accountability through on-air discussions between Mayors or officials and citizens, but this has yet to really take off (as it has in Uganda)
■ courts are potentially another mechanism of accountability, although they tend to be used by the better off (e.g. business organisations protesting about tax rates), and courts do not provide a satisfactory means of resolving complex issues.

Vertical upward accountability—council's accountability to the central government

■ given the weakness of downward accountability, upward accountability is crucial; but in practice that has also been weak, mainly because of the ineffectiveness of the Ministry of Local Government: serious delays in budget approval; approval of unrealistic budgets; and inspections which seem to be regarded as rent-seeking opportunities. The Ministry also seems unwilling or unable to take decisive action when LAs transgress regulations or where officers or councillors act corruptly.

Source: Devas 2002: 8–9. Reprinted with permission.

In addition to lack of technical knowledge, failures in local service delivery are often a function of "constraints and perverse incentives confronting local personnel and their political leadership" (Dillinger 1994). In Hungary and Slovakia, effectiveness in service delivery (defined as promoting efficiency, ensuring accountability, and encouraging participation), was found to hinge on factors that include "governance mechanisms to strengthen accountability and fiduciary responsibility" and "incentive mechanisms to ensure that agents deliver services of an acceptable quality at least cost" (Dethier 2000b: 1). Information asymmetries between central and local governments require that compliance be induced either by monitoring and reporting or through incentive mechanisms to align the utility-maximizing behavior of both actors. The key is to establish a framework (for example, financial management and accounting) and reporting requirements and to monitor compliance (directly and through public mechanisms). Proper management of funds and functions is also required and is served by transparency (of budget documents and processes and of annual financial statements) and enforcement (of standards such as audits of local jurisdictions).

Capacity and Participation

Latin American experience indicates that strengthening municipal capacity requires professional staff, citizen feedback mechanisms, increased output expectations of local public employees, and workforce stability (Peterson 1997). Citizen participation, public and market accountability, and own-source and intergovernmental fiscal instruments promoting appropriate incentives are also important.

Research on the Philippines (Azfar and others 2000) and Uganda (Kahkonen and Lanyi 2001) reveals several factors negatively affecting service delivery. First, local officials often have no authority to adjust service levels. Second, local corruption leaks funds and other resources, undermining efficiency. Third, pursuit of accountability through citizen participation is hampered by inadequate information dissemination. Fourth, exit as a motivation for public service improvement is weak because of limited mobility across jurisdictions. Fifth, local government capacity (personnel, materials, and equipment) is inadequate. Finally, services with significant interjurisdictional spillovers are hampered by coordination difficulties.

Citizen participation is recognized as a key contributor to effective service delivery. A review of 121 rural water supply projects found that the projects in which citizen participation in project selection and design was high were much more likely to maintain water supply in good condition (World Bank 1994: 76). The three keys to effective participation are directly involving beneficiaries, developing early project consensus, and acquiring beneficiary in-kind or cash contributions. The participatory municipal budgeting model used in Porto Alegre, Brazil, is thought to have contributed to positive outcomes in education, sanitation, and revenue mobilization and to have improved the allocation of resources to poorer areas (Bardhan 2002).

Political Capture and Providing for the Poor

A bias against providing for the needs of the poor may exist in local governance structures. Such a bias results from "low levels of political awareness among poor voters and lobbying by special interest groups that disproportionately represent the interests of the non-poor" (Bardhan and Mookherjee 2000: 5). Targeting of services to those most in need may decline if left to local discretion:

> The primary problem with the decentralized delivery mode is the proneness of local governments to pressure from local elites to divert supplies to them. These [sic] reflect weaknesses in the functioning of a fair electoral process at the local level, lower levels of political awareness among the poor, and the tendency for wealthier groups to form special interest groups that contribute to campaign finance of political parties. The anti-poor bias, and hence targeting failures . . . tend to be more severe in regions with high poverty rates (von Braun and Grote 2000: 35).

As von Braun and Grote (2000: 8) note, "[T]hose . . . in power . . . have few incentives to allow participatory institutions to develop."

Political decentralization (through the involvement of civil society) often benefits the poor and does so more than administrative decentralization or fiscal decentralization. A minimum threshold of subnational expenditure responsibility does, however, appear to be a precondition for poverty reduction. But expenditure decentralization can impair the delivery of critical social services (such as education and health) if institutional and managerial capacity and the local political power of the poor are inadequate.[6]

Representation is important in determining the distribution of policy outcomes. India's mandated representation of women in leadership positions at the local level is associated with increased female public participation and increased investment in infrastructure that provides for rural women's needs (Chattopadhyay and Duflo 2001; see Bardhan 2002). Foster and Rosenzweig (2001) find that fiscal decentralization and democratization increase the political representation of landless households (see Bardhan 2002).

Altered governance structures are also expected to be associated with increased economic output and growth. But in spite of economic improvements, the poor are often excluded because of capture and corruption. To mitigate local capture effects, sectors relevant to poverty reduction should have shared local and central responsibility, and mechanisms are necessary to ensure adequate participation and targeting (Dethier 2000a: 12).

Conclusion

Much of the substance and significance of local governments' budgetary processes depends on the intergovernmental structure within which the processes are implemented. Meaningful local processes require local discretion and local authority to marshal and manage local resources to fulfill local needs and objectives. Simultaneously, effective modes of communication and coordination among levels of government are essential. Multitiered institutions and actors result in complex and varied capacities for meaningful local budgetary choice.

Excessively constrained local authority is widespread in Africa, but a recent trend is more shared authority and greater local discretion and capacity. Cooperative intergovernmental systems are underdeveloped but evolving. A balance between hierarchal/coercive and cooperative/collaborative mechanisms (vertically and horizontally) has yet to be widely achieved. Nonetheless, the objectives and elements of effective local budgetary processes are essentially the same as at other levels. The process should include mechanisms to establish the following: needs, goals, and objectives to guide decision making and budget development; appropriate and effective programmatic and managerial responses; spending plans consistent with available resources and managerial and programmatic means of goal achievement; and feedback mechanisms to evaluate performance and ensure financial integrity. Effective systems are expected to promote fiscal discipline and expenditure control, strategic resource allocation, operational (managerial) efficiency, and responsiveness to local needs.

Process and environmental conditions are important elements of the local budget cycle. Critical factors are balanced institutional authority and proper representation of stakeholders. Fiscal discipline must be secured in a manner that ensures responsiveness to local populations. Effective budget formulation requires systematic incorporation of consultative local policy guidance within the context of realistic appraisals of local resource availability. Likewise, administrative and managerial initiative and flexibility should be fostered in the development of programmatic options. Effective legislative review requires meaningful legislative authority and the availability of pertinent information on which to exercise policy choice and oversight. Independent institutional capacity, submission of proposed expenditure plans in sufficient detail to hold operating units accountable, and discretion in making final spending allocations are all required. Mechanisms to ensure execution consistent with the approved budget are critical, as is balance between managerial flexibility and legislative control. Evaluation and reporting must be robust enough to ensure accountability for programmatic performance and financial integrity, and reporting must be made public. Timetables and technical details are important, but proper institutional relationships, capacity, roles, and stakeholder participation are critical to effective outcomes.

Participatory processes provide significant potential for improved planning and budgeting. However, to be effective, participation must be broadly based. Participatory processes too often provide access only to small subsets of local populations and can result in local elite dominance in a manner that channels resources away from populations in need. Mechanisms to promote open, communitarian participation are important to securing the benefits of participatory processes. Adequate social capital is a critical element. It both fosters and is fostered by meaningful local resource discretion and participation. Effective participation should be institutionalized in budget planning, development, and approval processes through channels such as community forums and budget hearings. Governments may need to establish procedures to ensure adequate representation of what might otherwise be socially excluded groups.

Attention to mechanisms to ensure accountability among institutions, among levels of government, and between institutions of governance and the public is critical. Both rule-based and performance-based mechanisms are required. Participatory processes take significant steps in this direction. However, accountability for results (ex ante) requires specific consideration. Accountability can be fostered through open reporting, meaningful sanctions, the appropriate organizational culture, program design and incentives, rule of law, and democratic institutions. Accountability requires measures to mitigate political capture and bureaucratic corruption. Mechanisms for independent evaluation and open information and voice are essential.

Establishment of proper process elements is one of the most important—and most complicated—aspects of effective local budgeting (and governance). It requires coordination across and between levels of government and among institutional actors, civil society, and the general local population. Such coordination requires the diligent performance of interdependent roles and functions by those officially and unofficially engaged in the process, including relatively independent institutions and actors. It also requires institutional and cultural development and sophistication. Coordination among processes and actors is probably the single most influential element in producing an effective and responsive local budgeting and governance system.

Annex 8A: South Africa as a Model of Intergovernmental Sophistication

South Africa has the most sophisticated and formalized approach to intergovernmental relations in Africa. The constitution specifically recognizes the importance of intergovernmental cooperation in governance and establishes both the "distinctive and interrelated" interdependence of the country's national, provincial, and local levels of government (PAIR Institute of South Africa 2002: 3). It requires that the spheres of government "co-operate with one another in mutual trust and good faith by fostering friendly relations; assisting and supporting one another; informing one another of, and consulting one another on, matters of common interest; co-ordinating their actions and legislation with one another; adhering to agreed procedures; and avoiding legal proceedings against one another" (Constitution of the Republic of South Africa 1996: chapter 3).

Parliament is required to create institutions and structures to promote intergovernmental relations and settle disputes and to ensure that disputes unresolved through established mechanisms are resolvable by the courts. The constitution establishes the structure and powers of each level of government, allows a higher sphere to delegate its powers to a lower sphere, and stipulates the legislative supremacy of higher spheres in conflicts among spheres with shared powers. However, all spheres, including municipal councils, are legislatively independent within proscribed matters.

Intergovernmental relations are defined arrangements for institutional, political, and financial interactions. Fiscal relations require recommendations from the Financial Fiscal Commission, with which Parliament is required to consult (along with provincial and local governments) in establishing the fiscal parameters of intergovernmental relationships. The Department of Provincial and Local Government also "guides and regulates co-operative government and intergovernmental relationships" (PAIR Institute of South Africa 2002: 10).

Provisions require local governments to encourage the involvement and consultation of communities and community organizations in municipal budget decision making. Local governments must establish ward committees to promote public participation in municipal governance. These committees assist the democratically elected ward representative to the city council in reflecting community interests. Their charge includes input into preparation of the municipal budget and service provision; implementation and review of systems of performance management; performance monitoring; information dissemination; and preparation, implementation, and review of Integrated Development Planning (IDP) (DPLG 2000a). The IDP process is also the basis for the "co-ordination of co-operative governance between spheres" at the "micro terrains of service delivery" (PAIR Institute of South Africa 2002: 11). Municipal government has a primary role:

> In accordance with this new intergovernmental development planning ethos, local government is the main/frontline planning arm of government, provinces would support and monitor this activity, and national government

would create the framework of norms and standards in which these developmental actions would take place. Collectively, and with each sphere fulfilling its specific mandate, the actions of the three spheres would dovetail into a joint intergovernmental effort aimed at achieving its key developmental objectives (DPLG 2000b: 8).

The IDP is a strategic plan incorporating both short-term and medium-term objectives. It is intended to serve as a guide to local government budgeting, service delivery, and management, and it supersedes all other municipal plans. Provinces assist in plan creation, monitor plan content and local performance relevant to required and desired actions, and ensure that regional and national priorities are reflected in plan development and performance. The formal plan development and approval process ensures coordination between spheres and seeks to ensure policy and budgetary conformity across spheres (see table 8A.1).

In South Africa, the national government can intervene if provinces do not fulfill an executive obligation. Intervention is focused on interregional uniformity, norms, standards, and national policy. The Intergovernmental Fiscal Relations Act of 1997 guides intergovernmental fiscal relations. It provides a consultation process and regulates budgeting, and it established the Budget Council and Budget Forum. IDP is the primary vehicle for coordination; spending in any portion of the republic is "traceable in municipal integrated planning frameworks" (PAIR Institute of South Africa 2002: 13). The Division of Revenue Act of 1998 also established a system for monitoring spending and allocating resources across spheres. This integration and cooperation increases uniformity in policy, while limiting local discretion in areas of broad priority.

Annex 8B: Estonia's Local Budget Process

Ainsoo and others (2002) provide a detailed description of Estonia's local budget process. Highlights of that description follow.[7]

Local Government Structure

Estonia's municipalities are governed by a representative council and have independent budget and revenue authority. The constitution forbids the central government's imposition of unfunded mandates for supplementary functions; delegation of such functions with sufficient compensation is hotly contested. The constitution also provides the right for cooperative unions among municipalities. Universal regulation governs all municipalities,

TABLE 8A.1 Integrated Development Planning in South Africa

Benefits of an IDP		Role of provinces	
Stakeholder	Benefits	Responsibility	Description
Municipal Council	■ Provides clear and accountable leadership and development direction ■ Develops cooperative relationships with stakeholders and communities ■ Obtains access to development resources and external support ■ Monitors the performance of municipal officials	Guidance	Guide municipal integrated development planning process and requirements in terms of (1) the most critical issues to be addressed; (2) provincial strategies, policies, and program and resource availability; (3) legal requirements; and (4) the need for coordinated municipal and provincial development and sector planning
Councilors	■ Provides councilors with a mechanism for communicating with their constituencies ■ Enables councilors to represent their constituencies effectively by making informed decisions ■ Enables councilors to measure their own performance	Coordination	Coordinate (1) provincial integrated development and sector planning, budgeting, and implementation processes within the province; (2) municipal integrated development planning, budgeting, and implementation processes among municipalities; and (3) provincial and municipal sector planning, budgeting, and implementation processes

(continued)

255

TABLE 8A.1 Integrated Development Planning in South Africa *(continued)*

Benefits of an IDP		Role of provinces	
Stakeholder	Benefits	Responsibility	Description
Municipal officials	■ Guides business unit planning within the municipal administration ■ Provides municipal officials with a mechanism to communicate with councilors ■ Enables officials to contribute to the municipality's vision ■ Enables officials to be part of the decision-making process	Support	Support municipalities with (1) integrated development planning, (2) sector planning, and (3) integration of municipal actions with actions of other spheres of government within provinces
Communities and other stakeholders	■ Gives them an opportunity to inform the municipal council of development needs ■ Gives them an opportunity to determine the municipality's development direction ■ Provides a mechanism through which to communicate with their councilors and the governing body ■ Provides a mechanism through which they can measure the performance of the councilors and the municipalities as a whole	Monitor	Monitor the extent to which all the required and desired actions take and/or took place in the required format, as well as monitor the contribution of the various (municipal and provincial) role players to the achievement of shared developmental objectives. This monitoring enables the provincial government to (1) extract local information for provincial planning, (2) determine whether and to what extent provincewide issues, strategies, and programs have been taken up in municipal planning, and (3) consider the effectiveness of engagement among the respective provincial sector departments and municipalities.

National and provincial sector departments

- Provides guidance to the departments as to where their services are required and hence where to allocate their resources
- Allows departments to coordinate their service delivery and development programs in a municipal area on the basis of local conditions and requirements

Private sector

- Serves as a guide to the private sector in making decisions about areas and sectors for investment

Source: Adapted from DPLG 2000b.

irrespective of differences in size and capacity. Municipalities can establish sub-levels in the form of municipal districts to which they can delegate functions.

Primary Institutional Actors and Roles

The primary local governing entity is the elected municipal council, which has "full control over the final decisions concerning local finances" (Ainsoo and others 2002: 280). The council is responsible for development planning, budgeting, local taxation, appointment of local administrators, establishment of administrative salaries, and management of municipal property. The functions of the council are specified in legislation, as is the formation of an audit committee composed of council members. The council appoints and removes the head of the local executive committee. The head of the local executive committee, with approval of the council, appoints executive-level administrators. A vice-governor with responsibility for finance and budget is normally appointed. The Local Government Organization Act prescribes the exclusive responsibilities of local government; actual assignment of responsibilities is complicated and confused. Responsibilities include health, education, social welfare, culture, recreation, transportation, economic services, and general public services.

Budget Framework

A strategic planning process is intended by law to drive local government budgeting. The local development plan has a three-year time horizon and establishes priorities on the basis of an analysis of the economic environment and social conditions. The time horizon is extended to cover longer-term commitments of the local government. However, because of training problems, failures to solidify content and format requirements, politically inspired adjustment, and unrealistic orientation, these plans are less than entirely effective as a policy or management tool. A separate capital budget is not required, but many of the larger cities use a separate capital programming process. Investment proposals often are five times budget capacity, suggesting questionable processes of prioritization.

Local budgets are classified by function, organizational spending unit, and object (economic article). Local budgets cover normal government operations (the council and agencies), organizations regulated by private law but owned by the local government, appropriations and contributions to nongovernmental organizations and foundations, cooperative participation in associations or enterprises with other public organizations or local governments, support to nonprofit or private organizations that deliver public services, contracted purchases from external organizations, and planning activities. The budgets of extra-budgetary entities are independently constructed. If the local government allocates resources to these entities' operations, it constructs the entities after adopting the local budget.

Local budgets are not comprehensive. Donations and external source revenues may be managed separately, but sometimes they are included in the budget retroactively in an attempt to avoid a reduction in funding by the central government. In-kind support is not comprehensively included. Earmarked funds from central ministries may be directly paid for execution of functions and not appear in the budget. Social assistance expenditures (administered by local agencies) also do not appear in the budget.

Budget Participants

Primary budget participants include the budget and finance department, the budget committee, the head of government, municipal council committees, and the municipal council. Secondary participants include temporary committees, agencies and spending units, organizations and individuals, the public, private enterprises, and civil organizations (see box 8B.1).

Budget Cycle

Central legislation regulates the local budget cycle. Local budgets are required to be adopted by April 1 or three months after approval of the state budget, whichever is later. The draft budget, approved budget, amendments, and execution report of the previous budget must be published, along with the audit report. The actual process varies substantially. Some budgets are approved with detail line itemization; others are approved for lump sum amounts by function and unit.

Actual budget preparation in municipalities in Estonia formally begins in March, 10 months before the January beginning of the new fiscal year for the state budget. During this time, local governments pursue the legislative approval and review and the executive preparation stages. The process begins with consideration of needs and resources and establishment of expenditure ceilings by permanent council committees and the council's Budget and Economic Committee. Guidelines for budget development are established, and draft subunit budgets are prepared during May and presented to the

BOX 8B.1 Participants in Local Government Budgeting in Estonia

Ainsoo and others (2002) describe participants in local government budgeting in Estonia as follows.

Primary Participants

Budget or financial department: This department conducts all analysis preceding budget preparation, produces all intermediate accounts and documents, and is involved in direct negotiations with all budgeting units. Committees of the council, especially the budget committee, are typically involved in these negotiations from the beginning.

Budget committee: This committee of the local council, which in smaller local government units has members from outside the council, is the main participant in the budget formation process. The role of the council committee is to discuss and harmonize the points of view expressed in preparatory papers.

Head of local government: This individual is responsible for preparation of the budget and ensures that all agencies follow the budget after its approval. Actually, the head of government delegates this responsibility to the vice-head of government, who in many local governments is responsible for local finances, or directly to the head of the budget department.

Municipal council committees: Committees such as the social, audit, budgeting, financial, and economics committees participate to some extent in the budgeting process. These committees discuss budgets of local government units and agencies.

Municipal council: This council has the right to adopt or deny the draft budget. It supervises and assesses the results of executive bodies' activities.

Secondary Participants

Temporary committees: These committees are formed in some local governments to fulfill specific tasks, such as preparation of a zero-based budget.

Local government agencies and units: These agencies and units should prepare their own budgets, but they are confronted with expenditure ceilings established at an early stage of the budgeting process. The room for maneuvering is small.

Other organizations and individuals: Those intending to get financial assistance from the local government must submit appropriate applications within a certain time period.

The public: The public can participate in the budget process at the council, because, as a rule, council meetings are open. The public typically is uninterested in participating in the process.

Private sector enterprises: Local government may enlist the help of these enterprises in preparing the municipal development plan and economic forecasts.

General public and civil organizations: Both can make suggestions to the municipal council concerning changes in the budget and municipal development plan. Thereafter, the municipal council will discuss these proposals in committees and present results to the government or council for preparation of the budget or municipal development plan.

Source: Ainsoo and others 2002: 304–05. Reprinted with permission.

government. These budgets are revised in June on the basis of analysis by the Budget and Economic Committee. Simultaneously, the municipal council approves revenue plans of agencies.

On June 15, subunit budgets are compiled to create a draft budget, which includes a transmission memo highlighting the previous year's revenue and expenditure totals, as well as subtotals classified by function, spending unit, and economic article. From June to August, the draft budget (augmented by supplemental statistical data) is presented to the Budget and Economic Committee of the council for further analyses, comment, and presentation to the municipal council for first reading. On August 10, council committees begin deliberation on the draft budget and formulate proposals. Adjustments are intended to offset increased expenditures and are submitted to the Budget and Economic Committee. The council can approve amendments rejected by the committee.

In December, the local government and the Budget and Economic Committee cooperatively prepare the final draft budget for approval. Failure to approve the budget by the start of the ensuing fiscal year results in an automatic continuing appropriation. The approved budget may be amended, usually on the basis of a finalization of central government transfers. By March 1, the previous year's execution report is submitted to the municipal council, along with the external auditors' statement. By July 1, the execution report is considered and approved by the municipal council. The approved report is then presented to the Ministry of Finance.

Detail in the originally adopted budget drives the process for midyear budget alteration (or supplements). Because only the municipal council can alter the municipal budget, much council time in jurisdictions that adopt detailed line items is consumed by budget adjustments throughout the fiscal year. In jurisdictions that adopt budgets with relatively little line-item detail, administrative changes by the government require no council intervention. The latter method provides administrative flexibility, a requisite in budget execution, in exchange for (sometimes quite meaningless) control.

Annex 8C: Participatory Local Budgeting and Planning in Uganda

In 1998, Uganda introduced the Uganda Participatory Poverty Assessment Project, which surveyed the poor in several rural and two urban districts to identify unmet needs. An assessment of these needs was incorporated into policy deliberation at the local district and national planning levels, influencing budget allocations on the priority of provision of access to clean water and security. The project surveys indicated the need for flexibility in the allocation of grant revenues to districts and the need to devolve service provision to urban and district authorities (ECA 2004: 11–12).

Uganda's Local Government Act requires that budget conferences be held and be open to the public at each level of local council from village, to ward, to division, to municipality, to district. The municipal and division conferences result in spending proposals for the ensuing fiscal year and a three-year rolling plan. At the village level, all adults are councilors. Therefore, the annual budget conference is an annual meeting of the citizenry. The executive committee members of each village attend ward meetings. The division budget conference includes the chairpersons of villages and wards, division councilors, and stakeholders. The municipal and district conferences include the leadership of local stakeholders, business groups, nongovernmental organizations, and community organizations. A review of the process in seven Ugandan municipalities showed that the actual level of representation and participation varies across jurisdictions. Some villages fail to conduct their annual meeting, and in others, representation is less than comprehensive:

> [S]ince invitations to the [upper-level] budget conference are in the hands of the local Executive Committee, it is unlikely that stakeholders who are not in the Committee's "good books" will be invited. Thus, participation in the budget conferences may be unrepresentative of important interests (DFID 2002: 4).

Conferences are intended to solicit the views of stakeholders and individuals. Actual participation is quite limited, however. Discussions at the division, municipal, and district levels are "mostly driven by technocrats, conducted in English and couched in formal, budget language, which may not be conducive to participation by ordinary citizens, let alone the poor. Better educated people also often exert disproportionate influence" (DFID 2002: 5).

Nonetheless, the process undertaken by the Jinja Municipal Council (a single-day affair) resulted in proposals for inclusion in the municipal budget with others referred to the division level and central government. It also provided a forum for direct accountability through discussion of the achievements and shortcomings of municipal administration and service delivery. The Mayor of Entebbe has also used the municipal conference to conduct budget outreach meetings in each of the city's 24 villages.

Although people appear "increasingly willing to speak out and challenge their leaders" at budget conferences, many hurdles remain to be overcome:

> Effective decision-making on allocation of resources is still made at the centre, and local councils have limited influence in determining what resources go to which priority areas. In addition, participation in practice is less than it might appear from the law, with village meetings being held less often than required, budget conferences attracting few who are not already involved in the system, and processes still dominated by the better off and better educated. The process is also still predominantly technocratic. Whilst there is a growing feeling of local ownership of local development process, there are also worrying signs of participation-fatigue and declining participation in local elections and local level development activities (DFID 2002: 11).

Notes

1. Treisman (2000: 2–3) identifies five forms of political decentralization: structural decentralization, decision decentralization, resource decentralization, electoral decentralization, and institutional decentralization. With the exception of the first, all have significant implications for local budget processes.
2. Urban jurisdictions (cities and municipalities) in Zimbabwe enjoy greater autonomy and independence, having "more complex systems of management with full-time executive mayors and town clerks" (Ndhlovu 2001: 8).
3. Execution entails actual implementation and greatly affects the role of the first two stages to the degree that budgets are modified (either explicitly or implicitly) during the fiscal year.
4. In France, subnational jurisdictions are responsible for education capital and maintenance expenditures, but education policy is established from the center. In Australia, the Audit Commission has studied the level of duplication between levels of government.
5. Political capture generally results from little political awareness on the part of voters and special-interest access. Bureaucratic corruption is a result of "an agency problem between elected politicians and central bureaucrats, arising from poor communication and information systems that prevent effective monitoring and performance evaluation of bureaucrats" (Bardhan and Mookherjee 2000: 5). Researchers assume that agency problems are reduced at the local level, because elected local officials either personally manage or closely monitor service delivery systems.
6. Von Braun and Grote (2000) give several examples. China's increase in economic inequality and significant rural poverty is attributed to governance factors such as "distorted incentive structure, existence of powerful elite, or inoperative legal systems" von Braun and Grote (2000: 12). India's decentralization allows the poor to exercise

voting rights at three levels of local government. However, patron-client relationships sometimes require the poor to vote on the basis of their landlords' preferences. Ghana's district assemblies establish a framework for implementing participatory, pro-poor focused projects. Although the general poverty rate has declined, the benefits of growth have not significantly accrued to the poor.
7. Reprinted with permission.

References

Ainsoo, D., A. Jaansoo, Tahve Milt, Eliko Pedastsaar, Georg Sootla, Aivar Surva, Paul Tammert, and Tarmo Tuur. 2002. "Local Government Budgeting: Estonia." In *Local Government Budgeting,* ed. M. Hogye, 273–327. Budapest, Hungary: Open Society Institute.

Antonio, V. 2001. "Local Government Reform in Mozambique." Case study on local governance, Southern African Development Community Regional Information Centre on Local Governance, Harare, Zimbabwe.

Azfar, Omar, Turgrul Gurgur, Satu Kahkonen, Anthony Lanyi, and Patrick Meagher. 2000. "Decentralization and Governance: An Empirical Investigation of Public Service Delivery in the Philippines." Working paper, Center for Institutional Reform and the Informal Sector, University of Maryland, College Park, MD.

Bardhan, Pranab. 2002. "Decentralization of Governance and Development." *Journal of Economic Perspectives* 16 (4): 185–205.

Bardhan, Pranab, and Dilip Mookherjee. 2000. *Decentralizing Anti-Poverty Program Delivery in Developing Countries.* Berkeley, CA: Center for International and Development Economics Research, University of California, Berkeley.

———. 2002. "Relative Capture of Local and Central Governments: An Essay in the Political Economy of Decentralization." Center for International and Development Economics Research, University of California, Berkeley, CA.

Calia, Roland, Salmon Guajardo, and Judd Metzgar. 2000. "Putting the NACSLB Recommended Budget Practices into Action: Best Practices in Budgeting." *Government Finance Review* (April): 1–9.

Campbell, Heather, and Robert Marshall. 2000. "Public Involvement and Planning: Looking Beyond the One to the Many." *International Planning Studies* 5 (3): 321–44.

Campos, Rocio, and Warren Krafchik. 2005. "Budget Analysis and the Millennium Development Goals (MDGs)." Working paper, case study 2, International Budget Project, Center on Budget and Policy Priorities, Washington, DC, 8–9.

Chattopadhyay, R., and E. Duflo. 2001. "Women as Policy Makers: Evidence from an India-Wide Randomized Policy Experiment." Unpublished manuscript, Massachusetts Institute of Technology, Cambridge, MA.

Constitution of the Republic of South Africa. 1996.

Crook, Richard, and James Manor. 2000. "Democratic Decentralization." Working paper, Operations Evaluation Department, World Bank, Washington, DC.

de Mello, Luiz. 2000. "Can Fiscal Decentralization Strengthen Social Capital?" Working Paper WP/00/129, International Monetary Fund, Washington, DC.

Dethier, Jean-Jacques. 2000a. "Some Remarks on Fiscal Decentralization and Governance." Paper presented at the Conference on Decentralization Sequencing, Jakarta, Indonesia, March 20.

———. 2000b. "The Effectiveness of Decentralization in Hungary and Slovakia." Paper prepared for the IMF Conference on Decentralization: Experience, Issues and Policies, Washington, DC, November 20–21.

DFID (U.K. Department for International Development). 2006. "Local Government Decision-Making: Citizen Participation and Local Acountability–Examples of Good (and Bad) Practice in Uganda." Building Municipal Accountability Series, International Development Department, University of Birmingham, Birmingham, England.

Devas, Nick. 2002. "Local Government Decision-Making: Citizen Participation and Local Accountability–Examples of Good (and Bad) Practice in Kenya." Building Municipal Accountability Series, International Development Department, University of Birmingham, Birmingham, England.

Dillinger, William. 1994. "Decentralization and Its Implications for Urban Service Delivery." Urban Management and Municipal Finance 16, Urban Management Program, World Bank, Washington, DC.

DPLG (Department of Provincial and Local Government, South Africa). 2000a. *Ward Committees*. Pretoria, South Africa: Department of Provincial and Local Government, Republic of South Africa.

———. 2000b. *Municipal Integrated Development Planning*. Pretoria, South Africa: Department of Provincial and Local Government, Republic of South Africa.

ECA (Economic Commission for Africa). 2004. *Best Practices in the Participatory Approach to Delivery of Social Services*. Addis Ababa, Ethiopia: ECA.

Edmiston, Kelly D. 2000. "Fostering Subnational Autonomy and Accountability in Decentralized Developing Countries." Working paper, Andrew Young School of Policy Studies, Georgia State University, Atlanta.

Forrester, John P., and Daniel R. Mullins. 1992. "Rebudgeting: The Serial Nature of Municipal Budgetary Processes." *Public Administration Review* 52 (5): 467–73.

Foster, A. D., and M. R. Rosenzweig. 2001. "Democratization, Decentralization and the Distribution of Local Public Goods in a Poor Rural Economy." Unpublished manuscript, University of Pennsylvania, Philadelphia, PA.

Gamedze, Benedict N. 2001. "Strategic Corporate Planning at the Municipal Level." Case study on local governance, Southern African Development Community Regional Information Centre on Local Governance, Harare, Zimbabwe.

Goodpaster, Gary, and David Ray. 2000. "Competition Policy and Decentralization." Paper presented at World Bank/Asian Development Bank/U.S. Agency for International Development/Australian Agency for International Development International Conference on Competition Policy and Economic Adjustment, Jakarta.

Gooptu, Bert Hofman, Ashoka Mody, and Vinaya Swaroop. 2000. *Indonesia: Public Spending in a Time of Change*. Washington, DC: World Bank.

Gurgur, Tugrul, and Anwar Shah. 2000. "Localization and Corruption: Panaceas or Pandora's Box?" Unpublished manuscript, World Bank, Washington, DC.

Kahkonen, Satu, and Anthony Lanyi. 2001. "Decentralization and Governance: Does Decentralization Improve Public Service Delivery?" *PREM Notes 55* (June): 1–4.

Kanyankole, Alex, and Darius Nzabakwiza. 2005. "A Case Study of Nyarugenge District Kigali City." Civic Participation in Municipal Governance in Rwanda research series, Rwandese Association of Local Government Authorities, Kigali, Rwanda.

Kingsley, G. Thomas. 1996. "Perspectives on Devolution." *Journal of the American Planning Association* 62 (4): 419–26.

May, Peter J. 1998. "Environmental Management and Governance." Paper prepared for the National Academy of Public Administration/National Institute for Research Advancement, U.S.-Japan-China Conference, Tokyo, July 26–29.

May, Peter J., and Raymond J. Burby. 1996. "Coercive versus Cooperative Policies: Comparing Intergovernmental Mandate Performance." *Journal of Policy Analysis and Management* 15 (2): 171–201.

Mikesell, John L., and Daniel R. Mullins. 2001. "Reforming Budget Systems in Countries of the Former Soviet Union." *Public Administration Review* 61 (5): 548–68.

Mosha, A.C., and O.L. Mabaila. 2003. "Financing Municipal Authorities for Sustainable Development: Case Study of Gaborone City, Botswana." Policy Brief on Governance Issues 7I, Municipal Development Partnership, Eastern and Southern Africa, Harare, Zimbabwe.

Musekiwa, Norbert. 2002. "Rural District Councils Capacity Building Programme: Best Practices from Zimbabwe." Case study on local governance, The Regional Information Centre on Local Government, Harare, Zimbabwe.

NACSLB (National Advisory Council on State and Local Budgeting). 1998. *Recommended Budget Practices: A Framework for Improved State and Local Government Budgeting.* Chicago, IL: Government Finance Officers Association.

Ndegwa, Steven. 2002. "Decentralization in Africa: A Stocktaking Survey." Africa Region Working Paper Series 40, World Bank, Washington, DC.

Ndhlovu, Ashella Tshedza. 2001. "Mobilization of Capital Funds by Urban Local Authorities: Zimbabwe." Case study on local governance, Southern African Development Community Regional Information Centre on Local Governance, Harare, Zimbabwe.

Norris, Era-Dabla, Jorge Martinez-Vazquez, and John Norregaard. 2000. "Making Decentralization Work: The Case of Russia, Ukraine, and Kazakhstan." International Studies Program Working Paper 00–9, Andrew Young School of Public Policy, Georgia State University, Atlanta, GA.

OECD (Organisation for Economic Co-operation and Development). 1997. "Managing Across Levels of Government, Part One: Overview." Paris: OECD. http://www.oecd.org/dataoecd/10/14/1902308.pdf.

PAIR Institute of South Africa. 2002. "Intergovernmental Relations and Co-operative Governance in South Africa." Best Practices Case Study Series, PAIR Institute of South Africa, Harare, Zimbabwe.

Peterson, George E. 1997. "Decentralization in Latin America: Learning through Experience." Viewpoint series working paper, Latin American and Caribbean Studies, World Bank, Washington, DC.

Parker, Andrew. 2001. "Promoting Good Governance with Social Funds and Decentralization." *PREMNotes* 51: 1–4.

Rondinelli, Dennis. 1999. "What Is Decentralization?" In *Decentralization Briefing Notes,* ed. Jennie Litvack and Jessica Seddon. Washington, DC: World Bank.

Schiavo-Campo, Salvatore, and Daniel Tommasi. 1999. *Managing Public Expenditures.* Manila: Asian Development Bank.

Schick, Allen. 2004. "Twenty-Five Years of Budgeting Reform." *OECD Journal on Budgeting* 4 (1): 81–102.

Shah, Anwar. 1998. "Balance, Accountability, and Responsiveness: Lessons about Decentralization." Policy Research Working Paper 2021, World Bank, Washington, DC.

Smoke, Paul. 2000. "Beyond Normative Models and Development Trends: Strategic Design and Implementation of Decentralization in Developing Countries." Management Development and Governance Division, United Nations Development Programme, New York. November 2000.

Spahn, Paul Bernd. 2001. "Intergovernmental Relations, Macro Economic Stability and Economic Growth." Topic 4: Intergovernmental Fiscal Relations and Local Financial Management Program, World Bank Institute, Washington, DC. http://info.world bank.org/etools/docs/library/128842/Spahn.pdf and http://www1.worldbank.org/ wbiep/decentralization/Topic04.8.htm.

Tanzi, Vito. 1995. "Fiscal Federalism and Decentralization: A Review of Some Efficiency and Macroeconomic Aspects." In *Proceedings of Annual World Bank Conference on Development Economics*, 295–316. Washington, DC: World Bank.

Treisman, Daniel. 2000. "Decentralization and the Quality of Government." Draft paper, Department of Political Science, University of California, Los Angeles.

von Braun, Joachim, and Ulrike Grote. 2000. "Does Decentralization Serve the Poor?" Paper presented at the International Monetary Fund Conference on Fiscal Decentralization, Washington, DC, November.

Wamwangi, Kinuhia, and Phillip Kundishora. 2003. "Decentralization Issues and Cross-Cutting Themes in the Eastern and Southern Africa Region. Harare, Zimbabwe." Research report, Municipal Development Partnership for Eastern and Southern Africa/The Federation of Canadian Municipalities, Harare, Zimbabwe.

World Bank. 1994. *World Development Report 1994: Infrastructure for Development*. Washington, DC: World Bank and Oxford University Press.

————. 2000. "Indonesia: Public Spending in A Time of Change." The World Bank, East Asia and Pacific Region, PREM, Washington, DC. April.

9

Local Budget Execution

KURT THURMAIER

The widely varying sizes of local governments make writing about local budget execution challenging. In a small rural state in the United States such as Iowa, local budgets are used for *cities* of 150 people. By contrast, New York City has more than 8 million residents (twice as many as the entire state of Iowa). A small city in Botswana has different needs and capacities for budgeting compared with a large city like Nairobi or Pretoria. Yet the citizens of all these cities—and other cities around the world—have the same fundamental needs and rights. They should be able to know for what purposes they are paying taxes and fees, and whether those taxes and fees are actually spent for the purposes determined by the governing body, the duly elected representatives of citizens in communities large and small. Local budgets meet these needs and support those fundamental democratic rights when the budget document is accessible and clearly communicates the sources of revenues and plans for spending them, and midyear and final reports on budget execution clearly present how the funds have been spent relative to the plan. Producing the budget document and appropriate financial reports requires a managerial approach to local budgeting. That is, the chief executive and governing body develop and execute a budget that realistically strives to achieve the city's goals and mission.

Budget execution is not the topic of much scholarly research, which is unfortunate, because it is an essential tool of public management. Many standard treatments of budget execution are found in budget textbooks (Axelrod 1995; see Lee, Johnson, and Joyce 2003;

Mikesell 1995). Few budgeting texts are explicitly aimed at local governments (see Bland and Rubin 1997; Giannakis and McCue 1999). These treatments cover expenditure-control mechanisms and revenue-monitoring activities. The best discussions of budget execution activities also explain the role budget execution plays in public management (Bland and Rubin 1997; Giannakis and McCue 1999). A small but growing literature addresses budget execution in developing countries within the context of the broader topic of public expenditure management (Fozzard and Foster 2001; IBP 2004; Killick 2005a, 2005b; Lienert 2003; Lienert and Sarraf 2001; Polidano 1999; Premchand 1993; Schiavo-Campo and Tommasi 1999; Schick 1998, World Bank 1998; Zody 1996).

This chapter treats budget execution as a critical management function and uniquely blends the basic tenets of budget execution for local governments with guidance on budget execution in developing countries. It focuses on budget execution in local governments. This discussion necessarily involves some discussion of national (and regional) budget execution as well. The relatively large dependence of many local governments on regional and central budget transfers for budget revenues means that local governments' capacity to effectively execute budget plans is dependent on central and regional governments' capacity to effectively execute budget plans.

The thesis of this chapter is that budget execution should be understood and treated as one of several instruments of administrative control to ensure democratic accountability and management flexibility. This approach recognizes political, legal, and management facets of budget execution. For example, to what extent are personnel controls implemented as legal, managerial, or political decisions during budget execution? To what extent are they a combination of all three? How are the transfers of money between line items viewed from these three perspectives?

The politics of budgeting cannot be separated from budget execution any more than politics can be excluded from budget development. Budget execution is not simply an accounting function, a perfunctory assignment that budgeters can easily pass off to the accounting staff. Instead, budget execution involves careful management of revenues and expenditures—and of the politics of budgeting.

The chapter first reviews the formal control model of budget execution, placing it in the context of budget cycle stages and reviewing central activities such as monitoring and expenditure control systems. The next section discusses budget execution as a management practice, including the management approach to using control systems. This approach must be viewed from the perspectives of both the chief executive and the program managers.

Practical concerns include the quality and availability of data required for monitoring and effectively using control systems. This discussion also includes the nexus of budgeting and policy making and the extent to which budget execution is used to inform and effect policy decisions. The chapter concludes by focusing attention on issues of budget execution practice in developing countries.

Before moving to the control model of budget execution, use of some key terms in this chapter should be clarified. Although the budgeting function can be administered in stand-alone budget offices, it is often located in the finance office of a local government, because no staff members are exclusively assigned to budget management. Therefore, *budget office* includes both stand-alone budget offices and finance offices that manage the budget function for a city. Similarly, *budget director* incorporates both stand-alone budget directors and finance directors, when they have responsibility for budget management.

This chapter focuses attention on cities to represent all types of local governments. Concepts can be adapted as needed to the different types of local governments found in a particular country. In this chapter, *department* encompasses all types of organizational units in cities, including agencies, departments, and municipal development agencies at the national and regional levels.

Chief executives in local governments are sometimes mayors and sometimes city or county managers. The term *chief executive* encompasses these officials, as well as governors, prime ministers, and presidents of regional and central governments. Many types of governing bodies are associated with the variety of local governments. The term *governing body* includes city councils; other types of local government legislatures; and state, district, regional, and national legislatures. Finally, many types of positions influence the budget process. This chapter distinguishes between *budgeteers* (staff who work in the city budget office) and *budgeters* (staff who work in city departments, as well as elected officials and chief executives who are actively involved in budgeting).

Control Model of Budget Execution: An Accounting Emphasis

Budget execution is often treated as the accounting phase of the budget cycle. The focus is on controlling expenditures so that public officials spend funds according to the wishes of the governing body. The role of budgeteers in the budget office is to monitor accounting reports to ensure that appropriations are not overspent and to monitor trends in spending to spot expenditure activities that might lead to violation of expenditure limits set by the governing body. The control model of budget execution is not incorrect, but it is incomplete, because it neglects the management focus of budget execution. Nonetheless, the control model provides a good foundation for the larger discussion of budget execution.

Evolution of Budgeting

Budget execution is rooted in the control function of budgeting. Schick's seminal 1966 article notes that budgeting has evolved over time from an emphasis on controlling expenditures to management of government activities through the budget, to use of the budget as a planning tool to forecast multiyear program expenditures. Thurmaier and Gosling (1997) extend Schick's framework to a current emphasis (beginning in the 1990s) on the budget as a policy tool.

Kahn (1997) discusses the evolution of U.S. budgeting as an instrument of democracy. Focusing attention on the activities and argument of the founding fathers of the executive budget concept, Kahn argues that William Allen, Henry Bruere, and Frederick Cleveland envisioned the executive budget as an instrument to define the local government jurisdiction. The executive budget was a tool that comprehensively placed all the activities of the local government in a single plan, a document that shed light on what the local government would do—and would not do—over the next fiscal year. The budget plan outlined how much would be spent on salaries, how much on contracts, and how much on fuel, for example. It identified public activities as separate and distinct from private activities.

The executive budget document included all of the departments and bureaus of the local government, and the transparency inherent in this assembly of data provided citizens with the information needed to hold department heads and mayors accountable for the money appropriated to their respective activities. The goal of the reformers was to encourage and facilitate the active involvement of citizens in what their city ought to do and how desired services should be efficiently and effectively delivered.

The reformers correctly argued that democratic accountability for budget execution depends on the quality of the initial budget documents. The budget document presents the spending plans that will be monitored during budget execution. A budget document that lacks sufficient detail and is not structured programmatically makes it difficult for citizens—even legislators—to effectively monitor budget execution.

Kahn's analysis also illustrates how the emphasis of the early municipal reformers on citizen engagement as instruments of democratic accountability at the local government level was replaced at the national level by an emphasis on professional budgeteers as instruments of democratic accountability. Whereas citizens were expected to monitor local spending using the transparency provided by the local executive budget, the responsibility for monitoring department budgetary activities at the national level was shifted to professional budgeteers in the central budget office. These budgeteers were expected to monitor department activities under the direction of the chief executive (the president) on behalf of the citizens.

The national executive budget improved transparency for the U.S. president and members of Congress, allowing them to view the scope of government activities in each department and to monitor adherence to congressional appropriations. More important for long-term budget evolution was the shift from the reformers' original emphasis on government performance measured against the budget's benchmarks. Unfortunately, at both the local and the national levels, the emphasis instead shifted to monitoring line item expenditures that illuminated what tax dollars bought, but not their effects. It would be almost 100 years before emphasis on budgets as instruments to gauge government performance was renewed. Today, performance measures are included in local, state, and national budgets in the United States and other countries to gauge the effects (outcomes) of government spending on policy priorities.

Yet the evolution of budgeting does not imply that when budgeting moves to a new emphasis it neglects the previous budgetary activities. The control, management, planning, and policy aspects of budgeting are all present in a specific budget process to one degree or another (Schick 1966; Thurmaier 1995a). A local government may emphasize the performance aspect of the budget, for example, but control activities remain essential features of any budgeting process. Basic budgetary bookkeeping practices (a very old practice predating modern budgeting) evolved into modern accounting practices (including fund accounting, managerial accounting, and cost accounting) and then into sophisticated financial information management systems (FIMS) that may incorporate performance and workload measures alongside basic revenue and expenditure data.

Recent fiscal transparency standards developed by the International Monetary Fund (IMF 1998), by the Organisation for Economic Co-operation and Development (OECD 2001) and by the International Budget Project (IBP 2004) are globally harmonizing what constitutes professional budgeting practices. The IBP report suggests that countries are doing a much better job at budget development than at budget execution and involvement of citizens and legislators in the budget process. Although the study dealt with only a sample of countries, the effort demonstrates fundamental values shared across nations for professional budgeting and democratic accountability.

Stages of Budget Cycle

Budget execution is a prominent feature of the budget cycle. The stages of the annual budget cycle are commonly distributed over a 12-month period. The annual budget cycle begins with a call for department budget proposals 6–9 months from the end of the current fiscal year (figure 9.1). Departments submit their requests for budget changes to the chief executive about three months later (usually through a central budget office). After reviewing the requests (a 2–3 month period), the chief executive proposes an executive budget to the governing body for approval. After discussing and adjusting the executive budget proposal (about 1–2 months), the governing body approves a final budget that is returned to the chief executive for implementation.

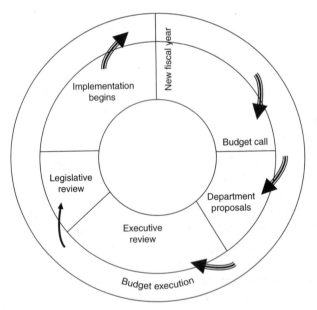

Source: Author.

FIGURE 9.1 Stages of the Budget Cycle

As seen in figure 9.1, budget execution continually takes place in the background of this cycle, because budgets are executed over 12 months, beginning with the first day of each fiscal year. The arrows indicate the flow of budget execution information into the various stages of the budget cycle. The departments use the year-to-date expenditure reports and other information to craft estimates of expenditures needed to provide services in the next fiscal year, and they use revenue estimates for program revenues to guide decisions about fee levels to set for the next budget. Budgeteers working for the chief executive review the same information to evaluate the budget requests from the departments. In concert with the chief executive, the budget director's authority encompasses the full scope of city departments, including public utilities.

The governing body depends less on budget execution information than the departments and chief executive officers, in part because the information has already been vetted twice, and more important, because the focus of the governing body is on the policy arguments inherent in the budget. Local governing bodies usually rely on the evaluation of the budget execution data by the city manager or mayor. Thus, the governing body can focus on the planning and policy issues implied by the budget plan.

Nonetheless, the ability of city councils and of state and national governing bodies to compare budgeted and actual expenditures is an essential element of their analysis and deliberations. They need and demand explanations when actual expenditures exceed budgeted limits, or fall substantially short of planned expenditures. The legislative allocation to appropriations reflects their policy preferences, and deviations from those allocations (high or low) affect the implementation of those policy preferences.[1]

Finally, as the departments and chief executive begin implementing the approved budget, budgeteers are entering data (appropriation levels, fee forecasts, and so on) into the budget and financial management system so that monitoring can begin as the new fiscal year starts. In a decentralized system such as the United States, the financial reporting systems of the central government, the states, and the local governments are independent entities. States usually require local governments to submit approved budget plans before the beginning of the fiscal year and summary reports on revenues and expenditures after the fiscal year is closed. Increasingly, these reports are submitted electronically to the state budget office. States and their local governments are not required to submit general budget reports to the federal government.

That said, substantial financial reporting requirements are mandated by the federal government in exchange for grants (subventions) to fund specific programs. In addition to providing budgets in the proposals that state and local governments present to federal departments to request grant funding, recipient governments must report how funds have been spent to achieve the goals of the funded program and for what activities.

Emphasis on Control and Monitoring of Department Spending

The control model of budget execution emphasizes the control and monitoring of department spending. This task is foremost a legal accountability issue: departments are not allowed to spend more than has been appropriated, departments may not spend funds on activities that have not been authorized by the governing body, and departments (and often chief executives) may not transfer appropriated funds between authorized activities without governing body approval. The ability to control expenditures depends on the accounting system for monitoring revenues and expenditures. These systems range from a basic bookkeeping system to a sophisticated FIMS. Except where specifically noted, *financial management systems* refer to the range of systems in use, especially the accounting component.

The level to which governing bodies appropriate funds at the local government level varies widely. Smaller local governments tend to use the traditional line-item budget, allocating funds according to objects of expenditure such as full-time personnel, part-time personnel, seasonal personnel, personnel taxes, pension expenses, and so on. In the pure line-item budget, the funds are allocated to these lines within an account or fund (such as the general fund), and little in the budget indicates that so much money is allocated for full-time police officers, so much for the city clerk, so much for the parks superintendent, and so on. Such information is gleaned in budget discussions that the governing body has with staff. The focus of the governing body's discussion is on inputs to the budget, not on the services that the funds will buy. In other cases, appropriations are made to line items within each department, which has its own appropriation(s).

A more sophisticated approach to the local budget organizes allocations to aggregated line items within defined programs, which are usually concurrent with departmental jurisdictions. Thus, the appropriations structure will be organized to mimic the departmental structure of the local government, with most departments receiving allocations through the general fund. In the U.S. system, the water and sewer utilities will be allocated within an enterprise fund so that they can operate more like a business based on fees received for water service. In the program budget structure, the line items are aggregated to only a few lines, usually personnel (including fringe benefits), supplies and services (including contractual services), and capital outlay.

The focus is on the activities each department will perform during the year; performance benchmarks are included alongside the financial information for each department's budget.

Accounting systems must be based on the structure of appropriations for a government or they will not be able to provide the information needed to evaluate budget execution. The building block for accounting and budgeting systems is the object of expenditure—what the government buys. Each purchase (goods and services) is placed in a category of similar objects of expenditure (salaries for full-time personnel, computer software, fuel, and so on). The set of objects are coded in a chart of accounts that lists the full range of potential government purchases. When governments use a line item budget format, they allocate funds according to each object-of-expenditure line in the budget (object codes). The line items are authorized within appropriations. Appropriations are usually grouped into funds, which are accounting entities with a self-balancing set of accounts (that is, each fund has its own revenues, expenditures, and fund balance). Local governments in the United States often have many fund accounts; sometimes, governments create a separate account or fund for each appropriation. Most other countries use only a general fund, trust fund, and contingency fund for all levels of government (Axelrod 1995).

When a department purchases gasoline, for example, the accounting system must be able to debit the correct appropriation in the correct fund for the correct amount of the correct type of purchase. Financial reports convey the accumulation of these debits (and revenue credits) monthly, semiannually, and annually. In each report and at any point between, the accounting system should be able to provide the current (year-to-date) balance of the appropriation remaining for each department and each fund; it also should present total spending by object of expenditure and by revenue source. The annual report is a comprehensive annual financial report that should present the financial data according to generally accepted accounting principles for governments.

Revenue and Expenditure Monitoring

The accounting system provides two types of valuable information for monitoring the budget. Monitoring revenues is essential to avoiding surprise shortfalls or illegal budget deficits at the end of the fiscal year. Monitoring expenditures allows managers and oversight officials to enforce legal strictures on budget spending. The essential aspect of monitoring activity is that it involves retrospective reporting of revenues and expenditures to date. As such, the accounting reports tell managers where the government has been; the managers must determine where the government is going. In that sense, revenue reports inform the managers and budget oversight officials of the status of the revenue constraints and whether the budget will balance by the end of the fiscal year, given current expenditure trends.

Revenues are forecast 18–12 months before the fiscal year actually begins. Given the unpredictable nature of economic activity that generates government revenues, the accounting system must provide current data on receipts for taxes and fees so that budgeters (including program managers, department directors, and chief executives) can monitor revenues against expectations. If revenues are not accruing as expected, spending may need to be decreased. Early warning of revenue shortfalls allows department managers to adjust expenditure plans to avoid deficit spending in accounts dependent on program revenues.

Likewise, budget directors can use expenditure control systems to withhold funds if revenues are not flowing into the general fund as expected. Withholding appropriated funds early in the process creates problems for program managers, but generally these problems are easier to work through at that point than if they find out 10 months into the fiscal year that they must *give back* some percentage of their total appropriation, effectively forcing them to stop spending or to *give up* contingency funds held in reserve.

Assumptions of Data Collection and Data Integrity

A strong assumption of data integrity underlies budget execution. The old adage, "garbage in, garbage out" survives because of its enduring utility. Accurate and timely data are essential to both revenue and expenditure reporting. Accurate data are not very useful if they are not timely. Managers facing revenue constraints need to know the status of those constraints on a frequent (at least monthly) basis; otherwise, they will be unable to adjust expenditures appropriately. Conversely, timely data that are inaccurate may be worse than no data if they incorrectly portray revenues greater than those actually collected, expenditures less than those than actually spent, or other errors. Forecasting a surplus that will not, in fact, occur can lead to overspending and illegal budget deficits; forecasting deficits that will not, in fact, occur can lead to abrupt spending cuts that are unnecessary and disruptive of critical program services.

Information in the financial system is not always accurate, even in developed nations. In developing countries, data accuracy can be a major problem. Sophisticated software systems with impressive financial reporting formats still depend on valid collection of data and accurate data entry. From where do the financial data come? Who is responsible for recording revenues and expenditures? How accurately and timely are the data recorded? How timely are they transferred within the financial management system?

Most central and local governments use a cash basis of accounting due to the historical emphasis on controlling government expenditures. Although cash-basis accounting has some significant weaknesses, the strength is that "what you see is what you have." If the cash is in the treasury, it can be recorded as available. If the cash is spent, it is removed from the treasury and paid to the vendor or staff salaries. This brief description simplifies a complex set of rules, but the point is that recording transactions in a cash system is relatively straightforward and does not require a highly skilled staff. Complicated procedures, such as using encumbrances, do not require substantially higher bookkeeping skills. Recording revenues and expenditures on a cash basis is a relatively straightforward operation, and data integrity should be quite high (absent the presence of theft and corruption).

Financial management software systems can improve the timeliness of reporting, because they allow fast transfers of data into central reporting systems and because they can provide instant looks at the status of revenues and expenditures. However, what is seen in such instant peeks depends entirely on the data entered to that point, and therein lies the pitfall of meshing sophisticated software systems for financial management with less-sophisticated systems of financial management personnel.

Assumptions of Financial Management Systems Reporting

Qualified personnel and appropriate technology must be complementary if a financial management system is to be effective. On the one hand, staff members must have the skills to use the system technology. On the other hand, the technology must be appropriately matched to the staff members' skills so that it can support decision making.

Personnel

A viable financial management system depends on personnel who are qualified to collect and enter data and manage the production of financial reports. Qualifications of the financial management staff in decentralized systems such as the United States are independently determined by each entity (local, state, and federal governments). In unitary governments, qualifications can be set by the central government, providing a uniform scale of ranks and qualifications across central and local offices. Although pay scales for financial management personnel vary widely in a decentralized system, they can be more uniform across similar positions in a unitary system. Even though qualification standards for personnel can vary widely in a decentralized system, professional organizations such as the Government Finance Officers Association of the United States and Canada (GFOA) can promote professionalization of budget and finance officers and highlight accepted professional practices that promote transparency and integrity in the financial management systems.

Skill sets for basic bookkeeping are useful for recording transactions in local governments. However, more sophisticated financial management systems require computer skills beyond simple data entry, and more important, they require managerial capacity to ensure that the proper data are entered accurately and in a timely fashion and that the software is correctly used to generate the appropriate reports. Beyond these simple technical skills, managerial capacity includes the staff member's ability to direct the information in the system to the appropriate program managers so that these managers can adjust program operations accordingly.

Technology

As paper bookkeeping is replaced by sophisticated FIMS, people may incorrectly assume that computers can easily communicate with each other and exchange information. In reality, software programs must be designed to exchange information, regardless of the computer hardware, and therein lies a problem faced by countless governments. The accounting system at one level of government may not be able to exchange information with the system of another level. One local government's system may be incompatible with a neighboring local government's system if the two governments use different operating systems. Merging disparate software systems into a unified accounting system can be a nightmare and require countless hours of labor, not to mention financial costs.

Alternatively, a comprehensive FIMS imposed by a central government to promote timely exchange may appear ideal in a "tabletop" implementation plan. Yet the system may require technical skills beyond those available at the local government level, as well as managerial capacities unavailable at the local, regional, and central levels. Although the goal of accurate and timely FIMS is absolutely correct and essential for good budgeting practice, it may be difficult to realize without major investments in the skills of the budgeters—the accountants and managers who will use the system. Whether in developed or developing countries, implementation of FIMS requires a major investment in training personnel, as well as the investment in software and hardware.

Expenditure control systems

Most budget control instruments are ex ante procedures to prevent unauthorized activity from occurring. The budget director has responsibility for ensuring the legal and political accountability of the budget. Several tools are useful for ensuring legal accountability, including allotments, encumbrances, personnel position controls, procurement controls, and line transfer controls. The tools are interrelated, working together to increase or decrease the flow of funds available to program managers.

Allotments

Allotments parse the full appropriation available to the department for an activity into quarterly or monthly installments for spending. The allotments can be tailored according to the expenditure history of the department or program instead of divided into equal installments. For example, a tourism department may let a large advertising contract early in the fiscal year and spend 100 percent of the appropriation for that activity. In general, quarterly allotments ensure that departments do not rapidly spend their entire appropriations and then find themselves asking the governing body for supplemental funds. In periods of fiscal stress, allotments allow the budget director to withhold funds from departments in light of revenues that are not meeting projected levels. Departments chafe at the level of micromanagement that allotments can entail during fiscal stress, but the prospect of recissions near the end of the fiscal year is worse.

Encumbrances

Encumbrances are mechanisms to ensure that the same money is not obligated twice. To protect salaries, for example, all spending required for paying the staff for the whole year can be encumbered at the beginning of the year, with the balance available for other expenses. Encumbered funds are entered into the accounting system as deductions from available fund balance at the time a commitment is made to purchase labor, equipment, or supplies. In this way, encumbrances mimic accrual accounting measurement in that the commitment to purchase staff time or equipment is spent from available funds at the time the commitment is made. If a staff position becomes vacant during the fiscal year, for example, the amount encumbered to pay the remaining salary for that position can be freed and returned to the general pool available to the program manager for spending on other salaries. If a purchase order is made for a capital item (for example, a utility truck), the budget director encumbers the funds so that they are available to pay the vendor when the truck is actually delivered to the program manager. The funds will not have been spent on buying other supplies or equipment for the program.

Purchasing/contracting function

The purchasing function is often associated with the budget director precisely because orders to buy goods and services require assurance that funds are available to pay for the order and that the funds will be available when the goods or services are actually delivered. In addition, the budget director can use purchasing controls to enforce organizational policy on the types of goods and services that can be purchased and to enforce rules about how purchases can be made.

Local governments can negotiate contracts with vendors for frequently purchased items; every department must then purchase the items from those vendors, paying the same price throughout the life of the contract. This strategy can often save governments money when prices are stable or rising; but contracts are less effective when prices for goods (for example, personal computers) are falling or are unstable, because the departments are locked into a price under the contract. The purchasing bureau of the budget office reviews each order to purchase goods and services to ensure that the order is placed to the appropriate vendor if a contract is in place.

Local governments are commonly governed by purchasing rules mandated by regional or central governments. Rules may stipulate that purchases larger than $5,000 must be advertised so that vendors can competitively bid to provide the service or goods. The threshold at which purchases must be bid rises to account for inflationary effects, but the level itself can vary widely in decentralized systems such as the United States.

Local governments may belong to a purchasing consortium that pools purchase orders from multiple local governments for bidding so that vendors provide lower prices that reflect the economies of scale inherent in bulk sales. Purchase officers also may work with two departments within the same city to buy five cars with the same specifications to get a better price than that possible when one department buys two cars and the other buys three cars that are slightly different. The budget office may encourage such collaboration by withholding allotments unless departments at least explore collaborative purchasing.

Personnel/position function

One of the most powerful and effective budget execution controls is management of the vacant positions in an organization. Governing bodies fully fund a position (salaries and benefits) with the expectation that the position will be filled 12 months of the year. Yet personnel turnover occurs regularly, resulting in unspent funds allocated to a particular position in a particular program. The chief executive has the opportunity to save money for the organization in several ways. First, the budget director can calculate the average salary (and benefits) savings realized from open positions each year. An average of 2 percent, for example, could automatically be encumbered from the department's appropriation(s) at the beginning of the fiscal year and be withheld from allotments, in reserve, by the budget director for contingencies.

A second model is to require department directors to request permission to fill vacant positions when they become open. This method represents an opportunity for the budget director and chief executive to require the department director to justify the continued activities provided by the position in the program. Depending on the rationale, the chief executive may decide to reallocate the position to a different use in the next budget (pending approval by the governing body) and hold the savings for contingencies. This option is not always available politically. Police officer or emergency response personnel positions are often filled quickly to ensure public safety, which is often a policy priority for local governing bodies.

A third option for position control is available in periods of fiscal stress. When revenues are not meeting expectations and the budget director fears a possible deficit at year end, program managers may face a *position freeze* that prohibits all hiring to replace departing personnel in order to save money and balance the budget at the end of the year. A blanket freeze may even affect police and other public safety personnel. During a position freeze, permission to fill a vacant position is rare.

Moreover, if the fiscal stress continues and the budget requires permanent spending reductions, the budget director may propose eliminating authorization for some or all of the vacant positions in the next budget. Once the position is deleted from a department's authorization, the department director will need to argue strongly to create a "new" position in a future budget to provide the services reduced by the lost personnel. Given the large share of local government budgets allocated to salaries and benefits, position control is one of the most powerful and effective tools budget directors can use to control spending during the year.

Line-item transfers

The level of detail in appropriations affects budget execution in two ways. First, the more aggregated the level of appropriation, the more flexibility the program manager or department director has in spending on various items included within a particular line item. For example, one appropriation line for personnel permits the police chief to spend the total allocation for personnel on the basis of the department's needs over the year. Although the requested amount may have been based on only 1,000 hours of over-time, if an officer vacancy occurs half way through the fiscal year, the chief can pay more overtime hours to existing officers to cover the service shortfall—without seeking governing body permission to shift funds from the full-time personnel line to the overtime line. In contrast, if the appropriation from the governing body is at the very detailed line-item level, the chief will need to go before the governing body for permission to transfer funds between the lines.

The level of control exercised at the line item level varies widely, depending on the organizational culture of the local government. In many govern-ments, the department director is given wide latitude in managing the funds allocated to the department for specified services. In others, the governing body or chief executive keeps a tight rein on spending in the departments, and managers must get permission to deviate even slightly from the approved line-item detail budget. In most cases, however, budget directors prefer to reserve permission control over transfers from personnel lines to other lines. This strategy ensures that their control over filling positions (discussed earlier) is not undermined by department directors taking money from vacant positions to spend on a consultant to provide the same service (or to use the salary savings to purchase some other goods or services). That tactic would defeat the purpose of controlling personnel positions to avoid deficits or to help create budgetary slack so that the chief executive and governing body can reallocate positions in the next budget.

Summary

This discussion of the formal control model of budget execution outlines the basic instruments available to budget directors, city managers and mayors, and governing bodies to enforce the spending plan identified in the budget approved by the governing body. The approved budget is the benchmark or standard against which spending and revenues will be measured. The orga-nizational culture of the city government will influence whether budget execution is flexible and oriented toward achieving city and departmental goals or whether it is oriented toward tightly controlling spending to minimize the possibility of deficits and to contain government spending generally. The formal control model tends to present a mechanistic view of budget execution. In practice, budget execution can be used as one of several management instruments to achieve organizational goals for the city.

Budget Execution Using a Managerial Approach

In a managerial approach to budgeting, the adopted budget is the blueprint to execute the management plan for the local government. Executing the budget is the means for executing the management plan to achieve the goals and mission of the local government. The oversight emphasis is not on legal compliance, but on whether resources are being used to provide effective services. A managerial approach requires a unified perspective on budget development and budget execution; the role of the budget director is to coordinate and direct the development and execution of the budget.

A managerial approach to budget execution does not neglect the monitoring functions discussed in the traditional control model. Understanding the current status of revenues and expenditures remains essential for managing the budget to achieve the goals of the local government. An important distinction, however, is the stronger reliance on ex post controls and a melding of program evaluation functions with budget execution. A managerial approach to budget execution uses the budget execution periods in the budget cycle to evaluate how well departments are accomplishing their goals and missions with the resources they are allocated in the budget. A managerial orientation to local budgeting focuses the governing body and the chief executive—and the department directors—on the long-term fiscal health of the city as a critical factor necessary for the departments to achieve their goals and succeed in their missions (Giannakis and McCue 1999).

Expenditure Control Systems

A managerial approach to budget execution still requires expenditure control systems to ensure against deficit spending. The issue is the degree to which allotments, personnel controls, and line transfer controls are used to constrain the flexibility of department directors. Monthly status reports on general revenues as well as program revenues and expenditures provide the department directors and the chief executive with the same critical information to measure budget execution against the budget plan. Often, however, the control tools are held in reserve by the budget director and only exercised in a managerial approach during times of fiscal stress.

Monitoring expenditures for legal compliance

Although legal compliance is an important value in a managerial approach, the emphasis is on ex post controls on purchasing, personnel, and line transfers. Instead of requiring department directors to get approval for purchases, hiring, and line transfers before actions are taken, the chief executive reviews the activities of each director at least annually to assess whether the director has effectively and efficiently used the budgeted resources to achieve the department's goals and mission.

Instead of pre-audits to review whether a purchase meets the city's policy guidelines, the director is subject to program audits on a regular basis (for example, every 2–3 years) to identify events and decisions (if any) that did not comply with current policies. (For example, how many times did the department purchase goods without using the preferred organizationwide vendor contract? What was the rationale?) Unless an across-the-board freeze is placed on filling vacant positions, the director is able to hire at will to replace departing staff; this strategy assumes that the director follows established policies on hiring personnel, including (in the United States) affirmative action and diversity requirements.

Alternatives to expenditure control systems

Where the organizational culture provides a large degree of flexibility and responsibility to department directors, the governing body and chief executive may use target-based budgeting (also called envelope budgeting) to give those directors lump sum appropriations for the fiscal year. The director has maximum freedom to reallocate funds as necessary to achieve the department's goals. Without allotments and position controls as constraints, the director is responsible for encumbering funds as needed to ensure that the department budget does not spend beyond approved amounts.

Accountability for results is achieved through an annual ex post review by the governing body and chief executive. The benefit for the program manager is a high degree of flexibility to achieve departmental objectives. The cost is that the department director generally has no recourse to appeal to the chief executive or governing body for supplemental funds if the budget is mismanaged during the year. Unless exceptional events (such as a natural disaster) occur, the manager must accomplish departmental objectives with the initial budget allocation.

The reports generated from the financial management system during budget execution will continue to provide the same basic information on expenditures and appropriation and line balances. The key difference is that this information is most useful to the program manager who must manage the program's resources to achieve objectives without exceeding legal and financial constraints. The discussion with the chief executive officer and the governing body will be about *how well* the manager achieved the objectives, not *how* the manager did it.

Nexus between Budget Execution and Policy Development

Budgets are inherently policy documents, even if the policies are not explicitly presented in the budget. The GFOA Distinguished Budget Presentation Awards Program (GFOA 2006) begins budget evaluations with a review of five criteria regarding the degree to which budget documents present city policies that are fundamental to the budget. A fundamental tenet of local government budgeting is that budgets exist to fund the programs that implement the policies of the governing body. There would be no need for a local government budget if there were no policies to be implemented by staff (and there would be no need for a staff). The critical question is how well the budget document and budget process are used to explicitly review the policies that the governing body has established, and how well department directors effect those policies during budget execution.

Formal Execution Phase

The extent to which local budgeting is meshed with policy analysis and development varies with the size of local governments. The smallest cities may argue that they have no capacity to generate the reports and budget documents to meet GFOA awards criteria. The argument rings hollow. To the extent that the smallest cities provide minimal services, minimal effort by the city clerk or governing body is needed to generate a budget document that makes the current city policies and priorities explicit. If the city provides only minimal services such as a city park, city sewer, and policing, the priorities are easily identified and discussed. Evaluating whether the city's goals are being met during budget execution during regular meetings of the governing body is easy. Sophisticated analysis is not required, but transparency is a necessary condition of good budgeting practice.

Medium-size and large cities with at least one person assigned to manage the budget and budget process can take advantage of the execution phase of the budget cycle to incorporate policy analysis and development into the budget process. Although budget development and executive review are extremely labor-intensive phases, the implementation and execution phases of the budget cycle provide the budgeteer in the budget office with the opportunity to analyze programs to determine how well they are achieving stated objectives with the appropriated resources.

Medium-size and large cities tend to use a program budget format, explicitly stating the activities and goals that each department is to achieve with its budget allocation. Increasingly, local government budgets in the United States incorporate meaningful performance measures and benchmarks into the descriptions and presentations of departmental budgets. Incorporation of performance measures into departmental budget documents enhances budgeteers' ability to analyze the department's performance, including achievements of the stated performance objectives.

Budget Monitoring as Program Evaluation for Policy Analysis

A managerial approach to budget execution transforms the role of budget staff members from bookkeepers to management analysts. This role is possible even without sophisticated FIMS technology. But supervisors must be committed to providing budget staff members with enough time to perform this function as well as their traditional functions.

Staffing requirements

Staffing levels in local budget offices increase as the size and scope of local services increase. The appropriate staff size depends less on a ratio of 1 budgeteer/100 employees or 1 budgeteer/10,000 citizens and more on the role of the budget office in the organization's culture.[2] Control-oriented budget offices require few if any staff beyond bookkeepers and accountants in the budget office. There is little work other than checking revenues and expenditures against line-item budget allocations. Policy-oriented budget offices, however, require enough staff so that each budgeteer can be assigned 4–5 department budgets to review and monitor.

Staffing roles

In a control-oriented budget office, the role of the budget staff is that of bookkeeper. The staff may serve a primary role as financial accountants in the budget office, and budgeting is merely a periodic diversion from regular duties. Policy-oriented budget offices require budget staff with the skills of a management analyst and budgeteers who can manage the technical skills of the budget as well as manage relationships with department personnel and serve as management consultants throughout the year. Budget staff with these extended responsibilities must have excellent written and oral communication skills; they must effectively communicate with the department directors and the chief executive and sometimes the governing body itself. They should have an understanding of organizational development and change, and other public management skills.

The policy-oriented budget office staff must have excellent working relationships with department directors. An in-depth understanding of the priorities and goals of each department director provides the budgeteer with the context in which future budget requests can be analyzed. (An important assumption is that the chief executive concurs with departmental priorities; this assumption is usually not problematic when the chief executive appoints the department director.) The budgeteer can use the budget execution phase for extended conversations with the department director and program managers about departmental priorities, emerging management issues, and revisions to departmental goals and objectives. The role of the budgeteer is not to replace the department director but to understand the departmental culture and mission and to know how to work with the department director to make sure the budget allocations support the department's mission.

Importance of site visits

Policy-oriented budget staff members who need to evaluate the effectiveness of programs and understand their management challenges cannot do so merely sitting at a desk and staring at a computer screen or written reports. Seeing is believing. The less intense budget execution period is an ideal time for budgeteers to make field trips to learn more about the activities described in the budget documents. If the budgeteer reviews the sanitation budget, he or she should schedule time to ride on a garbage truck for a shift. If the responsibility is the police department, the budgeteer should ride in a police car or walk a beat for a shift. The budgeteer who has the parks department can schedule a few days to visit the parks to evaluate the condition of the playground equipment, the picnic facilities, the trees and grass, and other features. Another day is scheduled to observe recreation classes for adults and children and to assess how many people use exercise equipment and the condition of the equipment.

Multiple methods of data collection are more reliable than paper (or electronic) reports alone. Arguments for policy and program changes and numbers in tables can provide helpful information to the budgeteer. Conversations with department directors and program managers can reinforce written arguments in formal reports; they can also uncover contradictions and missing elements of "the story" that may not have survived editing by the department director before submission to the budget office or chief executive. The site visits to the city garage, the city park, the fire and police stations, and other facilities provides yet another check on the arguments and numbers in formal reports.

Relationship between the Accounting Staff and the Budgeting Staff

Budget office staff members rely on accounting staff members to provide the expenditure monitoring for legal compliance. Budget staff can use the accounting reports for more than simple monitoring of fund balances. In partnership with department directors, budgeteers can analyze trends in different line items to identify activities that are driving costs or producing savings available for reallocation within the department's budget. In this capacity, the budgeteer acts as a management consultant to help the department director effectively and efficiently allocate departmental resources. In turn, accounting staff become facilitators of information integrated into the management decisions of the budget office (McCue 2001).

Producing of Insights versus Reports

The primary value of using the budget execution phase as a management tool is that budgeteers can give the chief executive useful insights into the operations and management of departments. Instead of producing reports with numbing tables of figures, the budgeteer can provide written and oral information that illuminates emerging issues and problems. Acting as a management analyst, the budgeteer compares and contrasts the accounting reports, the field data, and data gleaned from discussions with department directors and program managers. The depth of understanding provided by these multiple data collection measures prepares the budgeteer for discussions with the budget director regarding the department's requests for the next budget cycle.

When the department budget request arrives at the budget office for review during the budget development phase, asking for increased funds for park maintenance, the budgeteer for the parks department will have a better sense of how important the increased funding is and how it aligns with other departmental priorities. Instead of relying solely on departmental reports for evidence, the budgeteer can attest to the veracity of the budget claims or provide contrary evidence from discussions with departmental staff and field trips. The investment in evaluations that budgeteers make in the budget execution phase can pay handsome dividends in the hectic and harried budget development phase, when numbers are prominent ingredients of discussions. The value added of knowing what the numbers represent in terms of people, places, and things is very high.

Contracting with Third Parties

Local and central governments in industrialized and developing nations increasingly rely on nongovernmental organizations (NGOs) to provide important services. State and local governments in the United States, for example, have increased reliance on social service NGOs to provide a wide range of services, such as foster care and adoption management for children, drug rehabilitation, and other labor-intensive services. NGOs in developing nations may receive substantial funding from external donors, but they can also work under contract for central, district, and local governments.

Contracting with NGOs and private firms for services requires types of monitoring different from those for internal service production. Budget execution with contracts requires monitoring the contractor's work for performance rather than for financial transactions. This monitoring implies that performance standards are written into the contract and that specific actions are identified to reward (or punish) the contractor for its performance levels. Contract management requires management skills beyond bookkeeping; management analysts in a department budget office should have the skills to observe contractor performance and integrate that information with the budget expenditure reports generated by payments to the contractor. A growing literature addresses contract management for public managers (for example, Cooper 2003).

While an in-depth discussion of contract management is beyond the scope of this chapter, it is worth noting that improperly managed contracting can waste large sums of tax dollars. Moreover, managers often lack training in proper contracting techniques, from bidding to managing the contract. Program budgets implemented with substantial contracting require scrutiny to ensure that fair procedures are followed and that program managers know what they are buying when they sign contracts. The purchasing bureau will be responsible only for ensuring that the proper procedures have been followed for letting the contract. Purchasing officers are not responsible for how well the contract is managed.

Time Requirement to Build Culture of Compliance

Organizational culture is just as important in budgeting as in other aspects of public management. Thurmaier and Willoughby (2001) examine the conditions and consequences of having a policy-oriented central budget office versus a control-oriented budget office. These conditions and consequences hold true at the local government level (Thurmaier 1995a). An organizational culture that is focused on program outcomes and that gives much discretion to department directors—who are held accountable by the chief executive or governing body—should be reflected in a budget that uses a program format with highly aggregated line items. An organizational culture that is control-oriented is focused on the inputs to programs and the requirement to minimize departmental spending, holding the chief executive accountable to not exceed budgetary constraints; this culture does not permit department directors line transfer flexibility, and line transfers may even require governing body permission.

Whatever the organizational culture desired by the governing body, a culture of compliance from department directors and the general organizational staff takes time to build. An organization that moves from a flexible culture to a rigid control culture is likely to encounter resistance at multiple levels of the organization, because accountability for decisions has been moved to a higher-level (the chief executive officer [CEO], and members will feel the loss of responsibility. Organizations that move from a rigid control orientation toward a more flexible and mission-driven managerial orientation will likely find that it takes time for organizational actors to determine the extent of their flexibility and how to use informal discussions with the chief executive to ensure that departmental decisions are supported by the CEO and governing body.

A budget office in a large city fills an intermediary role between the mayor and manager on the one hand and department directors on the other hand. The orientation of the budget office can strongly influence the role that the budget plays in the organization's culture. A control-oriented budget office will be a central point of conflict in the organization as department directors attempt to exercise authority with budgetary flexibility, and budgeteers work to enforce budgetary discipline as directed by the CEO and budget director. However, budget staff in a policy-oriented budget office can serve a role more like that of a "consultant" and policy advisor by helping department directors determine how to use available budget resources to accomplish departmental missions and goals.

Summary

The discussion of the managerial approach to budget execution is meaningful only in the context of a larger managerial approach to the local government budget. A focus on the long-term fiscal health of the local government is essential if individual departments are to fulfill their missions and achieve their goals. Although some may argue that this approach applies only to medium-size and large cities, the argument is without merit. Small cities may provide a more limited range of services than their larger counterparts. This trait does not suggest that a managerial approach is infeasible; rather, it implies that the approach will be easier to implement and manage, because actors in the organization and changes to policies and programs are fewer. Similarly, the managerial approach to budgeting and budget execution is relevant to local governments in developing countries as well as in developed nations. The determining factor is not what the local government does, but whether the governing body and chief executive are intent on ensuring that local government activities are executed effectively and efficiently, within the legal and financial constraints imposed in the budget and other local government regulations.

Applications for Developing Countries

The challenges that developing countries face in applying the principles of sound expenditure control to local government management are not insurmountable. Weaknesses in expenditure control systems are overcome with feasible data collection methods free of political interference.

Weaknesses in Expenditure Control Systems

The weaknesses in public expenditure management systems in developing countries, including budget execution, are well known (Fozzard and Foster 2001; IBP 2004; Killick 2005a, 2005b; Lienert 2003; Lienert and Sarraf 2001; Polidano 1999; Premchand 1993; Schiavo-Campo and Tommasi 1999; Schick 1998; World Bank 1998; Zody 1996). The purpose of this chapter is not to critique the problems once more, but rather to offer viable suggestions for improvement. Keeping in mind that public expenditure management is necessarily country specific (Schiavo-Campo and Tommasi 1999), the suggestions in this chapter address three serious problems evident in the budget execution of many developing countries.

A serious problem underlying many other issues is weak institutional arrangements for managing expenditure systems. At root is a fragmented system of budgeting that places responsibility for budget development in a ministry of finance, strategic planning (multiyear budget planning) in a planning ministry, and expenditure management in spending departments. An essential feature of the executive budgeting system is that the central budget office coordinates—and controls—all three aspects of budgeting. In addition, nations that allow spending departments to maintain separate banking accounts thwart centralized cash management that enables effective expenditure controls such as allotments and positions controls.

A second problem is poor budget preparation. Chronic underestimation of revenues aside, budget development often lacks public sector input and significant governing body review. This paucity of input and review causes two kinds of problems. First, the lack of transparency means that significant errors in revenue and expenditure estimation are not brought to light before the budget is adopted. Second, budget documents that lack information by program and explanations of significant changes in spending, revenues, and staffing provide no benchmark for legislators, citizens, and the media to measure budget execution. Individuals cannot understand how well the budget is being implemented if they cannot understand the budget in the first place.

The third problem is budget execution itself, especially regarding timely and accurate reporting of expenditures by line, by appropriation, by department, and by fund on a monthly, semiannual, and annual basis. Blaming poor recordkeeping on inadequate administrative capacity to implement FIMS projects (that is, lack of skilled staff to develop and maintain FIMS software and hardware) is easy, but many countries had adequate expenditure control systems many years before sophisticated FIMS became available.

Basic budgetary functions simply must be executed with whatever technology is available. If accounting systems are poor because staff members are directed not to record certain transactions or to delay reporting transactions, the problem is a political and managerial problem, not a technical issue. If procurement and contracting systems are poor because managers deliberately avoid bidding procedures to favor certain vendors over others, the problem, again, is a political and managerial problem, not a technical issue.

The issue of position (or complement) control is central to budget execution problems. When "ghost" positions are placed on payrolls to siphon funds into unauthorized spending, or when the central budget office has no authority to hold positions vacant to capture savings, the budget director (or chief executive) is missing one of the most powerful expenditure management tools. Staff members represent a major share of public expenditures at all levels of government. Local governments in many countries are spending upward of 90 percent of revenues on salaries, leaving little for other operating expenses or capital outlay. Countries that have been able to centralize position control have been able to greatly reduce the number of positions in spending departments, freeing funds for other purposes, including transfers to local governments.

The extent to which the managerial approach to local budget execution is viable in developing countries thus depends on the political and managerial capacity at the central and local (and regional) government levels. Managerial capacity includes the efficacy of the accounting systems and the skill levels of program managers in the central and local governments. Political capacity includes the fortitude of political leaders at all levels to avoid excuses for government departments' performance failures and these leaders' insistence on a transparent budget process that allows media and interested citizens to hold program officials—and elected officials—accountable for program performance.

Political fortitude is a necessary condition for public managers to use the budget as a management tool. Such fortitude means that elected officials lose their tolerance of *leakage* as the funds appropriated in the national budget are transferred to line departments and local governments to fund programs. Whether the leakage is outright theft of public funds or gross mismanagement, a transparent budget execution system can identify the leakage source and allow the appropriate staff to be held accountable. Whether the process is transparent and whether staff members are held accountable is a political decision. As countries increasingly focus attention on ending corruption, the decision for elected officials is whether to fight the reforms or to promote them. A transparent budget execution system that provides access for citizens to monitor government expenditures is viewed as instrumental to reducing corruption and mismanagement in many nations (IBP 2004; Killick 2005a, 2005b; Polidano 1999).

Lack of data integrity

Both the accounting approach and the managerial approach to budget execution require data integrity if the accounting system is to provide valuable information for budget managers. The best software and countless hours of staff time are wasted if the data fed into the system are inaccurate. Developing countries' experience with implementing sophisticated FIMS projects is discouraging (Killick 2005a). Tanzania and a few other countries have successfully implemented new systems at the central government level and have extended them to many local governments. But Ghana and many other countries have struggled with multiple delays in fully implementing their own FIMS (IBP 2004).

Feasible data and evaluation models

Although sophisticated financial management systems are available to capture performance data, along with financial data, they provide little value added to a country's administration if the data and skills necessary to operate the system are unavailable. Until full-scale FIMS are successfully implemented, developing countries can focus resources on feasible data and evaluation models. A transparent procedure that tracks actual expenditures against budget expenditures by appropriation is not difficult, nor is tracking expenditures at the line item level. Object-of-expenditure tracking tied to purchasing decisions provides greater detail without requiring substantially more work of staff.

The key to success is the motivation to produce a transparent accounting of government spending at whatever level the spending occurs. If the central government provides an allocation to the ministry of health, and the ministry in turn provides all or a portion of that appropriation to district health offices, the accounting system should be able to account for how every bit was used at each level of government. Although budget execution reform is slow in some countries, progress is evident in others.

Examples from transitional and developing countries

Ghana's budget system has been called a "façade" and a largely "ritualistic" process with little relevance to actual spending (Killick 2005a). Transfers of funds from central to local ministries have high rates of leakage, and variances between budget and actual expenditures (when the data can be obtained) are found to be as high as 50 percent; salaries are consistently underbudgeted, and other expenditures are consistently overbudgeted compared with actual expenditures (Killick 2005a). Although the budget process is becoming more transparent, interested citizens—or even public managers—still find it difficult to obtain data on budgeted allocations for specific purposes (ISODEC 2006). The degree to which the budget system is transparent is a political decision; the increasing unpopularity of government corruption is creating incentives for elected officials to make the budget process, including budget execution, more transparent and more accurate.

However, Fozzard and Foster (2001) report significant progress with increased proportions of funds actually reaching schools in Uganda because of increased transparency in the education budget. Details of all fund releases and how they are spent are displayed down to the school level. The government also publishes details in national and local media of released funds, the schools for which they are intended, and the use to which they are to be put (see also DfID 1998).

Transitional states such as Ukraine and Poland offer further contrasting examples. A consultant in Ukraine who was tasked to help develop a budget execution system in the late 1990s met significant resistance within the budget office of the Ministry of Finance. Reports detailing the variance in revenues and expenditures by oblast (district) were at first said not to exist. When the monthly reports literally landed on the desk of the budget official during a meeting with the consultant, it was hard to deny their existence. A brief glimpse revealed that some oblasts were substantially in deficit. The consultant was quickly dispatched to the budget director, who questioned why someone would want to know such information; the director refused to release the reports. An appeal to a higher-level ministry official eventually resulted in the release of some reports. Citizens rarely have such privileged access. Where political fortitude is weak, budget execution suffers.[3]

In Poland before 1989, the amount to be spent by the local government was set by the central government; the local government budget reflected revenue and expenditure plans as approved by the central government. Local governments received allocations from the central government in several functional service areas that were treated as aggregate-level object codes. The local government budget was merely a table of accounts void of descriptive text to explain the various ways that the funds in each functional area were to be spent. Accounting staff members were charged with tracking expenditures within each functional area and with sending reports to Warsaw. Local government officials were never surprised to learn that the final local government budget report to Warsaw showed that the local government spent exactly what had been determined in the budget plan a year earlier. When local governments gained substantial autonomy in the decentralization program following 1989, political leaders encouraged heightened transparency, providing incentives for the accounting staff to present actual expenditures that varied from the initial budget plan.[4]

Part of the budget execution transformation in Poland after 1989 reflected a political desire to treat the local budget as a guide for local management decisions rather than as a directive from the central government. Cities such as Krakow and Lublin pioneered changes in the budgeting system to develop budgets at the program level and to include descriptive texts at the program and subprogram level, allowing governing body members and citizens to see how the funds were to be spent (Thurmaier 1995b). Mayors who reformed local budgets into a program format were pleasantly surprised at how much easier and how much more useful the governing body debates on the budget became. Debates turned from political accusations about missing information into focused policy discussions about spending programs and priorities (Thurmaier 1994).

Distinguishing between Poor Data and Corruption

Lack of data often stems from lack of data collection. Yet governments in developing countries seldom lack for staff members who can collect and report data. Reporting how much money has been spent on specific purchases and how much for salaries and contracts is the bedrock of accounting systems. These systems are based on recording transactions and aggregating the transactions into usable information for managers. Accounting staff can record transaction data, even on paper, and create monthly reports for managers at the local, district, and central levels. Recording transactions does not require sophisticated training and constitutes a fundamental budgetary responsibility of any government unit.

Lack of data can also be due to illegal behavior by reporting officials. Individuals can deliberately remove data from or alter data in reports to disguise corrupt behavior. Problems of administrative capacity are sometimes problems of corruption; placing blame on inept staff can disguise deliberate obfuscation of budget execution data. Political corruption that attacks the integrity of faithful public servants can drive honest staff out of public service, leaving behind staff compliant with political officers who use corrupt practices for personal gain. Increasing transparency to inhibit—if not prohibit—data alterations requires political fortitude and an organizational culture that values transparency and disclosure for public discussion. It also requires a transparent budget document, accessible to citizens and managers, so that budget execution can be measured against the appropriation benchmarks presented in the budget document approved by the governing body (IBP 2004).

Value of Informal Compliance Culture

Administrative control systems involve trade-offs between the benefits and costs of both internal and external enforcement (Thompson 1993). An organizational culture that values transparency supports a budget execution system that provides full disclosure of budget transactions. A transparency culture encourages informal compliance with accounting rules and procedures; staff members are rewarded for informal compliance by support from colleagues who share the same professional values. Staff members obey the rules and laws even as they focus their efforts on achieving the organizational objectives and mission.

Externally imposed compliance through ex post audits and legal enforcement actions is much less desirable for several reasons. First, external enforcement represents added costs; audit staff, legal proceedings, and associated costs are in addition to the actual costs of producing budget reports. Second, the absence of a culture of compliance increases the need for internal organizational enforcement mechanisms such as preaudits. Preaudits are costly financially and also in terms of slowed purchasing and organizational decision making. If every purchase and every transaction is subject to preaudit review for legality, the organization loses flexibility to quickly respond to opportunities and changes in the economic and political environment. These extra costs divert scarce resources from service delivery. Third, the traditional response of tightening controls for compliance is centralization of authority. Centralization may include preaudit procedures by the central government for local and district expenditures. It may manifest in increased preaudit authority from the ministry of finance, representing a decreased level of authority and flexibility for other central departments.

Centralization for compliance increases organizational rigidity without necessarily increasing transparency; although legal procedures may be followed, the central controlling department may not hold or enforce transparency values. Furthermore, effective external control and post hoc auditing requires an auditing authority that is independent of the executive and legislative branches and that is free from partisan political infiltration through the appointment of members. The U.S. comptroller general gains considerable independence through a 10-year term after the U.S. Senate approves his or her nomination by the president. Created in 1921 to balance the powers of the newly created budget bureau in the executive budget process, the U.S. Government Accountability Office (GAO) has not shied away from effective critiques of central (and local) government departments and programs. The current comptroller general, David Walker, (who heads GAO) has been a vociferous critic of U.S. budget deficits and a leading proponent of increased incorporation of performance measurements into budgeting procedures.

Collection of Information That Will Be Used

One way for governments to provide efficient data collection is to require only data that will be used at higher levels of decision making. Collecting data just because they can be collected does not add value to the organization. Central governments should avoid requiring data reports for information that will not be used in policy decisions. Some data will be used only by the line department or at the local government level; such data should not be required in reports forwarded to the central government. Financial and other data will be useful for program managers, as well as central government decision makers, and should be accurately collected and reported in a timely fashion.

Collection of Outcomes Data

Basic financial transactions data are essential for good budget execution. As the organizational culture of central and local government departments embraces transparency and professional values of compliance, administrative capacity can be increased to incorporate performance information into budgeting reports. The collection of outcomes data along with expenditure information facilitates program evaluation and policy analysis by the central and local government budget offices between the budget development phases of the budget cycle. As developing countries are able to implement sophisticated FIMS, budgeteers will be able to use performance data collected from departments to evaluate program performance. Given the current pace of FIMS implementation, that capacity could be several years away. Meanwhile, budgeteers can collect qualitative data on program performance in site visits to health clinics, schools, city garages, libraries, and other facilities. This type of performance data collection served many local governments in the United States very well before they installed FIMS projects (Thurmaier 1995a).

Complications from Dependence on Intergovernmental Revenue Transfers

One of the most significant constraints on local budget execution in developing countries is dependence on intergovernmental revenue transfers to fund local programs. As Caiden and Wildavsky (1974) have noted, developing countries often face recurrent problems of unmet revenue forecasts that result in canceled expenditure authority for municipal development agencies and canceled subventions to local governments. Unstable, undependable grants and subventions prohibit local governments from creating reliable revenue forecasts. Unreliable revenues wreak havoc on local budget execution, disrupting payrolls, delaying purchases, and postponing contracts for services. To the extent that local governments are allowed to rely on own-source revenues, they can mitigate the vagaries of central government transfers. Increased shares of own-source revenues have also been linked to greater success in meeting basic needs such as education and health care (Lindaman and Thurmaier 2002).

In the early days of transition from communism in Ukraine, central government policy makers were experimenting with the mix of revenues that would be allocated between central, regional, and local governments. How much of which revenue source (for example, income, value added tax) would be available to local governments was changing annually, and the final mix was sometimes unknown until well into the fiscal year. The unstable revenue environment created difficult problems for local governments; they had no way to create budgets, because forecasting revenues was impossible—they did not even know which revenues they would be allowed to collect.

The situation improved in 2001, when the central government passed a new budget code. The legislation substantially reduced the arbitrary influence of regional governors in the allocation of funds. The legislation assigned revenue and expenditure responsibilities to local budgets and used formula-based methods to transfer funds to local governments. The new revenue scheme included shared personal and corporate income taxes matched with mandatory expenditure assignments. The benefits to local governments included the ability to capture income tax revenues exceeding the mandatory expenditure assignments for use on other local government priorities. The scheme encouraged local governments to make economic development a priority, because increased local employment would generate greater income taxes.

Unfortunately, the central government in Ukraine has not sustained the reform. Numerous measures since 2004 have eroded local governments' capacity for budget reform. For example, in 2004, many local governments suffered the consequences of the finance ministry deliberately overestimating personal income tax revenues (the greatest part of city revenues) when Ukraine moved to the flat rate for income tax. In 2005, after local budgets were adopted, the central government removed one half of a dedicated city revenue source to cover other budget deficits at the national level. Intergovernmental budget transfers to cities were reduced by 5 percent with no offsetting city revenues. Without increased own-source revenues for local governments and without increased central-local transfers, cities were unable to achieve more than about 94 percent of budgeted expenditures because of revenue shortfalls in 2005. A consequence of these and other problems with central budgeting was that local budgets' dependence on central government transfers (including shared taxes) reached 97 percent in 2005, a trajectory opposite that promised by the 2001 budget reform act.

Effective budget execution is essential for both central and local governments. Ineffective, opaque budget execution at the central level has negative consequences for budget execution at the local government level. A culture of transparency and compliance at the local level is of little value when the central government fails to deliver the funds appropriated by the governing body for local programs. Thus, making budget execution transparency a political priority at the central government level will provide dividends for local governments as well.

Conclusion

This chapter argues that a managerial approach to budget execution yields a more effective budget process and a higher value to the long-term fiscal health of the organization, be it a central, district, or local government. A managerial approach goes beyond a simple accounting approach in two ways. First, it incorporates budget execution information into managerial decision making on a continuous basis. Second, it requires management information to be incorporated into budget execution reporting. Monitoring and reporting during budget execution is not simply a legal compliance exercise; it is an essential feedback loop that provides program managers with critical information to guide their implementation of policies and programs approved by the governing body.

Developing a managerial approach to budget execution does not necessarily require a sophisticated financial information management system with complex software programs. The most important ingredient is an organizational culture that values transparency and that encourages and rewards legal compliance as a professional value. Staff who value and receive political support for transparency can collect data on transactions and program performance in simple procedures. Timeliness of reports depends less on sophisticated software and more on a cultural imperative to efficiently and effectively collect and transmit the information to program managers and policy makers.

A supportive political environment is essential to fostering a managerial approach to budgeting and to maintaining an organizational culture that values transparency and compliance. Without the political fortitude of government leaders to confront information on corruption and inept management, line staff members have little incentive to collect data, much less transmit data in a timely manner. Political leadership that encourages and supports a culture of transparency also promotes a budget execution system that operates efficiently and effectively to support program managers.

Leaders who choose to develop an effective budget execution system should not tolerate leakage during budget execution. They should support accounting staff members who collect data that may indicate poor program performance, as well as budgeteers who conduct field visits to collect qualitative data on program performance. They should encourage managers to use the data collected during budget execution to improve the operations of their programs.

Notes

1. The degree to which legislatures are able to review and understand executive budgets varies widely and is beyond the scope of this chapter. See IBP (2004) for a full discussion of this important issue.
2. For example, the budget staffs for Milwaukee, Wisconsin (population of about 1.6 million), Kansas City, Missouri (population of about 441,545), and Charlotte, North Carolina (population of about 541,000), are all about 9 budgeteers, plus a budget director.
3. Information is based on the author's experience as a consultant in several projects in Ukraine.
4. Information is based on the author's experience as a consultant in several projects in Poland.

References

Axelrod, Donald. 1995. *Budgeting for Modern Government,* 2nd ed. New York: St. Martin's Press, Inc.

Bland, Robert L., and Irene S. Rubin. 1997. *Budgeting: A Guide for Local Governments.* Washington, DC: International City/County Management Association.

Caiden, Naomi, and Aaron Wildavsky. 1974. *Planning and Budgeting in Poor Countries.* New York: John Wiley and Sons.

Cooper, Phillip J. 2003. *Governing by Contract: Challenges and Opportunities for Public Managers.* Washington, DC: Congressional Quarterly Press.

DfID (U.K. Department for International Development). 1998. "Cost Sharing in Education: Public Finance, School and Household Perspectives." Education Research Paper 27, DfID, London.

Fozzard, Adrian, and Mick Foster. 2001. "Changing Approaches to Public Expenditure Management in Low-Income Aid-Dependent Countries." Discussion Paper 2001/107, United Nations University/World Institute for Development Economics Research, New York.

Giannakis, George, and Clifford P. McCue. 1999. *Local Government Budgeting: A Managerial Approach.* Westport, CT: Quorum.

GFOA (Government Finance Officers Association). 2006. Distinguished Budget Presentation Awards Program. Accessed May 20, 2006. http://www.gfoa.org/services/awards.shtml#budgetawards.

IBP (International Budget Project). 2004. *Opening Budgets to Public Understanding and Debate: Results from 36 Countries.* Washington, DC: Center on Budget and Policy Priorities.

IMF (International Monetary Fund). 1998. Code of Good Practices on Fiscal Transparency, updated March 23, 2001. Accessed May 30, 2006. http://www.imf.org/np/fad/trans/code.htm.

ISODEC (Integrated Social Development Centre). 2006. "An Open Letter to His Excellency." Integrated Social Development Centre, Accra.

Kahn, Jonathan. 1997. *Budgeting Democracy.* Ithaca, NY: Cornell University Press.

Killick, Tony. 2005a. "What Drives Change in Ghana? A Political-Economy View of Economic Prospects." Working Paper, Strategies and Analysis for Growth and Access Project, Cornell University and Clark Atlanta University, New York and Atlanta. http://www.saga.cornell.edu/images/killick.pdf.

———. 2005b. "The Politics of Ghana's Budgetary System." Policy Brief 2, Ghana Center for Democratic Development, Accra. http://www.odi.org.uk/PPPG/drivers_of_change/ODI-CDD_Policy%20Brief_2.pdf.

Lee, Robert D., Ronald Johnson, and Phil Joyce. 2003. *Public Budgeting Systems*, 7th ed. Boston: Jones and Bartlett Publishers.

Lienert, Ian. 2003. "A Comparison between Two Public Expenditure Management Systems in Africa." Working Paper 03/2, International Monetary Fund, Washington, DC. http://ssrn.com/abstract=879077.

Lienert, Ian, and Feridoun Sarraf. 2001. "Systemic Weaknesses of Budget Management in Anglophone Africa." Working Paper 01/211, International Monetary Fund, Washington, DC. www.imf.org/external/pubs/ft/wp/2001/wp01211.pdf.

Lindaman, Kara, and Kurt Thurmaier. 2002. "Beyond Efficiency and Economy: An Examination of Basic Needs and Fiscal Decentralization." *Economic Development and Cultural Change* 50 (4): 915–34.

McCue, Clifford. 2001. "Local Government Accountants as Public Managers: An Evolving Role." *State and Local Government Review* 33 (2): 144–57.

Mikesell, John. 1995. *Fiscal Administration: Analysis and Applications for the Public Sector*, 4th ed. Belmont, CA: Wadsworth Publishing.

OECD (Organisation for Economic Co-operation and Development). 2001. Best Practices for Budget Transparency. Accessed May 30, 2006. http://www.oecd.org/dataoecd/33/13/1905258.pdf.

Polidano, Charles. 1999. "The New Public Management in Developing Countries." Public Policy and Management Working Paper 13, Institute for Development Policy and Management, Manchester, England.

Premchand, A. 1993. *Public Expenditure Management*. Washington, DC: International Monetary Fund.

Schiavo-Campo, Salvatore, and Daniel Tommasi. 1999. *Managing Government Expenditure*. Manila: Asian Development Bank. www.adb.org/Documents/Manuals/Govt_Expenditure.

Schick, Alan. 1998. *A Contemporary Approach to Public Expenditure Management*. Washington, DC: World Bank Institute. http://siteresources.worldbank.org/INTPEAM/Resources/PEM_book.pdf.

Schick, Allen. 1966. "The Road to PPB: The Stages of Budget Reform." *Public Administration Review* 26 (December): 243–58.

Thompson, Fred. 1993. "Matching Responsibilities with Tactics: Administrative Controls and Modern Government." *Public Administration Review* 53 (4): 303–18.

Thurmaier, Kurt. 1994. "The Evolution of Local Government Budgeting in Poland: From Accounting to Policy in a Leap and a Bound." *Public Budgeting and Finance* 14 (4): 83–96.

———. 1995a. "Execution Phase Budgeting in Local Governments: It's Not Just for Control Anymore!" *State and Local Government Review* 27 (Spring): 102–17.

———. 1995b. "Using the Program Budget Model as a Tool for Local Development: Reforms in Lublin and Krakow, Poland." Monograph prepared for the Office of

Housing and Urban Programs, U.S. Agency for International Development, and the International City/County Management Association, Washington, DC.

Thurmaier, Kurt, and James Gosling. 1997. "The Shifting Roles of Budget Offices in the Midwest: Gosling Revisited." *Public Budgeting and Finance* 17 (4): 48–70.

Thurmaier, Kurt, and Katherine G. Willoughby. 2001. *Policy and Politics in State Budgeting.* Armonk, NY: M.E. Sharpe.

World Bank. 1998. *Public Expenditure Management Handbook.* Washington DC: World Bank.

Zody, Richard E. 1996. "Auditing in Africa: Some Unmet Needs." In *Public Budgeting and Financial Administration in Developing Countries,* ed. Naomi Caiden, 285–92. London: JAI Press.

10

Local Capital Budgeting

A. JOHN VOGT

A city with 120,000 people located in a fast-growing metropolitan area is spending $190 million over four years to expand the capacity of its wastewater treatment facilities by 5.8 million gallons per day. A local school district in the same metropolitan area serving a population of about 700,000 people will need to spend about $1 billion over the next 3 to 5 years to construct 15 new schools, renovate 11 existing schools, acquire new educational technology, and make other improvements to school facilities. A small town of 5,500 people is spending $465,000 this year to acquire police patrol and other automobiles, trucks for its sanitation and streets departments, and other equipment.[1] These expenditures, while different in purpose and amount, are alike in one way—they are all capital expenditures, and all were part of the jurisdictions' capital budgets.

The term *capital budget* is meant broadly. It embraces the identification, prioritization, and planning for capital needs over a multiyear future period; assessment of financial capacity; financial forecasting; development and use of suitable capital financing options; the evaluation, design, and costing of capital projects; project authorization and appropriation; and project implementation. This chapter emphasizes capital budgeting in local government, although many of the concepts and approaches discussed here are also applicable to regional or state-level governments or public entities. The chapter addresses the reasons for capital budgeting, defines capital expenditure, and discusses which capital expenditures and projects belong in the capital budget; it then identifies and discusses the steps involved in a full-fledged capital budget process. Those steps can be viewed as making up a model for capital budgeting against which actual capital budgeting practices in a jurisdiction can be compared. Most of the chapter is devoted to discussion of the steps involved in capital budgeting.

Why Capital Budgeting?

Why would a local government or another public entity have a special process for planning, making, and implementing decisions about capital projects and acquisitions? One reason has to do with the large amounts of money involved in many capital project and acquisition decisions, especially some infrastructure for meeting community water and sewerage, transportation, and other needs. Because much money is at stake in such decisions, a government should make sure that the decisions are the right ones and that the money for them is spent wisely. This approach creates a need for special procedures for planning and making the decisions.

The consequences of capital budget decisions often extend far into the future. The consequences are likely to last as long as the useful lives of the capital assets built or acquired. Thus, when a city builds a new city hall in a particular style at a downtown site, the city probably will benefit from or endure the results of that decision for 30 years or more. If planned and designed well and coordinated with private development, the new city hall can trigger new investment by businesses in the downtown area.

Debt is often used to finance major capital projects; this is another reason for having a special process for capital budgeting. When a jurisdiction's officials decide to issue long-term debt to finance a project, they obligate future officials to raise the money to pay annual principal and interest installments on the debt for many years in the future. In other words, present officials exercise authority over those who follow them— a fact that should cause the current officials to take great care in making capital project and financing decisions. In some places, certain types of debt—for example, general obligation or tax-secured bonds—must be approved by a community's voters in a referendum before the debt is issued. Officials taking a proposed bond referendum to the voters can use capital budgeting to make sure the projects to be financed with the bonds are well conceived and planned.

Another reason for capital budgeting arises because many project or acquisition decisions do not recur each year. In the annual or operating budget, most expenditures recur annually and officials can refer to recent experiences to guide them in making decisions for the coming year, which reduces the risk of error in these decisions. However, because most major capital projects have long useful lives, the decisions to undertake them recur infrequently. As a result, officials often do not have recent experiences to guide them in making decisions about projects this year. The consequent risk of error is higher for these decisions, which is a good reason to have a special process for capital budgeting to ensure that decisions on major projects are fully considered before they are made.

Capital budgeting can help a jurisdiction provide for the orderly and timely renovation and replacement of public facilities. Ensuring the adequacy of public infrastructure and quality of public services requires periodically renovating or replacing the facilities and technology involved. Capital renovation and replacement projects are too often postponed beyond the time when they should be undertaken. As a result, the projects end up costing more. A capital budget can help focus the attention of officials on capital renovation and replacement needs.

Finally, public infrastructure and facilities are essential in a jurisdiction's economic development plans. Many local communities are growing rapidly; the local governments serving them are hard pressed to provide the water and sewerage, transportation, and other facilities needed to accommodate the growth. Other communities, especially in more rural areas or where traditional industries are shutting down, are experiencing economic decline or stagnation. Local governments serving these areas are undertaking economic development programs that rely heavily on building new and upgrading existing infrastructure and facilities to attract new businesses. Capital budgeting can be a vital part of the economic development programs of both fast-growing communities and communities attempting to spur economic growth or change.[2]

Capital Expenditures and Capital Budgeting

This section presents alternative concepts of capital expenditure, discusses capitalization thresholds for identifying capital assets, identifies different types of capital assets, and considers which capital assets are appropriately included in a jurisdiction's capital budget.

What is a Capital Expenditure?

A capital expenditure yields benefits for many years or results in the acquisition of property that has a long useful life. Capital expenditures are often very expensive. Unlike current or operating expenditures, many capital expenditures do not recur each year. They recur irregularly, and long intervals of time elapse between periodic replacements.

Two definitions of capital expenditure are available in the literature. One is from economics, and it gives a broad meaning to the concept. The other is from accounting, and it provides a more restricted definition.

The economic definition suggests that a capital expenditure is an outlay that will produce benefits in future years, whereas a current expenditure yields benefits for only the current year (Quirin and Wiginton 1981).[3] Under this definition, whether the capital expenditure results in the acquisition of specific property is irrelevant. Thus, advertising expenditures made to attract new industry to a community, which accounting practices would charge to a current account, could be considered to be capital expenditures because they are made to obtain benefits in future years. This is a broad conception of capital outlay.

Accounting principles and practices, by contrast, define a capital expenditure as an outlay of significant value resulting in the acquisition of or an addition to property.[4] In the United States, "significant value" can be $1,000, several thousand dollars, or somewhat more, depending on the size of the jurisdiction. In the United States, financial reporting requirements under the Governmental Accounting Standards Board's Statement 34 (1999) have led many jurisdictions to use $5,000 as the limit for significant value, for the purpose of identifying capital expenditures and assets. If an item costs less than the significant dollar threshold, the expenditure for it is a current or operating outlay, even though it results in the acquisition of property that is used over many years.

The major difference between these definitions from accounting and from economics is whether property is acquired. Economics says that any expenditure that produces future benefits, whether or not specific property is acquired, is a capital outlay. To qualify as a capital expenditure under the definition from accounting, however, an expenditure must not only yield benefits in the future but also result in the acquisition of specific, long-lived property or add to or improve existing property. Indeed, it is through the use of the property or asset that the future benefits are realized.

The definition from accounting is the one generally used in government budgeting and finance, and that is the meaning intended for capital expenditure here. The usual categories of capital expenditure under this definition are as follows:

- *Land or rights to land:* This category includes not only the purchase price of land or land rights but also the legal and other fees related to such purchases. It also includes land preparation costs, such as for grading.
- *Buildings:* This category refers to permanent structures for housing persons or property, and equipment or furnishings that are fixed or attached

to such structures. The costs of construction contracts for buildings and for legal, architectural, and engineering services related to building construction or acquisition are also included. Costs here can also include costs incurred by a local government's own staff or workforce to construct buildings and the amounts paid to buy buildings.

■ *Infrastructure:* This category includes normally stationary and long-lived improvements (other than buildings) that add value to or improve land. Examples are streets and roads, bridges and tunnels, stormwater facilities, and water and sewerage, as well as other utility lines and infrastructure.

■ *Equipment, machinery, and other permanent personal property:* Examples of this category are automobiles, trucks, construction machinery, communications equipment or systems, computers, and office equipment and furniture. Equipment or machinery classified here must be movable rather than built into or attached to a building or to infrastructure. Other personal property can include works of art, historic treasures, or certain intangible property—for example, valuable communications or computer software programs owned and used by a local government.[5]

■ *Upgrades or renovations of facilities:* Upgrades or renovations are included when such projects add value to or improve the facilities or extend their useful lives. It is difficult sometimes to differentiate between major expenditures to maintain facilities and capital renovation projects. If structural or mechanical change is involved, an expensive renovation project is often classified as a capital project and the expenditures for it are capitalized. The expenditures for the project are presumed to add value to or extend the useful life of the project being renovated. If there is no structural or mechanical change—for example, complete repainting of a facility—such a project is usually classified as ordinary maintenance even though the project is expensive.

The capitalization threshold for identifying capital expenditure and assets is typically applied on an item-for-item basis. Thus, if a jurisdiction with a $5,000 capitalization threshold purchases 30 office desks, each costing $500, the desks would be accounted for as current assets or items—that is, fully expensed in the year acquired—rather than recorded and carried in the accounting records as capital assets. Correspondingly, the expenditure to acquire the desks would be an operating rather than a capital expenditure, even though the useful life of the desks spans many years and the total outlay to acquire the 30 desks is $15,000 (30 × $500), which is three times the capitalization threshold of $5,000. Although the capitalization threshold should generally be applied on an item-for-item basis, there can be exceptions when purchases of certain lower-cost, long-lived assets or property, such as water or sewer pipe for a city utility system or books for a local library, become a component or part of a system or set of long-lived property with material value in excess of the capitalization threshold.

Which Capital Expenditures Belong in the Capital Budget?

Not all capital expenditures need to be included in the capital budget. The operating budget is the better place for capital expenditures that do not cost a great deal of money. These outlays typically are for certain equipment, some purchases of land or buildings, and smaller construction or renovation projects. A cost cutoff, which may range (in U.S. dollars) from $10,000 or so for a small town to several hundred thousand or a half million dollars or even more for a large city or local government, is typically used for deciding which capital outlays and projects are large enough to place in the capital budget. Thus, while the accountant for a city with 200,000 people would be expected to classify an expenditure of $25,000 for a police patrol vehicle as a capital expenditure, the city's budget officer would probably include such an expenditure on a police department capital outlay line in the operating budget rather than put it in the capital budget.

The capital budget should generally not include expenditures for capital assets that recur each year. For instance, a local government that has a capital budget with a cost cutoff of $50,000 would ordinarily include an expenditure for a capital asset that cost more than $50,000 in the capital budget. However, if the local government replaces four residential refuse collection vehicles annually, each one costing $150,000, the annual replacement cost for these vehicles could readily be financed from annual revenues and included in the operating budget. Even though each vehicle is a long-lived capital asset, with a useful life of five years or more, and each vehicle costs much more than the $50,000 cutoff, the expenditure to replace the four vehicles recurs predictably each year and the operating or annual budget can handle this expenditure as readily as annual spending for salaries, fringe benefits, supplies, and the like. The capital budget therefore should be reserved for capital expenditures that are costly—that is, above a specified cost cutoff—and that do not recur each year.

If a local government has a major equipment replacement or infra-structure rehabilitation program funded each year with contributions from annual revenues, such replacement or rehabilitation capital spending would probably be better placed in the capital budget than the operating budget. Even though the funding occurs each year and may be similar in amount from year to year, spending for these purposes is likely to vary from year to year.

This variation, as well as the significance of a general equipment replacement or infrastructure rehabilitation program, makes it more suitable for inclusion in the capital budget than the operating budget.

Some might say that the capital budget should include all extraordinary, unusual, or large nonrecurring expenditures, not just those that result in the acquisition of capital assets. The reason is that these expenditures, whether current or capital, draw on the resources that a jurisdiction could otherwise use for capital budget spending and therefore should be planned in the capital budget process. Examples of such expenditures are a one-time outlay of $1 million to help low-income residents with home heating costs one winter, or $300,000 spent one year for management training. Helping with heating costs yields benefits for just one year and is a current rather than capital outlay under both the economic and the accounting concepts of capital expenditure. The outlay for management training could qualify as capital under the economic concept of capital expenditure but not under the accounting concept. The risk of putting large operating expenditures into the capital budget is that if the capital budget is financed with long-term debt, the door may be opened to long-term debt financing of current expense items. Debt to be repaid in the future should be used to finance only capital assets that will be used in the future.

Capital Budget Process

Capital budget process, as meant here, denotes an organized set of roles, policies, and procedures for planning, financing, authorizing, and implementing decisions about major capital projects and acquisitions. Although the process may occur in a year's time and be repeated each year, it focuses on capital needs over a multiyear period, unlike the operating budget that addresses spending for only a one- or two-year period. The capital budget process presented here consists of five general stages, each made up of specific steps[6]:

1. Organization of the process
   — Definition of the capital budget process
   — Development of policies for capital budgeting
2. Planning for capital needs
   — Identification of capital needs
   — Prioritization of capital needs or requests
   — Project evaluation, scoping, and costing
   — Preparation and approval of a capital improvement program (CIP)

3. Capital financing
   — Assessment of a jurisdiction's financial condition and preparation of a multiyear financial forecast
   — Identification of capital financing options
   — Development of a capital financing strategy and selection of financing for projects
4. Project decision making
   — Recommendation of capital projects and spending
   — Authorization of capital projects and spending and appropriation of money for them
5. Implementation
   — Acquisition and management of project financing
   — Organization and management of construction projects
   — Acquisition of equipment and other capital assets

A general sequence exists among these stages and steps. The process must be established and organized before effective planning for needs and the assessment of financial condition occurs; such planning and assessment should precede project decision making and implementation. The process is also cyclical, with experiences in the later stages providing the basis for redefining the process and improving what occurs in the earlier stages of the process.

Some steps in one stage of the capital budget process may extend into one or more other stages. For example, project evaluation, scoping, and costing is placed under the second stage, planning for capital needs, because determining project benefits and costs is an important part of planning. However, some project evaluation—for example, engineering-based feasibility studies—may occur later in the process, just before decisions are made to approve and fund projects. Moreover, although the CIP is placed under planning for capital needs and ahead of capital financing on the list, to be realistic it must be based on an assessment and forecast of a jurisdiction's financial condition. A CIP must also reflect a workable capital financing strategy. Thus, these steps should precede preparation of the CIP in practice. The CIP is placed where it is because it is the most important step in planning for capital needs. In many jurisdictions, it is the process in which capital needs are identified, prioritized, and initially evaluated.

The steps involved in capital budgeting often blend into one another in practice. However, it is useful to present each step separately to illustrate what is involved in capital budgeting. One might question whether the implementation of projects should be part of capital budgeting. The steps involved in implementation are a vital part of capital budgeting because failures here can sink the plans and financial strategies made and developed earlier in the process.

The stages and steps listed earlier make up a comprehensive capital budget process. Some local jurisdictions, mostly large ones, have capital budgeting practices that resemble the process here. Capital budgeting in other local jurisdictions, especially smaller ones, consists of only some of the steps. For example, while a specific local government may have a CIP, it may not be accompanied by a formal multiyear financial forecast. This is the case for many smaller local governments in the United States. The comprehensive model of capital budgeting presented here provides a checklist for officials in any jurisdiction to use to evaluate their capital budgeting practices. Each step of the capital budget process is now discussed.

Defining the Capital Budget Process

This stage involves identifying who will be involved in the capital budget process, what steps will make up the process, and how it will be organized. There are some important questions to address in defining the process: Who will be responsible for coordinating the process? What will be the roles of the governing board and chief executive officer in setting policies to guide capital budgeting and in reviewing and approving capital budget requests? Will citizen groups as well as a jurisdiction's departments submit requests? What types of information will be required to accompany each capital budget request? What criteria will be used to set capital project requests in priority order? Will there be a CIP? If so, how many years will it cover and what steps will be involved in preparing and approving it? In what ways will the CIP be linked to the annual budget process? What steps will be involved in authorizing capital projects, and what systems and procedures will be followed in constructing projects and for acquiring equipment or other capital assets?

Most, if not all, of these questions need to be addressed as a jurisdiction first undertakes, organizes, or reorganizes capital budgeting. However, the questions are seldom, if ever, settled once and for all. Actual experiences in planning, financing, decision making, and implementation will, of course, reveal ways in which roles and procedures can be better defined or improved.

Developing Policies for Capital Budgeting

Policies can help define the capital budget process by identifying roles in the process, establishing responsibilities, and referring to the general steps to be followed in capital budgeting. If a jurisdiction's governing board formally adopts the policies, this action can give legitimacy to the process. Governing board–approved policies can, in effect, become the infrastructure for the capital budget process itself.

Some policies may originate from legal requirements. Others may be adapted from practices recommended by debt-rating agencies or other authorities on capital budgeting and finance. Still others may reflect a local government's own financial condition, prospects, and needs and the goals and preferences of its governing board, other top officials, and citizens.

Specific capital budgeting policies can address capital planning, for example, requiring a jurisdiction's chief executive officer to prepare a multiyear CIP. Other policies may relate to capital financing, for example, creating and funding capital reserves for the replacement of major equipment and the rehabilitation of infrastructure, identifying the types of projects for which debt will be considered, and limiting debt by reference to ratios that measure the jurisdiction's debt-carrying capacity and perhaps encouraging departmental staff members to seek intergovernmental grants to help finance projects. Other policies can address the authorization of projects and set guidelines for project implementation.

The policies that a jurisdiction has to guide capital budgeting can be numerous and elaborate or relatively few and simple. A larger or fast-growing local government facing major capital improvement needs is probably better served by having more extensive and specific capital policies. For example, one fast-growing city of 150,000 in a high-growth region of the United States has about six pages of policies that address the city's CIP process, funding for capital projects, debt limits, equipment replacement, and reserves. By contrast, a smaller, slower-growing local jurisdiction probably can get by with a limited number of key policies that address capital budgeting. As an example, a city of 30,000 people in a slow-growing farming region of the U.S. heartland has just six one-sentence capital budgeting and finance policies. One simple but very important policy provides for a level tax levy for annual debt-service payments. This not only helps ensure that resources are available for current debt repayment but also provides resources, as existing debt is repaid and annual debt service drops, to support new debt to meet future capital needs.

Identifying Capital Project and Equipment Needs

In many local governments, the identification of capital project and equipment needs occurs entirely within the context of preparing the CIP. Departmental directors and staff submit CIP requests to replace equipment, to renovate facilities, and to fund projects or purchase equipment to meet service improvements related to economic development. Citizen or neighborhood groups, nonprofit organizations, and community business associations may also be allowed or encouraged to identify project needs and submit CIP requests related to their specific interests.

Long-term master or strategic planning is used in some communities to identify future capital improvement and equipment needs. Such planning starts with broad community goals over a long-term future planning period, then attempts to translate the goals into infrastructure, capital facility and service requirements for the local government serving the community. The time horizon for master or strategic planning is long—extending anywhere from 5 to 20 or more years depending on the needs faced, the visions of those leading and participating in the process, and the realities of the situation. Participation in master or strategic planning is typically based on boards, involving not only local public officials but also leaders and representatives of neighborhoods and different economic sectors.

A master or strategic plan usually identifies future infrastructure and capital project needs in a general way, providing information about the nature of each need, the reason for it, when it is needed, its relation to goals in the strategic plan and to other project or service needs identified in the plan, and rough or general cost estimates. Once completed and generally accepted by local officials, the strategic or master plan can be a springboard from which identified capital projects and acquisitions are launched into the CIP. Local government departments and perhaps other groups make CIP requests drawing on needs or projects identified in the strategic or master plans. Master or strategic plans, once made, need to be updated annually or periodically to keep them current with changing conditions. This may be done by the same group of officials and citizens who formulated the initial plans or, if such a group does not continue in existence, by a smaller, ongoing, executive committee of the original group or by local government officials.

One example of local government use of master or strategic planning to identify capital project needs is provided by a city with 35,000 people in the southeastern part of the United States. The city currently has 14 master plans that set goals and identify capital infrastructure and facility needs in a variety of functional areas. These plans include a 10-year, citywide landscaping plan; a 10-year parks and recreation master and service plan; a 20-year sidewalk and bikeway plan; and several plans that address facility and service needs in specific city neighborhoods. The city began its master planning program in the 1990s. Once formulated, a master plan is updated annually by city staffs working with interested community leaders and citizen groups. The city council approved the original or initial master plans and also reviews and generally approves each updated plan. Most project requests made in the city's annual CIP process come from the master plans.

Capital renovation and replacement needs are often neglected beyond when they should be undertaken. As a result, the costs for such projects, when the projects are eventually done, can be much higher than what the costs would have been had the projects been undertaken in a timely way. To identify capital renovation and replacement needs, some local jurisdictions have developed and use capital asset management systems. Such systems rely on engineering-based analysis to evaluate the condition of existing roads, water and sewerage infrastructure, and other facilities and buildings. For example, one city with a population of 250,000 has its engineering staff assess the condition of major city buildings, such as fire stations. This assessment determines the general condition of the building, projects the year when renovation or replacement will be needed, and estimates renovation or replacement costs. The city is currently revamping, strengthening, and extending this system. Many local governments have equipment and vehicle replacement policies and schedules that help officials determine when it is most economical for replacement to occur and what the costs will be. Capital asset management systems such as these can be important tools that local governments use to identify capital expenditure needs for existing facilities and equipment.

Prioritizing Capital Project and Equipment Requests

Few, if any, jurisdictions have sufficient resources to meet all their capital needs. Only a portion of the needs identified and requests made can be funded at any one time. Capital project and equipment requests compete with one another for available resources, and the requests must be set into priority. Although such ranking occurs throughout the planning and decision-making stages of capital budgeting, a formal ranking of requests should occur as the CIP is developed. The CIP allocates the costs of capital projects among the years of the CIP forecast period; projects allocated to the first few years of the forecast period have a higher priority than projects and spending allocated to the later years. Thus, prioritization necessarily occurs as the CIP is prepared.

Different approaches are used to prioritize capital needs. Decision makers can set capital requests in priority order on the basis of their general familiarity with the needs underlying the requests and their judgments about the relative need for each request. While prioritization based on the judgment of key decision makers is an important part of any budget ranking system, prioritization based solely on experienced-based judgment falls short under certain conditions: decision makers are not familiar with some requests; there are many requests on which to decide; the requests involve complex needs or technical considerations; there are multiple decision makers who have different perspectives about the needs; or resources are especially short.

One or more of these conditions usually prevail in capital budgeting; therefore, ranking approaches or systems are often used to help decision makers prioritize capital requests. Many of these systems are composed of so called "urgency of need" ranking criteria, such as the following:

- Reduces or eliminates threats to public health and safety
- Is mandated by law or regulation
- Remedies a pressing facility or service deficiency
- Is consistent with governing board goals
- Facilitates more efficient operations
- Promotes economic development
- Uses available outside funds
- Is linked to other projects
- Is supported by the community

Officials in a small county (50,000 people) located on the edge of a fast-growing metropolitan area in the United States have incorporated these as well as several additional criteria in a weighted rating system to prioritize requests made in the county's CIP (table 10.1).

The county has used the rating system in table 10.1 for more than 10 years. Its rating criteria and weightings were generally approved by the county commissioners (governing board) when the system was first proposed for use. The county manager and staff are the ones who actually use the system for prioritizing requests when they develop the proposed CIP each year for presentation to the commissioners.

Another approach is to prioritize capital requests in terms of program priorities or goals. A key element of the philosophy underlying this approach is that the same program needs and goals should drive both the capital and the operating budgets. Thus, if the governing board of a local jurisdiction decides that transportation and public safety are a jurisdiction's most pressing needs, that should weigh very heavily on if not determine the rankings

TABLE 10.1 County Weighted Rating System for Prioritizing Project Requests

Rating criteria	Definition or explanation	Maximum points	Percentage weighting
Goals/objectives	Extent to which project meets goals and objectives of county commissioners	25	15.9
Safety	Extent to which project eliminates, prevents, or reduces an immediate hazard to safety	14	8.9
Mandates	Extent to which project helps county meet existing or new mandates	13	8.3
Timing/links	Extent to which project is timely, a continuation of a project currently under way, related to other high-priority projects	12	7.6
Economic impact	Extent to which project enhances economic development in county, or directly or indirectly adds to the tax base	11	7.0
Efficiencies	Extent to which project contributes to savings in county operating costs or capital spending	10	6.4
Maintaining current level of service	Extent to which project is necessary for county to continue to provide one or more services at current standards	9	5.7
Improving access	Extent to which project improves citizen access to current services	8	5.1
Service improvement	Extent to which project improves the quality of existing services	7	4.5
Service addition	Extent to which project increases the quantity of existing services	3	1.9
Operating budget impact	0 to 15 for projects that lower future operating expenses; 0 for projects that have no effect on operating expenses; 0 to −15 for projects that increase operating expenses score	0 to 15, 0, or 0 to −15	9.5
Community support	Extent to which project has broad or strong support from the community	10	6.4
Financing	Extent to which project can be financed with non–general fund revenue sources	15	9.5
Timeliness of submission	Extent to which project request is submitted in a timely way	5	3.2
Maximum points, all categories		157	100.0

Source: Office of the County Manager, Chatham County, North Carolina.
Note: The weighted rating system shown in this table was initially created by the assistant county manager, who also serves as county budget director. This rating system was used through the 1990s. The rating system currently used excludes "goals/objectives" and adds up to only 132 points. At this writing, the county commissioners are not setting goals and objectives to guide CIP and budget prioritization.

among capital budget requests. Similarly, if a jurisdiction's governing board sets specific program goals as the top priorities—for example, reduce traffic congestion in the downtown area and increase recreational opportunities for youth—these goals should strongly influence if not determine the priorities among CIP requests.

The rating system in table 10.1 includes consistency with commissioner goals and objectives among the criteria for rating project requests. Indeed, this factor is weighted more heavily than any other, at 25 points. However, this factor is only 1 of 14 criteria that make up the system and accounts for only 15 percent (rounded) of the maximum points that any project could receive under this system.

Program priorities and goals must be an important part of any ranking or prioritization system used in capital budgeting. However, such priorities and goals often do not represent the full range of needs, pressures, and goals that must be considered in prioritizing projects in capital budgeting. Prioritization in capital budgeting should consider legal mandates, threats to public health and safety, deteriorating facilities, and community support for specific requests, whether or not such considerations are incorporated into governing board program goals or objectives. The weighted rating system shown in table 10.1 addresses governing board goals and objectives, and still other important factors.

When program priorities or goals are used to prioritize capital requests, it is typically sufficient for officials to identify their top priorities and goals, and not to label some programs or goals as low in priority. Labeling low priorities runs the risk of generating adverse political reactions from those working in or served by the low-priority programs.

Ranking or rating systems do not determine priorities or make project decisions. Rather, they contribute to or aid prioritization and decision making by helping to make sure that a broad range of factors are considered in the prioritization process. Moreover, the criteria and systems provide decision makers with a common framework for prioritizing requests and for explaining their decisions to the public. Nor does the use of ranking criteria or a rating system make prioritization and decision making objective. The resulting rankings remain subjective in that officials select some ranking criteria and not others and, if weighted ratings are used, officials assign the weights. Finally, it is important to recognize that ranking criteria and weights can vary from one type of request to another. For example, while local governing board goals may drive priorities for projects where external mandates do not exist, external legal mandates are likely to drive priorities in areas where those mandates exist and are strong.

Evaluating, Scoping, and Costing Capital Projects

Capital project and equipment requests are evaluated in various stages or steps of the capital budget process: generally when capital needs are first identified; when requests are prioritized in terms of urgency of need or other criteria; when projects are scheduled by year in the CIP; when feasibility studies or analyses are done; and for larger projects, when architectural or engineering plans are prepared. Project evaluation is placed here in the planning stage of capital budgeting because it begins to occur at this stage and is linked to prioritization and preparation of the CIP. Moreover, for some projects, elaborate feasibility studies are done as the CIP is prepared.

Generally, the purposes of evaluation are to identify project benefits, to define project scope, and to estimate project costs and their effects on future operating budgets. For construction projects, evaluation extends to the preparation of construction plans and documents. For larger projects or those involving technical considerations, project evaluation is usually contracted out to a consulting firm that has expertise with the type of project being evaluated.

The benefits to be derived from public improvement projects are often defined in terms of one or more of the criteria for prioritization discussed in the previous section: fulfillment of legal mandates, reduction or elimination of threats to public health and safety, remedy of a facility or service deficiency, and so forth. Some project benefits can be quantified. For example, if a request is to build a new school, the evaluation can specify the number of students who would attend the new school, perhaps some of them being moved out of temporary classroom facilities and others from existing permanent but overcrowded classrooms. Many public enterprise projects will generate future operating revenues, which can be estimated and included among the benefits. Some projects will result in savings in operating outlays in future years. Many public sector projects have certain benefits that are difficult or impossible to quantify, yet such benefits are very important in determining the priority of the projects. For example, cultural facilities such as libraries and parks or open space can contribute greatly to a community's quality of life, which by definition is essentially an intangible rather than quantifiable benefit. Many projects have external benefits that are not directly associated with the project but that spin off from it and contribute broadly to well-being in the community or make other projects more valuable. Some external benefits may be fairly certain to occur. Others are likely to be potential. In either case, both can be listed and discussed in any evaluation of a requested capital project, with the discussion indicating the likelihood of each benefit being realized if the project is implemented.

Evaluation also involves specifically defining a project's scope. The scope and parameters of some capital projects may be readily apparent. The precise scope of other projects may be difficult to determine; this is especially true for large projects and for those for which views differ about what the project size, capability, and quality should be. For example, if a local jurisdiction's emergency communications system needs to be replaced, law enforcement officials may have different views from other emergency response officials about what specific capabilities a new communications system should have; all these officials may want a more powerful and expensive system than the jurisdiction's budget staff think is needed. Even after agreement is ostensibly reached on a project's scope, there can be upward "scope creep" as a project is designed and implemented. For example, professionals to be served by a project and the architects designing it may include components in the design phase that were not addressed in the agreed-on project scope and that add significantly to the project's cost. After the project scope is defined, on the basis of project evaluation, it needs to be monitored by budget staff through the design and implementation phases of the project.

The usual categories of cost for a construction project are land acquisition and preparation, planning and design, construction, and equipment and furnishings. Equipment and furnishings can be attached to the project or movable. Even though movable equipment and furnishings are not capitalized as part of a facility's cost for accounting purposes, they should be included among project costs if the equipment and furnishings are needed to make the facility operational. A contingency line is also typically included to allow for unforeseen cost items. If a project will not be built for a year or more or if it will take many years to build, an allowance for inflation is likely to be needed in estimating costs. Testing costs associated with project design should not be overlooked; the costs and time to obtain environmental clearances need to be considered. Legal fees related to land acquisition, construction contracting, and financing are project costs. Project management fees or costs, whether contracted or done in-house, can be significant and should not be overlooked. Interest on debt that is paid during construction is appropriately charged to a project. Outlays for project feasibility studies done before a project is approved are usually funded initially from other sources (the general fund), but if a project is approved and financing is obtained for it, such costs are reimbursable from project financing proceeds. Finally, when construction is finished, there are usually project activation costs, including moving expenses.

The evaluation of costs for a capital project should consider not only the construction or acquisition costs themselves but also any resulting ongoing operating and maintenance costs. All the capital, operating, and maintenance costs that occur over a capital asset's useful life are called life-cycle costs. While it is difficult to estimate operating and maintenance costs to be incurred far into the future, such long-term, life-cycle costing can be useful in deciding on components and quality features to include in the design of the project and in evaluating a project's overall benefit. For example, a choice may exist for a project between incurring higher initial capital costs and thereby lowering future operating costs, or reducing project quality and capital costs and thereby likely resulting in higher annual operating costs for the project. Life-cycle costing, which considers both future operating costs as well as the capital costs for a project, can provide a basis for comparing and choosing between such alternatives.

The methods used in project evaluation range from informed judgment to sophisticated statistical or engineering-based analyses. Informed judgment can be reliable when a project is relatively small to modest in size, when cost estimates for it are well established, when decision makers have experience with that type of project, and when there are no viable alternatives to the project as requested. Evaluation methods that rely on quantitative analysis can be useful when capital projects are large, where cost estimates entail significant uncertainties, and of course where there are quantifiable or financial benefits.

Financial analysis techniques are commonly used in business to evaluate proposed capital projects. These techniques can be used to help evaluate public sector projects that generate annual revenues or savings during the useful life of a project. One set of financial techniques that can be used to evaluate such projects relies on interest rate formulas that convert cash flows occurring over time to comparable values. Formulas are available for calculating the present value of future cash flows and comparing that value with a project's original capital costs. There are other formulas for amortizing a capital cost incurred today to an equivalent annual value over a project's useful life and for converting capital and future annual costs to a present value or to a single value at one time in the future. The use of these interest rate formulas requires the selection of an interest rate for discounting and an estimated useful life for a project. Even though assumptions about interest rates, project useful lives, and other factors create uncertainties about such financial analysis methods, more applications of the methods are occurring in evaluations of certain types of public sector projects—for example, projects for public enterprises supported by user charges.

Preparing and Approving a Capital Improvement Program

The CIP is at the center of planning for capital projects and acquisitions. The CIP is also a key part of financial planning and a basis for recommendations to authorize specific projects. A CIP is a multiyear forecast of major capital infrastructure, building, equipment, and other capital needs; the project appropriations or spending that must be incurred to make those needs a reality; the sources of financing for the projects; and the impact of the projects on future operating budgets. The CIP includes the higher-priority capital needs that have been identified in the initial planning stages, and it documents the specific benefits and costs of individual projects. The CIP is essentially a plan, with projects and spending in the first year of the CIP forecast period typically becoming the recommended capital budget for that year.

Most CIPs forecast five or six years into the future. Experience suggests that this provides sufficient time to identify and plan most capital projects and arrange financing for them, yet is not so long as to result in too much "wish listing." Although 5 or 6 years is the norm, some jurisdictions find it useful to extend the CIP forecast period to 10 years or even longer. These are usually fast-growing communities that face many major new capital improvement needs. The out-year projections in these CIPs are typically more general than the near-term projections. A jurisdiction with a five- or six-year CIP can accommodate needs in the years beyond that period by including a list of projects that are not in the CIP but that remain under consideration. Some smaller local governments have CIP planning periods of only three or four years. Such a forecast period is suitable when most capital projects are modest in size.

Table 10.2 presents a prototype summary form of a CIP with a six-year forecast period for a city's general fund. A general fund supports public safety, streets, schools, and other governmental services that are financed with general taxes and revenues. The essential feature of a CIP is the apportionment of project spending, financing, and operating budget effects among the years of the CIP forecast period. The columns in table 10.2 designated "prior years" and "current year" are for capital projects that are in process. The column labeled "year 1 budget" is for capital projects and spending that will occur in the upcoming year. Such projects and spending may be considered to be the recommended capital budget for that year. The amounts in this column may include spending for projects in process that were begun in earlier years and spending for new projects getting under way in the budget year. The columns for year 2 through year 6 are for capital projects and spending that are planned for one or more of those years.

The CIP is conceived of as an annual process, and most jurisdictions with a CIP repeat it each year. Annual repetition provides for a recurring assessment of capital needs and updates the CIP to account for new needs and changing conditions. Use of a CIP presumes that capital needs are foreseen and that requests will be placed initially in the CIP in one of the distant planning years.

TABLE 10.2 CIP Summary Prototype Form, General Fund

Item	Prior years	Current year	Year 1 budget	Year 2 plan	Year 3 plan	Year 4 plan	Year 5 plan	Year 6 plan	Years beyond year 6	Totals
					Forecast period					
Project and acquisition expenditures by function										
Public safety										
Streets and transportation										
Recreation and culture										
Community development										
Technology										
General government										
Total project expenditures										
Financing sources										
Operating revenues										
Fund balance										
Capital reserves										
Equipment/vehicle replacement fund										
General obligation bonds/debt										
Capital lease debt										
Other bonds or debt										
Impact/development fees										
Grants										
Other sources										
Total financing Sources										

Impact on operating budget
Debt service: bonds and certificates
   of participation
Capital lease payments
Increased operating costs
Decreased operating costs
Increased/decreased revenues
Total operating impact

Source: Adapted from the CIP summary form presented as exhibit 3-1 in Vogt (2004: 34).
Note: The author formulated the CIP summary form from the financial forecasting form in figure 11.2 in Lawrence and Vogt (1999: 342).

Then the requests are reviewed each year, when the CIP is repeated. When the requests that survive reach the budget year, they are approved and funded, although even at this final stage of review some projects may be rejected or perhaps postponed another year. Not all capital needs can be recognized five or six years ahead of the time they are needed. Some will have to be approved almost immediately upon first request. However, if this happens for many requests, the CIP loses much of its value as a planning tool.

As table 10.2 shows, the CIP also identifies the financing sources for projects and the impact of projects on future operating budgets. The CIP can be very valuable to officials in planning capital financing for projects and coordinating the capital and operating budgets. Subsequent sections of this chapter discuss capital financing options and financial forecasting that considers the impact of the CIP on future operating budgets.

The CIP serves various useful purposes. It allows time for the design of projects, giving architects and engineers the opportunity to more carefully define project scope, prepare plans, and estimate project costs. The CIP provides time to arrange financing for projects; this can include establishing and funding capital reserves, searching for and obtaining grants, securing authorization and community support for issuing debt, or pursuing private investment in public projects. The CIP can also provide officials with time to find suitable sites for projects and negotiate for the purchase of land on favorable terms. A CIP can help officials spot the relationships among different projects and schedule them for implementation in a way that saves money.

The CIP preparation process usually involves the review of requests by different officials and public bodies from different perspectives. A planning board often makes one review that focuses on the needs that requests fulfill and their conformity with development plans and land use or environmental restrictions. The chief executive officer and administrative staff usually review CIP requests in terms of their feasibility, benefits, costs, and alternative ways to meet the needs for which requests are made. The governing board of a jurisdiction makes a final review of CIP requests, considering the community's views about the requests and the taxes or other revenues that will be needed to fund projects. Public hearings are often held, to give citizens the opportunity to comment on the proposed CIP or specific projects. When its review is finished near the end of the CIP preparation process, the governing board usually adopts a resolution approving the CIP. This formalizes the CIP process. However, such a resolution typically neither commits funds to a project nor gives the go-ahead to start a project. The resolution is basically a statement of governing board support for the general plan of projects, spending, and financing in the CIP. Authorization of projects and appropriation of money for them usually occur by governing board approval of a capital budget, encompassing projects and spending in the first or budget year of the CIP or those by other board actions that specifically authorize or appropriate money for capital projects and spending.

Assessing Financial Condition and Preparing Forecasts

Any capital budget process should involve an assessment of a jurisdiction's current financial condition and a forecast of the jurisdiction's capacity to fund future needs, including both ongoing services in the operating budget and capital projects or acquisitions included in the CIP.

Analysis of current financial condition and trends

A jurisdiction's financial condition depends on its revenues, spending, fund balances and other reserves, and debt. Financial practices also underlie a jurisdiction's financial condition and prospects.

Annual or operating revenues support all spending, including expenditures for capital projects. Such revenues provide resources to pay operating spending and pay-as-you-go capital financing and to pay debt service on bonds or other debt issued in the past to finance capital projects. The growth or change in major local revenue sources, such as the property tax or sales or excise taxes, should be tracked over a period of recent years. Such growth or change should be compared with growth or change in a jurisdiction's population, overall operating spending, spending for debt service, and other relevant spending purposes. The analysis of specific revenues should distinguish among growth or change in the tax or revenue base caused by economic expansion or change, redefinitions of the base, and changes in the tax or revenue rate. If some revenue sources are not growing or growing slowly, the causes should be identified.

Expenditures for salaries, wages, and fringe benefits account for the largest share of operating spending for most government services. Growth or change in spending for such purposes in recent years should be tracked. Analysis should identify the reasons for growth or change and compare them with growth or change in major revenue sources. Expenditures for other major recurring operating budget items, perhaps public assistance payments or certain contractual services, should be similarly tracked and analyzed.

Available general and other operating fund balances are very important to a jurisdiction's financial condition. They provide the working capital to fund cash flow shortfalls during the year, and they serve as "rainy day" funds to cover unanticipated or emergency spending. Their role in capital financing is addressed in the next section. Available operating fund balances are usually measured in relation to general and operating fund spending. An analysis of current financial condition and trends should identify changes in operating fund balances in recent years and the causes of the changes.[7]

An analysis of outstanding debt, including capital lease obligations, is crucial in any assessment of a jurisdiction's financial condition. If a jurisdiction is already heavily in debt and is making large annual debt-service payments, its ability to incur debt to finance new capital needs is limited. Growth or change in annual debt service, including periodic lease payment obligations, should be tracked and compared with growth or change in overall operating spending and in major revenues. Various debt ratios are used to assess a jurisdiction's debt capacity. These are discussed in the section on developing a capital financing strategy.

A jurisdiction's financial practices sooner or later affect its financial condition. Budgeting, accounting, and tax and revenue administration practices need to be examined and compared with applicable standards or benchmarks in any assessment of a jurisdiction's financial condition. For example, the assessment should compare actual spending with budgeted appropriations and actual revenues collection with budgeted estimates, evaluate accounting and financial reporting practices in terms of generally accepted accounting standards, and compare tax collections with taxes levied or billed.

Preparation of a multiyear financial forecast

A financial forecast builds on the assessment of current financial condition and trends; considers likely changes in the local economy over the forecast period; and projects future annual revenues, spending, and fund balances. The forecast supports both the operating budget and the capital budget. Generally, for any year during the forecast period, annual revenues less annual operating and related spending and contributions to operating fund balances leaves the amount that is available to support pay-as-you-go capital financing and annual debt-service payments. A financial forecast should cover the same future period that the CIP covers.

A jurisdiction can prepare a multiyear financial forecast using a format such as that presented in table 10.3. The format is for a city's general fund, which includes public safety, schools, streets, and other needs financed with taxes and other general revenues. Table 10.3 uses the same yearly format as the CIP prototype summary form in table 10.2. A similarly organized form, albeit with different revenue and spending lines, could be used to forecast enterprise revenues, spending, and financing.

TABLE 10.3 Financial Forecast, General Fund

Item	Prior years	Current year	Year 1 budget	Year 2 plan	Year 3 plan	Forecast period Year 4 plan	Year 5 plan	Year 6 plan	Years beyond year 6	Totals
Beginning fund balance revenues										
Property taxes										
Sales and use taxes										
Intergovernmental revenue										
Fees and charges										
Other revenues										
Transfers in										
Total revenues										
Operating expenditures										
General government										
Public safety										
Streets and transportation										
Cultural and recreation										
Debt service and existing debt										
Other expenditures										
Total operating expenditures										

(continued)

331

TABLE 10.3 Financial Forecast, General Fund *(continued)*

Item	Prior years	Current year	Year 1 budget	Year 2 plan	Year 3 plan	Year 4 plan	Year 5 plan	Year 6 plan	Years beyond year 6	Totals
					Forecast period					
CIP impact on general fund										
Debt service, new bonds, and debt										
Operating expenditures										
Revenues										
Net annual impact of CIP										
Forecast bottom lines										
Annual surplus or deficit										
Ending fund balance										
Ending fund balance as percentage of spending										
Debt, existing and new										
Debt service, existing and new, as percentage of general fund										
Tax rate impact of surplus or deficit										

Source: Adapted from figure 11.2 in Lawrence and Vogt (1999: 342).

A forecast of annual revenues considers past trends and evaluates how economic events are likely to affect revenues during the forecast period. Because different revenues often grow at different rates, a forecast is needed for each major revenue source. For many local governments, the major general fund revenue sources are property taxes, sales or value added taxes, revenues or taxes collected by a state or provincial government and shared with local governments, and user fees and charges. Many less important taxes and revenues can be combined and forecast together. In an enterprise fund, such as a water and sewerage utility, service charges to customers are the major revenue source. They should be forecast separately from the other sources in the enterprise fund. In forecasting, present tax and user fee rates are generally assumed to continue through the forecast period, unless a policy has already been approved to provide for changes in the rates during the forecast period.

Once annual revenues have been projected, the amounts that will be used to finance operating spending each year during the forecast period need to be estimated. This can be done by line-item categories—salaries and wages, fringe benefits, contractual services, and so on—or by department or function. If the forecast is by line-item category, forecast amounts are less likely to become a floor for annual budget requests from departments of the local government. However, forecasts of spending by department or function are likely to be more understandable to governing board members and most other local officials. The forecast in table 10.3 shows spending by function. The forecast should separately set forth debt-service requirements each year over the forecast period. Like annual revenues, operating expenditure forecasts should consider trends and changes in spending in past years and also how events expected to occur during the forecast period will affect spending by line item, department, or functional category. In some cases, the trends can simply be carried forward; in others, they will have to be adjusted for expected changes.

The impact of the CIP on future annual revenues and operating spending should be highlighted in the forecast, as shown in table 10.3. Such information can be very helpful to officials as they make capital budget decisions. The major operating budget impact of a CIP that includes projects to be financed with debt will be new annual debt-service payments. Increased operating costs for new positions or other recurring items are also likely to result from some capital projects included in the CIP. A few CIP projects may improve productivity and result in lower operating spending in future years. Some projects may have an up or down effect on future annual revenues. All these expected increases or decreases in annual revenues or spending should be shown in the forecast.

To be meaningful for decision-making purposes, a financial forecast should show one or more bottom lines. The forecast in table 10.3 depicts several such lines: an annual surplus or deficit, the ending fund balance, the ending fund balance as a percentage of operating spending, the existing and new debt, the debt service on existing and new debt—both a dollar amount and as a percentage of the general fund, and the change in the tax rate associated with an annual surplus or deficit. Showing one or more of these bottom lines can entail some risk. Elected officials, the press, and others need to understand that annual surpluses or deficits and changes in the tax rate are not decided. The forecast presents such information to show what the future might be if potential projects are approved and implemented and the projected financial situation or scenario actually occurs.

Identifying Capital Financing Options

The specific capital financing options available to a local jurisdiction vary from nation to nation and sometimes within a nation, from province to province or state to state. For example, in the United States, some states confer broad "home rule" powers on some types of municipalities; one effect of this is to give such municipalities a broader range of financing options for capital improvements than other local governments in the same states or non–home rule local governments in other states have. National laws relating to development, banking, finance, and taxes can also have a great effect on the capital financing tools available to local governments in a country. For example, in the United States, Internal Revenue Service (IRS) laws and regulations affect the financing choices that local governments in that country have. Generally, IRS laws and regulations exempt the interest paid to investors on state and local government debt from federal income taxes. This has had the effect of creating a huge pool of private sector lower-cost financing for local government capital projects in that country. Finally, the availability of national or federal and state or provincial grant and loan programs for local capital improvements is very important in local capital budgeting in many nations, especially where private debt or financing markets are limited.

The familiarity of officials in a local jurisdiction and their experience with specific capital financing sources can effectively affect the range of options that are legally available to a jurisdiction. As a result, officials may select sources that are not as suitable as or that are more expensive than other available financing methods. It is important in financial planning for officials to be aware of the full range of capital financing sources that are legally and practically available to a jurisdiction.

Capital financing sources are commonly divided into two general categories: pay-as-you-go sources and debt sources. Additional sources have evolved specifically for financing projects related to economic development. Some jurisdictions also enter into intergovernmental or public-private partnerships, in which they draw on capital contributed by other parties to help finance projects.

Pay-as-you-go sources

Pay-as-you-go sources are comparable to equity or owner financing of capital needs in the private sector. In such financing, businesses secure equity capital through sales of stock, which make the stockholders owners of the businesses, and from other contributions of capital funds by owners or partners. Pay-as-you-go capital financing by local governments or public entities comes from taxes and other annual revenues contributed by taxpayers and citizens who pay fees when they use certain services. Portions of the annual taxes or user fee revenues are earmarked and allocated directly to finance capital improvements and assets. Public pay-as-you-go or private equity financing stands in contrast to debt financing, in which the public entity or private firm borrows capital and incurs debt to finance capital projects and then pays it back with interest over a portion or all of a project's useful life. The advantages of pay-as-you-go financing are that it avoids the interest costs associated with debt and that, because the cash must be raised before a project is undertaken, it tends to encourage more economical projects. One disadvantage of pay-as-you-go financing for major, long-lived projects is that it is often very difficult or impossible for a local government to accumulate enough pay-as-you-go money to undertake the project when the money is needed,

The U.S. bond rating agencies recommend that local governments finance a portion of their capital budget from pay-as-you-go sources (Prunty and Jacob 2002). Doing so helps a jurisdiction preserve flexibility in future operating budgets. If annual revenues level or fall off in a recession, pay-as-you-go capital financing can be reduced to help respond to revenue limitations. Annual debt-service and lease payment obligations cannot be cut to respond to revenue shortfalls. Pay-as-you-go sources include the following:

- *Annual taxes or revenues that are spent on capital projects:* The taxes and revenues are raised and go directly to finance the projects or assets rather than to fund capital reserves or periodic payments on debt that had previously been incurred to finance projects.
- *Operating fund balances:* If operating fund balances are accumulated above the levels needed to support the operating or annual budget, the excess balances can be drawn down to finance capital projects.

■ *Capital reserves:* A capital reserve is a savings account. Taxes or other revenues are raised, set aside for a period of time, and then drawn down and used to finance capital spending. Capital reserves can be separate funds that exist apart from the general or other operating funds, designated portions of general or other operating fund balances, or revolving funds for ongoing capital asset replacement or rehabilitation programs.

Debt sources

Financing from debt for local capital projects may come from placement of the debt with local banks or investors who are investing in the community. In nations with developed financial markets, debt financing may also come from public sales of local government debt or bonds or from debt underwriters who resell the debt to any interested investors, including individuals, businesses, and financial institutions, who buy the debt for their investment portfolios. Debt financing for local projects may also be provided by national or state-level public agencies that make loans to local governments, often at interest rates lower than those available from other sources.

The advantages of issuing debt to finance capital projects is that it spreads the capital costs of a project over much or all of the project's useful life through the annual debt-service payments that the issuer makes to repay the debt with interest. This allocates the capital cost of the project to those who use and benefit from the project. They pay the annual taxes and revenues that cover the annual debt service over the project's useful life. The repayment term for debt should not exceed a project's useful life. Debt financing also enables major capital projects to be undertaken in a timely way. The major disadvantage of debt is that it adds interest or financing expenses to a project's costs. Of course, such interest or project expenses recognize the fact that money has a time value, that is, that it declines in value as time goes on.

Types and classifications of debt depend on national and state law and vary from country to country and often within a country. Nonetheless, debt can be classified generally by the collateral that is pledged to secure the debt. The names used for the following different types of debt distinguished in terms of security or collateral are those commonly used in the United States. Other names or terms are likely to be used in other nations to refer to these types of debt. Using the criterion of collateral pledged to secure debt, the following options are identified for financing local capital projects with debt:

■ *General obligation (GO) bonds:* These are secured by the full faith and credit or taxing power of the issuer. Any available taxes or revenues are pledged to secure and repay the debt. In most states in the United States, the taxing power pledged to secure and repay local GO debt is the power to levy a property tax. For the debt to be considered "full faith and credit" debt, that power to levy property taxes to repay GO debt may not be limited in any way. Moreover, in most U.S. states, the authorization of such GO debt requires approval by the voters in a referendum. A GO, unlimited tax, or full faith and credit pledge for debt is generally considered to be the highest-grade security for debt. If a local government defaults on GO debt, the holders of the debt can go to court to obtain an order requiring the local government to levy taxes to repay the debt. GO bonds often have the lowest interest rates among the different types of long-term debt issued to finance local capital improvements.

■ *Revenue bonds:* These are secured by and paid from the net revenues of a self-supporting public enterprise or activity that is organized and financed separately from the general fund and other activities of a local government. Revenue bonds or debt are often used to finance infrastructure and improvements for local government public enterprises, such as water and sewerage, electricity, gas, airports, ports, public transportation, and other enterprise systems. Jurisdictions that issue revenue bonds must set fees and charges for the enterprise services at a level to more than cover operating costs, including annual debt service, for the enterprise. This is required by the contract between the local government issuing the revenue bonds or debt and bondholders or investors. The bondholders or investors might appoint a trustee to represent their interests and oversee rate setting and management of the enterprise by the local government. Because specific rather than general revenues are pledged to secure revenue debt, such debt is likely to have a higher interest rate than GO bonds or debt.

■ *Capital lease debt, including certificates of participation:* Such debt is typically secured by the property financed with the debt. The local government issuer, in effect, mortgages the property financed with the debt; the mortgaged project or facility, rather than general taxes or any specific revenue source, secures the debt. If the local government issuer defaults on the debt, the debt holders can seize the mortgaged property or asset through court or legal proceedings. In most states in the United States, capital lease or property-secured debt includes a nonappropriation clause that technically makes the debt a year-to-year rather than a long-term obligation under state law. As a result, the debt is not classified as long-term GO debt and does not have to be approved in a voter referendum. Another result is that such capital lease debt typically has higher interest rates than GO debt. Capital lease debt was first used by local governments in the United States to finance expensive equipment. It is now being used by many local governments in that country to finance the construction of schools, prisons and jails, water and sewerage infrastructure, and other facilities. Such capital lease debt to build major facilities is usually issued in the form of certificates of participation (COPs). COPs are shares in the capital lease debt that are marketed and sold as securities to interested investors.

■ *Special or limited obligation debt:* This category includes a variety of different types of debt secured by limited or special taxes or revenues and issued to finance public facilities to meet special needs or for special governmental districts or authorities. Included here would be so-called special assessment debt issued by a local government to finance street, water and sewerage, or other public improvements that benefit specific property owners. The debt is secured by and paid from assessments that the local government imposes on the benefiting property owners. Such assessments are considered to be user charges, rather than taxes, and they are typically levied only against property that borders on or lies very near the project for which the assessment is levied. Usually, a special assessment district, limited in size, is formed and assessments are levied only against property in the district. The assessments may vary within the district depending on how much various properties benefit from the project for which the assessments are levied. Usually, property owners pay the assessments in installments, with interest, over a period of years.

■ *Variable-rate demand debt:* The interest rates on the types of debt listed previously are usually fixed over the term or life of the debt. Fixed-rate debt protects local debt issuers from the risks of changing market interest rates. The local issuer knows what interest rate it will have to pay for however long the debt is outstanding. This facilitates planning and budgeting for the local debt issuer. However, some local jurisdictions, mostly larger, more sophisticated ones, issue variable-rate debt to finance a portion of their capital needs. The interest rates charged on such debt are subject to frequent change (weekly, monthly, or quarterly) as market interest rates change. The debt therefore is treated as short-term debt and, because such debt is seen to have less risk than long-term debt, usually carries a lower interest rate than long-term debt. This enables the local issuer to reduce interest expenses. The downside of variable-rate debt is that the issuer assumes the risk of changing market interest rates. Authorities suggest that only financially strong jurisdictions with adequate debt management capacity use such debt and that it account for no more than a quarter or so of a jurisdiction's outstanding debt.

■ *Loans from national or state government "bond banks" or loan pools:* Many nations and states or provinces within nations have set up government-financed and government-administered "bond banks" or revolving loan programs that provide investment capital to local governments for public improvement projects. The debt or loans typically are provided on very favorable terms—at lower than market interest rates and for long repayment terms. Such debt or loan programs can be crucial to smaller and poorer local governments that do not have strong enough credit to obtain debt financing at reasonable rates and terms in the commercial debt markets.

Sources for financing economic development

Specific financing sources have evolved and become available to local governments in certain places for financing public facilities that are needed to support private economic development. Impact fees and tax-increment debt are two of these sources.

■ *Impact (or development) fees:* Impact fees are charges levied against new development to help finance the public improvements that are needed to serve new development. Such fees have the effect of transferring the capital costs of such improvements from existing residents to the new residents who come into the community to occupy or use the improvements. The fees are typically paid when new development is approved. Fees for residential development are most often charged per household or residence, while fees for business property are typically based on square footage. The developers who pay the fees include them in the price they charge to the residents or businesses that buy into the new development. In most localities that have impact fees, revenues from the fees may be spent for new or expanded facilities anywhere in the jurisdiction that levies the fees. Zones are sometimes required for certain impact fees, so that revenues resulting from the fees imposed on new development in one zone must be spent on public facilities in that zone. Impact fee revenue may not be used to renovate or upgrade public facilities serving existing residents. If projects to serve new development are not ready to build when impact fee revenue is collected, the revenue must be held in a capital reserve until such projects are ready to build.

■ *Tax-increment debt:* Such debt is issued to finance public improvements needed to support private development in a specific tax-increment district; the debt is secured by and paid from growth in property and other taxes and revenues that occurs in the district after it is established. The tax and revenue growth results from new private development that occurs in the district after it is formed. In some jurisdictions, the proceeds from tax-increment debt are also used to finance business loans and incentives, such as sites and facilities, for businesses that locate or expand their operations in the district. Some local governments establish tax-increment districts and issue such debt only if private development in the district is assured. Other local governments form districts and issue tax-increment debt on a speculative basis, expecting but not assured that private development will occur in the district. To be successful, the plans for tax-increment districts and debt must be tied into general development plans for a local government.

Contributions of outside capital and joint projects

Outside capital to help a local government finance the facilities it needs can come in the form of grants from higher levels of government (the national, state, or provincial government), participation by other nearby local governments in joint projects that take advantage of economies of scale, or partnerships with private firms in public-private sector projects.

- *National, federal, state, or provincial grants:* National and state or provincial governments vary in the extent to which they provide grants to local governments to help finance projects. In the United States, such grant revenue is far less today than it was in the past, as the U.S. government has cut federal discretionary spending while struggling to balance its own budget and pay for the rising costs of the nation's social security and medical care for the poor and elderly. Nonetheless, even in the United States, federal grant money is available to local governments for certain types of projects. This is even more the case in most other parts of the world. Local officials in any nation need to inform themselves about the availability of national, federal, state, or provincial grants for local improvement projects, and they need to aggressively pursue such grants. Obtaining grant money can significantly reduce the local costs of those projects.
- *Joint projects with other local jurisdictions or with private sector partners:* Such projects are occurring more often now than in the past. Such projects generally are customized undertakings that require a great deal of planning and negotiation among the partners. The negotiation typically centers on the respective responsibilities and financial contributions of the different partners. As mentioned earlier, joint local projects may arise to take advantage of economies of scale, or smaller

surrounding local jurisdictions may piggy-back onto a project organized and operated by a much larger neighboring local government. Among other reasons, public–private sector projects may arise to enable the private sector partners to take advantage of tax benefits and to allow the public partners to take advantage of the management experience of the private firm.

Developing a Capital Financing Strategy and Selecting Project Financing

With a good understanding of its financial condition and of available capital financing options, a jurisdiction is in a position to develop a strategy for financing capital projects and to select financing for specific projects. Capital financing involves major decisions and long-term commitments that require planning as deliberate as the planning for capital needs. Without a strategy to guide capital financing decisions, some jurisdictions may rely on a few, familiar financing sources; as a result, these jurisdictions may not meet certain capital needs in the most cost-effective way. Other jurisdictions, accustomed to borrowing to meet project needs, may fail to develop pay-as-you-go sources and obligate too much of future operating budgets with heavy debt-service payments. A capital financing strategy for a local government should include the following objectives:

■ Meeting higher priority capital needs yet limiting the cost of doing so
■ Ensuring financial strength and flexibility over the long term
■ Maintaining or strengthening the jurisdiction's standing with creditors, investors, regulatory agencies, and any debt-rating agencies

Ten policies are presented as follows that can constitute or at least contribute to a capital financing strategy. All are important, but the relative emphasis given to any one by a specific local jurisdiction should depend on the capital needs that it faces, its financial condition and prospects, and its general situation.

1. Maintain adequate operating fund balances.
2. Fund low-cost and annually recurring equipment and projects from the operating budget.
3. Create and fund capital reserves.
4. Use suitable debt financing for major capital projects.

5. Determine and remain within debt capacity.
6. Achieve a workable balance between debt and pay-as-you-go financing.
7. Maintain or improve the jurisdiction's credit standing or bond ratings.
8. Develop and implement policies for financing economic development projects.
9. Seek grants and other outside sources of essentially free funding for capital projects.
10. Look for opportunities for joint local and public-private sector projects.

The significance and role of each of these policies in capital finance is briefly explained here.

Operating fund balances

Operating fund balances are important in capital budgets for several reasons. When there is an unexpected shortfall in annual revenues, operating fund balances are a reserve that can be used to help meet annual payment obligations, including debt service on bonds issued in the past to finance capital projects. Operating fund balances can be drawn on to fund unanticipated capital spending in response to emergencies—for example, the repair of buildings damaged by storms. For many local jurisdictions, especially smaller ones with limited access to the debt markets, operating fund balances can be accumulated and then used to help fund planned capital projects.

Operating capital

The operating or annual budget can be geared to fund capital assets that are low to modest in cost or that recur annually at about the same cost. Such items are sometimes called "operating capital"; annual revenues raised in the operating budget can just as readily fund such capital assets as recurring, current spending for salaries and wages and other operating items. This allows the capital budget to be focused on financing large and long-lived projects and helps a jurisdiction avoid overreliance on debt financing.

Capital reserves

A capital reserve can be an effective tool for funding expensive equipment and small construction projects and for providing down payments for major projects. A capital reserve must be funded to be effective. Options for funding a capital reserve include excess operating fund balances if they develop, an annual appropriation from the operating budget to the capital reserve, earmarked special revenues or a portion of general revenue, or depreciation or usage charges on capital equipment, facilities, or infrastructure. An example of the last funding method is provided by a U.S. city that makes use of a revolving reserve fund for equipment replacement that is funded with annual usage charges to all city departments that use equipment. The revenues from such annual charges are transferred from the city's departments that use equipment and vehicles to the equipment replacement fund, which then uses the money to pay cash to replace vehicles and equipment.

Suitable debt financing for major projects

The fourth through seventh policies of the capital financing strategy presented here relate to debt financing. Bonds or debt are often the only way to finance very costly projects. Sufficient pay-as-you-go money cannot be accumulated in a timely way to finance major projects when needed. Debt financing spreads the costs of a major project over much of its useful life through annual debt-service payments that must be made on the debt after the project is built. Such payments also effectively charge the costs of a large project to those using or benefiting from it through the annual taxes and fees that they pay. The taxes and fees partly go to cover the debt-service obligations on the debt issued for the project.

Different types of debt are suitable for different projects. If GO bonds can be authorized without a voter referendum, their low interest rates and issuance costs make such debt the most suitable choice for general government projects, such as local government office buildings, jails, or other public safety facilities. If a voter referendum is needed to authorize GO bonds, such debt can be a good choice for projects that are visible, used directly by citizens, and popular with the voters, such as school or park projects. GO bonds authorized by a voter referendum are also suitable for projects that are new initiatives for a local government. The referendum allows officials to obtain a measure of public support for the project before deciding whether to undertake it.

Revenue bonds are suitable for financing major capital projects for public enterprises or special activities that have their own revenue sources and strong records of self-sustaining operations. Such enterprises or activities are organized into separate funds apart from the rest of local government; their revenue sources are reserved or protected legally to support the enterprise or special activity. Revenue bonds or the equivalent are commonly used for capital financing for local government water and sewerage, electricity, airports, ports, and toll roads. Revenue bonds are used less often for solid waste and parking facilities because in many local jurisdictions those activities have less certain revenue streams or face competition from private sector providers of the services.

Capital lease debt came into use initially to finance expensive equipment, such as fire trucks, construction equipment, and computer systems. Such debt continues to be a suitable form of financing for these and other kinds of expensive equipment. The debt typically has a term of 3 to 10 years, depending on the equipment's useful life; it is usually placed privately with a local bank or financial institution. Some local governments have developed master capital leasing arrangements to finance all or most of the expensive equipment that its agencies use. Capital lease debt that is issued in large amounts and is publicly sold is suitable for major, mandated projects for which it would be difficult to obtain voter approval of GO debt. For example, many prisons and jail facilities in the United States have been financed with capital lease debt using COPs (defined earlier in the discussion of debt options).

Special or limited obligation debt is suitable for financing specific needs for which other types of debt are not well suited. For example, one U.S. state authorized its local governments to issue special debt that is not voted on and that is not secured by taxes, to finance solid waste projects. The debt may be secured by any revenues available to a local government except the taxes that the local government itself levies. This type of debt was authorized for local governments in the state because local voters were unwilling to approve GO bonds for solid waste projects. Revenue bonds were unsuitable because the revenue streams, mostly tipping fees paid by the waste haulers, were not sufficiently reliable. Capital lease debt would not work because lenders were unwilling to hold a mortgage on a landfill or other solid waste facilities.

Debt capacity

Knowing or determining the capacity of a local government or any public entity to issue and carry debt is vital in capital budgeting. A community's wealth and economic growth and the ability of a local government to generate revenues from its local economy ultimately underlie the local government's debt capacity. Certain debt ratios are at the heart of determining the capacity of a jurisdiction to issue and repay debt. One set of ratios pertains to net debt. Net debt consists of any debt that is repaid from generally available revenues. Such debt includes most GO bonds, much capital lease debt, and some special or limited obligation debt. Net debt excludes revenue bonds. One key ratio is annual debt service (principal repayment and annual interest) on net debt as a percentage of general fund and other general-purpose spending. Some authorities say that this ratio should not exceed 15 to 20 percent, depending on a jurisdiction's size and financial strength (Standard & Poor's 2007). For a jurisdiction that relies heavily on the property tax, a second measure of safety in borrowing is net debt as a percentage of its market or taxable value of property. Per capita net debt is a third measure widely used to compare the debt burdens of jurisdictions. Care must be exercised in applying and interpreting these and other measures of debt capacity. While a fast-growing local jurisdiction may have issued considerable debt and have relatively high debt ratios, development in the future can generate considerable annual new revenue to support new debt issuance as well as meet current debt payment obligations and support other spending.

Balance of debt and pay-as-you-go financing

As already mentioned, financing a portion of the capital budget from pay-as-you-go sources helps preserve flexibility in future operating budgets. Having a policy that specifies a target balance between pay-as-you-go and debt financing can help a jurisdiction preserve such flexibility yet issue substantial debt to meet major project needs. Such a balance can compare the sum of annual debt-service and lease payment obligations with the sum of annual cash payments for capital assets plus contributions to capital reserves. The appropriate balance between pay-as-you-go and debt financing will vary from one jurisdiction to the next. A fast-growing, larger local government might safely finance 80 percent of its CIP using debt and 20 percent from pay-as-you-go sources, while a mature or built-out jurisdiction with a strong tax base probably could rely much more on pay-as-you-go financing.

Bond ratings

Bond or debt ratings assess the ability and willingness of an issuer to repay debt and make periodic interest and debt service payments when due. Good bond ratings broaden the market for debt and reduce or hold down interest rates and costs. A full faith and credit or GO bond rating for a jurisdiction depends on the strength, growth, and stability of its economy; the jurisdiction's financial condition, prospects, and practices; its net debt burden and capacity, including the rate of pay-down on existing debt; and the leadership and management provided by elected and top administrative officials. A revenue bond rating depends mainly on the profitability and prospects of the enterprise or activity for which revenue bonds are being issued. The pledged net revenues of the enterprise or activity must exceed or cover annual debt service on the bonds each year. Ratings for capital lease debt for general government facilities depend on the general creditworthiness of the issuer and the essentiality to the issuer of the project financed with the debt. The assumption underlying essentiality is that a debt issuer is unlikely to stop making annual payments on capital lease debt, even though it is subject to annual appropriation, if the debt finances a project that is essential—for example, a local jail. Special obligation or limited tax debt is rated in terms of the strength of the revenue stream that supports the debt.

Policy for financing economic development

In some nations or states and provinces within nations, the laws may limit the use of tax and other public revenues to spending for public services and projects. However, in other nations, many state and local governments have broad legal authority to finance incentives for businesses and for private nonprofit organizations in order to foster economic development. In return, the businesses and private nonprofit organizations are expected to make investments that create jobs, raise incomes, and produce additional taxes and revenues for the governmental entities that provide the incentives. The incentives can include the construction of public infrastructure (streets, water and sewerage lines, and the like) that serves just the business or private organization; provision of low- or no-interest loans to finance business or private organization investments; grants of cash to help a business or private organization buy and improve land, build facilities, or acquire equipment; and forgiveness of future tax obligations for a period of years. If a local jurisdiction has the legal authority to provide these or other incentives to finance private economic development, it should have a policy to guide its financing decisions in this area. Such a policy must be based on the laws authorizing the incentives. It should identify the kinds of financing to be provided; eligible businesses and organizations; and the additional jobs, income, or taxes that the businesses or private organizations would produce in the community.

To limit competition with other local governments offering incentives, a local economic development policy could also favor projects involving multiple jurisdictions. In other words, neighboring local jurisdictions in a region could join in offering incentives that subsidize private investment in one or more of their communities; the participating local communities could share in the growth in taxes resulting from such private investments.

A local government's economic development policy can require financial contributions from private developers for certain types of development to help the local government finance infrastructure and public facilities needed to serve new private development; such contributions could be in the form of impact or other development fees.

Grants

As already mentioned, grants from higher levels of government can be a very important source of capital financing for local governments' capital improvements in many nations. Even in countries where national and state or provincial grants for local projects are generally limited, grants are often available to finance certain kinds of local improvements, especially for smaller and less well-off local communities. A local government should have a policy that encourages its leaders and officials to pursue grants to help finance capital projects. Success in obtaining outside grants can significantly lower the local costs for such projects.

Joint projects

As already mentioned, joint projects can involve multiple jurisdictions collaborating on a project or public–private partnerships. Two examples of joint projects developed by a small city of 17,000 people highlight how effective such projects can be in providing public facilities and fostering economic development. One project is the rehabilitation of an old unused textile mill, converting part of it to shops and condominium apartments that will generate tax revenue for the city and the other part into space where city offices are now housed. The rehabilitation project was undertaken by a private developer; it involved federal and state income tax credits for historic restoration taken by the private developer and entailed a five-year lease between the developer and the city. In the second project, the city is involved in a joint local government project with the county and four other towns in the county to purchase and develop a large tract of land for industrial and business use. Although the site is in the unincorporated area of the county, all the participating local governments will share proportionately in new property and other taxes resulting from new industrial or other business development on the site. Of course, these not only are joint projects involving public infrastructure, but also are economic development projects for the city and the other participants in the projects.

Recommending Capital Projects and Spending

For local governments with a CIP, the first year of the CIP forecast period includes the recommended capital projects and spending. That CIP's first year is typically called the budget year, and the projects and spending proposed for that year are often considered to be a jurisdiction's capital budget that year. A few local governments have a two-year capital budget that includes proposed projects and spending in the first two years of their CIP forecast period. If a local government does not have a CIP, it may nonetheless have a capital budget, consisting of major capital projects and spending that are recommended for approval and funding in the upcoming year. Such projects and spending may be approved and funded with the annual or operating budget or separately but parallel to operating budget approval.

Whether recommended capital projects and spending come from the CIP or are only a special part of or related to each year's operating budget, for any project or item the capital budget should address the need fulfilled, the benefits, the scope, the costs, and the impact on future operating budgets. All this information comes from the planning, prioritization, and evaluation of capital project and equipment requests done earlier in the overall process. Similarly, the capital budget for any year should recommend financing for each project or item, which would be based on an assessment of the local government's financial condition, a forecast of its financial capacity, and the capital financing strategy that officials have approved to guide financing decisions. The recommended capital budget for any year or other period sets the stage for the authorization of projects and the appropriation of money for them.

Authorizing Projects and Appropriating Money

Authorization refers to approval of a capital project or acquisition, while *appropriation* is legally making financing available to spend for it. Typically, it is the governing board of a local government that authorizes and appropriates money for capital projects. Occasionally, a local governing board provides a lump sum of money for certain capital needs and delegates to the chief executive officer or to a committee of the governing board the authority to approve and appropriate money for specific projects or spending. When this is done, the projects are usually relatively modest in size. Similarly, a jurisdiction's governing board may sometimes delegate to the chief executive or to one of its committees the authority to approve changes in a project's scope and the amount appropriated to be spent for the project. When such delegation or amendment authority for projects occurs, it is usually limited in some way and the changes must typically be reported to the board after they are made.

The authorization of projects and the appropriation of money for them often occur simultaneously, with authorization taking place by means of one or more appropriations for a project. Authorization and appropriation for other projects or acquisitions, especially larger ones, occur in separate actions and at different times.

The authorization of larger projects often occurs in a series of decisions, one of which is for appropriation. For example, a major construction project may be approved generally in concept when the governing board approves the CIP in which the project first appears, perhaps in one of the later planning years of the CIP forecast period. The board may then authorize a consultant to do a feasibility study of the project to identify its benefits and costs. If the findings from that study are favorable, the project remains in the CIP. Several years later, more definitive authorization of the project occurs when the board approves the CIP in which the project is in the CIP's first or budget year—that is, the recommended capital budget for that year. The board may then approve the architectural design and scope and specific cost estimates for the project. Next, the board could approve a bond order authorizing a voter referendum to finance the project with GO bonds. If the voters approve the bonds, the board would then approve their issuance. Finally, the board would appropriate the bond proceeds, along with any other resources that will be spent for the project. Such appropriation could occur through a capital projects ordinance (explained below). Depending on legal requirements and the nature of the project, the governing board may also have to approve the acquisition of one or more sites for the project and specific construction or other contracts related to project implementation. In the early and middle stages of this authorization process, board decisions do not irrevocably commit the local jurisdiction to go ahead with the project. For some projects, final authorization does not occur until the actual issuance of debt or other action to raise money for a project and enter into contracts to build the project.

The approval of bonds or debt for a project is a key step in the overall authorization process. The governing board itself may have the authority to authorize the use of debt, as with the revenue bonds or capital lease debt issued by local governments in most U.S. states. In addition to governing board approval of debt, citizen approval in a local referendum may be legally required, such as with GO bonds issued by local governments in most U.S. states. State or federal regulatory authorities may need to approve local government issuance of debt for local capital projects or other purposes.[8] Even after the authorization of debt for a project, officials may still choose not to issue the debt, either because they do not intend to go ahead with the project or because they intend and are able to use other sources of financing. Of course, this is an exceptional situation. Debt is typically issued and spent for a project after it is authorized. The steps involved in authorizing debt are usually considerable and often complex. Therefore, officials go through the authorization process only if they fully expect to issue and use the debt. After properly authorized debt is issued, no further action by a local governing board may be needed for proceeds from the debt to be spent for a project. However, the law may require separate appropriation of debt proceeds by the governing board in some type of budget or appropriation ordinance before the proceeds can be spent.

The usual methods of appropriating money, including bond proceeds, for capital projects are through a local government's annual or operating budget ordinance or resolution, or in one or more capital projects ordinances or resolutions:

- *The annual or operating budget ordinance or resolution:* Appropriations for capital projects in an annual or operating budget usually lapse at the end of the year or period and must then be readopted in the subsequent year's or period's budget for projects that continue into the next year or period. Alternatively, the appropriations for ongoing projects may continue or automatically renew from year to year or fiscal period to period without specific action by the governing board. Recommendations for governing board appropriations for capital projects may come to the board after the annual or operating budget is adopted. In these cases, the board can adopt an amendment to the annual or operating budget incorporating the available funding and appropriating it for spending on the project.
- *A capital projects ordinance or resolution:* Such an ordinance or resolution appropriates money specifically for a capital project or acquisition, and it is enacted separately from the annual or operating budget ordinance. A project ordinance provides ongoing spending authority for a project that continues until the project is finished. Such spending authority does not lapse or end at the close of any fiscal year or period. A jurisdiction's governing board may enact a separate capital project ordinance for each individual capital project or acquisition. This is likely to occur when projects are brought to the board for approval and funding throughout the year. Alternatively, a local governing board could adopt a comprehensive capital projects ordinance for recommended capital projects and spending included in the first or budget year of the CIP. Such a comprehensive projects ordinance could be enacted by the board shortly after it approves the full CIP.

Each of these methods of appropriating funding for capital projects has advantages and disadvantages. Appropriation in the annual or operating budget helps to ensure that capital project decisions are coordinated with operating budget decisions. Moreover, because operating budget appropriations are usually only for a year or two, this provides for periodic review of capital projects in process.

The disadvantages of appropriating money for capital projects in the annual or operating budget apply mainly to large multiyear projects. First is the incongruity of appropriating money for a project for only a year or two at a time when spending to build it occurs over several years. Second, while the annual or operating budget includes mainly current spending to benefit only a year or two, spending for a capital project, by nature, is intended to provide benefits that span many years. Including appropriations for major capital projects in an annual or operating budget fails to recognize this distinction.

The disadvantages of appropriating money for capital projects in the annual or operating budget are overcome by using a capital projects ordinance. This type of ordinance, whether comprehensive and embracing all projects approved in a year or broken into separate ordinances for individual projects, continues in force until the projects are completed. By appropriating money for capital projects separately from the operating budget, current expenditures and the benefits flowing from them are matched more reliably with annual revenues. Large capital projects with benefits that occur over many years are segregated from operating budget decisions that provide benefits for one or two years. This can help local officials explain to the public the benefits and costs of each type of spending more effectively.

One disadvantage of relying on a capital projects ordinance to appropriate money for capital projects is that decisions about such projects may not be coordinated sufficiently with operating budget decisions. This is more likely to occur if capital project ordinances are enacted at different times from the annual or operating budget.

Acquiring and Managing Project Financing

Much of this step in the capital budget process is concerned with the issuance and management of debt that occurs after or as a project is authorized. Obtaining capital financing other than debt depends on implementing the pay-as-you-go, grant, and joint project policies that have already been discussed. Money accumulated for pay-as-you-go capital financing in capital reserves or operating fund balances should be invested at interest to increase financing capacity.

Debt provides much or most of the financing for major capital projects. Effective debt issuance and management can limit debt issuance and interest costs; the resulting savings can be quite significant, especially when large amounts of debt are issued for major projects.[9] Some of the key steps involved in planning the issuance of debt and then managing debt proceeds are set forth and briefly explained as follows:

■ *Develop effective working relationships with debt-market professionals who can advise on and assist the local government with issuing debt to finance its capital program.* Such professionals might include attorneys who specialize in local government debt issuance and who can provide advice about the legal requirements of debt issuance; a financial adviser who advises on planning specific debt offerings of the local government; bankers and investment bankers who invest in or buy and resell local government debt; key officials in state or provincial and national regulatory agencies who oversee the issuance of debt by local governments; and credit or bond rating agencies that provide reports or ratings on the creditworthiness of local governments. Because of the complexity of debt issuance, even larger local governments that have in-house debt expertise are likely to find it necessary to seek outside assistance in planning and issuing debt.

■ *Plan debt issues effectively.* Doing so includes limiting the size of any debt issue for a capital project to the amount needed to complete the project, including a reserve for contingencies; not issuing debt in excess of a jurisdiction's debt-carrying capacity; setting the repayment term to be equal to or less than the project's useful life; and structuring annual debt service (principal repayment and interest) to match the local government's annual payment capacity for debt, considering other annual payment obligations.

■ *Choose a cost-effective method to place or sell each debt issue.* The ways in which local government debt is sold depend on the laws and to what extent debt markets have developed in a nation. If debt markets do not exist or are very limited, a local government seeking to issue debt to finance capital projects is likely to have to place the debt privately with one or more banks, financial institutions, or investors who are familiar with the local government and are willing to finance the local unit's projects. If debt markets exist, a local government may be able to sell its debt in a public sales process to investors in those markets. In a public sale of debt, the debt issuer may sell the debt itself directly in the market or, what is more likely, through investment bankers or debt underwriters who buy the debt from the local government and then resell it to investors. In the United States, most local government debt is sold publicly through investment banking firms. These firms compete against one another to buy the debt and then resell it to individuals, mutual funds, insurance companies, banks, and others who buy and hold the debt in their investment portfolios. In this process, the local government may sell the debt in a competitive process to the investment banking firm that offers it the lowest interest rate. Alternatively, the local government may sell the debt in a negotiated process in which it selects an investment banking firm that it judges will be most able to sell the bonds in the most cost-effective way. That firm then plans the debt issue, buys the debt from the local government, and resells it to investors. Finally, in many countries, national, state, or provincial agencies may buy local government debt, often at low interest rates. Local governments should take advantage of such public credit or debt sources wherever they are available.

■ *Decide whether and when to use short-term debt for capital financing.* Such debt includes variable-rate debt for long-term capital financing and short-term debt for construction financing, such as bond or grant anticipation notes. The section on capital financing strategy addresses the use of variable-rate debt for capital financing.

■ *After debt has been issued and before it is spent, invest the proceeds to produce investment income.* Such income can be a significant source of project revenue and reduce the amount of debt that is issued for a project. The investment of debt proceeds must comply with applicable laws and restrictions and must generally be for short terms so that debt proceeds are available when needed to cover construction bills and other payment obligations in a timely way.

■ *While debt is outstanding, take advantage of re-funding opportunities that lower annual debt-service costs.* Such opportunities arise when market interest rates fall after debt has been issued. New debt can be issued at lower interest rates to replace the existing outstanding debt that was issued at higher interest rates in the past.

Managing Construction Projects

This stage involves the selection of delivery systems for the management of construction projects and additional issues related to construction design and contracting. The importance of project implementation and construction to capital budgeting lies in the fact that mistakes and cost overruns in the construction of major capital projects can wreak havoc with capital plans, can require the raising of amounts of financing that are much larger than expected, and can severely squeeze future operating budgets because of debt-service costs that are higher than expected.

Project delivery systems

Project delivery system refers to the way in which the construction process for a capital project is organized. It involves design, contracting, and construction management.[10] Several basic construction delivery systems are used by local governments and other public entities: design-bid-build, construction manager at risk, and design-build. There are also variations in these basic systems and the ways in which they are applied. Legal requirements and construction industry norms and practices in a country are important in determining which of these systems are used for construction projects.

The traditional public sector project delivery system is design-bid-build. The use of this construction delivery system is mandated by law for local governments in many U.S. states. The system consists of three general steps:

1. Design of a project and preparation of construction plans and documents (blueprints, specifications, and so on); for all but small projects, this is typically done by a contracted architect or engineer.
2. Public bidding, in which contractors compete with one another to work on a project, and selection of one or more contractors to build the project; the contractors selected are often but not always the ones offering the lowest-cost bids.
3. Construction of the project by the selected contractors, with oversight during the project provided by the architect or engineer who designed the project, the jurisdiction's own engineering or construction staff, a contracted construction management firm, or some combination of these parties.

Two general approaches to design-bid-build are used—multiple prime and single prime contracting. With multiple prime contracting, a local government contracts directly with several contractors to build the major components of a project—for example, a general contractor who is responsible for all phases of construction not done by the other prime contractors, a heating and air conditioning contractor, a plumbing contractor, and an electrical contractor. Depending on the customs of construction contracting, different types of contractors may be used. Under single prime contracting, a jurisdiction contracts with one contractor who is responsible for all phases or components of construction. That contractor then builds the project, using its own workforce or hiring subcontractors as needed. If a construction project is large or if a local government has many projects under way, the jurisdiction may hire a construction management or advisory firm to help oversee construction. This is more likely to occur when a local government relies primarily on multiple prime contracting for construction projects.

The design-bid-build construction delivery system gives a jurisdiction the benefit of separate design and construction expertise. The approach also fosters competition among contractors, especially when multiple prime contracting is used; this can hold down construction costs. It also offers more independent contractors direct access to public construction projects. The disadvantages of design-bid-build are that it often falls short of centering responsibility for construction and that it can involve many disagreements between the architect and contractors and, if multiple prime contracting is used, among construction contractors. This can lead to construction delays, mismatches in different phases of construction, and cost overruns. The contracting local government often ends up responsible for most of the additional costs.

Because of the problems with design-bid-build, other project delivery systems have emerged and are available legally to local governments in many places. One alternative is called construction manager at risk. This system has two general stages. The first is design of the project and preparation of the design documents by an architect or engineer. The second begins with the selection of a construction manager or contractor, on the basis of qualifications rather than project price or cost. The construction manager examines the design documents and proposes a guaranteed maximum cost for construction and completion of the project. Officials of the local government and the construction manager then negotiate to arrive at a final price. The negotiation can involve changes in the project's scope, components, and design. A guaranteed final cost or price is then set. The construction manager hires all contractors, is responsible for construction, and must deliver the project within the guaranteed price. A performance bond is typically used to assure the local government that the project will not cost more than this price. If the construction manager builds the project for less, the construction manager keeps the savings.

Design-build is another alternative to the traditional design-bid-build approach. In design-build, a jurisdiction first develops a rather specific development plan for a project. Then design-build firms or partnerships that have both design and construction capabilities are asked to submit proposals that focus on their qualifications to design and build the project. Several of these firms or partnerships are selected; each is then asked to develop detailed design documents and cost estimates for the project. The firm or partnership that offers the most acceptable and lowest-cost bid is selected. Unlike the construction manager at risk approach, the design-build approach does not necessarily guarantee a maximum construction cost for the project.

Four general criteria are often used to evaluate alternative construction delivery systems: control of construction costs, delivery of a project on schedule, assurance of project quality, and limitation of administrative burden. According to a survey in one U.S. state (Riecke 2004), public construction managers have the least confidence in design-bid-build approaches that use multiple prime contractors for meeting these performance criteria. Their view is that the selection from among the other delivery systems—design-bid-build (single prime), construction manager at risk, and design-build—needs to be made with consideration of the type of construction project to be built. If a project involves a standard design and conventional construction, either design-bid-build (single prime) or construction manager at risk can be the most cost-effective choice. However, if the project involves unusual design or construction, design-build may be the most suitable choice.

There are variations of these major project delivery systems. For example, a construction manager may not provide a guaranteed maximum construction price. In this case, the construction manager is serving as an agent; the contracting local jurisdiction has the major financial risk. In some instances, the design-build approach has been expanded to design-build-operate. The firm selected to design and build a project will also operate and maintain it under an ongoing service contract. Finally, time and materials contracts rather than performance contracts are often used for construction projects that are relatively small. Such contracts are also used for unusual projects when contractors are unwilling to specify the amounts they could charge to work on the project. With a time and materials contract, the contracting local jurisdiction is responsible for total project costs.

Additional design, contracting, and construction management issues

Certain design, contracting, and construction management questions arise regardless of the type of delivery system that is used to build a project. The more important of these are mentioned here.

- *Important questions concerning design:* What types of design qualifications are needed for a project? Are both architectural and engineering skills needed? Does the law require a local government to contract for architectural and engineering design services? In some U.S. states, the design of a project that costs more than a certain amount must legally be contracted out. Can a less expensive standard design be used, or is a more expensive customized design needed? Will the design proceed through phases going from general plans to specific blueprints? Who will approve plans and documents at each phase? What site or other testing will the architect or engineer perform in designing the project? How reliable are the architect or engineer's project cost estimates? Is the proposed construction schedule realistic? What role will the architect or engineer have in guiding or overseeing construction? On what basis and schedule will payment of the architect or engineer occur? While professional standards exist to help answer most of these questions, interpretation of the standards is usually necessary for a construction project of any size.
- *Important questions about construction contracting:* Has there been an evaluation of the construction market, and what is the likelihood that bids

will be submitted within cost estimates for a project? Does the bidding process comply with legal requirements? Are construction bidders required to prequalify? Prequalification helps exclude bidders who may be interested in bidding but would be unable to perform work as needed for a project. Is there a prebid conference for prospective construction bidders? Such conferences can help bidders submit more responsive bids. Do the bid request documents address participation by minority contractors? What criteria are used to evaluate the bids and select contractors for the project? Does the law specify criteria—for example, "lowest, responsible bidder … consider[ing] quality, price, and performance"?[11] To what extent are officials constrained to accept the lowest-cost bid? How can lowball bids be excluded? These questions suggest the wide range of issues that affect construction contracting.

■ *Key questions concerning the construction process itself:* Who will be involved in managing and overseeing construction, and what will be their respective roles? Other questions concern procedures to ensure that construction occurs in accordance with the contracts, as well as procedures for approval of phases of completed work, progress reporting and meetings, payments to the contractors, monetary incentives and sanctions, and the control of project cost during construction. How does the construction contract define "substantial completion," and what procedures are there for addressing the punch list and contractor closeout?

Acquiring Equipment and Other Capital Assets

Acquisition of equipment and other capital assets is another important part of implementing a capital budget. The process for purchases of equipment must comply with applicable legal requirements. Whether legally required or not, procedures should be followed to take advantage of competition among potential vendors. Leasing and purchasing options should be compared to determine which is more cost-effective. Finally, the timing of equipment acquisitions can make a difference in the successful implementation of this part of the capital budget. If annual revenues from the operating budget are used to acquire equipment, scheduling equipment acquisitions in cash-rich months of the fiscal year may be necessary.

Conclusion

One concluding question that might arise from this overview of capital budgeting is whether a local government should have a separate and identifiable capital budget process. However, the experiences of local jurisdictions in making decisions about capital projects suggest that this would not be the most useful question to ask. Most governments of any size already use some or many of the steps that are described here as elements of capital budgeting. Therefore, the better question to ask is to what extent the steps that make up the process of capital budgeting described here should be used by a specific jurisdiction. Criteria that can help the officials of a local government answer this question go back to the reasons cited for capital budgeting at the beginning of the chapter. Thus, the more of the following conditions that are present, the more likely a local government is to benefit from having a separate and well-developed process for capital budgeting: (a) the local government is experiencing substantial growth, or it is not growing and is investing in public infrastructure to spur growth; (b) the jurisdiction faces large capital needs requiring the investment of substantial amounts of money; (c) meeting these needs is likely to shape the basic features of the community; (d) debt will be incurred to finance major capital projects; and (e) operating budget and other procedures are not well suited for planning and financing the capital needs that the local government faces.

Notes

This chapter is a revision of another chapter written by the author and titled, "Capital Budgeting," to appear in a forthcoming book, *Budgeting: Formulation and Execution*, 3rd ed., edited by Jack Rabin, W. Bartley Hildreth, and Gerald J. Miller, to be published by the Vinson Institute of Government of the University of Georgia, Athens. The expected publication year for this book is 2007.

1. These examples of local government capital projects and spending were provided by the budget officers of these jurisdictions. Information about these projects is also available in the jurisdictions' capital improvement programs and other budget documents.
2. A study of Florida municipalities in the United States suggests that infrastructure issues are significant in determining governing board elections. See McManus (2004).
3. This broad concept of capital expenditure is not used by all economists. For example, one well-known economics texts uses a definition of capital expenditure very similar to the one used by accountants. See Baumol and Blinder (2005).
4. Definitions of capital asset and capitalization threshold appear in Gauthier (2004). Also see Freeman, Shoulders, and Allison (2006).
5. Works of art, historic treasures, and certain intangible property are not included in the list of capital assets presented by Freeman, Shoulders, and Allison (2006). They are added here based on their inclusion among capital assets by Gauthier (2004) and because of their growing importance in local arts, museum, and historic preservation programs.
6. An in-depth treatment, with illustrations, of local government capital planning, budgeting, and finance appears in Vogt (2004). A more succinct overview of capital budgeting is provided by Westerman (2004). The Economic Development and

Capital Planning Committee of the Government Finance Officers Association of the United States and Canada has put a useful and detailed outline on capital budgeting on the Association's Web site: http://www.gfoa.org.

7. The U.S. bond rating agencies consider general fund and other operating fund balances to be a very important factor in assessing a local government's financial condition. For example, see Jacob and Rosso (2005). Also see Moody's Investors Service (2004).

8. In the U.S. state of North Carolina, a state agency must approve all debt that a city, county, or other local government plans to issue. The state agency is called the North Carolina Local Government Commission. The commission not only approves all local government debt in North Carolina, but also sells the debt in the U.S. municipal (state and local) debt markets. The commission is highly respected in these markets, and its role in approving and selling the state's local debt results in lower interest rates for the debt than specific local governments could obtain on their own. See Larkin and Schaub (1999).

9. One of the best books on debt financing and management by local governments in the United States is Ehlers (1998). Also see Vogt (2004), especially chapters 7–11.

10. This discussion of construction project delivery systems is based on Riecke (2004). Ms. Riecke is an architect.

11. In North Carolina, construction contracts entered into by local governments and other public entities are subject to formal bidding requirements. Such contracts must be awarded to the "lowest responsible bidder, or bidders . . . taking into consideration quality, performance, and the time specified in the proposal for the performance of the contract." See North Carolina General Statute 143–129 (b).

References

Baumol, William J., and Alan S. Blinder. 2005. *Economics: Principles and Policy*, 9th ed. Mason, OH: Thomson Southwest.

Ehlers, Robert I. 1998. *Ehlers on Public Finance: Building Better Communities*. Rochester, MN: Loan Oak Press.

Freeman, Robert J., Craig D. Shoulders, and Gregory S. Allison. 2006. *Governmental and Nonprofit Accounting: Theory and Practice*, 8th ed. Upper Saddle River, NJ: Prentice Hall.

Gauthier, Stephen J. 2004. *Governmental Accounting, Auditing, and Financial Reporting*. Chicago: Government Finance Officers Association.

Government Accounting Standards Board. 1999. *Statement No. 34 of the Governmental Accounting Standards Board: Basic Financial Statements—and Management's Discussion and Analysis—for State and Local Governments*. Norwalk, CT: Governmental Accounting Standards Board.

Jacob, Karl, and Baltazar Juarez. 2005. "The 2005 Annual Review of 'AAA' Rated U.S. Counties." *Standard & Poor's Public Finance*, September 21, pp. 1–8.

Jacob, Karl, and Jennifer L. Rosso. 2005. "Annual Review of 'AAA' Rated U.S. Municipalities." *Standard & Poor's Public Finance*, June 9, pp. 1–8.

Larkin, Richard P., and Jeff Schaub. 1999. "State of North Carolina Local Government Commission." *FitchIBCA Public Finance*, March 29, pp. 1–6.

Lawrence, David M., and A. John Vogt. 1999. "Capital Budgeting and Debt." In *County Government in North Carolina*, 4th ed., ed. A. Fleming Bell and Warren J. Wicker. Chapel Hill: School of Government, University of North Carolina.

McManus, Susan A. 2004. "'Bricks and Mortar' Politics: How Infrastructure Decisions Defeat Incumbents." *Public Budgeting and Finance* 24 (1) Spring: 96–112.

Moody's Investors Service. 2004. "The Six Critical Components of Strong Municipal Management." *Rating Methodology*, March, 1–6.

Prunty, Robin, and Karl Jacob. 2002. "Top 10 Ways to Improve or Maintain a Municipal Bond Rating." *Standard & Poor's Public Finance*, February 4, 1–4.

Quirin, G. David, and John C. Wiginton. 1981. *Analyzing Capital Expenditures: Private and Public Perspectives.* Homewood, IL: Richard D. Irwin, Inc.

Riecke, Valerie Rose. 2004. "Construction Contracting: Project Delivery Methods." *Popular Government* 70 (1): 22–33.

Standard & Poor's. 2007. *Public Finance Criteria 2007.* New York: Standard & Poor's.

Vogt, A. John. 2004. *Capital Budgeting and Finance: A Guide for Local Governments.* Washington, DC: International City/County Management Association.

Westerman, Nicole. 2004. "Managing the Capital Planning Cycle: Best Practice Examples of Effective Capital Program Management." *Government Finance Review* 20(3) June: 26–31.

Index

Boxes, figures, notes, and tables are indicated by b, f, n, and t, respectively.

access
  institutionalizing of, 239–40
  in limited discretion environments,
    240–41
accountability, 5, 8–9, 18, 90, 295
  African local government, 243b8.4
  in budgeting, 152–53, 241–46,
    247–48b8.6, 263n5
  citizen-centric performance
    budgeting, 166–68
  execution of budgets, 272–73
  participatory budgeting, 245–46,
    247b8.6, 263n5
  for corruption investigations, 119
  downward, 245, 247–48b8.6
  for expenditure controls, 286
  horizontal, 220, 247b8.6
  in Kenya, 247–48b8.6
  link to democratization, 183
  link to own-source revenues, 98
  on local discretion, 242, 243b8.4
  for outcomes of financial
    management, 99–100
  outputs-based, 161
  and performance measures, 146
  of performance of public officials,
    244–45
  and tax evasion, 116
  and technical capacity, 45, 49n40

upward, 245, 247–48b8.6
vertical, 220, 245, 247–48b8.6
voice-accountability systems, 243b8.4
accounting systems, 65, 69, 277, 294
  cash-basis, 279
  as function of fiscal administration,
    30–32, 47n19
  incompatibility of, 280
  to monitor revenues and expenditures,
    277–78
  relationship between accounting and
    budgeting staff, 289–90
accrued liabilities, 194
acquisition of property, 310
ADB. *See* Asian Development Bank
  (ADB)
administrative capacity, and performance
  budgeting, 165–66
administrative decentralization, 216–18
administrative-dominated budget
  systems, 224–25, 226–27, 242–43
administrative units, and budgets,
  141–42
advertising, expenditures for, 310
Africa
  accountability in local government,
    243b8.4
  constrained authority in, 218–20, 251
  and fiscal discipline, 84